Sunday
Best

PETER LINEHAM

Sunday Best

How the Church Shaped New Zealand
and New Zealand Shaped the Church

MASSEY UNIVERSITY PRESS

School children play outside the Catholic Church of St Mary's, built in Manuka Street, Nelson, in 1856 and destroyed by fire in 1881. The school was established by the first priest, Fr Antoine Garin, and had a high reputation with Protestants and also ensured an ecumenical atmosphere in the town. COURTESY MICHAEL GRAHAM-STEWART

To Allan Davidson,
friend and collaborator
over many years

Contents

Introduction
page 10

❶

The Sacred Day
page 26

❷

The House of God
page 48

❸

Gathered to Worship
page 100

❹

The Music and Words of Faith
page 134

❺

Clergy Culture
page 168

❻

Convictions of the Faithful
page 198

❼

The Money in the Bag
page 224

8

A Sociable Religion
page 242

9

The Gendered Church
page 274

10

Children and Young People and Church
page 308

11

Status, Hierarchy and Faith
page 338

12

All Change
page 378

Glossary
page 386

Notes
page 390

Index
page 450

About the Author
page 462

Introduction

Previous The Church Missionary Society church at Tūranga (Gisborne) in 1852, showing the reading desk with Māori reader, and the pulpit with a Māori clergyman. This, the second chapel (sometimes known as Manutuke) at Tūranga was erected from 1849 by Māori, and used traditional panels with simple manaia motifs. It was 45 ft by 90 ft (13.7 m x 27.4 m) in size and was an interesting blend of European and Māori styles. ALEXANDER TURNBULL LIBRARY. REF: B-051-017

NEW ZEALAND WAS ONE of the last countries in the world to be settled, with Māori probably not arriving from the islands in the centre of the Pacific until about 1300. By the time of initial European contact (Abel Tasman in 1642, James Cook in 1769), tribal groups were established along the coast of all of the North Island and some of the cooler South Island. When Samuel Marsden, the Church of England chaplain for the Australian prison colony, persuaded the Church Missionary Society (CMS) to commence a mission in New Zealand, there was already some contact between Māori and Europeans. But the mission, which began in December 1814 with a Christmas Day service, was the first permanent settlement of Europeans.

Missionary work of this kind was a very new approach in the 1810s. Voluntary Protestant missionary societies were first established in the 1790s, and they had little experience of how to choose successful missionaries and what their goals should be. New Zealand was an experiment. The CMS mission of three lay missionaries and their support staff was confined to the Bay of Islands, and had very unstable beginnings. There were no converts until 1826, by which time half of the early missionaries had been sacked by the mission. The appointment of Henry and Marianne Williams in 1823, followed by Henry's brother William and his wife Jane, stabilised the mission, and from 1823 it was a strong presence in more and more Māori communities.

In 1822 the Wesleyans arrived, and they began to establish a mission station at Whangaroa to the north of the Bay of Islands. Whangaroa was the site of an 1809 massacre in which the sailors on the *Boyd* were killed and eaten after insults to Māori on board the ship, and in 1827 Wesleydale was attacked and had to be abandoned. The Wesleyan missionaries established a new mission the following year at Mangungu on the Hokianga harbour, on the west coast of Northland. In 1838 it was agreed that the Wesleyans would expand down the west coast as far as Taranaki and in the South Island, while the CMS would expand down the east coast and then around and up the coast as far as Wanganui.

The CMS was a vastly bigger mission than the Wesleyans, but Henry Williams had been cautious about expanding its operations. He built a boat, the *Active*, and preferred to use this to make briefer visits to the Bay of Plenty, while the mission consolidated in various sites around the Bay of Islands, and inland at Waimate North. The turning point came in the 1830s, as numbers increased at the services held by the mission, and converts sought baptism and received portions of the Bible that from 1835 were translated into Māori and published for the mission by William Colenso. Still, the number baptised was deliberately selective, as the mission sought to insist on attested evangelical conversions. There were extensions of the mission to the Bay of Plenty and Waikato from 1835, and in 1840 to the East Coast and the

Waikanae and Ōtaki area of the south of the North Island.

In 1838 Bishop Jean-Baptiste Pompallier and a very small team arrived in New Zealand as part of the Catholic plan to use the Society of Mary to plant Catholicism in the western Pacific. A very different strategy of baptisms and extensive travel created two very different kinds of Christian mission.

The CMS worked closely with the British government's emissaries in the arrival of the British resident, James Busby, in 1833, the Declaration of Independence by the northern tribes arranged by the British in 1835, and the annexation of New Zealand and the Treaty of Waitangi in 1840. But these attempts to control the settlement of New Zealand by Pākehā and to protect Māori had a long-term effect on the mission. From 1840 Māori focused on political issues, and did not need the mission to help them: the various missions remained significant to Māori, but not essential.

The missionaries remained vigilant about the terms of the Treaty of Waitangi and were increasingly critical of the British government's changing policies about Māori land. Their role was made more complex by the arrival of a bishop appointed by the British government: George Augustus Selwyn, the very epitome of muscular Christianity. Selwyn was not well received by the CMS missionaries, who valued their independence. Serving as a member of the governor's council, Selwyn supported Governor Grey's decision to attack the mission's land purchases when they opposed his land policies, and he advised the mission to abandon these purchases. Henry Williams, unlike most of the missionaries, declined to give up his land (aware of his family's needs and convinced of his own integrity) and the tragic result was that the bishop advised the CMS to dismiss him. The consequence for the credibility of the mission was massive.

The land wars of the 1860s were a further development of the strategy of securing Māori land, this time by the newly established settler government, which manipulated the governors. Missionary protests about this were real, and Selwyn was equal in these protests. But Māori had increasingly decided, on the basis of a reading of the Old Testament by Wiremu Tāmihana (a great Māori Anglican), that they needed to become an independent people. The King Movement was a profound challenge to British government legitimacy, and the mission was bound to choose the British side; for safety's sake it had to evacuate almost all of its mission fields. There were tragic consequences: Bishop Selwyn became a military chaplain and was wrongly accused of being present at massacres in Rangiaowhia in 1864. One of the missionaries, Carl Sylvanus Volkner, returning to his station in Ōpōtiki in 1865, was accused by the invading Kīngitanga troops of being a spy for the British (which was true enough) and was killed.

During the wars, a former Wesleyan turned prophet, Te Ua Haumēne, created

Pai Mārire or Hauhau, a movement that brought together Christian and traditional themes, and identified Māori with Israel. In 1867 Te Kooti Arikirangi was accused of spying for the rebels while fighting on the British side and was sent to the Chatham Islands. Here he had a series of visions, and later led his followers back to the East Coast, where in dramatic circumstances he disrupted the settler world and created a spiritual movement based on Old Testament karakia (prayers), which became what we know as Ringatū. In Taranaki another prophetic political movement developed at Parihaka under Te Whiti o Rongomai. In November 1881 Parihaka was invaded by 1600 armed constables who arrested the prophet and many of his followers, who responded with passive non-resistance.

Meanwhile the Māori Anglican Church was re-established gradually, by a small group of missionaries and some Māori ordained priests, especially in the territories of Ngāti Porou on the East Coast, which had been staunchly kūpapa (supporters of the British government) during the wars. The Catholic mission, which had anyway weakened when Pompallier fell out with the Marists, was re-established by a new Catholic religious order, the Mill Hill Fathers, and a number of nuns including Suzanne Aubert in Meeanee, Hiruhārama (Jerusalem) and elsewhere. The Wesleyan mission and a new Presbyterian mission also worked in the central North Island, but the Māori population and the number of churchgoers had dropped hugely.

No great recovery in Māori Christianity occurred until Tahupōtiki Wiremu Rātana had a spiritual vision on his farm south of Wanganui in 1918. For a while he led a team from many churches in encouraging Māori back into a new spiritual covenant, but tensions within these churches over control led the movement to secede and create its own independent Rātana Church in 1925. The net effect of these trends was that the Māori churches were by and large on a very different trajectory to the European churches, and therefore can be covered in only a limited way in this study.

OVER THESE YEARS THE denominations of churches became organised in New Zealand as independent bodies. Their organisation and structures matured into national bodies, and they created local congregations or parishes across the whole country. There is a rich literature on the formation and development of these denominations. Since this book is focused on the story at the local level, some background on the formation and character of each denomination is required.

The stories of the major denominations are all complex in different ways. Given that New Zealand was a British colony, the Anglican story was the key one. The Church of England was one of the national branches of the Catholic Church which broke away in the sixteenth century Reformation (notoriously, the result of Henry VIII's many marriages). It retained more remnants of Catholicism (bishops, vestments, liturgy, parishes) than any other Protestant church, but in the end the Church of England was subject to the Houses of Parliament as a state body. During the next three centuries it was an important instrument of the state and not allowed to choose its own bishops, while parish priests were mostly chosen by lay patrons. Bishop Selwyn had to figure out how to turn a state church into a working New Zealand denomination. Various attempts to get permissive legislation from the British parliament failed, and so the solution was an act of voluntary compact, agreed by lay and clergy leaders (all of them Europeans) at St Stephen's Chapel in Auckland in 1857.

Defining Anglicanism as based on using the Book of Common Prayer prepared by Archbishop Cranmer in 1552 and revised in 1662, and accepting the Thirty-nine Articles of Faith, the church as envisaged by Selwyn reformed many of the inconsistencies of English Anglicanism, thus modelling what a truly national church ought to look like. It also restored a system of self-government in which bishops were answerable to synods and a periodic General Synod which comprised elected laymen, clergy and the bishop from each diocese. Those dioceses (Christchurch, Nelson, Wellington, Waiapu and Auckland, which was the remnant of the original Diocese of New Zealand) initially had Crown-appointed bishops. Dunedin was created later in a poor exercise of authority by Selwyn out of the southern part of the Christchurch Diocese; the bishop he allowed to be ordained was unacceptable to Dunedin lay people, and was forced to resign his office.

The New Zealand church, unlike the Australian church, was relatively consistent in its style of Anglicanism. At this time Anglicans in Britain were moving in several divergent directions, one group strongly evangelical (and initially represented in New Zealand by supporters of the CMS and by the Diocese of Waiapu, which was highly dependent on the CMS for most of its clergy, and who ministered to Māori), and another that was affected by the Oxford Movement, which had emerged in England in the 1830s and sought to revive the Catholic traditions of the church (a movement for which Selwyn had some sympathy).

Anglicans showed a gradual trend towards more Catholic ceremony, although the Nelson Diocese reacted sharply against this and became an evangelical diocese. And in the Diocese of Waikato, carved out of the southern part of the Auckland Diocese in 1926, Bishop Carrington was unsuccessful in his efforts to push it in a strongly Catholic direction. The Anglican Church was a relatively middle-of-the-road body. Bishops were mostly appointed from England until the 1960s. The Māori Church had longed for its own bishop, fitting the original vision of the CMS, but only in 1928 was a Māori Bishop of Aotearoa appointed, and he was a bishop without a diocese, dependent on the willingness of other bishops to allow him to have any role. In 1992 the General Synod of the Anglican Church adopted a new constitution, Te Pouhere, by which the church was separated into three parallel tikanga — Pākehā, Māori and Polynesian — each with its own bishops, meeting only at General Synod. In recent years it has also had three presiding primates.

The Presbyterian Church has an even more complex story. Presbyterians were shaped by John Calvin's vision of the Reformation, in which bishops and priests were replaced by elders (the 'presbytery', or meeting of elders), and biblical justification was sought for all church practices. John Knox made this form of church part of the Scottish way of life and, after bitter struggles with England, the state church of Scotland. Given the demand for biblical justifications, there were frequent schisms from the state church, and the largest of these happened in 1843 when the 'evangelical party' (those more committed to Bible-based reform) created a new Free Church, insisting that each congregation should select its own minister.

A congregation of the state Church of Scotland was formed by the Rev. John Macfarlane at the first Wakefield settlement of Wellington in 1840 (this was the first church in Wellington). The first significant group of Scots came with the settlement in Otago in 1848, and was commenced in the name of the Free Church. So the Otago church was very determined to maintain strong reformed and biblical principles, and the settlement remained a tiny enclave until gold was found at Gabriel's Gully in Otago in 1861.

In 1862 the Presbyterian congregations throughout the colony met in Auckland and agreed to create a system of presbyteries (regional bodies with authority over local congregations) and an annual General Assembly with supreme authority over the church. Unfortunately, a few months later, when the Presbyterians of Otago heard of the more liberal trends in the northern Presbyterian congregations, they became alarmed and formed the Synod of Otago and Southland, which remained separate from the national Presbyterian Church. Since this part of the church had many more resources and a theological training plan, this was a massive obstacle for Presbyterianism. Only in 1901, when the southern Presbyterians had accepted the use of organs and hymns, did they enter the united church. The Presbyterian Church of New Zealand began as a very strong force in New Zealand, considering the relative sizes of the Church of Scotland and the Church of England in the United Kingdom.

The Catholic Church in New Zealand began with the Vatican's establishment of a Vicariate of the Western Pacific, and Bishop Pompallier, with wide responsibilities for the islands north of New Zealand, worked with the newly founded Society of Mary, based in France. The Catholic Church had been profoundly affected by the schisms of the Reformation, and in the Council of Trent (held in three sessions between 1545 and 1563) had revised and clarified many aspects of church life. So the 'tridentine' Latin Mass, the central service of the church, was defined, religious orders were restructured, and the training of priests in seminaries was introduced. The next reforms took place in 1870 while New Zealand was a colony, at the First Vatican Council, when the infallibility of the pope was declared a fundamental doctrine of the faith. The First Vatican Council in 1870 inspired the creation of the separatist Catholic school system, since Protestantism and secular society were viewed in a very negative way.

Traditionally, religious orders had a high degree of independence, and the missionaries of the Society of Mary grew very discontented at Pompallier's imperious and lavish style, and petitioned the Vatican for a new regime. They were satisfied in 1850 with the creation of the Diocese of Wellington, which covered the whole of New Zealand south of Lake Taupō. The French Marist priests were largely withdrawn from their Māori ministries, and placed in parishes ministering to European settlers, most of them Irish. Pompallier had to recruit 'secular' priests, who were not members of religious orders. He also brought the Sisters of Mercy to Auckland, and this order became the largest of the numerous female orders which attached themselves to dioceses.

Once Pompallier was replaced, the Diocese of Auckland had bishops from a striking range of traditions: Irish, English and New Zealand secular and Benedictine bishops. The Marists were very strong in Wellington and in the later Christchurch Diocese, while the Dunedin Diocese had a very strong secular Irish tradition in its bishops, and a high profile in hostility to the Protestant majority in Otago and in New Zealand as a whole. There were small minorities of other nationalities in the church, including Germans at Pūhoi and Italians in Wellington, but New Zealand — unlike Australia — welcomed relatively few southern European Catholic migrants after World War II. Thus the New Zealand church remained dominated by Irish Catholics, and dependent on Irish clergy and nuns.

The Second Vatican Council in the 1960s shook the church in New Zealand as elsewhere, and parishes and religious orders were transformed, while the church struggled to recruit priests and nuns for its work.

Methodism was a movement to bring the people of Britain to a personal experience of faith, which began through the preaching of John Wesley and others in the eighteenth century. The Church of England was very suspicious of it, even though Wesley was a devout Anglican priest, but the state allowed the movement to continue, and it flourished in some parts of England and in America. After Wesley's death it split into several groups, the largest of which called itself the Wesleyans.

It was the Wesleyans that sent missionaries to New Zealand from 1822, but the Primitive Methodists sent preachers in 1840, and two other small Methodist denominations also established a modest presence here.

Initially the Australasian Wesleyan churches as a group were granted independence by the British Wesleyan Conference, but the New Zealand Methodists, who were enjoying rapid growth, were not happy under Australian control. When the merger with the Primitive Methodists of New Zealand took place in 1913, the New Zealand Conference became independent at the same time. But by then rapid growth had ceased, and Methodists struggled with competing pressures from liberal and evangelical forces, which resulted in 1999 in the separation of the more evangelical members into the Wesleyan Methodist Church. Since the 1970s the strongest forces in Methodism have come from migrants from Tonga, Samoa and other parts of the Pacific, but some of these have formed Samoan and Tongan denominations rather than join the New Zealand Methodist Church.

Members of other British denominations also established congregations in New Zealand wherever numbers made this practical, but this mostly restricted them to the cities. The Congregationalist Independents, descendants of the Nonconformists or Dissenters who had been expelled from the Church of England in 1662, had made an impact among the urban middle class of England but gained only a small foothold in New Zealand, perhaps because few of the middle class migrated to this country. Similarly, Baptists had few separate congregations in the nineteenth century but their numbers grew rapidly, taking advantage of an evangelical surge, from the middle of the twentieth century. These denominations had very weak central structures, and struggled to develop a national network.

The Salvation Army was only founded in the late nineteenth century in England under General William Booth, but when two missionaries were sent to Dunedin they made a very dramatic initial impact, especially among the poor. There were other denominations among ethnic minorities (for example, German and Scandinavian Lutherans) and with particular emphases, including Quakers, Churches of Christ and Brethren. Overall the smaller denominations amounted to just 5 per cent of the total population. Many of their lay members did well in New Zealand, however, and their denominations often reflected trends in the mainstream of church life, and so a few of their stories will also be found in this book.

Pentecostalism is often traced to the Azusa Street revival in Los Angeles in 1906, but it reached New Zealand through British preachers in the 1920s. Then, in the 1950s and 1960s, there was a huge burst of interest in Pentecostal phenomena, especially speaking in tongues, within mainstream denominations. The result was the charismatic movement, which attracted many young people — indeed virtually a whole generation of Protestant young people and many Catholics as well. Some remained in the mainstream churches but many others joined Pentecostal denominations, and those churches were evolving. Increasingly, large megachurches, with very strong leaders, became the feature of this movement.

From 1901 there were increasing calls for some kind of unification of the various denominations in New Zealand, reflecting broader world trends. In a land with a small population the duplication of churches seemed an extravagance. In many communities the first church had been a joint Protestant community church; the denominational range increased with the population. Then in 1901 the Presbyterians became a single denomination, and in 1913 so did the Methodists, and ideas of a single evangelical Protestant denomination circulated at this time. These discussions slowly developed, especially between Presbyterians and Methodists. The formation of the National Council of Churches in 1941 also increased denominational cooperation, embracing all the larger Protestant churches. Then in 1965 the Joint Commission of Church Union, embracing five of the larger Protestant denominations (not Catholics, Baptists or the Salvation Army), began discussions for union. The plan would have succeeded but for Anglican caution, which led to the withdrawal of the Anglican Church in 1976 and the collapse of the proposal.

Since then many church people and churches, including the Catholic Church after the reforms of the Second Vatican Council, have cooperated on a range of activities. People have moved more freely between denominations, but the denominations themselves have stopped seeking organisational unity, and have concentrated on the significant decline in membership which all have experienced. Meanwhile the National Council of Churches was replaced in 1987 by the Council of Churches in Aotearoa New Zealand. The Catholic Church joined, but the Baptist Union did not. In 2006 the council was closed down after other denominations withdrew their support. Various bodies — including one of church leaders, the evangelical New Zealand Christian Network (which arose out of the Evangelical Fellowship of New Zealand) and a series of Vision congresses — have been established, while in 2016 Anglicans, Methodists and Catholics attempted to create a new ecumenical body.

I N THE HISTORY OF the churches in New Zealand one issue that assumes central importance, although it is largely irrelevant in the context of this book, is the lack of a formal link with the state. Bishop Selwyn had been appointed by letters patent, the normal mode of British Crown appointments, and in his case one in which the Queen took a real interest. It was intended that the bishop would organise the provision of the Church of England in the Crown colony, including

The laying of the foundation of the Wesleyan Methodist Church in Moxham Avenue, Hataitai (or Kilbirnie), Wellington, in 1896. The church was part of the Wellington circuit, where Josiah Ward was the main minister, and he is probably the speaker while Mrs Ward is seated at the harmonium. The church seated 100 people and was built beside the state school for the sum of £39.15 using donated materials.
ALEXANDER TURNBULL LIBRARY.
REF: 1/2-075654-F

the work of the CMS missionaries, the provision of chaplaincy to the British forces and the creation of parishes for the settler community. The position of the bishop was therefore financed one-third by the CMS, one-third by the Colonial Office and one-third by one of the inter-diocesan Anglican organisations, the Society for the Promotion of the Gospel.

Part of the bishop's function was to solicit clergy and funds for the establishment of local churches, since the Anglican government had ceased to provide this kind of support since 1829, when the British state had opened its doors to Nonconformist Protestants who were not part of the state church, and to Roman Catholics. New Zealand was founded at a time when the state role in supporting Anglicanism was significantly less than it had been in either Australia or in the South African British colonies. Relative neutrality was urged by some of the Govenor's Council, but Selwyn was also on that executive and expected some degree of state support. This primarily consisted of the provision of land for building churches of all denominations. A scheme to support clergy of all denominations was opposed by Selwyn and negated in England.

The later stages of the separation of church and state awaited the advent of the settler parliament in 1854, when the members refused to recognise the military chaplain as the chaplain to the parliament, insisting on perfect equality of all denominations but requiring the speaker to open each day by reading a Christian prayer. This remains the situation. A year later the settler government declined to take over the share of Bishop Selwyn's salary previously paid by the Colonial Office.

In 1877, when the parliament turned its attention to a compulsory system of primary education, it insisted that this education must be non-sectarian, and the strongest protests against this were not Anglican but Catholic. Attempts to get non-sectarian Bible readings and prayer into the curriculum over later years failed, the final attempt interrupted by the outbreak of World War II. Instead, a scheme of voluntary classes on a non-sectarian basis during the first half-hour of the school day became an informal, and later formal, system when approved by the school committee. This curious expedient — the living proof that no grand principle underlay the decision — remains a source of tension to this day. Meanwhile the Catholics' demand for support for their system finally, in 1975, led to integration into the state system with some reserved rights for the proprietor, and today's education system is looser than that in the nineteenth century.

So the state remained interconnected with the churches, but its attitude to these links varied somewhat in different periods. During the world wars, the state encouraged the churches to cooperate in providing chaplains for the army serving overseas in large numbers. During the era of the Cold War in the 1950s, the church here as in America was sometimes described as essential to the fabric of Western values. Just why the state used the church in this way is outside the scope of this book. Instead this study focuses on the neglected role played by the church in society.

The churches have campaigned for many causes, the obvious ones including making religious education a compulsory subject (or, in the Catholic case, gaining state support for their separate educational system); the attempt to ban the use of alcohol; attempts to help the poor, women, refugees and those with disabilities; and campaigns against eugenics, prostitution, abortion, nuclear arms, rugby games with South Africa, and refugee quotas. In many cases a minority of the churches joined in these campaigns, and often they allied with other groups. The particulars of these crusades have been explored by Laurie Guy in his fine book *Shaping Godzone*.[1] The subject of this book is less the crusades and more the style of the church as a crusader — sometimes a reluctant one. It is about the Christian values and community experience that provoked activism.

A final theme that is not the subject of this book is the way in which the churches have experienced decline among their traditional supporters, and a rise in their attraction of new migrants. Church involvement had never been a high priority to most New Zealanders. Although until 1971 more than 89 per cent of the population professed a Christian denominational link on their census form, church attendance came nowhere near such figures. From 1971 the figures declined rapidly to 76 per cent in 1981, just over 60 per cent in 1996, 52 per cent in 2006, and 46 per cent in 2013. The age distribution of this religious adherence strongly suggests that the decline will continue as older people, with their higher levels of adherence, pass away.

Although European and Māori numbers have declined, the rapid change in New Zealand's ethnic distribution has created new concentrations of religious adherence. In particular, Pacific peoples, who have come to New Zealand in large numbers since the 1950s, have much higher levels of nominal religious adherence and regular attendance at church. Although this now seems to be declining, some denominations, notably the Methodist Church, are now dependent on Pasifika people. The migration of Europeans has diversified the Catholic Church and brought groups of Dutch people into the Presbyterian Church, but had little effect on other Anglo-Saxon Protestant denominations. The increase in Asian migration from the 1990s has mostly aided the growth of other religions, notably Buddhism, Hinduism and Islam, but it has also brought large numbers of mainland Chinese who have been subject to generations of anti-religious propaganda. Koreans and Filipinos have strong Christian affiliations, and this has been very significant for the Catholic Church in particular. Suggestions of how this has changed the culture of the churches are explored at the end of most chapters, but much remains to be seen or to be researched.

ALL THE FACTORS MENTIONED above are legitimately part of church history, but my concern is about what church people believed, and the way in which their churches cohered and touched their lives and their communities. The ambitious hope of this book is to unlock this largely forgotten story.

To do so, it is necessary to go beyond an examination of one denomination. Certainly a collective story suppresses some of the extreme ends of the story. There was a vast difference in the experience of religion between a Catholic parishioner and the member of a Salvation Army Corps. I have sought to incorporate aspects of the culture right across the spectrum, but individual denominational and even congregational stories need to be told. Moreover, the book may create an impression that there was a long century of relatively unchanging church culture, followed by very rapid change. History rarely happens like that, but the book is undoubtedly centred on 'the world that was lost'. Again, the details look different within each denomination; undoubtedly, for example, church morning teas follow denominational trends, as do the changing patterns of prayer.

Sunday Best seeks to provide a narrative of overall trends, but the shrewd reader will soon identify 'patches' in the book where unusual detail is offered on particular themes, be they coffee bars, curtseying to the bishop, soirées, Christmas, Scripture in Song or the furnishing of the parsonage. These topics could be subjects on their own, and some of them I have described in detail in other places, but the aim of the book is to set them in a cultural tradition, in a stream of development. I hope, further, that some of the other stories which I touch on will be picked up by others, who can test my arguments, and hopefully give them additional value.

The argument of this book is that understanding religious culture is highly desirable for our understanding of New Zealand society and culture as a whole. A history of the culture of New Zealand Christianity is not a history of its political significance, organisational developments, or social impact. Each of these is important, and superb recent writing has highlighted all these themes, but the lack of an understanding of the culture of New Zealand church life is evident in a number of contexts. For example, religion is regularly dismissed as of no significance because its impact was largely in the private sphere. Yet historians have repeatedly identified the importance of the private sphere. Religion sat partly in the private sphere — and indeed is a critical part of it for some people — and gaining an understanding of this ought to unlock explanations for many aspects of society and culture, including music, literacy, cultural memory, class consciousness, family formation and gender identity.

I am by no means the first to work in these areas, and I am immensely grateful to friends and colleagues who have contributed so much to my understanding. In some fields I simply summarise their fine work, and seek to give the credit where credit is due. I would particularly mention Geoff Troughton, Allan Davidson, Chris van der Krogt, the late Hugh Laracy, Martin Sutherland, Stuart Lange, Laurie Guy, Noel Derbyshire, Margaret McClure, Hugh Morrison, Janet Crawford, John Stenhouse and Alison Clarke. I am very appreciative of various archives where I found documents and photographs. I also particularly mention the Grey Lynn Group, which has met in my house once a month for nearly two decades, trading historical and theological stories. Also, so many students over the years have enhanced my understanding of specific topics as they have explored various themes. I hope all can see now that I was listening to their arguments. There are some other aspects where I have found that very little work has been done. My attempt to make sense of the field awaits revision by the new generation of students and researchers.

I have used the anachronistic term 'Anglican' in general to refer to the Church of the Province of New Zealand, and I have used the terms Methodist and Catholic rather freely. Other religious terms are explained in the glossary.

I am a collector of parish histories. These little works are in sheer bulk as common as the histories of schools, and obviously were meaningful to the people who wrote them. In a way I am suggesting that such accounts would do well to focus on this cultural theme; the very best of them have done this very well. Meanwhile I have been delighted to have had an excuse to read so many of them, and to look for what is told, casually and in an off-hand way, which reveals so much about their life and community.

The Sacred Day

Previous John Kinder's watercolour painting *Onehunga, Manukau Harbour and Heads*, 1860. Kinder portrayed an idyllic English scene with the Onehunga village church in the centre, although this was only how it looked from one angle. The current St Peter's stands on the same site. AUCKLAND ART GALLERY TOI O TĀMAKI, GIFT OF HARRY KINDER, 1937

AT THE HEART OF traditional religion lay a different notion of time. The idea of a sacred day of worship is not as familiar today as it was in preceding generations. Historically — or perhaps one should say, in anthropological terms — it formed part of an extensive code of holy and unholy things, or in Māori terms, tapu and noa formed the framework of community life.

The Christian church from the fourth century observed an annual cycle that was more significant than its weekly routines. Great festivals followed the pattern of Jewish annual festivals, but Passover was converted into the Christian Easter, while further festivals reflected the traditional rural year. In this way the church sought to replace paganism while adopting some of its customs. These traditions diverged in the Catholic western European world from the Orthodox eastern European world, and Christmas and Easter customs reflect this.

At the time of the Reformation in the sixteenth century, the Protestant reformers disagreed about the value of the church year. Lutheran and Anglican churches continued the church year with modifications, although they did not add new saints and holy days. Presbyterians and the separatist churches, the 'Anabaptists', rejected the value of holy days, and Puritan attempts to abolish the celebration of Christmas in the period when the royal government and Church of England were overthrown in the seventeenth century reflected this view.

While the secular tradition of a New Year's Eve celebration, Hogmanay, flourished in Scotland, Presbyterians rejected Christmas, instead focusing entirely on the Christian Sabbath, Sunday. Chapter 21 of the Westminster Confession of Faith of 1646, the formulary for Presbyterians in Great Britain, insisted that Sunday was the Christian Sabbath, and worldly employment and recreation were forbidden. In contrast, Anglicans followed James I's Book of Sports, issued in 1617, which permitted 'harmless recreations' on Sunday after church.[1]

The Sunday Observance Act of 1677 protected the day, prohibiting all work except that of necessity or mercy, but it did not restrict leisure and it was not well policed. In the late eighteenth century the evangelicals — the 'Church Methodists' — in the established church campaigned to enforce the regulations rigorously. William Wilberforce, the respected evangelical advocate of the abolition of slavery, persuaded George III to issue the Proclamation for the Encouragement of Piety and Virtue in 1787, and a society was founded to prosecute Sunday traders.

Sabbatarianism grew rapidly as a political campaign while the evangelicals were in the ascendant. The Lord's Day Observance Society, formed in 1831, was a highly successful pressure group, which closed Sunday trading by the post office in 1849, Sunday opening by museums in the 1850s, and ended Sunday trains for a period. The campaign was primarily directed against leisure, for some Sunday work was unavoidable in an industrial society.[2] One scholar calls the Sabbath 'almost a sacrament' in Protestant eyes.[3] A sacrament is supposed to connect Heaven to Earth, and it was certainly viewed as a requirement for a Christian society; it placed the community in a religious framework, reminding them every week of the Christian sense of time. The culture of sabbatarianism was very significant. It was the foundation for cultural practices that were shared or respected by church people despite their theological differences. In a profound way the Sabbath was part of the British way of life, especially during the Victorian age.

MĀORI OBSERVED RITUAL CELEBRATIONS (hahunga) around harvest time based on their lunar calendar.[4] From the very first, the evangelical missionaries of the Church Missionary Society who brought Christianity to New Zealand in 1814 were emphatic about observing the Sabbath. Samuel Marsden, who brought the missionaries to Aotearoa, sought to persuade Māori to adopt the pattern of the Sabbath, and the facilitator of the missionaries, Ruatara, told fellow Māori 'that it was a Day of Rest, and that God would be angry with them for working and selling things on the Sabbath — They were much afraid, and told him that they now believed that there was a Sabbath — I had given Instructions to the Master of the Active to be very particular in keeping the Sabbath.'[5]

Sabbath-keeping was the initial priority of the early missionaries. On his second visit to New Zealand, in 1820, Marsden spoke to Māori every Sunday, explaining the nature of the creation, the goodness of God and the institution of the Sabbath.[6] By 1823, long before any Māori had been baptised, the Sabbath had widespread respect. Henry Williams, who became the senior CMS missionary, noted this soon after his arrival in 1823: 'Their observance of the Sabbath is, for them, very great; they know when it arrives as well as we do, and distinguish the day by wearing their European clothes and abstaining from work; our Settlement on that day is perfectly quiet.'[7] Augustus Earle, the secular artist, made the same observation when he visited in 1827.[8]

Māori Christianity began with sabbatarianism. Perhaps it was easy for Māori to respect these rules, and it became a uniform characteristic of Māori Christianity. Many early observers noted how strictly Māori observed the day, perhaps with the zeal of people wanting a simple formula for Christian blessing. 'Rā Tapu' literally applied a tapu to one day in the week.[9] According to missionary Richard Davis, British troops exploited this adherence to the Sabbath when they attacked Māori on that day at the battle of Ruapekapeka pa during the Flagstaff War, catching them off-guard (although the details are disputed).[10]

Opponents of missionary Christianity loathed their sabbatarianism. Religious

Natives assembled to celebrate the Lord's Supper at Orona, Taupo, New Zealand, 1845. The image was probably drawn by Bishop George Selwyn and published in the English magazine *The Ecclesiologist*. The preacher is in the left tent, the presiding priest in the one on the right. ALEXANDER TURNBULL LIBRARY. REF: PUBL-0180-1845-084

groups that developed in the wake of Christianity included Pai Mārire, the religion that emerged during the New Zealand Wars, and Ringatū, the religion of the prophet Te Kooti, which made the twelfth day of every month sacred, offered an alternative sacred day, Saturday, and lunar sacred days.[11] Māori Anglican clergy sought to reinforce sabbatarianism, for the loss of this habit undermined communal adherence to faith.[12] Southern Māori, evangelised by Wesleyans, were described as being as strict in their sabbatarianism as the Scottish community in Otago.[13]

In the earliest days of Pākehā settlement, law and order was only loosely observed, attitudes to Sunday were largely pre-Victorian, and the settler community had few weekly patterns. The small group of Protestant pastors in Wellington who formed the Evangelical Alliance in 1848 were very concerned to strengthen Sabbath observance, and reprinted material by Wilberforce in favour of the legal protection of the Sabbath.[14]

The New Zealand prohibitions were based on the 1676 British Act for Better Observation of the Lord's Day, and the 1781 Act for Preventing Certain Abuse and Profanations on the Lord's Day. For religious politicians like the Dunedin Presbyterian politician Downie Stewart, the logic of this legislation was clear: New Zealand was a Christian country and therefore the Sabbath should be enforced. But it was not that simple, even in Otago.

During the early years of the colony there was a real battle over the Sabbath. While there were attempts to strengthen its enforcement in line with British legislation, at the same time many colonists were cynical about the whole sabbatarian framework. Debates centred in different towns on public transport and public facilities, where the law was somewhat ambiguous. And people took liberties. Protestants sometimes saw liberalisation of the Sunday legislation as opening the door to Popery.[15]

The sacred calendar was in essence a communal one. But historians have argued that the success of Protestantism, and of Catholicism after the Protestant Reformation, was the way it made the household the key sphere of faith, in which the master of the household was in effect its priest. The issue led to many debates, but this book instead explores the experience of sabbatarianism, for it was a rhythm of life and a framework for community life.

The scholar who has explored this framework of sacred time most profoundly is Alison Clarke. For Presbyterians, as Clarke has indicated, but also for Anglicans, the state announced fast days and feast days to respond to military and royal occasions.[16] Anglicans continued to observe the church year, with some modifications. The Catholic Church after the Reformation made few changes to the Christian year, expecting the faithful to attend Mass on the key saints' days. Irish Catholics used St Patrick's Day, the day of the patron saint of Ireland, as a celebration of their faith.

Most non-Anglican Protestants regarded the Christian year as an archaism, happily left behind in England. Christmas was a time for festivities, but not primarily for religious observances. And antipodean Anglicans, too, seemed to make less of these customs, partly because the patterns of the calendar had been upended, and therefore made less sense. Bishop Selwyn commented, 'the general laxity of morals, and defect of church principles, in the new settlements... render it almost impossible to keep up that high tone of religious character and structure of discipline which is required'.[17] Christmas, with all its secular associations, flourished in New Zealand, while Easter languished.[18]

Ethnic differences increased the complexity of the situation. Good Friday was profoundly significant to German and Scandinavian Lutherans, who found themselves at odds with other Protestants (especially as many of them were forced to worship in other denominations). English migrants were horrified by Otago Presbyterian attitudes to their sacred calendar. More recent Filipino migrants have been puzzled by the more relaxed Kiwi Catholic attitudes to Good Friday.

O N 8 DECEMBER 1862 the Otago provincial government sought to introduce an additional ordinance to restrict Sunday work, but it was disallowed by the Governor of New Zealand, Thomas Gore Browne. However, an ordinance of 4 September 1863 was approved, and licensing legislation in 1865 introduced tight controls on Sunday sales.[19]

In Scotland, Sabbath protection was a standard feature of church and social life, for in a very significant way the preservation of a quiet Sabbath was seen as a repeated community honouring of God's law in public life. Thomas Burns, the first pastor of Dunedin, eloquently described the character of the settlement in those years: 'The stillness of our Sabbath and the crowded state of our churches, and the highly respectable and becoming appearance of our congregations, I have been told by visitors (strangers from the neighbouring colonies) are not to be paralleled anywhere out of Scotland, more especially in our country congregations.'[20]

This tone was undermined by the gold rushes that began in 1861. In 1866 Presbyterian ministers were forced to defend the Sabbath from the pulpit in the face of criticisms.[21] In 1871 the Rev. George Sutherland, minister of First Church in Dunedin, decried Dunedinites who went to the port on Sunday to see a visiting American ship during the hours of worship. The result was a stormy newspaper correspondence.[22] Sutherland was dedicated to maintaining a strict Sabbath and in the debate he presented an ideal view of how the Sabbath functioned for the good of all: 'In days not far distant it was customary for families to attend church in the forenoon, returning home to a light meal, to resume attendance at church in the afternoon; immediately thereafter the Sunday School was held; and, public duties over, the whole Sabbath evening, the purest, sweetest, and most peaceful of all the hours of life, was free for home life.'[23]

This may have been so for church attendees, but as Dunedin became larger others demanded the right to live their own way. There was a sharp debate about the opening of the Athenaeum reading room in 1874.[24]

After the provinces were abolished in 1876, regulation of permitted Sunday activities devolved to local bodies. There was a sharp protest from church ministers at the permission given for the naval band to play in the Dunedin botanical gardens in 1885. In the debate that followed, the mayor's casting vote prevented this entertainment.[25] So Otago was able to retain its Sabbath restrictions at least in part.

The Sabbath was much less strictly enforced in the provinces other than Otago, and the end of the provincial administration meant that apart from legislation for the whole colony, the only option was enforcement by local bodies at the behest of community agitators. The vigour of the advocacy of Sabbath controls was a very public aspect of Protestant life. So, for example, in 1906 Christian Endeavour held a parade to condemn Sabbath desecration.[26] Many Protestant churches became involved in such protests. The Presbyterian Church maintained a Sabbath Observance Committee which reported to the General Assembly.[27]

Christchurch, as a nominally Anglican settlement, was more relaxed on the issue, but there was a burst of agitation in the 1870s about a proposal to open the museum on Sundays. The museum authorities hoped that it would thus become popular with the working-class community. Congregationalism was the strongest of the historic Protestant churches in England, and William Habens as its minister in Christchurch was an influential voice. He was troubled by the proposal, for while he was a great advocate of free education and believed in the virtue of museum attendance, he was also minister of a Sabbath-keeping community.[28]

The agitation became more vocal as a result of new legislation in 1880. A Christchurch magistrate interpreted the legislation as permitting more activities on the Sabbath, causing alarm to some church people.[29] In 1881 the governors of Canterbury College (the Christchurch branch of the University of New Zealand) decided to open their library on Sunday.[30] Other reading rooms followed suit.[31] But Sunday opening of public facilities went no further for the next 60 years.

THESE WERE MINOR CONCESSIONS. Most Protestants gave lip service to a sacred Sabbath as a healthy and wholesome pattern of regular rest from work, and it became ingrained in communities. It was imposed on people whether or not they went to church. For many it was simply how they lived. James McCaw, the son of a Presbyterian minister, many years later recalled his experience of Sunday; the restrictions irked him, but he and other children found other ways to enjoy themselves, and hospitality, country rambles and family time were significant. But he still recalled being whacked for whistling on the Sabbath.[32]

Sunday was a rather formal day. For example, there were strict rules as to dress for church in order to honour God. Even working-class men who did not go to church had their Sunday best, which they would wear if going out on that day. Young Presbyterian parishioner Margery Ayrton recalled that her Sunday clothing was a red velvet dress with a lace collar, and shiny leather shoes.[33]

Sunday food in areas where the Sabbath was strictly observed was generally cold, cooked on Saturday and sliced and eaten on Sunday. Sometimes the dishes were not washed until Monday.[34] In contrast, most English colonists enjoyed a hot Sunday roast, although some households served it up reheated after church on Sunday morning. The advent of the electric stove made it easier for mothers to prepare the meal, and Sunday became dominated by the big meal.

In the strict Protestant household, boots were polished on Saturday and domestic work kept to a minimum on Sunday. There was a strong emphasis in colonial society against Sunday work except where absolutely necessary. Yet there were no laws against it until the passing of the Police Offences Act in 1884. This was maintained by subsequent legislation, although there were always exceptions for sellers of fresh food and meals. In 1920 the law was made stricter, but exceptions were allowed for small shops. A list of exempt goods was created in the 1955 Shops and Offices Act. This raised some serious issues for dairy farmers and others whose work forced them into daily activity. In a dairying culture the cows still had to be milked, but non-essential work was seen as inappropriate. Dairy farmers were sometimes told from the pulpit to avoid fixing fences on the Sabbath.[35]

By 1945 these patterns were changing. Unpaid work became acceptable. Even the Brethren (who often preserved Protestant traditions long after others had abandoned them) weakened in their observance. Chris Collins cites a Brethren male who, for the sake of 'the testimony' and the weaker brother, would not mow his lawns on Sunday nor paint the front of his house, but was prepared to paint the back of the house if necessity intervened.[36]

Transport raised some troubling issues for Protestants. Some church members were horrified at people travelling by steamer on a Sunday.[37] Joseph Clark, the minister of the Baptist Tabernacle in Auckland, told a 1903 audience that he was happy if he lost the more scattered members of his congregation due to the banning of Sunday trams.[38] Mount Albert Baptist Church was founded in 1913 by two families in the newest Auckland suburb who found it too far to walk to the Tabernacle on Sunday morning.[39] Yet some church boarding schools sent their students to church by tram, and no church complained lest they deplete their congregation.[40] Eventually private transport palliated some of these rules. The Rev John McKenzie, Clerk of the Presbyterian General Assembly in the 1930s, would not use a tram on a Sunday to get to a preaching appointment, but once he owned a car he was happy to drive, because no one else had to work.[41] Car owners avoided buying petrol on Sunday. I had a relation who would not purchase petrol on Sunday, but accepted my father's offer to syphon petrol from our car to his!

This issue, however, became an increasing subject of debate. In Auckland there was a running debate about whether the trams should be permitted to run on Sunday. In 1887 the city council decided to ban them, but the debate recurred in 1895.[42] Then, in 1903, the council took a poll on the issue and there was a slender majority in favour of letting the trams run on Sundays.[43] As the Baptist historian Laurie Guy explains in his study of the subject, this was a very serious showdown, which provoked deep divisions in the community. In certain respects it put churches on the defensive, and some believed that congregational numbers declined as a result.

THE MOST DELICATE ISSUES surrounded leisure. After all, Sunday was designated a day of rest, not of church attendance, which was not particularly high in the colony. Moreover, in many country areas church services occurred fortnightly or even monthly. One horrified speaker told the Albert Street Congregational Church in 1867 that in a district he knew, 'the settlers employed their Sabbaths alternately in attending divine service, cattle hunting, and rifle shooting', but that reflected the irregularity of church services in the countryside.[44] In urban areas Sunday morning was recognised as the time that people went to church. Yet many people were not in church. As the Methodist President for 1908 told their conference, 'Walk down our central streets at the hour when the factories and workshops begin to empty themselves of their workers and try to reckon how many of their faces are ever seen from a pulpit; or disguise yourself and spend a few hours with them during their meal time. It will surprise and pain you to hear with what contempt they speak of ministers and of church members.'[45]

Lady Mary Anne Barker, the noted writer and Canterbury sheep station runholder, noted that, 'At every turn one is met by disheartening warnings: "oh the

The inscription of this 1901 cartoon is entitled 'Hope' and reflects the debate over Sunday recreation. ALEXANDER TURNBULL LIBRARY. OBSERVER, 20 JULY 1901

people here are very different from those in the old country; they would look upon it as an impertinence if you suggested they should come to church".' She held services in the homestead but found that many hesitated to enter a private place for worship.[46]

Strict Protestants were busy on Sunday afternoons at Sunday school, but they were taught that leisure on Sundays was restricted to improving magazines such as the *Sunday Herald*, and scripture memorisation. Once the harmonium and piano became cheaper, singing hymns became common. Alison Clarke cites examples where families competed to memorise chapters of the Bible, but were suspicious of anything too enjoyable. The daughter of the Rev. William Will (the second minister to come to the Otago Settlement) was advised by her mother: 'Papa and I would not like you to go walking for pleasure on the Sabbath; we would like you to do as we do at home — take a turn in the garden, or take your book and read there if you like, but don't go either to the sea-beach or to the Botanical Gardens.'[47]

Such regulations could be resented. There are many accounts of people who, in old age, remembered childhoods of endless church services, being dressed up in their best all day and forbidden to run around and play, or even watch, games and sports.[48] This was the model British Sunday, which was so often contrasted with the 'continental Sunday' with its lack of regulations, and it did not appeal to colonial children.

Hotels were permitted to sell alcohol on Sunday until the Licensing Act of 1908 restricted this. Advocates of restriction on the sale of alcohol were especially horrified at the thought of drunkenness on the Lord's Day. The Women's Christian Temperance Union (WCTU), for example, was alerted by the prominent nineteenth-century politician Sir William Fox about the sale of alcohol at Auckland railway station on Sundays.[49] So rules became stricter. In 1909 Miss Lill of the WCTU sent a circular on Sabbath observance to every pupil in New Zealand schools.[50]

This strict attitude did not persuade the majority of people to attend church, and men and boys quietly pursued gambling, games and relaxed drinking, especially where hotel hours were not policed.[51] In 1904 the prime minister himself, Dick Seddon, was criticised for going fishing on Sunday — although he then tried to wriggle out of the accusation that he had breached the Sabbath.[52] No laws prohibited free Sunday entertainment, and Anglicans and Catholics were very comfortable with it. In the 1880s a huge debate focused on this issue when the Police Offences Act introduced legislation prohibiting paid Sunday activity. Several denominations were engaged in the campaign; for example, the Australasian Wesleyan Methodist Church (to which the New Zealand Wesleyans were affiliated) passed a resolution supporting the prosecution of Sabbath breaches at its 1884 triennial conference.[53] But no regulations forbade providing free entertainment in the theatres on Sundays.

Richard Turnbull, MP for Timaru, expressed concern in Parliament about a theatre in Masterton providing a Freethought lecture. Robert Stout, as the Minister for Justice, insisted that the Police Offences Act did not prohibit such events.[54]

This legalistic culture survived a very long time in some church circles, but public sympathy was lost in the early twentieth century. A Brethren source in the 1920s lamented: 'We have had repeated evidence that many children of believers are sadly out of hand, disobedient to parents, lawless, etc., and being allowed to drift to Hell instead of being trained for God. Novel reading and picture going among Christians are having their effect on their children.'[55] Similarly, a conservative Methodist minister, Henry Ryan, lamented in 1930 that there had been a steady decline in attendance at church and Sunday school and attributed this to the modern spirit: 'More people than ever are spending their Sundays motoring, rambling, and in recreations, and turning their backs upon worship, service and meditation.'[56] By the 1930s churchgoing was effectively unfamiliar to many. An ecumenical survey in 1935 of many hundreds of homes in Onehunga revealed astonishing levels of basic ignorance about Christian beliefs and denominations. Only a tiny number were hostile to religion, but radio broadcasts of church services were about as close as most got to church.[57]

The community's sympathies had also shifted towards less enforcement. A debate, provoked by Rationalists, broke out in 1930 about the closing of children's playgrounds on Sunday, and this broadened to a general debate on permitted Sunday leisure.[58] There was still a strong group that held that it was wrong to pay for entertainment on Sunday, and in 1932 they mounted a strong reaction to Sunday train excursions.[59] Perhaps the sharpest debate was over Sunday movie screenings. During World War I the WCTU had expressed concern about golf being played and movies being screened on Sundays.[60] As Laurie Guy has explained, churches seeking to attract a working-class congregation recognised that their services would need to pass as entertainment, so they too experimented with clips from movies to enhance their services. But restrictions continued, and some of the compromises were ingenious. During World War II the Wellington City Council permitted paid movies as long as a brief talk was given by a minister before the film began, providing pious remarks on the events of the day.[61]

Movie-going became very popular on Sundays, and eventually the edifying talks ceased. Finally, the rules were most fully undermined by the arrival of television in the 1960s. For in the privacy of the home, and given the limits on programming on that day, who could be criticised for looking at it?

SUNDAY SPORT, WHICH THE church had never managed to suppress, remained a subject of critical debate. In male-dominated workplaces, and among youth, team sport rose rapidly in the late colonial period, and the church was too weak in such areas to inhibit games on Sundays. Under the 1884 Police Offences Act, games and pastimes were allowed, but it was illegal to charge for them. However, church leaders continued a community battle against such leisure activities as cycling, football, cricket matches, shooting and fishing.[62] The WCTU expressed its alarm that young men tended to spend their Sundays in leisure, lolling about on barges, and in 1891 it established a Sabbath Observance Committee, led initially by Mrs Jane Costall of Wellington, wife of the Government Printer, and then by a Miss Minchim.[63] The committee was proud to report in 1910 that firing practices on Sundays had been stopped by the prime minister, Sir Joseph Ward.[64] In 1922, sport was again permitted on a Sunday, despite protests, as long as tickets were not sold.

Anglicans were less troubled than others by the issue. They felt that 'an enlightened view of Sunday observance' was required, rather than rules and regulations.[65] Anglicans had a tradition of Sunday cricket, and in the 1930s, in an effort to attract men to church, the vicar of Merivale encouraged the men of his fashionable Christchurch parish to come to the 8 a.m. communion service once a month in their golf or sport clothes if they wished.[66] So the old rules were gradually set aside, and club cricket matches were scheduled for Sunday. This was problematic for some Christian sports players. Vic Pollard and Bruce Murray were well-known Baptists who refused to play cricket on Sunday, with the encouragement of the 1967 Baptist Assembly.[67] And despite the changes, churches struggled to allow their own premises to be used for sports on Sunday. In 1950 the St Stephen's Tennis Club in Lower Hutt approached the elders of the Presbyterian congregation requesting that they might play tennis on the church courts on Sunday afternoons. Session was intransigent, and finally in 1965 the club was disaffiliated from the church and leased the court as the Glen Iris Tennis Club.[68]

By the 1930s Protestant visions of the Sabbath were slowly recast. Individual recreation, including golf and physical exercise, was justified, perhaps because it was an act of individual consciences, whereas team sports might entice the 'weaker brother' to go against their conscience. Tennis and non-contact sports also became more acceptable. Playing team sport remained taboo with many, and for Protestants even watching team sport raised moral issues. As schools began to schedule matches on Sundays, families faced acute dilemmas. A strongly evangelical member of the Brethren commented in the 1980s:

> I mean what do you do? So on a Sunday we started off saying no. Then they wanted [my son] in the representatives, and they practised on Sunday. We really soul searched that one, and we decided, well, yes do it, it would be silly not to. We made a deal that we said, we want you to come to church as a family with us when you can . . . we are not going to stop you advancing in your sport.[69]

By the 1970s, faced with the risk of causing anger and recalling their own bitter disappointments, even strongly Protestant families compromised in order to preserve relationships.

IF WE CAN OBSERVE a decline in rules around Sunday, we can also see more churches adopting some parts of the church year. For practical reasons an annual cycle of church activities made sense. A new festive calendar developed within Protestantism, which included anniversary teas, Sunday school anniversaries, harvest festivals and the like.[70] Meanwhile the state set aside holidays at Easter and Christmas, and also for St George, St Andrew and St Patrick, the patron saints of England, Scotland and Ireland. Then the state added to the sacred calendar when Anzac Day was deemed sacred by statute in 1920 and 1922.[71]

For Catholics the liturgical year remained very strong, although it underwent reform in the late twentieth century. Meanwhile Anglicanism became more focused on the church year due to the growing influence of Anglo-Catholicism, the English Anglican movement that commenced in Oxford in the 1830s and which sought to assert a stronger religious tone in secular society. Lent, the six weeks preceding Easter, was supposed in the church year to be a period of self-denial, and was observed by Catholics and a few Anglicans.[72] Anglo-Catholics sought to revive forgotten observances of saints' days and seasons like Lent. Because the New Zealand bishops were suspicious of divisive practices, such customs were slow to spread in the colony. However, in 1935, for example, a Procession of Witness was organised by the New Zealand Church Fellowship in Auckland, associated with one high-church Anglican parish, in which people processed in penitential robes.[73] Gradually the church year became more strictly observed by Anglicans.

Other Protestants were happy enough to take holidays at Christmas and Easter — even in Otago — but they held no special services. Easter certainly was used by churches for conferences and Bible class camps, but such events simply took advantage of a holiday rather than focusing on a sacred calendar.

Christmas Day was a great day in New Zealand from the very first arrival of Pākehā, but not at first on account of any religious celebrations. In the nineteenth century, Anglicans in New Zealand followed the Church of England in limiting their celebrations to the Eucharist on Christmas morning, while Catholics had a midnight Eucharist. Both events attracted huge numbers of people. Anglicans began to hold midnight services in the 1920s, while most Protestant churches rarely held Christmas Day services until after 1950. Community carol-singing was not a church tradition, but as in England informal wassailing, as it was called, was conducted by groups of people wandering the streets on Christmas Eve. Then churches began to offer choir-led carols as a form of outreach in the community.

Not until 1951 did the prominent Knox Church in Christchurch hold a Christmas Day service, and in 1969 for the first time it held a midnight communion service.[74] But Protestants remain less formal in their Christmas celebrations, and their Christmas Day services are often poorly attended by families preoccupied by Christmas festivities. It was in the lead-up to Christmas that churches took advantage of the season, and those churches that ignored the season of Advent (the four weeks in the church year preceding Christmas) indulged in Christmas carols to excess.[75] Church attendance was much higher in the month leading up to Christmas, as parents came out to Sunday school anniversaries and pageants, and residual religiosity was thus reignited. Yet the cultural role of Christmas celebrations was full of the contradictions of a festival that had a powerful northern-hemisphere midwinter flavour in which Father Christmas (or later, Santa Claus) presided over scenes of snow and feasting while New Zealanders prepared to head to the beach.

Christmas customs slowly changed in the late nineteenth and early twentieth centuries. The advent of department stores led to a commercial focus on Christmas giving, and churches marked the season with carol services, performances of Handel's *Messiah* and elaborate church decorations.[76] Christmas became more popular with Protestants as churches looked for opportunities to focus on the sacred in a secular climate. Christmas had obvious relevance with the happy coincidence of seasonal shopping. Christmas services became common in churches that observed no other aspect of the church year, and in those that did the weeks of Advent, which precede Christmas, were increasingly overshadowed by Christmas themes.

Lent, the six-week period from Ash Wednesday until Easter, in which self-denial of luxuries was supposed to be practised (hence Mardi Gras, Fat Tuesday, preceded it), was emphasised by Catholics, but it made little impact on nineteenth-century Anglicans to judge by the number of weddings that took place in that season.[77] Even among Catholics it was imperfectly observed. A Catholic woman married on Ash Wednesday in 1949 recalled being required by her mother to leave the ash sign of the cross on her forehead during her marriage so she covered it with powder; she also endured a service with no music and a symbolic coffin in the church, common

Lenten customs. In theory, weddings were prohibited in Lent, but that did not seem to bother her or the priest.[78]

Easter services also varied according to the denomination. Good Friday services in the traditional Catholic format included the stripping of the altar and the shrouding of the cross. Anglican practice included the three-hour service, a lengthy meditative service.[79] Most Protestants made little of Good Friday, and in an 1882 survey in Auckland Protestant congregations were smaller at Easter except in Anglican and Wesleyan churches.[80] About this time Baptists, Presbyterians and Methodists often held combined services on that day.[81] In 1930 the Presbyterian General Assembly officially recognised Good Friday, urged by its Auckland Presbytery that 'there is a feeling among many of our people that it should not be turned into a common holiday and that its observance would not tend to superstitious beliefs and practices'.[82]

As for Easter Sunday, the associations of this day and the powerful message of its promise in the face of death were universally appealing. Again it was Anglicans and Catholics who made the most of it with elaborate services that drew large numbers of people, for this was a time when Anglicans were expected to take communion.[83] Churches were elaborately decorated and choral anthems abounded (especially excerpts from the *Messiah*). Popular Protestantism embraced Easter Day in the interwar years.

Easter is full of rich associations with spring and new life after the deadness of winter in the northern hemisphere, and at Easter time churches there were filled with spring flowers. New Zealand parishioners (including Protestants who did not otherwise recognise the church year) installed elaborate displays of greenery and flowers. Some of these were very exuberant, but they could not make the association with the new life of the northern-hemisphere spring.

It was not until the 1960s that most Presbyterians regularly observed the Christian year in their set Bible readings for services. Other Protestant churches have increasingly observed selective highlights of the Christian year in the hope that they have a vestige of public support, and that it can become an occasion for outreach.

Meanwhile one very popular festival was observed, even by those who did not follow the traditional church seasons. The harvest festival was a nineteenth-century British innovation intended to attract the community to church.[84] It was popular in New Zealand country districts by 1870.[85] The date of the celebration could be as early as February and as late as June. Most secular New Zealand people thought little of Easter, and the churches perhaps missed an opportunity of holding their harvest festivals at Easter time.[86] Certainly the harvest festival was a popular occasion. In Bunnythorpe Methodist Church a 'dutch auction' would be held after the service to sell off the goods, including, on one occasion, an improbable auction of the pig's tail, where everyone was required to donate a shilling to take part.[87]

FROM THE 1920S THE Protestant concept of the Sabbath lost recognition in general society, especially after World War II. Churches slowly changed their own practices. Already in the 1960s some churches held picnics on Sunday.[88] Presbyterians sought to modify their objections to Sunday cricket in 1960, but remained concerned at the impact on church attendance by youth.[89]

The commercialisation of Sunday remained a hot issue. In the 1970s, a government advisory committee noted changing attitudes towards Sunday shopping, but did not recommend a change. The 1977 Shop Trading Hours Act and its amendment in 1980 permitted Saturday shopping and special permission to allow Sunday shopping. Exceptions were permitted in specific shopping areas, including Paraparaumu, north of Wellington, and New Brighton, near Christchurch. Items on a restricted list were also sold through dairies and service stations.

Meanwhile commercial forces initiated a battle in the 1980s. The Shop Trading Hours Advisory Committee was established in 1988 and heard strong submissions for deregulation. The 'Save Our Sundays' group led by Tom Quayle and the 'Keep Sunday Free' group organised by my Massey University colleague Robin Gwynn opposed change, focusing mostly on the impact on employees, although the former group seemed to be guided by traditional sabbatarian concerns. In 1990 the Shop Trading Hours Repeal Bill came into effect, reflecting the Fourth Labour Government's emphasis on deregulation; the regulations were suspended by executive order even before the law had been changed.[90] Pressure to remove the restrictions on shopping at Easter have mounted since then.

The significance of the outcome of this debate is doubtless that the churches lost their previous ability to protect the Christian calendar by legislation. Thus 'Christendom' lost momentum. The Christian community also lost its energy to seek support of its role from the state.[91] At the present time, the commercial sector is focused on the removal of the remaining restrictions for the sacred days of the Christian year at Christmas, and particularly at Easter, and the strongest voices against this are from the unions, not the churches.

Yet there has been a revival of some aspects of sabbatarian life in the last generation. The Protestant missionaries in the Pacific, most of them from Congregationalist churches of England and America, and the Methodist churches, were more effective in instilling sabbatarian rules in the Pacific islands. As Pasifika people came to New Zealand they brought their Sabbath code with them. Former All Black Michael Jones

A harvest festival at Masterton Methodist Church (later called Wesley Church) about 1930. In front of the central pulpit and organ sits the fruit and produce provided by the congregation. MASTERTON DISTRICT LIBRARY ARCHIVE, 04-166/66

set an example as someone who was not willing to play sport on a Sunday, long after resistance had collapsed in general. This was a largely working-class community, and Sunday work was unavoidable, but Sunday sport reflected their struggles with the secular environment of New Zealand, especially as the Pasifika community took immense pride in its successful sports people. The next generation of Pasifika sports people have not been so observant of these rules, but they remain anxious to attend church with their community.

MOST CURRENT CHURCH MEMBERS prefer a clear separation of church and state, and view the church as a minority with a primary concern to defend its right to freedom of worship. As a result they find it difficult to understand the view that the state should defend Christian principles and 'Christendom'. New Zealand never had a state church and most Anglicans never wanted one, but they believed that the state ought in some way to be Christian. They believed that Christianity sought to influence society through Christian principles for the good for all. Sunday observance was viewed in this light, but it never gained acceptance to the degree that pious people sought. In modern society there has been strong pressure for allowing services and industries to continue uninterrupted, and the best working people could hope for was preferential rates of pay for work on Sundays and public holidays.

Sunday observance provided a rhythm of life for most New Zealanders and the law strengthened Christian churches. Without such regulations, the Christian community has struggled, although Sunday remains the day on which churches expect to hold their services, and Christmas and Easter remain significant in Western societies. The state is a very strong force in modern society. The Christian community is so diverse and porous that it was difficult for the churches to maintain a separate code. As the Russian educationalist Lev Vygotsky argued back in 1934, individuals are formed within a society, and learn to understand themselves in terms of the way in which they act within the rules of culture.[92]

We can also observe how Christian culture has changed. Untidy edges risk undercutting the coherence of the community. The churches in New Zealand have never been united on what a Christian timetable looks like, and some degree of pragmatism shapes when churches hold services and keep the Christian calendar. The increasing belief by Christians and non-Christians alike that Christianity existed solely for the benefit of its adherents led to the privatisation of behavioural codes.

So has the notion of a Christian culture completely broken down? If that was the case, the Christian community would have no external forms, and without these forms it would struggle to survive, leaving individual Christians to practise Christianity in any way they chose. Actually the sense of sacred time remains, despite its weakening, and there are many more cultural features of Christian practice than this — and, as this book argues, some of them are much less fragile.

The House of God

Previous St Peter's Anglican Church, Te Kopuru, on the west coast of Northland, in 1937. Photographed by the Rev. W. H. Stych, vicar of Hokianga parish. AUCKLAND ANGLICAN DIOCESAN ARCHIVES

NEW ZEALANDERS ARE SOMETIMES described as nature-worshippers. The rich, fertile land awaiting clearing and taming enthralled early settlers.[1] Yet many inhabitants of this land who came here from Britain began with a sense of spiritual vacuum in this space. A confident Presbyterian hymn-writer penned the words:

> Far from our ancient home, sundered by oceans,
> Zion is builded, and God is adored:

And later in the same hymn:

> Beauteous this land of ours, bountiful Giver!
> Brightly the heavens thy glory declare;
> Streameth the sunlight on hill, plain and river,
> Shineth thy cross over fields rich and fair.[2]

But a far more typical response has been that the places of association with spirit in the old land are replaced with a bare, empty land. The nationalist poets of the 1930s picked up this theme.[3] Yet mountain climbers and trampers often responded to the landscape with a sense of awe and reverence at the glories of nature.

Blanche Baughan puts the paradox like this:

> Yet only in my poor blind human way
> Sense I the splendour of this place and day;
> And my sight passes Collie's, it may be,
> But by this mean degree —
> That passionately I know I do not see!
> An eye to gaze, a mind I have, to read
> A heart, a soul, to exalt in this great scene —
> But ah! What faculty to fill my need
> Of knowing what its dazzling scriptures *mean*?[4]

And in the art of Colin McCahon, great questions and cries echo over the space that is defined and shaped as sacred, mysterious, other.

Several recent books have enhanced our appreciation of the buildings erected for worship in New Zealand.[5] It is not my intention to repeat their analysis. I want to focus on the much more ordinary places of worship and understand how their special function affected the way they were designed, constructed, used and modified.

IN MĀORI TRADITION THE land itself was seen as sacred, the place where the burial of the placenta made the people tangata whenua. This is radically different from the European view of land as a resource to be employed profitably. Tom Brooking, the Otago historian, has commented that: 'One of the great misfortunes of New Zealand is that it has been settled by two peoples who are romantic and even sentimental about land and imbue it with magical properties that move past logic into the realms of the supernatural and transcendental.'[6]

While there are certainly imposing religious buildings in New Zealand, in only a few places do they dominate the landscape. The dream of spires and crosses which enhanced Anglo-Catholic thought never really happened in New Zealand, except perhaps in Christchurch. The images of other cities include few spires.[7] There are a few examples of attempts at religious sites in public spaces, but they are few and far between. A striking example of this is the absence of crosses from Anzac memorials, which, as historian Jock Phillips has remarked, were replaced by the neutral obelisk.[8] Anzac memorials certainly are increasingly viewed as sacred spaces, especially the National War Memorial in Wellington.

Every district also has a sacred place in its cemeteries. A few very old churches (notably Christ Church in Russell and St Stephen's in Parnell) have graveyards around them, but local authorities were quickly charged with providing cemeteries. Public these cemeteries may have been, but all nineteenth-century cemeteries had Anglican, Catholic and 'other' sections, which were consecrated for the deceased of their affiliation.[9] This sacred space was mediated by the state, and the way the state has subsequently put roads through cemeteries and urupā does not inspire confidence in its vision.

There were, in the days when denominationalism was less competitive, some attempts to create a church presence, but they have always been controversial. Consider for example the cross over the clock tower in the Square in Palmerston North, which was erected in 1981. It became very controversial in subsequent years, attacked by Ashraf Choudhary, New Zealand's first Muslim MP, and defended by Winston Peters, founder of the New Zealand First Party.[10] In 1958, Father J. S. Dunn, from the local Catholic parish, commissioned a Dutch artist to build the statue of Our Lady of Lourdes on top of a hill at Paraparaumu.[11] His hope was to make it a site of pilgrimage, commemorating the vision at Lourdes. Poet Allen Curnow thought it amusing:

> Who hasn't sighted Mary
> As he hung, hot-paced
> By the skin of the humped highway

South from Waikanae
Three hundred feet above the
Only life-sized ocean?
Tell me, mother of mysteries
How long is time?[12]

However, modern Catholic tastes are less inclined to this form of devotion and the tradition of pilgrimage has not flourished at Paraparaumu. The use of contemporary and more symbolic art remained more unusual, despite the significance of religious art in New Zealand modern art.

The notion of sacred space is, on the face of it, more closely akin to Māori than Pākehā conceptions, given the depth of Māori associations with the land. For Māori, sacred associations were created by the places where the afterbirth was buried, and the urupā, the sacred places where bodies were laid to rest. Thus the land was marked with sacred places, wāhi tapu which could not be used for mundane purposes without tapu-lifting ceremonies. Early Europeans, including missionaries, realised this significance and respected these places. Their successors did not show the same respect and viewed the land in a utilitarian light.[13] For Europeans, sacral associations came slowly. Philip Carrington (1892–1975), a member of a significant Canterbury family who was later the Anglican Archbishop of Québec, took the journey earlier than most, in his extraordinary poem 'Rangiora':

The land has no antiquity
(Said the little voice in my head.)
After all it has no history . . .
(No history, it said.)
I was riding along by Rangiora,
And considering how through endless blue August days
I had ridden from village to village
In the holy land of England;
And every turn in the road
Was full of remembrances and histories.
And that is why the voice said, No history,
No history, it said
But what is history?
So I looked at the sacred fields of harvest
Consecrated by the labour of man and the blessing of heaven,
And strove to see their story.

> And I saw the swamp and the bush of long ago . . .
> So the Maori heads the procession
> That consecrates this land with labour and blood.
> Then comes the white men with the axe and gun . . .

And he goes on to imagine seeing Mary and her child in the land as well.[14] But others conceive of the end of the story in a land where Tāne Mahuta and Papatūānuku rule:

> I close the door and step into the early
> Summer morning, hushed above me, high
> And still as a cathedral. Here patiently
> The ancient gods anoint the earth, cry
> Blessings on the season.[15]

Europeans found it inappropriate to recognise any presence in the previous gods — idols they would have called them — in the land.[16] The first Christian missionaries had no such sense of the divine presence. So while the first Christian service in New Zealand was conducted out of doors, they did not want to connect with the existing holy spaces of New Zealand, the marae before the meeting houses and the sacred trees.

Nevertheless the whare was an obvious place to conduct worship, and indeed it was sometimes used as a venue. Soon, however, separate buildings were erected, sometimes raupō (or rush) huts open at the sides. The CMS missionaries were anxious to worship the Christian God in consecrated Christian buildings. Latter-day observers may observe that the success of the early Christian mission owed something to its willingness to adapt its services so that they could be conducted in the open air or in the meeting house. In the eyes of the missionaries, however, Christian worship needed to be led by Christian missionaries, and the meeting houses were polluted by pagan associations. So they set about creating their own mission buildings.

The first 'church' was constructed by the missionaries of the CMS at Paihia in 1827–28. Lathe and plaster and shingles were used, so it was very unlike the Māori buildings. Drawings suggest that it was Georgian in style, looking rather like a house from the exterior.[17] At Kerikeri the pulpit was placed behind the altar, for preaching was the primary activity.

The surviving chapel at Russell, the rebuilt chapel at Waimate North and the rebuilt great church at Ōtaki (Rangiātea) are very suggestive of evangelical Christianity, even though the interiors of these buildings have been altered to place the altar at the

Rangiātea Church in Ōtaki, about 1860, painted by Charles Barraud. Rev. Octavius Hadfield is in the pulpit and Māori stand or sit as in a meeting house. Rangiātea was named after the original homeland of Māori and the place to which the dead departed, and this high building, fashioned with a single tōtara ridgepole, was completed by Māori in 1851 as a result of cooperation between the unconverted rangatira Te Rauparaha and the missionary Octavius Hadfield. It blends Māori and European concepts. ALEXANDER TURNBULL LIBRARY. REF: D-010-002

centre of the east end. Initially a central pulpit was featured in all of these chapels, for the buildings and their benches were primarily places to hear instruction. People sat on the ground rather than on pews, and were able to move around, as on marae. The first church erected at Waimate North was elaborate, with Gothic windows, and was very bright inside, 'quite like a greenhouse' as William Cotton commented.[18] It had a flat ceiling and was in effect a preaching box. On his arrival, Selwyn reorganised the building, placing a font and a reading desk inside, moving the pulpit to the side, creating more focus on the altar. The Anglican missionaries (who were 'Low Church', opposed to Catholic ritual) were suspicious of this layout.

Richard Sundt, an American expert on Māori architecture, draws attention to some Māori Christian places of worship that were modelled on marae. He points to Rangiātea as a demonstration of this. Rangiātea indeed is a remarkable building. Unlike most missionary buildings it was initiated by Māori, not Europeans; it was commissioned by the missionary Octavius Hadfield, with the support of the unconverted rangatira Te Rauparaha. The great tōtara tree which formed the ridge pole of the building was chosen by prophecy, and earth from Raiatea, the ancestral homeland of the Māori, was placed under the building. The three supporting central pillars created a link between the old and the new worlds, the building being envisioned as bridging the two.

While Rangiātea was exceptional in its links back to Māori tradition, it still looked like a European building. The entrance, the open space and the lack of carving were all unprecedented for Māori. Rangiātea's huge length and height made it distinctive, along with the soil from Raiatea that was placed underneath it, presumably by the authority of Te Rauparaha. Richard Sundt makes much of the Māori design of these churches, but acknowledges that others had a more European character. The missionary Robert Maunsell's chapel at Maraetai was designed by Frederick Thatcher in 1845 and was the first of his 'Selwyn churches', and his first attempt to grapple with local needs.[19] Overall the missionary buildings were shaped primarily by a European vision.

Along with the erection of these buildings went a striking change in the clothing worn by those entering the buildings. James Buller, the Wesleyan Methodist missionary, claimed: 'A dirty blanket-clad congregation has always been associated in my mind with a hospital of the diseased rather than a company of Christian worshippers; and I have now the pleasure from Sabbath to Sabbath, of addressing not very large but generally very clean and very well clad congregations of natives.'[20]

At Ōtūmoetai, near Tauranga, the Catholic mission erected a small chapel in 1840 which reflects a very different tradition. Brother Luke Macé, who had built 'Pompallier House' at Kororāreka (the earlier Māori name for Russell) using earth bricks, was responsible for its construction. Although Jean-Baptiste Pompallier, the bishop sent to found a Catholic mission in New Zealand, suggested that he would pay for the building, in fact the erection of the chapel was funded by the small Catholic congregation in Tauranga. That first little chapel was made of raupō, and included a home for the resident priest, Fr Pezant, with a set of drawers to hold his vestments, sacristy material and personal possessions. There was a crucifix and an image of the Virgin Mary.

The next chapel was dedicated on 8 September 1847 and is rightly described by William Gisborne as 'an exquisite piece of workmanship', with a delightful curved altar end with tukutuku panels ('as in the manner of Tonga'), and carvings. Throughout the chapel were Māori inscriptions seeking to encourage devotion to God and to Mary, the most moving of which was 'Kia wehi koutou ki toku aroaro' (Approach my presence with holy awe). A canopy over the altar portrayed the heavens, and two carved receptacles held holy water. An 1865 painting by Lieutenant Horatio Robley shows how well this building deserved recognition as what Pompallier described as 'one of the most beautiful churches erected by native workmen'. It was later abandoned and finally collapsed.[21]

A remarkable Māori image of virgin and child now held in Auckland Museum's Gilbert Mair Collection shows the way in which Catholic imagery could enable Māori to rework traditional highly sexualised imagery. Some have suggested that this image is a work by Patoromu Tamatea of Ngāti Pikiao intended for a church at Ōhinemutu, and that the local priest rejected the work because its Māori style was unacceptable to Pākehā worshippers.[22] Certainly, devotion to the Virgin and to the reserved sacrament was a significant aspect of worship for Māori Catholics.

WHEN EUROPEAN MIGRANTS ARRIVED from 1840 on, they came with virtually no sympathy for the missionary endeavour, let alone for Māori. Johann Karl Ernst Dieffenbach, the German naturalist who accompanied the settlers to Wellington in 1840, called the newcomers 'an imported race of shopkeepers', and if this is harsh, it may explain the very utilitarian approach taken towards the spiritual in general, and church buildings in particular, in the early days of the colony.[23]

In small settlements any available public building was used for worship. Courthouses were used in both Auckland and Wellington, while schoolhouses were used in many country districts. It made sense to borrow or rent a hall if it existed, and if a community hall or school was erected ahead of a church. In Napier, Methodists met at first in the Council Chambers in 1874, and then were forced to move to the

Major General Horatio Robley's painting of the Roman Catholic chapel at Ōtūmoetai, Tauranga, 1865. This was the second chapel built by Catholics. The inscription in its woven flax chancel reads 'Kia wehi koutou ki toku aroaro' ('fear my face'), which is probably based on 2 Chronicles 7:14 in the Old Testament. MUSEUM OF NEW ZEALAND TE PAPA TONGAREWA. REF: 1992-0035-1705

Oddfellows Hall; the need to tidy it after Saturday-night dances overrode the fact that there was no charge for using it.[24] Catholics used homes for the early celebrations of the Mass and even hotels if the publican was Irish. For example, on the West Coast the Commercial Hotel in Charleston and the Harp of Erin Hotel in Westport were used for celebrations of the Mass and for Catholic weddings by a visiting priest in 1866 and 1867, but parishioners demanded to have their own churches.[25] Meanwhile courthouses and schools continued to be used in rural areas for the next hundred years, especially where church was held less regularly.

Kathleen Hawkins's poem 'Church Sunday' reflects a world when church services were not held in a sacred space:

> To-day the School-house dons its Sunday dress.
> This is no fane where Beauty moves to prayer
> Here grace lies but in comely homeliness
> And colour comes from things a child finds fair.
> . . . here people come;
> Plain folk from all the little farms around.
> And some in the harmonium's wheezy hum
> Will hear the far-off echoes of the sound
> Of clear boy-voices soaring to a roof
> Of carven arches, grey with storied age;
> And hearing, feel that pang which is the proof
> Of birthright to the ancient heritage.[26]

Building was deferred if there was no one to take responsibility for raising funds for it. Across South Canterbury, for example, there was no religious building of any description until the first Anglican church, St Mary's, was built in Timaru in 1859 — a point noted as surprising when the building was replaced, for generally the Wesleyans were the first in the field.[27]

THE ERECTION OF CHURCH buildings has often been viewed from the vantage of the architects who designed them, or sometimes from the denominations. It is helpful to turn the focus to those who decided to build them, who funded them and kept them functioning.

The design of churches tells us much about the shared religious views of settlers, because they were almost all paid for and built by local settlers for use once a week or less frequently. Many country churches were under the control of no denomination,

Above Laying of the foundation stone of St Margaret's Anglican Church in Taihape in 1902, photographed by Cecily Pickerill. When the town was laid out in 1898, section 13 was reserved for the Anglican Church. Rev. Percy Clarkson, curate of the Marton parish, arrived to collect funds for a church and within a week had £100, so he commissioned John Swan of the De Clere partnership to design a small church, which was begun in July 1902 and finished by September. ALEXANDER TURNBULL LIBRARY. REF: 1/2-040713-F

Below Laying of the foundation stone of the new stone Anglican St Matthew's Church, on the corner of Wellesley and Hobson Streets in Auckland, 23 April 1902. Frederick Pearson of London was commissioned to design a cathedral-style replacement in Ōamaru stone for the old wooden church, and his Excellency the Governor Lord Ranfurly laid the foundation stone. The building took three years to complete. AUCKLAND ANGLICAN DIOCESAN ARCHIVES

or were used by several Protestant denominations even though owned by one. Consequently distinctive denominational features were avoided.[28]

Providing a church began with the collection of money or subscriptions for a building. Sometimes a section of land was made available (although sometimes, as in the case of the church by Lake Pupuke, on Auckland's North Shore, it was not surveyed out but a building was permitted to be erected on spare land). Usually a community subscription was opened and enough money raised by a small group of zealots to justify commissioning a builder. (In the nineteenth century, buildings did not have to have council approval before erection began.) In the case of simpler buildings, voluntary labour was often involved.

Those little churches were very utilitarian constructions, for the early settlers hated waste, and it was impossible to borrow money for a building with no title deeds. They were in effect small boxes, single rooms with a pulpit and table at one end and a small vestibule at the other. There was sometimes a vestry for ecclesiastical robes. There were slight variants for Anglican churches, but mostly the building of a chancel, providing space around the altar, came later. Such buildings can be seen throughout New Zealand, although many have in recent years been converted into antique shops or homes.

The buildings typically had side clapboards (although the Selwyn churches had vertical slats). They were hot buildings in summer and cold in winter, being built with very little lining; communities soon lined them to keep them warmer, and to prevent rotting. Seating was on long solid pews, which were more common in Methodist than Anglican churches, because most Anglican churches in England had rented pews provided by the lessee. They were frequently altered to suit changing needs or space requirements.

The décor of the churches might include a few texts or religious pictures. Worshippers expected a harmonium, hymn books, frosted glass, but rarely blinds or curtains. Carpet went down the centre aisle. Any lining was simple and often stained rather than painted wood inside, although the exterior was painted. Effectively these were multi-purpose open spaces, with as few denominational symbols as possible. Even the pulpit was plain.

By the end of the century most districts had a church. Sometimes, as in rural Canterbury, churches were only a mile or so apart. But the villages were complete communities, and there was a natural desire to worship locally, sometimes overriding denominational loyalties, but at other times leading to an impossible number of small churches. Presbyterians, Methodists and Baptists were thin on the ground in Mid Canterbury but they each had a network of small churches as alternatives to Anglicanism.[29]

Above Laying of the foundation stone of the Unitarian Church in Ponsonby Road, Auckland, in August 1901. William Jellie was the first Unitarian minister in New Zealand. The denomination was too theologically liberal for most people, and in the absence of notable guests the two foundation stones were laid by the first pastor, William Jellie, who had recently arrived from England, and Captain Lamb of Mahurangi Heads. SIR GEORGE GREY SPECIAL COLLECTIONS, AUCKLAND LIBRARIES, NZG-19010824-359-2

Below Laying of the foundation stone of St George's Takapuna, on Auckland's North Shore, on 26 April 1902. The building was rather advanced by this stage, but Presbyterians wanted the Governor, Lord Ranfurly, to lay the stone on the same visit to Auckland during which he laid the foundation stone of St Matthew's. Inset is a photograph of the minister, Rev. Robert Ferguson. The large house to the right was owned by Henry Brett, proprietor of the *Auckland Star*. SIR GEORGE GREY SPECIAL COLLECTIONS, AUCKLAND LIBRARIES, 7-A563

A church was not a heavily used building. So there were hopes that the church could double as schoolhouse, as it did in Takapuna. And there is a very long tradition of the church serving as a community resource; for example, many church halls were used as polling booths.[30]

For soon the churches began to proliferate, as denominational communities became large enough to erect their own. In Greytown, the secretary of the Methodist trustees, when justifying the erection of their own church in the 1860s, explained that the Methodists felt that 'there's no place like home' and applied this to church as well as family. 'When a community of Christians of any denomination gets sufficiently strong, it is their imperative duty to build a church of their own.' He then acknowledged that no permission had been sought or given by the Methodist conference before they began, and this was very often the case.[31]

IT WAS A DEEP Victorian conviction — one could say myth — that inadequacy of church accommodation was a key reason for low levels of church attendance. In New Zealand the issue of the adequacy of accommodation had been raised by the 1851 religious census, and occasionally colonial authorities thought in the same way. A census of churches was carried out in Auckland in 1882. It showed that there were 19,157 seats available in Auckland churches — approximately half the number of seats required for the population of 37,912. Altogether for the two Sundays measured, attendances at morning services were 27 per cent of the population, and in the evening 16 per cent on one wet Sunday and nearly 23 per cent on a finer evening.[32]

The census regularly recorded attendance figures until 1926 and also supplied a record of the number of seats available in churches. In 1874 a total of 548 churches and chapels, and 138 schoolhouses and 18 dwellings hosting services were recorded in New Zealand, with seats for 113,597 people, although just 69,155 attended services.[33] By 1878 the number of churches had risen to 831, while the schoolhouses stayed at 136. There were seats for 158,705, but 100,510 attended.[34] In 1881 there were 834 churches, with accommodation somewhat expanded to 189,155, but 117,817 attending.[35] In 1886 church buildings had expanded very significantly to 1063 churches along with 290 schoolhouses and 146 private homes, seating 256,151, but the attendance had only increased modestly to 164,033.[36]

Accepting the inadequacies of these figures, the denominational patterns are revealing. In 1874 there were 172 Anglican churches, 125 Presbyterian churches, 124 Methodist churches of various different types and 86 Catholic churches. Presbyterians were far and away the largest users of schoolhouses (63 of them), perhaps because in Otago church and school were allied. Anglican seats were only a few more than Presbyterian seats (30,983 compared to 30,188). At that time these four denominations accounted for 91 per cent of all the seats; there were just 58 buildings from other denominations.

By 1891 there were 345 Anglican churches and 63,204 Anglican seats; 246 Presbyterian churches and 86 schoolrooms, with 59,839 seats. There were 282 Methodist churches and 76 schoolhouses — a huge increase — making them close to Anglicans in places of worship, although the number of seats available was much lower at 42,599, and 181 Catholic churches with 44,062 seats. There were 271 places of worship with 52,905 seats provided by other denominations or in non-denominational chapels, the figures revealing that these were smaller buildings than those of the larger denominations.

In 1906 there were 516 Anglican churches and 72 schoolrooms, with some 85,185 seats; 382 Presbyterian churches and 147 schoolrooms, with 80,558 seats; 386 Methodist chapels of all types plus 51 schoolrooms, with 71,710 seats; and 290 Catholic churches, with 65,565 seats. It is noticeable that other denominations by 1906 provided nearly 19 per cent of the seats, although only 16 per cent of the attendees went to these churches.

By 1926 there were 755 Anglican churches, but the striking growth was in Presbyterian churches — to 596 — while there were 444 Methodist churches, and 362 Catholic churches. These four denominations accounted for 82 per cent of all accommodation and 84 per cent of all attendees out of a total of 2471 churches. Catholics filled their churches most efficiently, with 63 per cent of the seats occupied, while most Protestants filled between 40 and 50 per cent of the seats. Methodists fell just below 40 per cent, but most of the small denominations chose to have a lot of space, with 38 per cent of Brethren seats filled, for example.

The implications of this level of accommodation may be read in various ways. The editor of the *Auckland Star* noted in 1882, 'The eagerness of Church members to provide commodious buildings has somewhat outrun the wants of the time, and has saddled the present generation with financial burdens for the requirements of their successors.'[37] Certainly there was nothing like this degree of building after the 1920s.

BISHOP GEORGE AUGUSTUS SELWYN, appointed by the British Crown as the one and only Bishop of New Zealand from 1841, had an immense influence in this country because he had so clear a sense of what he wanted to achieve. Selwyn had emphatic views on architecture, as he had on the overall shape that the Church of England should take in New Zealand. The late art historian Jonathan Mane-Wheoki noted that Selwyn was attracted to the idea of bishop as church builder, literally, and called this 'a fantastic moment in the story of church building in New Zealand'.[38] Fantastic and in many respects fantastical. Selwyn was unable to achieve much without significant compromises, and this is true of his buildings as in other aspects of his plans. His collegiate plan for St John's College in Meadowbank, Auckland, left a heritage of a cluster of buildings. This was also the site on which some other churches were prepared, including Howick's All Saints, before they were carted off for assembly onsite.

There has been some debate about Selwyn's ecclesiastical principles, especially as he denied that he had even read the controversial Oxford Tracts, which led to the Oxford Movement, or Anglo-Catholicism, pushing the Anglican Church in a Catholic direction. He was certainly not a modern Anglo-Catholic, for he wore only traditional Anglican vestments during his time in New Zealand. But although Selwyn avoided the taint of that movement, he accepted many of its basic principles, holding that the Anglican Church needed to recover its inheritance in the early patristic 'church fathers' and later Catholic tradition, and avoid state erastianism (in which the church existed to serve the state). He also believed that the Church must avoid compromise with and defilement by the Protestant Dissenters or Nonconformists, those who had left the Anglican Church in the seventeenth century because it had not, in their view, been fully reformed according to the scriptural pattern.

Before he came to New Zealand, Selwyn had joined the Cambridge Camden Society, whose members insisted that Anglicanism needed to be renewed in its architecture as well as in other aspects. He asked the Camden Society to supply him with standard designs for a parish church, which they recommended should be executed in Norman or early English Gothic style since the church was so very young and primitive.[39] In view of these principles, Selwyn insisted that the ancient layout of Catholic churches should be revived. This meant that the church should ideally face east, should have a spacious chancel which was set apart from the nave with an altar up a few steps, and with the pulpit to the side.[40] The ideas of Augustus Pugin — a Gothic Revival architect and convert to the Catholic Church — on church design included a strong emphasis on verticality, a steep roof, careful placement of the altar and a large east window, although we often observe in those early buildings three narrow windows on the west wall.[41]

Architects designed these buildings, but they were rather busy in early New Zealand and may not have valued commissions from bodies that might not be able to pay. Selwyn used Sampson Kempthorne and his friend Frederick Thatcher, an architect who trained in St John's in the early days to become an Anglican priest. Thatcher designed St Mary's New Plymouth in 1846, Christ Church in Nelson in 1851,

Jane Ussher's photograph of Old St Paul's in Wellington, the Anglican Pro-Cathedral designed by Rev. Frederick Thatcher, then minister in Wellington, under the supervision of Bishop Selwyn and built in 1865–66. Here, wooden Gothic Revival architecture achieved Selwyn's vision of the parish church.
JANE USSHER

St Mary's Parnell in 1860 and St Paul's Wellington in 1866, and had some role in the chapel at St John's College and in All Saints Howick.

Bishop Selwyn's vision of buildings was enhanced by a carefully thought out philosophy of building. These buildings are distinctive, although less influential than one might expect. Selwyn wanted to bring to mind the parish churches of England. The buildings took the first steps towards a future ordered society, where the church would be a central player. But the use of exposed beams proved very unsuitable for the damp and humid climate of northern New Zealand, and there was an increasing need to address the challenges of timber construction. Later architects including Benjamin Mountfort, the Anglo-Catholic church architect of Christchurch, recognised that care needed to be taken with the use of undressed timber framing in the face of the humid conditions.[42]

All Saints Howick is the most charming of these Selwyn churches, and in this building one may observe familiar British elements in miniature: a conjuring of sacredness through a cruciform shape, a bell tower, and space for clergy and parishioners and even for the guns of the military settlers which were to be laid down in the porch. At Thatcher's crowning achievement, St Paul's in Wellington, still standing on Mulgrave Street, the same principles were writ large. There are some other so-called Selwyn buildings that lack these elements, and are simple country churches, but in his key buildings the exterior and interior buttresses, and the evocative use of timber and mullioned glass, all convey sanctity.

There were hopes that stone buildings could be erected, but the first of these had serious problems. Sampson Kempthorne's stone St Stephen's chapel in Judge's Bay, Parnell, intended as a private chapel for the bishop, lasted for only three years before a hurricane brought it down.[43] Cyril Knight, the architectural historian, believes that light foundations were responsible for the cracks that closed St Thomas Tamaki, built in 1847, but he acknowledges that the use of scoria and sandstone may have caused crumbling.[44]

The glorious St Mary's in New Plymouth was the first significant stone Anglican building. This was a Thatcher building, built of stone from Mount Egmont (Taranaki), and with a very steep roof. It was begun in 1845 and completed the following year. The church was carefully extended in 1862 and 1866, and in 1893 a second aisle was added; much of its charm comes from these additions, which enhanced the original design.[45]

This architectural vision succeeded in expressing Anglican worship despite the church's loss of establishment status in the new colony. These buildings combined intimacy and holy space, impelling a sense of reverence. Other factors were also at work. Anglicans thought of the space as sacred (and hence were less likely to use schoolhouses for worship). The service of consecration, which took place once any mortgage over the building was paid off, included an episcopal act to 'separate and set apart the said church from all common and profane use whatsoever', dedicating it to the service of God.[46] Such words were particularly important, since for many Anglicans the erection of the building was more important than attending it.

The artist and school teacher John Kinder often photographed, sketched and painted Anglican churches, and in his images the church is often the dominating presence in the neighbourhood.[47] Certainly where churches had spires they were often the tallest, but in the northern cities the church was not a dominating physical presence except in the religious imagination.

WHILE SELWYN INSPIRED ANGLICANS to build in a way that expressed their aspirations, other denominations were also in on the building act. Among them, it was the Methodists whose buildings were the most lavish. Methodism had a particular approach to expansion, using buildings to attract people. The Methodists were very dynamic in all the four main centres. The very first stone church in Christchurch was the Durham Street Methodist Church (originally the Wesleyan Chapel), erected in 1865, which was destroyed in the 2011 Christchurch earthquake. This substantial building was expensive, with its masonry exterior and rich mahogany interior, very much in the tradition of British Methodist architecture, but Methodists were eager to give their money to the cause.

Stone was also used in Auckland's Pitt Street Wesleyan Chapel, erected at the same time, but many of the other early Wesleyan chapels — Wesley Church in Wellington, and High Street Chapel in Auckland, for example — were built of wood, with elaborate Gothic motifs, especially on the exterior.

All these are buildings designed to accommodate very large congregations upstairs and downstairs, congregations that sing, congregations with choirs, congregations where the preachers alternate and compete with each other, where the sacred rituals are performed by the congregation not the clergy, and so there is no chancel. The pulpit is central, for these are in effect preaching barns. At Wesley Church in Wellington and a number of other Methodist churches (following patterns in England at the time) the choir was placed behind the preacher, and the pulpit was set high between nave and gallery. Later ecclesiastical taste has often removed these fascinating features.

The cost of erecting these elaborate buildings was much greater than for community churches. Liardet Street Wesleyan Church in New Plymouth cost £1100 in 1856.[48] That was a huge expense for a small community and involved mortgages and constant fundraising, but as we shall see this was no obstacle.

This style of urban building, making aspirational statements but designed to maximise seating, was quite common in the nineteenth century. A surprising number of Protestant churches were in the Gothic style. St John's Presbyterian Church on Wellington's Willis Street and Knox Presbyterian Church in Dunedin, for example, were elaborate Gothic buildings. There were other more intimate Gothic buildings, such as Trinity Congregational Church in Christchurch, which was designed by Benjamin Mountfort even though the architect Samuel Farr was a member of the congregation. R. B. Keey, historian of the church, suggests that the style was intended to negate the sneer that they were mere Dissenters.[49] Over time these buildings were much altered, for wooden buildings can be easily changed, and in some cases stone parts were attached to original wooden buildings.

WHILE FREDERICK THATCHER had a brilliant eye which helped to fulfil Selwyn's vision, he was never a fulltime architect, and apart from St Paul's in Wellington his buildings are essentially modest parish churches. Anglican architecture rapidly

Durham Street Wesleyan Methodist Chapel, designed by Samuel Farr, opened on Christmas Day in 1864, the first stone church in Christchurch, putting Anglicans to shame on their home territory. The photograph shows the church in the 1920s. CHRISTCHURCH CITY LIBRARIES. REF: PHOTOCD 12, IMG0038

became more ambitious. The leading Anglican architect of the period was Benjamin Mountfort. Mountfort had been a Canterbury 'pilgrim', and his work in the colony extended over a long period. Although he was not thought good enough to design the ChristChurch Cathedral or St Michael and All Angels, he did supervise the construction of the former. He therefore played a significant part in adapting the plans prepared for the cathedral by the famous British Gothic revival architect Sir George Gilbert Scott to the colonial context.[50]

Mountfort's first work in New Zealand was a design for Holy Trinity in Lyttelton, an expensive stone building that suffered problems on one wall and had to be closed. In this first building Mountfort showed his commitment to the principles of the 'ecclesiologists' (Anglo-Catholic theorists of pure church design), creating a building of Norman or early English Gothic — a clean, simple, but clear structure with all lines leading to the altar, and strong vertical lines. But after the structural problems at Lyttelton he recognised that colonial buildings needed to be adapted to the high costs of labour and the distinctiveness of colonial building materials.

Holy Trinity Church, Avonside, Christchurch. The wooden part of the church was built in 1855, with a stone chancel designed by Benjamin Mountfort added in 1869 and 1873. Soon after this photograph was taken in 1905, the wooden nave was replaced by a stone building designed by Cyril Mountfort. The beautiful Anglo-Catholic building had to be demolished after the 2011 earthquake.
CHRISTCHURCH CITY LIBRARIES. REF: PHOTOCD 9, IMG0085

THE HOUSE OF GOD   71

Mountfort's architecture is usually associated with stone buildings in Christchurch, although he is also responsible for brick buildings, and the Church of the Good Shepherd at Phillipstown in Christchurch exploits brick very effectively. Dispensing with internal columns, he was able to achieve a sense of a wide nave.[51] This architecture also reflects changes in the tone of Anglicanism. Mountfort was a deeply committed Anglo-Catholic, and his masterpiece was Holy Trinity Church in Avonside, in east Christchurch (sadly demolished after the 2011 earthquake), the chancel of which was erected in stone with rich colour and detail.[52] When he became a worshipper in the Church of the Good Shepherd (also demolished after the earthquake) Mountfort conceived of a space that suited a parish Eucharist conducted by clergy robed in white vestments and the singing of Evensong according to the Sarum usage, the ancient ritual used in Salisbury Cathedral.[53] Then he designed St Thomas's in Auckland (demolished to make way for the Auckland motorway), although the only innovation in ritual at St Thomas's was a processional cross, not even lighted candles on the altar.[54]

Later in his life, Mountfort was commissioned to work on three cathedrals. 'Old' St Mary's, the pro-cathedral for Auckland built from 1886 to 1898, uses wood to create a golden Gothic effect — high, wide, with steps leading up into a large chancel. It has a very wide open feel and yet there are also high pillars and a striking ceiling. It is a building that fills with worship in a very rich sense.[55] Mountfort was not the only architect using wood in this way. Many fine wooden buildings remain from this period, among them Holy Sepulchre in Auckland, St Michael's in Christchurch, and Thatcher's St Paul's in Wellington.

PRESBYTERIAN CONSTRUCTION WAS VERY extensive in early New Zealand, perhaps because Presbyterians were more prepared to put money into churches. The first stone church in Auckland was St Andrew's, which used solid if rather porous volcanic blocks. Such a building could not be the result of voluntary labour. St Andrew's in Christchurch was a very fine Gothic wooden construction. There are many other examples of fine nineteenth-century Presbyterian churches.

In the south, it became customary to use Ōamaru stone for public buildings. Although in the long run it did tend to deteriorate, it enabled massive buildings and soaring spires to be built. Robert A. Lawson, the great architect of Dunedin, himself a committed Presbyterian, used this to great effect.[56] When First Church was built on the levelled Bell's Hill in 1863, it dominated all other buildings in the city. The exterior of this building invites one to crane the neck and look upwards. The interior

First Church of Otago, Dunedin, photographed in 1925. There had been three previous First Church buildings, but the decision was made in 1868 to place the central church of the Presbyterian settlement on the levelled Bell Hill in Moray Place. Robert Lawson designed the soaring building, which opened in 1873. ALEXANDER TURNBULL LIBRARY. REF: 1/1-008297-G

is very different; it is no Gothic cathedral, but a Presbyterian communal sacred space with only a small recess for its magnificent pulpit. Knox Church, on George Street, close to the university, a later building by Lawson, is more conventional in its church shape, but combines simplicity and magnificence. In both cases, though, all eyes focused on a high and lofty pulpit, for the expounding of the word of God was the central task of the Sunday service.

The aspirations of Presbyterian builders were most clearly expressed, however, at the opening of St Paul's Church in Ōamaru, designed by Thomas Forrester (who was influenced by Lawson's design for First Church). In this strongly Presbyterian community, the first religious gathering was in fact Anglican, but in April 1865 St Paul's was opened. The local newspaper obliged with a fulsome description of the early English design, the lancet windows, the bell tower, and the robes fit for a bishop which were given to the minister, although a few days later it admitted that the building in the partial form in which it had been opened lacked a little in contours. This did not stop Dr Burns in his elaborate sermon and prayer comparing it with the temple in Jerusalem.[57] The English view of sacred space seemed to be taking over from Presbyterian utilitarianism.

SACREDNESS IN CATHOLICISM IS much more concrete than in other religious traditions. The real presence of Christ in the Mass implies very definitely that the reserved sacrament is adored because Christ is actually on Earth. Catholic buildings were in effect temples for the holy presence in the material world.[58] This presupposed a very different worldview from Protestants, and it necessitated separate buildings, for how could a meeting house be a temple?

The elevation of the Host, when the consecrated wafer and cup were held up by the priest kneeling at the altar with his back to the congregation, was thus the moment in Catholic worship in which one adored a present God. Catholic ceremonies were designed to create a sense of awe, so that one observer of a ceremony of First Communion commented in 1880, 'I left Napier convent grounds yesterday evening with a thorough conviction of the beauties of the ceremonies and devotions of the Catholic Church.'[59]

The first Catholic missionaries did not have the money to erect many buildings. The old Ōtaki Catholic Church, now the oldest-surviving Catholic building in New Zealand, has the same basic design as Protestant buildings, except for more space around the altar.

Naturally, some of the most loved of the Catholic buildings were Gothic in design. St Patrick's in Auckland was a very plain Gothic building, and a series of renovations and extensions have not obscured this. The Gothic could be more elaborate, however. One of the Catholics' favourite architects was Frederick de Jersey Clere, who was in fact a devout Anglican; in the 1880s he was the Wellington Anglican diocesan architect, designing many small district churches. His Catholic buildings show that he understood the Catholic aspiration for gorgeous altars and buildings reminiscent of the glories of Catholic worship in Europe. St Patrick's Palmerston North and St Mary of the Angels in Wellington show him to be a master in using ferro-concrete to create aspirational French Gothic churches.

The Catholic aura was achieved through distinctive furnishings as well as design. Images and statues, stations of the cross and objects for personal veneration, notably the blessed Virgin, distinguished these buildings. Tastefully done, the stations of the cross and the statues of the Virgin and of the sacred heart of Christ, and the grand high altars, created a theatrical atmosphere that hinted of the dazzling qualities of the rococo churches of Europe. Some of these furnishings were rather tacky and overly elaborate, especially the monstrances, dazzling containers in which the reserved sacrament of the consecrated were carried around for reverence by the congregation. A report in the *Colonist* in 1891 describes one such scene:

> At the conclusion of High Mass the procession was formed, and presented to the onlooker a very picturesque appearance. First came the cross-bearer, then several acolytes in scarlet cassocks and white surplices, and carrying lighted tapers; then the altar boys, also in scarlet and white; these were followed by the various girls religious sodalities, the Children of Mary, in blue with white veils, and the members of the Sacred Heart Society, in scarlet cloaks with white veils. These were followed by a number of sweet little girls prettily dressed in white, and carrying baskets of flowers, with which they strewed the path. Then came the thurifer [swinging the incense], and then beneath a beautiful canopy of white satin heavily fringed with gold, came the Rev Father Landouar, wearing a magnificent cope, and carrying the Blessed Sacrament in a very handsome gold remonstrance. The Very Rev Father Mahoney, wearing a black cassock and beautiful surplice of white cambric and lace and a cloth of gold stole, acted as general director. The congregation came last, first the men and boys and then the women and girls.[60]

Some of the bric-a-brac was dumped unceremoniously after the Second Vatican Council of 1962–65 reviewed and transformed many Catholic traditions.

MANY CATHOLIC CHURCHES WERE erected in Neoclassical and Baroque style, rather than Gothic. They could not be mistaken for Anglican or other Protestant buildings. John Ruskin, the English artist and cultural historian, had laid down that Gothic was a proper architecture that was more truly Protestant. Augustus Pugin's dream of spires linked the Gothic revival to Anglo-Catholicism. Eventually leaders of most denominations accepted the same conventions for their churches. Gothic revival was used in England by Catholics and Nonconformists as well as Anglicans, but inevitably ecclesiastical differences were reflected in these buildings. Nonconformist and Presbyterian Gothic was bound to use space differently from Anglicans or Catholics. The need for a chancel was much reduced, and the choir played a larger role. Nevertheless, on the exterior, St Andrew's Presbyterian Church in Christchurch, St Joseph's Catholic Cathedral in Dunedin and St Patrick's Catholic Cathedral in Auckland were little different from each other or their Anglican counterparts. It is interesting that while the first Knox Church in Dunedin was a Classical building, its successor was a soaring Gothic building, albeit with a pulpit in the small chancel.

Yet it is striking that the Catholic minority

The Basilica of the Sacred Heart, Timaru, designed by Francis Petre and built in 1910–11 after the old wooden church burned down. The finest, if not quite the largest, of Petre's several Byzantine and Romanesque churches, it was a symbol of the strength of Catholic presence in the town. Photographed by Ben Thiem in 1911. SIR GEORGE GREY SPECIAL COLLECTIONS, AUCKLAND LIBRARIES, AWNS-19111012-16-5

used very different designs in some of the places where religious tensions were high. The basilicas in Timaru, Invercargill (St Mary's) and Ōamaru, all designed by Francis Petre, a prominent Catholic architect who was based in Dunedin from 1872, were particularly notable. The greatest such building, the Cathedral of the Blessed Sacrament in Christchurch (which George Bernard Shaw rightly complained was so appallingly located by the gasworks and the railway station, and which was badly damaged in the 2011 earthquake) showed the Baroque style at its best when light from the dome lit up the high altar. The second Catholic cathedral (Sacred Heart) in the Archdiocese of Wellington is another example of Petre's work. Petre was equally able to design in the Gothic style, as he did at St Joseph's Cathedral in Dunedin, for many of his clients obviously believed that churches should be Gothic.

Neoclassical was also used by some churches. St Andrew's in Auckland is perhaps not a good example, because its columns were added 40 years after the thick scoria walls were erected. Better examples are St Paul's Presbyterian Church in Christchurch, and St Andrew's Presbyterian Church in Wellington. Perhaps the most pristine example was the Beresford Street Congregational Church in Auckland, now the Hopetoun Alpha. There were smaller examples as well, such as Caversham Baptist Church in Dunedin, but the interiors of these buildings were rarely Classical: Oxford Terrace Baptist Church in Christchurch and the Baptist Tabernacle in Auckland had no Classical allusions inside. The Metropolitan tabernacle, built for the famous Baptist preacher Charles Spurgeon in London, was a very influential example of Neoclassical design outside with tiered galleries within, and Auckland's Baptist Tabernacle (where Spurgeon's son was the minister) was a miniature of this famous building.

IT COULD BE ARGUED that the first cathedrals to be built in New Zealand were in fact Presbyterian, for First Church was surely cathedral-like in its aspirations, a place of gathering for the whole community. Unfortunately this building was not placed in the Octagon, and it was left to the Anglicans to claim this prime site.

The main cathedrals were inevitably Anglican, but the dioceses created in 1858 were slow to build. Anglicans in New Zealand lacked the energy and commitment to erect diocesan central churches. Parish churches were nominated as pro-cathedrals, and served *pro tem* as the seat of the bishop partly because they were larger churches. The finest of these was St Paul's in Wellington. The site for ChristChurch Cathedral was left bare for many years and then built section by section. In Nelson there were grand hopes to replace the wooden church on the central hill with a fine stone cathedral, and the foundation stone was laid in 1925, but in the 1950s financial constraints forced the abandonment of the pitched roof for a flat ceiling. The building was finally completed in 1967.

Three cathedrals were begun in the postwar era. St Paul's in Wellington and Waiapu Cathedral (St John's) in Napier were completed in ferro-concrete. Each reflected very traditional conceptions of what a cathedral should be, although each lacks a proper transept or cruciform style. Projects were rarely quite completed as intended. Wellington's cathedral took a long time to complete. The original plan for Auckland's Holy Trinity Cathedral began with the building of a high ferro-concrete Gothic chancel, but was completed with a wide Pacific-style fale as its nave, which was executed in the 1990s. Waiapu Cathedral, which was finished on schedule as a replacement for the church destroyed in the 1931 Napier earthquake, was the least distinguished of the three.

Māori churches were somewhat distinctive. Ringatū, the church founded by Te Kooti in the Bay of Plenty, sought to reclaim Christianity as a Māori-Jewish experience, and therefore returned worship to the marae. The great Ringatū house Rongopai at Gisborne, and Ōtewa at Te Kūiti (where Te Kooti spent his last years) are carved (or in the case of Rongopai, painted) houses.

The story is profoundly different for the constructions erected for the followers of Tahupōtiki Wiremu Rātana, the Māori healer and prophet who offered new hope to his people in the years after World War I. Reflecting their radical attempt to reshape Māori spirituality, their churches, and especially the temple near Wanganui, are rich with symbolism, with colours, towers and designs. The architecture represents their beliefs about T. W. Rātana, whom they recognised as Te Māngai, the mouthpiece of God. The outside of the temple gives little idea of its exotic internal appearance, yet even here Methodist influences are evident in its two aisles and the tiered seating at the front for the choir, brass band and clergy. The most striking aspects of the building are the great symbolic painted lines on its walls, leading at the back to the balcony doors and converging at the front on Te Māngai's seat, where he could be the mouthpiece of God. Such a structure expressed the values that gave many Māori fresh hope for their people.

THE DESIRE THAT A church should look like a place of worship rather than a secular hall led some builders to place a steeple or a bell tower on top. This was the statement that it was a place dedicated to worship, as for example the Greytown pioneers of 1879–80 acknowledged when they insisted that their church have a spire.[61] These steeples were in a sense not only irrelevant, but they had also certainly symbolised for some in England the notion of a parish, and therefore

Ans Westra's photograph of Rātana ministers, with the Āwhina (Sisters of Mercy) in the background, outside the Rātana temple on the prophet's birthday celebration, 25 January 1963. ANS WESTRA

were inappropriate or even false symbols of faith (for example, the Quakers talked not of parish churches but of steeple houses). In New Zealand, however, the steeple and the bell seemed symbols to be appropriated by all, although the neat American church and steeple was beyond the reach of most communities.

Moreover, many a church found that the steeple was the part of the building most vulnerable to the strong prevailing winds and had to be removed. All Saints Ponsonby was an Anglican church from which the steeple was removed (leaving the Methodists over the road with the dominating presence), and in Eketāhuna the 1898 Wesleyan church creaked and groaned so much as the winds caught the steeple that the redoubtable Masterton businessman Charles Daniell solved the problem by ripping the steeple off, towing it with his Hudson Terraplane car.[62] In other churches, towers may have been difficult to maintain and to paint but they were the best recognised religious symbol. The congregation of St James Newtown, having almost decided to remove its tower at a cost of £75 in 1964, instead placed a cross on top and added floodlighting so that Wellington Hospital patients over the road might be given hope.[63]

Another important symbol of religion, at least for Anglicans, was the bell. When George French Angas, the early New Zealand artist, left England on his voyage to New Zealand, 'The last parting sounds from the shore were the gentle and distant tollings of the Sabbath bells. Were ever Sabbath bells so full of meaning before?'[64] Religion's cultural symbols provided therapeutic support to settler life.

A bell had practical value in the age before clocks, but it was now largely symbolic for Pākehā New Zealanders. It was invaluable to summon Māori to mission services, since they had a very different sense of time and place, and it continued to carry strong symbolism for Māori. The bell that had been given by Māori to Pompallier for the church in Ōtūmoetai was moved to a belfry alongside the church built in Tauranga, but around 1895 Māori from Te Puna arrived to take it for their chapel: '. . . the bell that called our parents to church must call us; no other bell will do; we do not want a bell but that bell'. The priests of the respective churches resorted to fisticuffs, and refused to accept an episcopal ruling on the subject.[65]

Bells were still valued in other contexts. At St Peter's in Upper Riccarton the bell was housed in an independent bell tower, but more often, as at All Saints at Howick, the church erected in 1847 for the Fencible soldiers, the bell-pull hung in the aisle of the church. Bells were tolled at lunchtime during World War I and II, reminding people to pray for the outcome of the war.

Usually there was just one bell — carillons of bells were rare in New Zealand. St Matthew's in Auckland and ChristChurch Cathedral held them, and there was a single-octave carillon at St Barnabas, Fendalton, erected in 1926 with the new church. There were secular carillons at Dunedin Town Hall and in the National War Memorial in Wellington, where it was decided to hang a set of 49 bells when it opened in 1932, but even these were part of a wider religious world. When it was proposed that a carillon tower be erected as a war memorial in Palmerston North's Square, the support of the churches was sought by arguing that it could save them from having to install their own, an argument scoffed at by Methodists.[66]

One supporter of the carillon in Wellington remembered that 'I could stand on a hill on my farm in England and see seven beautiful old village churches, and on a Sabbath the peals and chimes from those church bells sounded very heavenly', and suggested that the bells could stand on the site of the future cathedral and encourage its building.[67] In 1950 Mr & Mrs A. K. Firth gave St Mary's in Merivale (demolished following the 2011 Christchurch earthquake) eight bells cast in England, on the condition that they not be used to play hymns![68] When they were built in 1958, both All Saints Ponsonby and the chapel at Selwyn Village, in Point Chevalier, Auckland, had small carillons installed. There were no such restrictions and the bells still frequently toll out hymns.

Bells were not always viewed benignly by the adjacent population. There were occasional criticisms of the sound of bells when ringing was especially vigorous. As a complainant within earshot of St Peter's in Wellington noted,

> A man finishes a heavy week's work and looks forward to a quiet read and sleep after luncheon both on Saturday and Sunday, but no sooner is one settled down when these all-out-of-tune bells are set going, and all hope of rest and quiet is taken away, and that in one's own house, and in a locality where the high values of the land and the heavy rates mean high rents, for which one is entitled to look for decent comfort, and a church is the very last body from which the infliction of pain and discomfort ought to come, for both pain and discomfort are inflicted by these bells.[69]

Salvationists found this sort of thing amusing given how often their drums and band were criticised for disturbing people.[70]

In Auckland the bell installed in the church of St Philip's in St Heliers in 1961 was rung 21 times at 6.45 a.m. on weekdays and 7.45 a.m. on Sundays. This led to court action by F. Chidwell and Brian Rudman to restrain the ringing before 8 a.m. on weekdays and 9 a.m. on Sundays. In the end, despite a high-level protest in support of the rights of the church, it was agreed that the bell be muffled.[71]

Today, the sound of bells is rare. Occasionally new churches have sought the semblance of tradition in a different format. So, for example, the new St Peter's

Above Recast bells being installed at St Matthew's Anglican Church, Auckland, in 1972. Only St Matthew's, ChristChurch Cathedral and the National War Memorial in Wellington had full carillons, and these were cast in England in 1862, originally for use at Bishopscourt in Parnell. They were installed in the new St Matthew's tower in 1906, but after some cracking they were returned to England and recast by the Whitechapel Foundry. Later No. 4 bell cracked again and had to be sent back. AUCKLAND ANGLICAN DIOCESAN ARCHIVES

Below St Hilda, Mount Wellington, with the vicar of the parish, Rev. Frank Truman, at the doorway. A branch church of the Ellerslie Anglican parish, the rudimentary building was erected in 1950. The church had a large working-class following through its Sunday school. PARISH OF GREATER ELLERSLIE (WELLS CAMPAIGN BOOKLET), AUCKLAND, 1956

Presbyterian Church in Tauranga had electronic chimes installed which could also play hymn tunes, in place of the traditional bell.[72]

Once the church was built, the next priority was its furnishings. In Anglican churches, fixed furniture could signal theological changes or inappropriate gifts, and therefore had to be approved by means of an application for a 'faculty' from the diocese. Other churches were much more permissive, and often it was left up to the priest or pastor, or even the ladies. The ladies were certainly expected to fund changes if no wealthy donor appeared. Thus at St Michael's in Christchurch the Ladies' Working Guild raised large sums of money for chancel furnishings, putting their energies into fairs and other fundraising efforts, consciously seeking to beautify the building.[73]

Dim gas lighting was a striking feature of European Christian buildings, although from about 1900 (and particularly in the 1920s) installing electric lights became common, making evening services more efficient.[74]

Although the Selwyn buildings had mullioned windows, some devout early settlers quickly saw the opportunity of commissioning stained glass to serve as memorials and apt conduits to sacred space. Admittedly the earliest stained glass in New Zealand was in fact put in the Canterbury Provincial Buildings in 1864, and the next in the Barbadoes Street Cemetery Chapel, which was a civic building.[75] The stained glass in the chapel Thatcher designed as the centrepiece of Selwyn's chapel at St John's College in Auckland was the first in a church.[76] Some of the early glass came from the Wellington studio of the brother of an early New Zealand artist, Charles Barraud. By the 1880s and 1890s Victorian architects were encouraging the installation of stained glass commissioned from England in new churches. Yet not a lot of glass was installed in the nineteenth century, perhaps because the debts for construction constrained other expenditure.

World War I was probably the most significant influence on the production of stained-glass windows. In one way or another, the sacrifices of war were commemorated by artistic renditions of Christ's followers, who had imitated His love in their manly acts of war.

Other displays in the altar area were not uncommon. Texts were painted on the walls of St Peter's Riccarton by the architect.[77] Paintings were used in many Catholic churches, although typically these copied European examples rather than showing much originality.

The Protestant love of plainness came into conflict over such issues. While it was acceptable to display texts, even plain crosses alarmed some Protestant sensibilities. The Wesleyan Thomas Sharplin complained to his denominational magazine about the use of crosses in churches: 'Yes, Sir, I have seen four of them upon one [church]

— gilded crosses, glittering in the sun and defiling His rays, mocking the true cross, pleasing the votaries of error — a sight at which angels might weep, demons laugh, and every right-minded Methodist shudder.'[78] Décor and decorum became increasingly important in central-city Methodist churches, and attitudes to display relaxed significantly in the twentieth century.

Catholic buildings faced no such restrictions. Robed priests, altar boys and candles were required for 'all the imposing rites peculiar to that faith'.[79] Images and paintings set the scene for this worship. Thus, for example, Fr Antoine Garin was extraordinarily cautious about spending on the church at Nelson, but in May 1872 he spent significant funds on two cherubs for either side of the altar. When no one in the parish was willing to contribute to this extravagance, he paid for them himself.[80] Many churches were similarly furnished. Almost a hundred years later, in the 1950s, Fr Francis Bennett, in a South Dunedin parish, built a 30-foot-high statue of the Virgin Mary using wire netting, plaster, wood and steel; his achievement was so admired that he was invited to assist in designing and building film sets in Hollywood and Spain.[81]

THE CHANCEL OF THE church inevitably demonstrated what was of central importance to parishioners and how it was understood. In Catholic churches the altar stood in the central position. Catholic worship was conducted by the priest with his back to the people, facing the altar, kneeling or standing, while members of the congregation knelt in reverence, hearing very little — and that in Latin. Anglican churches erected by the CMS followed Low Church practice and had a central pulpit with a table in front of it, but when Selwyn arrived he expressed his disapproval of this, as evidenced by the rearrangement of the Waimate North church.[82] The Russell church was also rearranged, with an altar displacing the pulpit.

The evangelical clergy of the CMS and Bishop Selwyn followed the Prayer Book guidance of saying the service from the 'north side' of the altar. There was very little room for this in many of the churches, which gave an excuse to follow the Anglo-Catholic eastward position with the priest's back to the congregation. The Rev. Henry Edwards adopted the eastwards position at the altar at St Michael's Christchurch in his brief period as vicar 1873–76.[83] There was some debate about this in Anglican churches, and the Prayer Book's preference for the northwards-kneeling clergyman was practised by a few parishes, but the eastward-facing position became standard practice for most churches (and some, including St Mary's Merivale, strongly objected when liturgical reform placed the priest on the other side of the altar).

In traditional Greek worship the iconostasis protected the place where God dwelt on the altar from the people, and in 1215 the Fourth Lateran Council of the Catholic Church, which finalised many Catholic doctrines, decreed that the sanctuary needed to be protected. Rood screens between the chancel (containing the altar) and the nave, where the congregation sat, were one solution. However, these were removed during the Reformation and by the order of the Council of Trent, which reformed some of the practices of the church. They were replaced by altar rails, so that the congregation could watch the consecration. In Catholic churches these were ornate and often marble or stone, serving the dual purpose of fencing the sanctuary and being the place where kneeling parishioners received communion.

In the churches of the Reformation, altars had no place, and altar rails were theologically abhorrent to Puritans and thus to Presbyterians because they implied that communion was the prerogative of the clergy. Archbishop Laud, the seventeenth-century Anglican leader who steered the church away from the teachings of John Calvin, urged the installation of altar rails. They became common in Anglican churches in the seventeenth century, and were universal in New Zealand Anglican churches. Curiously, as the Methodists became more formal altar rails were added, for example in Mount Eden Methodist Church in 1938, for the purposes of identifying the sanctuary, not for kneeling to receive communion.[84]

Altars were another issue. Catholic altars were intended to be ornate (although appearances could be deceptive; when they were moved or removed in 1970 some proved to be wooden boxes with a false appearance of marble). Until the twentieth century Anglican holy tables were genuinely tables. The massive slab of marble that comprises the high altar at St Matthew-in-the-City in Auckland suggests a growing formality in worship, at least for significant churches. Again the liturgical renewal of the early twentieth century, which emphasised that liturgy should engage all the worshippers, changed this. Other Anglican and Catholic churches preferred to create a separate freestanding table, although at St Mary's Merivale the old grand altar retained its place in worship.[85]

The most valuable items in the church were typically the communion vessels. Here was a great opportunity for individual endowments, using gold or gilded or silver work. This gave much scope for lavish donations.

Altar linen was symbolic as well as practical. Presbyterians 'dressed' the church, adding starched linen to the ends of pews, because they 'sat at the table'. The altar in Anglican churches was covered with an elaborate linen cloth, and a brocaded cover when it was not in use for communion. Adornment of the altar gradually became more acceptable. The altar at All Saints in Foxton was embellished by an altar frontal that a soldier during the South African War removed from a private chapel at Jammerberg in the Orange Free State, purloining it to serve as a saddle cloth and

The chancel of Holy Sepulchre church in Khyber Pass Road, Auckland, decorated for Christmas in 1891. The colours are green and red, with the name Bethlehem across the altar. AUCKLAND WAR MEMORIAL MUSEUM. REF: PH-CNEG-C22785

later bringing it home. Peace was later made with the owner and the frontal remains at Foxton.[86]

Candles have a story all their own, reflecting the evolution of religious practices. A lavish Pontifical Mass was always dignified by glittering candelabra ('those showy adjuncts which are usual in the Catholic ritual').[87] Anglicans in the nineteenth century generally were not allowed to have candles on the altar.[88] At Merivale Anglican parish a gilt cross on a retable (a shelf behind the altar) was permitted in 1881, but in 1882 the vestry put 'the offending object' in storage; in 1900 a Mrs Sabine gave two altar candlesticks and the gilt cross was restored to its place behind the altar.[89]

In 1912 the Rev. Cecil Watson caused a storm when alongside changes in his priestly robes or vestments he proposed to light candles at Evensong at St Paul's Church in Auckland.[90] By the end of the twentieth century altar candles were lit during services in most churches and some also allowed visitors to light a candle as a prayer. In any number of liturgically minded Presbyterian and Methodist churches candles have become strangely popular, for today the candle has a curiously undogmatic religious meaning.

In Protestant churches the pulpit was all-important, especially to the minister, for the sermon was the major part of the service, most of which was conducted from the pulpit. In a large elaborate church like Knox in Dunedin or Durham Street in Christchurch there were high central pulpits. When Thomas Spurgeon initiated the building of the Baptist Tabernacle in Queen Street in Auckland, he followed the pattern of the great preaching barn that was the Metropolitan Tabernacle in London, and made the pulpit large enough for the preacher to move around in. Since for most Protestants the whole service was conducted from the pulpit, the high position enabled people in the gallery pews (generally those too poor to rent pews) to hear and see the preacher. There may have been sounding boards in New Zealand to assist, but I know of none. Preachers were often chosen for the strength of their voices.

Anglican and Catholic churches, where the text of the service or liturgy was prescribed, had a different arrangement, with a reading desk on the side in the apse, and then a pulpit to the left or right of the sanctuary. Eventually, as sermons shortened and ritual became more important, most Presbyterian and Methodist churches moved the pulpit to the side, and as congregations shrank, sermons were delivered from the lectern. Many Anglican churches installed heavy eagle-shaped metal lecterns, almost impossible to move and therefore forcing the provision of a step for short people.

From the point of view of parishioners, long sermons could become very tedious, and it became common to install a clock on the back wall where the preacher could see it. At Rangiora Wesleyan Church the Sewing Guild paid for the installation of an eight-day wall clock, the loud ticking of which so annoyed the Rev. Joseph Smalley one Sunday in about 1880 that he halted his sermon and asked one of the worthies of the congregation to stop the beat.[91]

WHAT A UNIQUE THING is the church pew. These massive objects were virtually immovable fixtures among church furnishings that came and went. It puzzles me that more science was not devoted to their design. The English tradition of boxes is still evident on the walls of New Zealand's oldest church, Christ Church, Russell, while Māori generally stood or sat on the ground during services. Pews soon became standard, however, and anyone who has sat in pews will know that they are not suitable for staying long. The pews in poor churches were simple benches. Bunnythorpe's Methodist Church, opened in 1887, had backless pews, amazing a later historian who had heard exaggerated tales that sermons lasted for hours.[92]

From the outset regulars had their own pews. At first this was because they literally rented the pew, which would have their name on it, but, as a later chapter will show, eventually this practice was abandoned. Thereafter pews did not require those hefty wooden ends. Actually most families still had 'their pew', reflecting the stability of the congregation and its interrelationships. Consequently ushers were important, for their task was to direct families to their own pew, and to direct strangers to pews where they might sit without offending the regulars.

Along with the pews went kneelers. These were helpful aids to comfortable worship in an Anglican church, but in the nineteenth century also useful in other churches where one knelt to pray. Although the standard was of a wooden slat hinged to the bottom of the pew, from early on cushioned pew-kneelers were sewn or embroidered by women of the parish.

Another aspect that reflected the inadequacies of nineteenth-century churches was the inadequate provision of heating. Wooden buildings, many of them with no real lining and with high ceilings, proved almost impossible to heat in winter, while those with low ceilings were stiflingly hot in summer. Churches tried various methods to heat their buildings. The huge auditorium of Oxford Terrace Baptist Church in Christchurch was heated by a coke-fired boiler lit by a volunteer at 11 p.m. on Saturday night, until finally in 1957 an automatic oil-fired boiler was installed.[93] At Christ Church Wanganui steam heating, gas heating, electrical heating and water heating were all tried; the gas heater took so long to warm the church that the 8 a.m. services were distinctly unpopular. Cooling required air circulation, and at least most of the smaller churches had windows that could be opened, but at Wanganui vents in the ceiling could not be properly shut because the sun had warped them, adding to the chill in winter.[94]

I N THE TWENTIETH CENTURY very extensive changes were made to old church buildings to suit changing needs. Connecting electricity and providing a toilet were the two obvious priorities. In St Christopher's Sunday school hall in Blenheim, the Ladies' Guild in 1945 funded an entrance porch sheltered from the weather, an enlarged kitchen with a sink board and copper, two lavatories and electric power points.[95]

Heating and fresh air were also given more attention in an age much more concerned about health. The solutions were not always easy. Rangiora Methodist Church installed gas heating from overhead burners in 1926, and this remained when electric lighting was installed in 1928, but in 1937 they moved on to electric heaters.[96] In the 1970s, as flexibility of worship space became more important, separate chairs began to be introduced. Almost all churches gained vestibules, to supplement the existing minimal racks for hats and coats.

From the applications for 'faculties' issued by bishops for the furnishing of Anglican churches, it is possible to spot the growing proportion of 'gear' required. Altar, processional cross, two brass candlesticks, three chalices and patens, alms dish, credence table, font, silver bread box, two glass cruets, prayer desks, bishop's chair, flower stand, alms table, hymn boards, bookstall for the foyer piano, organ and clock were all on the 'must have' list. All were useful items for individual donors. They proved expensive for one church, totalling more than £500 in 1966. Pews at £60 each, carpet for the sanctuary at £400, and a bell at £220 greatly added to the expense of worship.[97]

Even with all these adaptations, most of the nineteenth-century churches had never been intended to be permanent, and pious congregations often aspired to replace them. Most of them had been much adapted and altered, but there was a feeling that buildings in permanent materials were required, with more space and lower upkeep costs. (Little thought was given to earthquakes, which had such a devastating effect on the churches built in permanent materials in Napier — the Cathedral and St Mary's Meeanee.) The roofs of many of the early churches had proved inadequate; some had to rope off areas of the church when it rained. Nevertheless, the costs of building were high, especially after World War II when the boom in housing construction increased the costs. Many churches stumbled their way through these issues, and most that could afford to replaced their old buildings, often predicting a rise in church attendance which never eventuated.

Increasingly, church building had to choose between utilitarian and elaborate styles. In wealthy suburbs and in central places, fine buildings went up. A building constructed of 'permanent materials', rather than wood, was the goal. St Matthew's in Auckland, built with Ōamaru stone in 1905, was intended to be a public statement, replacing the wooden church of 40 years earlier (which remained alongside, as in so many cases, as a Sunday school and parish hall). Ōamaru stone was the mark of the public building designed to last. Brick was sometimes used as a compromise. St David's in Khyber Pass Road in Auckland, intended as a solders' memorial, conveyed magnificence within although necessary economies forced a plain brick exterior.

In the wealthy suburbs, village Gothic revival stone constructions were favoured. St Barnabas Fendalton and St Mary's Merivale in Christchurch were fine Anglican examples of this, but the finest may be St Luke's Presbyterian Church in Remuera. Its delightful traditional, even Anglican, cruciform style belies the fact that it was built in 1931–32 by James Fletcher, who was just beginning his great career as a builder. There are also a number of attractive stone chapels on Canterbury sheep stations, beautifully designed, among them at Longburn and Cass.

Just occasionally the architecture was distinctive. St Michael's, built in 1933 on Beatrice Road, Remuera, behind St Luke's, had a zany Romanesque or Art Deco style. First Church in Invercargill had a stunning brick Byzantine style. More generally, however, churches were very formulaic.

I**N THE NEW SUBURBS** of the cities very simple wooden churches were erected, mostly styled like the nineteenth-century community churches, and in some cases they were the same buildings, slightly altered, or even dragged onsite. In contrast to the wooden churches, other community facilities were built in concrete.

Various fundraising campaigns were undertaken, beginning with the Presbyterian New Life Movement, which funded utilitarian buildings in new suburbs. Anglican churches approached an American fundraiser, Herbert F. Wells, whose organisation had extended to Australia immediately after World War II. The Wells funding scheme focused on mobilising members of a parish to attend a 'loyalty dinner' at which pledges were announced and celebrated. For a share of the profits, the Wells organisation provided lavish tools and methods for canvassing the parish, including very nominal members. The organisation was used to raise funds to build Auckland's Holy Trinity Cathedral and many other Anglican churches in the diocese, and some Presbyterian and Methodist churches also used it.

Many of the buildings that were funded by this means have a striking similarity. Slab construction enabled high roofs to be achieved without complex buttressing, but the result was bare and spartan buildings, perhaps a little out of place in suburbs. St Mary's Anglican Church in Levin and St Peter's in Palmerston North are two examples. This style was also used for some of the Anglican cathedrals that were funded by the Wells method, notably at Napier (replacing the building destroyed in the 1931 earthquake) and the new St Paul's in Wellington. The rigid barn-like style has not worn well.

In 1960 the Methodist Church published a book of guidelines for building, where the focus was 'as clearly as possible to give expression to the fact that the church is a community — not a collection of isolated individuals'.[98] So a corner site was recommended, on a main road, and car parking was even proposed. But the guidelines also reflected growing liturgical emphases that seemed to run quite counter to this: 'There is in our midst a deepening awareness of the power of simple beauty and dignity in a place of worship to uplift the soul of man to God.'[99] A sanctuary was to be up one step, with a central wooden communion table and a pulpit on one side. The choir was also to be in the sanctuary, on one side, and certainly not facing the congregation. There was also recognition that significant rooms needed to be provided for Christian education.

Branch congregations were established in many suburbs by the larger denominations in the period of rapid suburban growth after the war. The Presbyterian New Life Movement was funding new congregations with the status of mission stations, and they were financed by levies from existing congregations. Thus across the Bay of Plenty Presbyterian church halls were erected. St Peter's in Tauranga established an offshoot in Mount Maunganui in 1936 and a second site was added in 1960, but eventually the buildings were both sold and replaced by one more centrally located church.[100]

One very common practice in the 1960s was to build a so-called 'Keith Hay' church (named after the commercial builder and Christian politician from Mount Roskill), which took a custom-designed house shell and, with slight amendments, turned it into a church at the cost of about £2250. For example, the congregation of Howick Methodist Church had long outgrown their tiny wooden church (which had been relocated twice) and so on their newly acquired site on the Pakuranga–Howick highway they erected a Keith Hay building while they raised money for the large new church.[101]

Often the little church halls were very versatile. The little Presbyterian church hall erected at Ngaio had blue velvet curtains around a small alcove at the side, which when drawn revealed a pulpit, a lectern, a table and three seats for the minister and elders. The hall was in constant use by the community, and the funds from renting the building helped to pay back the loan needed for its erection.[102] In many cases

A side altar of St Mary of the Angels in Wellington elaborately decorated for a Novena to the Blessed Peter Chancel in the 1930s. Francis Petre's soaring Gothic building is elaborately decorated in honour of the future saint, martyred in Futuna in 1841.
MARIST ARCHIVES

these buildings did not attract the unchurched population in the way expected, and the halls were not quickly replaced. The Wellington Anglican Diocese funded the building of St Philip's in the 'Pepper Block' (a new housing area north of the railway line in Wanganui East parish). While it was relatively successful as a community facility, numbers at its services were so low that these were reduced to a monthly communion service. Finally even this was discontinued, and the building was sold to the Plimmerton parish as a church for Pukerua Bay.[103]

MEANWHILE NEW THEOLOGICAL VIEWS on worship began to be reflected in architecture. As Anglicans began to see the parish communion as the central service, then liturgical dress became more justifiable. All Saints Anglican Church in Ponsonby, designed by Richard Toy and built in 1958, deliberately sought a more homely suburban feel, and the altar was freestanding so that the priest standing behind it could be father of the congregation. Other churches were reorganised along these lines, including All Saints, Wanganui East. More traditional churches, often in country areas, resisted this; for example, at Warkworth there was firm opposition to the removal of the altar frontal and hangings, even though other church renovations were approved.[104]

Once the Second Vatican Council had authorised changes to Catholic churches, radical alterations took place. In New Zealand altar rails were rapidly removed in almost all churches and people stood to receive communion. The Futuna Chapel in Karori, Wellington, was an extraordinary example of a church designed with the new approach to worship central in the mind of the architect, John Scott.[105] New Catholic parish churches in many suburbs experimented with worship in the round, with very wide apses, central altars and a feeling of community and celebration. This style was sometimes extravagant, and the church of the Blessed Sacrament in Gore, designed by Oakley Pinfold and Turvey, has a striking series of fibreglass features reminiscent of Le Corbusier's architecture. At Ōtaki the old wooden church, the oldest Catholic church in New Zealand, sits alongside the semi-circular building that dates from 1992. This pairing loudly proclaims the vast gulf between the old conception of worship centred on the priest and the new where the priest leads the people in their worship. In an age when church attendance is less regular than in the past, this was the right note to strike.

Protestant buildings were less affected by these conceptions, particularly non-Anglican churches where the Eucharist was less important. Yet there was a renewed sense of the gathered community here, too, and the decline in denominational loyalty meant that styles of church converged.

There was a degree of understated luxury about these buildings. Salvationists, Brethren and Baptists aimed to show that they were more than mission halls, as their members aspired to upward social mobility (for this reason the Brethren renamed their buildings 'chapels').

The new church buildings that were built after the 1960s are on the whole fairly utilitarian. When the old All Saints in Tauranga was destroyed by fire, the new church was designed to serve as an auditorium as well, and so a large and wide sanctuary included an altar on rollers. Baptists rapidly grew in numbers around this time, and did a great deal of building. Central Baptist in Palmerston North and Opawa Baptist Church in Christchurch are typical, with dominant central pulpits, the baptistery tastefully surrounded with indoor shrubs, and a great deal of space for music groups and movement. Windsor Park Baptist Church, the very large church on Auckland's North Shore, is a converted old pub with the sanctuary placed on the long side of the building. Spreydon Baptist Church in Christchurch, which grew rapidly under the Rev. Murray Robertson's long ministry, in 1977 replaced its church with a large square building seating 400 people, and then with a huge flexible gymnasium-style building for double that number in 1994.[106]

Pews were dispensable in such buildings. Individual seats were both more comfortable and more flexible, as concepts of worship and discussion and interaction became increasingly common. A semi-circular layout was natural in this style of worship, but caused some apprehension among those with a traditional outlook. When the pews were thrown out of the Anglican church of St Mark's in the Rai Valley, near Nelson, there were protests that they had been provided by the community, and the church had no right to dispose of them.[107] Where pews remained, kneelers became increasingly colourful and idiosyncratic. At the Cathedral of St Peter in Hamilton, 'the Ladies of the Order of Fine Things' formed in 2002 to repair and embroider coverings and vestments for the church.[108] In Tarras in Central Otago the local Women's Division of the Federated Farmers furnished the Anglican church with elaborate needlepoint kneelers illustrating each family's history to celebrate Women's Suffrage year in 1993.[109] American historian Tom Isern commented that, 'The Tarras kneelers are evidence not only of a powerful sense of place, recorded in collective memory, but also of the definite pull of community.'[110] Yet this was a display of distinctiveness unimaginable before the 1970s.

There are other modest features in recent refurbishments, for example in representational painting rather than paintings of biblical scenes in imagined Middle Eastern styles. Banners are now striking features in many churches.

The growing appreciation of contemporary culture has meant that at times there is a very bold use of stained glass, for example in the Erebus window in St Matthew's in Auckland, or the brilliant side windows in the nave of the Anglican Cathedral of the Holy Trinity in Parnell, designed by Shane Cotton and Robert Ellis. They are effective because they are exuberant and evocative of Polynesian interpretations of the faith, rather than specific in their subject matter. The vast expanse of the East Window at the back of the nave of the cathedral is by Nigel Brown, and includes portrayals of the arrival of European and Māori boats and a colourful plethora of images of Aotearoa. This is very typical of the indigenous themes that now dominate New Zealand art.

The Pentecostal form of Christianity appeared in New Zealand in the early 1920s, with its dramatic expectations of signs and wonders and healings in services. Early Pentecostal buildings were simple churches on the Baptist model, but later buildings overturned most of the traditions of church architecture. While early Pentecostalism played down the status of the clergy, later massive auditoriums were opened where worship could be loud and exuberant and the preacher could dominate. Many of these buildings were either remodelled theatres (most notably Majestic House in Christchurch) or converted warehouses. They were intended for high visibility and a powerful sense of presence and drama. In such buildings the flat open space gave room for worship and movement, but also room for the spectacular. The new Destiny Church centre at Wiri in South Auckland, a renovated factory, has a huge video wall some 30 metres long which offsets the speaker.

The first places of worship used by Polynesian communities in New Zealand were borrowed Congregational, Methodist and Presbyterian churches and halls. Soon, however, there was a desire among some to have their own buildings. For climatic reasons it was not possible to use the fale style, and the church buildings of the Pacific reflect the Nonconformist architecture of Victorian England, although rendered with thick stone walls and whitewash.

When the churches erected their own buildings in New Zealand, they often made very utilitarian decisions, adapting houses and halls for the many demands of the Polynesian community, where the building had strong social functions. Very large spaces were required, but there was little money for elaboration, and the Nonconformist tradition meant that there was little desire for towering naves. Tithing meant that money was raised quite quickly, but the buildings were often cheaply constructed. South Auckland has some huge Methodist and Presbyterian churches for Tongan and Samoan worshippers, but the buildings have few touches of grandeur other than demonstrating a penchant for elaborate chandeliers. The buildings seem to wear out quickly.

A CHURCH LIFE SURVEY THAT has been conducted in many churches over recent years asks, among other things, whether people sense the presence of God in worship. In the 2001 survey, 44 per cent of Catholics said they always felt the presence of God in worship.[111] For Catholics, indeed, the Mass is the centre of all religious experience. Protestants' responses, however, were very different. Nearest to Catholics were Pentecostals, of whom 34 per cent always sensed God's presence in their style of worship, which was focused on singing and preaching. Among Anglicans, 28 per cent sensed God in worship all the time, and among the less ritual-focused, 24 per cent of Brethren but only 21 per cent of Baptists always had this sense of a life of worship.

Looking at the same figures by age spread, older people were far more likely to sense the presence of God always in worship: 35 per cent of those over the age of 60 felt a sense of worship in church services, compared to 21 per cent of 15- to 29-year-olds. It is clear that expectations as well as experiences are part of the issue for a generation reared on magnificent productions on television.

The 2007 survey also asked participants about their sense of the presence of God at work, at leisure and in nature.[112] It was clear that many people struggled to have a sense of God apart from the church building and church service. Cross-correlations indicated that people were more likely to sense the presence of God in nature if their faith was sustained not just by church attendance but also by their own private devotions.

Western notions of church attendance may enculturate people into a very limited notion of the divine presence. Christianity historically had a much broader impact on culture than just its churches and services. A significant confinement of religiosity has shaped the experience of church in New Zealand. Yet curiously, when the Anglican Church wanted to bulldoze the damaged cathedral in the centre of Christchurch and replace it with a modern building, an unlikely combination of secular leaders demanded that it be rebuilt. As the historian Katie Pickles commented, it 'existed for many as a hollow icon with good branding potential . . . It called out "Christchurch" in all its multiplicity of meanings, promising everything and nothing at once.'[113] The resonance of sacred space oddly survives even in the secular wasteland.

Gathered to Worship

Previous Audience and choirs at the Associated Church of Christ's annual conference held in the Nelson School of Music in 1913. This evangelical denomination was founded in Nelson in 1850 and congregations from all over the country attended its annual conference, all dressed in their Sunday best. PHOTOGRAPH BY FREDERICK NELSON JONES, ALEXANDER TURNBULL LIBRARY, REF: 1/1-011349-G

ANYONE WHO VISITS A new church is at risk of suffering a degree of nervousness. What rules govern behaviour? When do you sit and when do you stand? Do you have to kneel? What about the books that have been placed in your hands? Sometimes references to numbers in these books are very unclear. Most of the denominational rules are less extreme than they once were, but there are still divergences. In Anglican churches in some places people kneel during the Eucharistic prayer (the prayer of consecration at Communion), but in other places they stand. Sometimes congregations are thrown into confusion by uncertainty over whether to sit or stand. Customs for the collection and for the distribution of Communion seem to have many local variations.

Imagine, then, the experience of the first Māori attending the service on the beach at Oihi (Hohi) in 1814, where Samuel Marsden conducted an Anglican service complete with hymns and even a sermon delivered in 'pidgin Māori'. The culture of faith is at its most impenetrable in its forms of worship.

There has been some debate about when the first service was held, since John Dunmore claimed that the Mass was surely said on board the French explorer Jean François Marie de Surville's ship *St Jean Baptiste* in 1769. Nevertheless, the first service held on New Zealand soil was without doubt the service on Christmas Day 1814. Much has been written about the event. The careful setting up of the site by Ruatara, who had formerly lived in Australia, shows that he knew what was required for morning prayer, or Matins, according to the Anglican liturgy, and the readings were those laid down for Christmas Day. The hymn 'All people that on earth do dwell' was not particularly Christmassy, but there were at that stage relatively few Christmas hymns, and carols were regarded as folk traditions rather than as hymns. The sermon was the key part of the service of Matins in its eighteenth-century form.

Māori church services developed over the following years. Laymen were permitted to read the service but discouraged from preaching. By the 1820s, the CMS had a cycle of services held throughout the Bay of Islands, which were announced by the ringing of bells. Increasingly, Māori catechists (non-ordained agents of the mission) led these services and provided brief homilies.

Communion was held quarterly, and ordinary Māori who had not been baptised and admitted to Communion were not invited. The celebrations were also held at Christmas and Easter. Marsden's diary indicates that Communion was celebrated on board the brig *Active*, anchored by the beach at Rangihoua or Hohi in the Bay of Islands, on the evening of 25 December 1814, hours after the first service held on land.[1]

Thus gradually patterns of worship became part of the Māori routine. The moment in 1833 when the senior missionary Henry Williams visited Thames and heard Māori repeat the liturgical responses from the service — even though this was the first service a missionary had ever conducted there — shows how liturgy had become part of Māori knowledge.[2] About 1827 there was an attempt to translate the Lord's Prayer into Māori, which was printed by the other missionary group that had arrived, the Wesleyans. The second set of scriptural selections printed in Sydney under the supervision of William Yate in 1830 includes a Māori version of morning prayers, with some key prayers for the king, the royal family and the missionaries; in addition there was a short Catechism listing Christian beliefs, which was also printed separately.[3] The Anglican missionaries would only baptise the small number of adults who learned the Catechism and demonstrated that they were believers. The liturgical content was based on the translated words of the Book of Common Prayer. The American scholar Richard Sundt comments critically that 'the church in New Zealand remained strictly English in the measured tones and conduct of its liturgy and spaces'.[4]

As for the Catholics, the first Mass was said in the Irishman Thomas Poynton's parlour at Totara Point in the Hokianga on 13 January 1838, three days after the missionaries landed there. The rituals of the Mass followed by Bishop Pompallier and the other Catholic missionaries reflected a different form of religion than that of the Protestant missionaries. Doubtless most of their services were Mass, but most of these would have been low Masses, in which only the priest takes Communion. Pompallier was very free in baptising converts who often had a very limited Christian understanding, believing that it was his calling to shed God's grace in the world, whether or not his actions made sense to others. Because the Mass was said in Latin, nothing needed to be changed to suit the congregation except the Bible readings (which were read by the priest in Latin and given a loose translation) and the sermon. The sermons were generally short homilies. Mass books in Latin were also provided.

IN THE EUROPEAN WORLD, the church service was a public event in a formal place, where due formalities were expected to be observed. This sense of occasion showed the central role of church to the community, and the loss of this status shook its sense of identity.

People dressed up to go to church: everyone had their Sunday best. Until the 1970s, families insisted that children don their best clothes to go to church. Both Protestants and Catholics followed this pattern.[5] Many a child was lectured on the need to dress up properly because they were going to meet with the king (viewing God as the supreme monarch). The same logic (reinforced by texts from St Paul's Epistles in the Bible) required women to wear hats. This was a formal occasion, and reverence was required. So children should shut up and be seen and not heard, and laughter (all too easy when pompous language fell flat in this homely setting) had to be stopped by stuffing one's mouth with a handkerchief. People's voices and accents reverted to the formal, the intoned, the reverent. 'Parson's voice' always made people lose concentration.[6] The problem was that in the small, stuffy buildings of the nineteenth century, Sunday best sometimes meant being rather overdressed for the temperature. But when, for example, during an Anglican mission at Christ Church, Warkworth, the Rev. A. H. Colville, the visiting missioner, told the men to come in their shirt sleeves, few took the invitation seriously, and they had to endure a stifling atmosphere.[7]

So usually at 11 a.m. on Sunday (although ministers regularly held services in many places, at various times in the afternoon or evening) the service commenced. Those churches that followed a formal liturgy memorised by parishioners experienced a quite different form of service from those where there was no written liturgy. In liturgical churches familiar words (even if in Latin) were intoned or sung and said. The sermon and the hymns were an intrusion on this central experience. There was a great difference between a sacramental service, where Communion was central, and a service where preaching lay at the centre. It was the difference between acts and words.

The regular morning service for Protestants consisted of a sequence of hymns, prayers and sermon, almost all said by the minister or approved lay reader. This, too, was a ritual, but one that resided in the minister's head, following patterns from the denomination as followed in Britain. Few congregations were asked to say the Lord's Prayer because a recited prayer was viewed as Catholic (and to this day it is rarely said in Baptist churches).[8] The minister always delivered the scripture reading. Even in a church as community-minded as Mount Eden Methodist Church it was only in 1974 that lay people were assigned to do this reading.[9] In the more Protestant churches (Baptists and Brethren, for example) the preacher read the Bible text before preaching. So just one speaker dominated the whole service. The larger churches gradually added more dignified ceremony as they became more respectable. Music played an increasing role in these services. The first minister of Napier Presbyterian Church, Peter Barclay, observed in 1871 that there was less formality in New Zealand and less hypocrisy in the church than in the settlers' homelands.[10] Perhaps for this reason denominational distinctions waned more easily, although this may minimise the ingrained nature of different denominational traditions, even within the several types of Presbyterianism in Britain.

Anglicans tried to keep their distinctiveness by reviving English church traditions. Some Anglicans reproduced a number of curious ceremonies and traditions, including 'clipping the bounds' by walking around the parish boundaries, and boys' choirs. Many Anglicans held a high view of the state in the purposes of God and some declared profound affection for Britain. A few professed the British Israel teaching that England had inherited the Old Testament promises to Israel. Many church leaders were active Freemasons. Joseph Feron, vicar of Rangiora and then of St Albans in Christchurch, and a forthright critic of lazy Anglicans, was an ardent Freemason and passionate believer in the doctrines of British Israel.[11] The ceremonies of Anglicanism had some appeal as the middle class grew, but the casual informality of the late twentieth century left many Anglicans uncomfortable.

Before the revolution of the 1960s and 1970s, Anglicans followed the Book of Common Prayer, and the Anglican liturgy both for Matins (morning prayer) and for Communion had limited congregational responses. Until the 1950s the main service at Anglican churches was Matins, which the clergyman led while kneeling or standing at a prayer stall. There was a gradual move to involve the congregation more; in 1965 the Rev. Colin Venimore gained written permission from his bishop for the congregation in Wanganui East to join him in saying some of the prayers in the Communion service.[12] He was unusual in this, and seeking formal permission was advisable given that he was proposing changes in the Prayer Book. The attempt to authorise a revised prayer book in England in 1928 had been overturned by the House of Commons, where suspicions of Catholic trends in the established church created a great storm.

People have long had deeply felt reactions to the form of worship shaped from childhood. The patterns of private prayer and devotion probably reflected this: Catholics prayed the rosary; others detested this as vain repetition. Some people were very uncomfortable at a formal liturgy, while others refused to attend churches where the words were not familiar.[13] Many Presbyterians were suspicious of written prayers, but others agonised at long-drawn-out extempore prayers that mentioned every needy person or place the minister could recall. A Presbyterian service, according to the Rev. Peter Barclay, writing in 1870 out of his experience as a Presbyterian minister, could be 'cold and somewhat repellent to emotional natures'.[14] New Zealand Methodists, like Presbyterians, rarely used liturgies in the nineteenth century, even though their founder, John Wesley, had prepared a purged prayer book.[15] The only interruption to the voice of the minister would be congregational singing, or the choir anthem. Yet within Methodism there was powerful emotion and a sense of the mystery of religion expressed in the spirituality of the Wesleys, an aspect of Protestantism that is not unlike the Orthodox Churches in its devotions.

This divide in forms of worship remains. Bishop Richard Randerson, the Dean of the Anglican cathedral in Auckland in the early 2000s, describes in his

St Paul's Anglican Church, Waiwhetu, Lower Hutt, in 1960. The church was built in 1959 after a Wells fundraising campaign. The vicar and curate are at the front; the choir is in the back gallery. The women all wear hats. Probably E. C. Barber was vicar. EVENING POST, WELLINGTON, 24 JUNE 1960, ALEXANDER TURNBULL LIBRARY, REF: EP/1960/2271-F

autobiography his panic at having to lead an unscripted Presbyterian service in the 1980s.[16] Anglicans failed to appreciate the ways in which each part of the Protestant service could be carefully directed by the minister, thus guiding the aspirations and values of members of the congregation. The sermon was not necessarily the high point, but rather an introit to the intensity of the long prayer and the fervency of the final hymn and blessing. Bower Black, the eloquent and popular minister of St David's Presbyterian Church in Khyber Pass, Auckland, was famed for his preaching. But the historian of St David's (himself a distinguished minister) notes that 'One of Mr Black's greatest contributions was his gift of conducting a service as one integrated and compact act of worship where every part contributed to bring every member of the congregation into the presence of God.'[17]

A very significant change for Presbyterians was brought about by the Church Service Society founded by the Rev. Duncan Hercus and friends in 1936. This organisation (modelled on a similar society in Scotland) encouraged the rediscovery of liturgy, the church year, and ways to encourage an understanding of the act of worship within a reformed framework.[18] Laity were much less influenced by the liturgical movement, however, and resisted the growing formalising of traditions.

A factor not exactly in the liturgy but of some significance was what was called in polite Protestant parlance the 'intimations' (although in our debased language today they are simply the church announcements and notices). Churches puzzled over where to place them to keep them from interrupting the act of worship yet in a place where they could not be missed or forgotten (which argued against the natural timing prior to the service). These intimations could be almost as long as a sermon. In the Baptist tradition they were delivered by the church secretary, and in more recent times, as the church has become more like a family, they have become an opportunity for anyone to stand up and give news of a forthcoming event. In the Presbyterian tradition they came at the end of the service and were given by the minister.

Gray Dixon, a former professor of English language and literature at the Imperial College of Engineering in Tokyo who was later ordained, was from 1900 the minister who was responsible for the flourishing of St David's Church in Khyber Pass. As one parishioner commented: 'It was a treat to hear Mr Dixon give out the intimations, especially when there was a good batch of them. As he dealt with them they became a gladdening recital of the conduct and progress of the everyday activities of the church.'[19]

Baptism was a significant ritual that was viewed in different ways by the different denominations. There were two forms of baptism, and many ways of administering it. The early CMS (Anglican) and Wesleyan missionaries recognised each other's baptisms as valid, but when Bishop Selwyn arrived in New Zealand in 1842 he rejected Wesleyan baptisms as invalid because in his view the missionaries were not ordained. Moreover, Selwyn held the traditional Anglican view of 'baptismal regeneration' — viewing the sacrament as the basis of salvation. Fashionable Anglicans viewed baptism as a celebration of birth, using the ancient term 'christening', and the elite preferred private christenings to be held in the church on Sunday afternoons rather than during the church service. There was a theoretical requirement that baptism be held within a regular service of the church, but when Hubert Carlyon was charged with adopting Catholic practices at the Anglican church in Kaiapoi in 1877 the charge that he had conducted private baptisms was dismissed, reflecting that this rule was commonly ignored.

There were also disputes by those who queried making the sign of the cross on the baby at their baptism. Some Presbyterian ministers sought to exclude the children of errant parishioners from being baptised, causing great anger in the community, which again viewed it not as a sacrament but as a celebration of birth.[20] Methodists used christening as a form of outreach.[21] Jasper Calder, who founded the Auckland City Mission in 1920, and who frequently defied the rulings of his own Anglican Church, held seaside baptisms for his friends in the sailing fraternity, pushing even Anglican practice to the limit.[22]

Infant baptisms these days are less common, as they have ceased to be the custom for those who do not attend church, even in the best families. Some Anglicans are choosing not to baptise their children, leaving it to the children to 'make up their own minds' about religion. There also seems to be much less emphasis on baptism generally, and churches often do not ask whether their communicants have been baptised.

T**HE SHEER VARIETY OF** names around the Holy Communion service — Mass, the Eucharist, the Lord's Supper, the Communion service — tells us that the Christian sacrament was a matter of sharp divergence between the churches, and the name itself could be a source of controversy. Anglicans who used the term 'Holy Eucharist' rather than Communion (as some did from the 1860s) were indicating that they wanted to distinguish their rite from that of other Protestants.[23] Only the Quakers and the Salvation Army had no such service, for they did not recognise the need for sacraments.

The Latin Mass standardised Catholic rituals whether for Māori or for Europeans. Catholics knew the responses by heart, but for long periods of the service their minds were disengaged. They joined in a timeless ritual with its dramatic display at the moment of consecration. The Mass could be simple or magnificent. Catholics could draw on Gregorian chant and the Masses of Palestrina and Mozart and, as one Catholic author has commented, 'Faith meant primarily the way one worshipped, ie the Liturgy, the rituals, the ceremonies, all of which presented a mystique, a sense of awe and reverence. A solemn High Mass was a drama.'[24]

The responses were said in Latin although many parishioners brought to the service their small Mass books, which included the Latin and English translations (except for the Eucharistic prayer) and devotional prayers which devout Catholics said during the ritual. When it came to the prayer of consecration, the priest spoke 'sub secreto' in a hushed voice so that only the altar boys could hear. Only the priest drank the consecrated wine. Laity knelt at the altar rails and the priest placed the wafer on the tongue while the acolyte held the paten underneath to catch any crumbs.

While it was the standard form of the Mass, most Catholics, taught to fast for all the hours prior to receiving the sacrament, would not take Communion except on special days, while the priests were obliged to fast until lunchtime on Sunday. So the experience was effectively a sacred spectacle. If a priest was not available, the Māori church would hold a 'dry Mass' with prayers but no consecration.[25]

The Eucharist was not part of the weekly ritual of most Anglicans before the 1950s. General Synod had laid down that it should be celebrated on the third Sunday of the month, and often on those Sundays it was an abbreviated addition to Matins; some members of the congregation would leave before it commenced.[26] Anglicans were encouraged to receive the bread and wine, but recorded numbers at the Eucharist especially in the nineteenth century indicate that many Anglicans rarely took Communion, perhaps viewing it as a little scary. Choral settings of the Eucharist were sometimes held in the evening to attract congregations.

The forms of the ritual were tightly regulated by early Anglican bishops in order to prevent the divisions that had happened to the church in England. In the late 1850s, Bishop Harper of Christchurch laid down that the bread and wine were to be placed on a credence table on the north side of the chancel, and they were placed on the table or altar prior to the consecration prayer; the clergyman would kneel at the altar during this prayer, usually with his back to the congregation.[27]

In the early twentieth century, Anglican practices began to vary. Priests fought their bishops to be allowed to introduce more Catholic ritual. St Michael and All Angels in Christchurch led the way by beginning a weekly Communion in 1871, and numbers taking Communion increased to a higher proportion of worshippers (although the majority still did not do so).[28] After 1910, St Michael's was permitted to adopt full Anglo-Catholic ritual for the Eucharist. In most Anglican churches

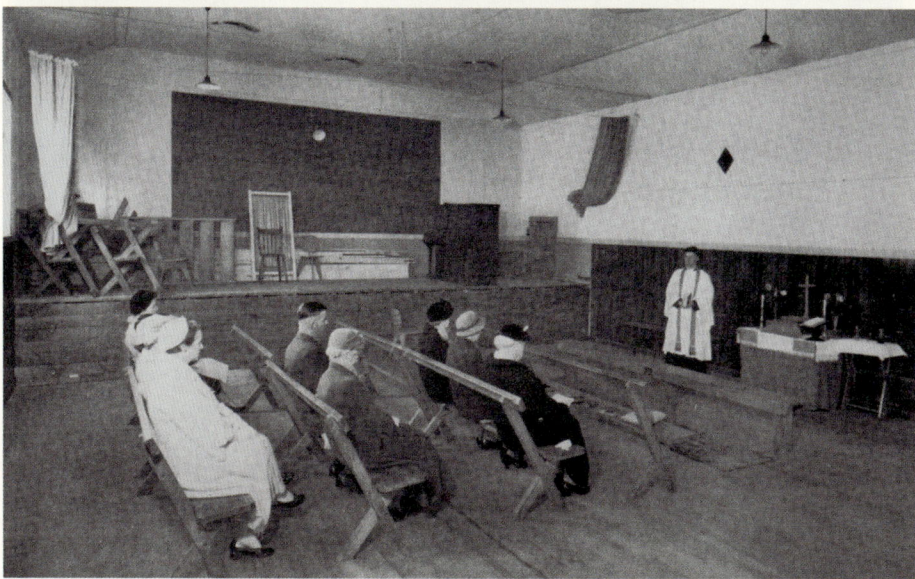

Above The Anglican church St George's, Papatoetoe. This photo appeared on the cover of the Wells Campaign booklet urging pledges to support the parish so that a new and bigger church could be built. The campaign was successful and a new church was built in 1961. G. O. Adams was the vicar of this parish. PAPATOETOE PARISH (WELLS CAMPAIGN CANVASS BOOKLET), AUCKLAND, 1956

Below An Anglican church service in the public hall in Takanini, south Auckland. This image also appeared in the Papatoetoe parish's Wells Campaign publicity booklet. Roy Everell, the vicar, is in robes as the Communion service is about to begin. FAITH IN ACTION! (PAPAKURA WELLS CAMPAIGN CANVASS BOOKLET), AUCKLAND, 1956

congregations resisted Catholic innovations. When the English priest Creed Meredith was appointed vicar of Christ Church Wanganui, the vestry quickly discovered that he planned to introduce wafer bread, altar lights, and a processional cross on festival days in order to improve the spirit of worship, arguing that this would 'serve to associate [the parish] with the great Central Church movement in the Church of England, which aims at safeguarding the Church against extremists'. The members of the vestry were outraged and resisted all the way.[29] The number of Anglo-Catholic churches in New Zealand was small.

In most Protestant churches Communion was celebrated quarterly in the nineteenth century, and monthly in the twentieth century, not because they cared little for the sacrament but because they regarded it as profoundly important. The Presbyterian traditions of quarterly Communion were particularly elaborate in Otago, following Scottish customs. Alison Clarke has described how Communion Sunday once every three months was a major event in the southern Presbyterian communities.[30] It was a very exclusive event. A preparatory sermon was given in the preceding week. Church elders distributed Communion tokens or cards at least a week before the service (and members often brought these with them when they came, for this entitled them to a place at the table). On Communion Sunday the pews were dressed with starched white linen. The elders seated around the Lord's table at the front of the church ensured it was a solemn occasion, but they spoke of 'sitting down at the table' for they still reflected the Reformation concept of a Communion meal.[31] Ordinary white bread was cut into small pieces, the elders delivered it to each row and people served one another in the pews. A simplified version of these customs remains in more traditional Presbyterian churches.

The Methodist version of the same service was notified to members by Communion tokens. It was generally held quarterly and then on the first Sunday of every month. Members would sometimes sit in alternate pews to receive the bread and wine, with the minister walking down the empty rows to deliver the 'elements', the bread and wine.[32] In many churches the plates of diced up bread and thimbles of Communion grape juice were passed along the rows. Protestants disliked going forward to receive Communion, which seemed to them too Catholic.[33]

In Baptist churches the minister was joined at the table by a selection of members, one of whom would give the prayer of consecration. At Kaiapoi Baptist Church there was once a disaster when the member called on to pray was unable to utter a word.[34] Professor John Condliffe, Professor of Economics at Canterbury University College in the 1920s, sometimes attended Oxford Terrace Baptist Church in Christchurch, and described the Baptist Communion, 'in its simplicity and intensity', with its corporate sense of 'imminent Presence and a consciousness of brotherhood and election', as very different from going forward to the altar in an Anglican church.[35]

In the late nineteenth century the experience of Communion changed for most of the Protestant churches. This was when alcoholic wine was replaced with grape juice and the shared chalice by individual cups. These were first proposed by a New York writer in 1882, and the practice spread rapidly in an age obsessed with hygiene, reflecting new understandings of how germs transmitted disease.[36] The practice soon reached New Zealand; individual glass thimbles were introduced at Queenstown Presbyterian Church in 1905, and doubtless this was typical of many other congregations.[37] Hygiene, as well as views of the immorality of alcohol, lay behind the substitution of grape juice for alcohol as well.

These practices became deeply ingrained in Protestant practice, although they left the more liturgically minded uncomfortable. When a group of Catholics visited a Methodist youth conference in 1955, a common cup was deemed appropriate.[38] The Brethren, almost the only Protestant church with a weekly Communion within a completely unscripted service, kept the shared cup until the 1990s, when they became much more like other Protestant services in their format. In recent years many Protestant churches have offered multiple options, including coming forward to drink from a common cup of wine, or receiving a thimble of grape juice in the pews.

WHEN BISHOP POMPALLIER ARRIVED in 1838, Māori were immensely impressed by the grandeur of his vestments compared to the black ankle-length cassocks and white surplices (the wide-sleeved robe worn during services) of the Low Church Anglican missionaries. The story of the Anglican robes and vestments from that age until today is complex. Bishop Selwyn was High Church Anglican, unlike the missionaries, but his ecclesiastical dress was very like theirs, including the bishop's white rochet gown and black chimere cloak. The Oxford Movement, or Anglo-Catholicism, which gained momentum in England from the 1850s, increasingly sought to express its view of the priestly status and the Communion as the act of partaking in the body of Christ by garbing priests in traditional Catholic colourful and elaborate Eucharistic chausubles during the Communion, and copes (elaborate sleeveless capes) at other times. Stoles, ornate scarves in the colours of the liturgical season, were also worn. Suspicions were often aroused by this kind of dress in congregations concerned at the undermining of Protestant rejection of the priestly role.[39]

Hubert Carlyon, vicar of Kaiapoi in the 1870s, was the first New Zealand Anglican priest to revert to the ornamented liturgical robes, until this was banned by his bishop. The Rev. Hannibal Gilbert, vicar of Good Shepherd Church in Phillipstown in the east of Christchurch from 1880 to 1897, is thought to have pioneered the use of Eucharistic vestments, and he was succeeded by the Rev. Harold Ensor (from 1899 to 1917), who used appropriate vestments for the different liturgical seasons. Coloured liturgical stoles appropriate to the season of the Christian year were also introduced at about this time. Vestments were adopted by St Michael's in Christchurch, at St Paul's in Auckland in 1912, and St Luke's in Christchurch in 1913, and key members of the team of British Anglican priests brought to New Zealand for the Mission of Help in 1910 modelled and encouraged a positive attitude towards Anglo-Catholic practices.[40]

In 1927, Archbishop Alfred Walter (Wally) Averill indicated that the bishops would permit greater variation in vestments and allow the wearing of stoles (which were often elaborately decorated, indicating the office held), thus allowing New Zealand Anglicans to follow new English customs. St Peter's Hamilton later set the pace in the wearing of vestments and stoles.[41] Significant sums of money had to be set aside for these vestments, for High Church worship was magnificent and lavish, and they sometimes cost hundreds of pounds. Advocates always emphasised the combination of gravity, celebration and drama that they conveyed.[42] Culturally this expressed a ceremonial reinforcement of the church's tradition, history and authority. Stoles were coloured according to the different church seasons (for example, violet for Advent and Lent; white for Christmas, Easter and commemorations of the saints; red for Pentecost), suggesting a desire to restore a more visual aspect of worship. The Low Church parish of St Matthew's in central Auckland used the vestments of the very High Church St Thomas's when the two parishes merged in the 1960s, not with any High Church theology as a justification but simply because Anglicanism was now much more ceremonial than in the past.

The Protestant churches other than Anglicans (often called non-episcopal because they did not have bishops) were highly suspicious of these trends. John Dickson, a Presbyterian minister from Northern Ireland who conducted sensational debates with the Catholic priest when he was minister in Temuka in 1896 — the so-called Temuka Tournament — challenged the trend and was critical of Bishop Julius and others for their tolerance of the Anglo-Catholics. 'It is not Christianity. It is Ritualism, Romanism, heathenism,' Dickson argued.[43] At the heart of this concern lay a complex interconnection of Protestantism and English nationalism, in which non-Anglicans considered themselves the proper guardians of the Church of England (although in New Zealand the Church of England was just another denomination).

Methodists and Presbyterians had historically worn Genevan gowns, the black preaching robe common among Calvinist or Reformed churches in Europe and

Scotland. Presbyterian ministers often wore the academic hoods of their degrees, for their formal title was as a teaching elder. Many lay preachers and ministers, however, conducted worship wearing suits. A surprising variety of robes was worn by Protestant clergy. In the Malvern parish in North Canterbury in 1959 robes were worn by the Presbyterian minister in some but not all of the district churches, reflecting whether the issue had been debated in the congregation.[44]

Yet in the postwar years Protestant clergy also wanted to wear more formal dress while conducting worship. Methodists became more formal, especially in the larger churches. In 1940 the Durham Street Church in Christchurch invested in pulpit gowns for visiting ministers who came with none. Raymond Dudley, the minister at the time, was renowned for his great dignity.[45] The growing recognition of education led some Methodists, for example, to demand that academic gowns be worn by ministers.[46] The result, as Alan Walker from Sydney's Wayside Chapel told Methodists in 1956, was very strange dress worn by clergy, strange religious voices, and a widening gap between people and clergy.[47]

Baptists mostly wore suits to conduct worship. In 1951, at the time of the Canterbury Centennial, the Rev. L. J. Boulton-Smith, minister of the grandest of all the Baptist churches, Oxford Terrace Baptist Church in Christchurch, was invited to a reception with the Archbishop of Canterbury. Feeling that he ought to be suitably garbed, he borrowed a robe from the Moderator of the Presbyterian Church. The Archbishop concluded he was speaking to a Presbyterian (used as he was to dealing with the Church of Scotland) and Boulton-Smith was forced to confess, 'Alas, my lord, I am only a bush Baptist in borrowed plumes.'[48]

IT MIGHT BE ARGUED that Christian churches may be classified by whether they focus on ritual acts — for example Catholics, Orthodox and some Anglicans — or on the content of the confession of faith and individual profession of it. While this is an inadequate view, for all churches have rituals and most churches have creeds, there is some truth in it. In the Sunday service, Protestants viewed the sermon as the central event. Much attention was given to the length and rhetorical style of these sermons.

There were renowned preachers in every denomination, and their sermons were often reproduced in denominational magazines, so we know something of the style, content and duration of those sermons. In general, Baptists and Presbyterians vied for length, but Presbyterians surpassed all in erudition. None could rival the eloquence of Rutherford Waddell or John Elmslie or (from a later era) Owen Baragwanath. These were silver-tongued preachers who attracted vast congregations. Salvation

Army sermons were always entertaining in their use of the working-class vernacular. Anglican and Catholic preachers aimed for brevity.

In the Anglican world the sermons were very different. Some of the most highly regarded preachers could be extremely concise. Matthew Calder, for example, from a notable family of ministers, was vicar of St Mark's by the Basin Reserve in Wellington in the 1960s. A popular broadcaster, whose sermons were published as 'Sin in the City', he spoke typically for 15 minutes, but made every word work with his intimate and direct tone.[49]

In Baptist circles, one of the most renowned preachers was John North (1871–1950), minister at Wellington Central and Oxford Terrace Christchurch, and later first principal of the Baptist College in Auckland. A recent Baptist scholar has identified North's strength as lying in his ability to combine scriptural references with fervour and a sense of urgency.[50]

Baptist preachers in the nineteenth century often preached for at least half an hour. Thomas Spurgeon, minister of the Baptist Tabernacle in Auckland in the 1880s, and Frank Boreham, minister at Mosgiel from 1895 and author of 46 books of sermons, who went on to a notable career in Australia, were masters of this art. Boreham gripped hearers with opening stories that illustrated the relevance of his message. Preaching in this tradition was a way of expressing the personality of the preacher. As Boreham wrote, 'the most solemn trust committed to each of us is his own personality — the self, the ego — call it what you will. It is the thing that makes me me; a creation quite unique, having no duplicate in all of God's eternities. And the supreme thing that we each have to do in the theatre of life is to give that individuality its full and natural expression.'[51] His sermons did just that.

The Methodist tradition of preaching was different again: long, passionate, using scriptural texts and alliterative subsections in a tone that reasoned as well as stirred the emotions. The Catholic sermon was sometimes an impassioned harangue, and sometimes a plea for funds or a political statement in favour of Ireland. When Fr Dean O'Donnell, who was parish priest of Ashburton from 1892 to 1944, became old, he often forgot to preach, to the relief or amusement of the congregation.[52]

In the twentieth century amplification began to be introduced in churches, although the quality of reproduction left much to be desired, and loud sounds of static became a familiar part of the audio experience. Few parish histories describe this. At St Mary's Merivale a new system was installed in 1970, but Canon Froud lamented, 'I am dead scared that every time I raise my voice, some of you will be blown out of your pews by the volume.'[53] The effect of amplification was most marked on preaching, leading to a significant change in the style of sermons as a flat conversational style became common.

Radio and later television broadcasting made church people more aware of good preachers. Jasper Calder conducted the first broadcast church services in April 1923, and the range of churches selected for broadcasting was later widened as regional stations relayed local services, according to a formula developed by the Central Religious Advisory Committee established by the National Broadcasting Service in 1943.[54] The services were appreciated mostly by those who were unable to attend church due to sickness or incapacity, and who therefore knew what a service should be.[55] There were masters of the art, and their ordinary services were reshaped in the process. The Rev. Bob Lowe of the Anglican parish of Fendalton, St Barnabas, conducted his services as drama, blending the traditional and the informal (the lights were dimmed during the sermon), playing up his avuncular and personable style.[56]

This is not the place for a history of religious programming, but radio specialists soon realised that church services did not always make for good radio, and they could be even poorer television unless there was some dramatic action such as an ordination or Communion. Outside broadcasts were gradually reduced, until today they are only broadcast at Christmas. The legislative requirement of public service content for television undercut this tradition of broadcasting, and religion in the media faded with very significant effects.[57] By the 1980s the state-owned broadcasters employed staff to prepare their religious content in-house. Most broadcasting thereafter was sponsored by large Pentecostal 'televangelists'.

SUNDAY EVENING SERVICES HAD a different natural market than morning services. Those services had been made easier by lighting with gas lamps in the 1880s, succeeded by electricity in the 1920s. Domestic servants, who in the morning were at home preparing the Sunday lunch or carrying out other duties, were generally sent to church in the evening. Evangelical churches such as the Methodists cultivated an evangelistic atmosphere in the evening services, with hot sermons and regular altar calls in which, using nineteenth-century revivalist methods, they invited would-be converts to come to the front. They also used distinctive and emotional hymns. This became a service directed at the working class and the young, and they could be a spectacular success if sermons were advertised in advance with titles like 'The worth of a working man'.[58]

The Salvation Army congregations were much larger on Sunday evenings than in the mornings, and often attracted a rowdier audience. These services were designed to appeal and attract rather than to support the community, and this meant that attendance declined if the excitement was lost.[59]

Catholics had little use for such a service, although sometimes Benediction was offered on Sunday evenings. Anglicans used Evensong, which previously had been held in the late afternoon. In the smaller Protestant churches it was more common for the morning congregation to also attend the evening service, and sometimes numbers were significantly larger in this service, which was often more informal. In 1920, in a suburban church such as Somervell Presbyterian Church in Remuera, 190 might attend in the morning and 110 in the evening.[60] In city churches, more accessible by public transport, such services were more important from the 1920s and even today, and perhaps less controlled by the clock.

From the 1950s, the expectations of evening services changed significantly. Evangelical churches made extensive use of the American evangelical Moody Bible Institute's 'Fact and Faith' films, beginning with *God of the Atom* in 1951.[61] Other forms of entertainment became common during services, especially solo and group singers. Youth services and other special services were often held in the evenings.

In the 1960s attendance at evening services began to decline.[62] The lighting of the television screen largely marked their demise. They remained significant to young people, however, and in the evangelical mega-churches, which were more entertainment-focused, they gained a new following.

In Chapter 1 we noted the significance of special services linked to the observance of the traditional Christian year. Every denomination had its own special rituals and services. Methodist adherence to weekly class meetings (small groups for spiritual accountability) declined in New Zealand, but Methodists continued to observe New Year's Eve as a watch night, at which they were supposed to renew their covenant with God.[63] Such distinctive services slowly declined as churches became more like each other in their patterns of life.[64]

Many Protestant churches also held a mid-week church meeting. For example, at the large Knox Church in Dunedin, the prayer meeting was a major occasion each week, attended by more devoted members. In some churches there were also regular lectures on Bible passages mid-week.

Within the Protestant community there was an increasing emphasis (going back to the Methodist revival of the eighteenth century) on reaching the uncommitted members of the local community. Churches were very aware that they had little contact with the majority of people. This was a broad Western problem, a product of the end of state requirement to attend church, and a more secular state. The New Zealand churches were acutely aware of the issue, and the evidence of censuses from 1874 to 1926 was a cause of great concern to many.

Some churches put massive energy into evangelism, and individual Christians were caught up in this. Colporteurs (paid agents) delivered Bibles under the aegis of the Bush Mission.⁶⁵ The Flying Angel Mission wooed seamen to services with food and Saturday football matches.⁶⁶ The various city missions focused on the working class.

It was the smaller evangelical churches, from Methodists down, which were most energetic in trying to reach the 'lost'. Unlike Anglicans and Catholics, the evangelical denominations wanted personal conversion, not just the christening of children.

Furthermore, the evangelical denominations incorporated evangelism into their church services. The Sunday evening service became the gospel meeting. This had similar goals and formats across a wide range of denominations. Hymns and message focused on the call for commitment to Christ, and a gospel appeal was always given, in which people were invited to become Christians. The service was stereotyped by notions that had developed first under the American evangelist Charles Finney in the 1840s, including the 'altar call' where converts were asked to come forward. The service focused on personal choice and decision, and the message emphasised that the cross of Christ could provide reconciliation with God and salvation. This service was often much more innovative than others because of its aim of reaching the lost. This was best seen in the gospel preaching of the Salvation Army.

ANOTHER ASPECT OF RELIGIOUS convictions and commitments was the attempt to convert people to Christianity or (more usually) to their form of it. Different churches approached this in very different ways.

Māori were by the twentieth century more inclusive in their approach to religion, for a marae-based religion meant that few Māori had much awareness of denominations. The marae or the hapū functioned among Māori much as the local church did among middle-class Europeans. Many Māori attended whatever service was taking place on the marae. As a result, Māori families may have been more mixed in their religious affiliations than Europeans.

In the early years Te Hāhi Mihinare (the Māori name for the Anglican Church) was the largest Māori church, but it made few demands on its adherents. Confirmation levels among Māori were very low, but a small group of European missionaries continued to seek the spiritual and physical wellbeing of Māori. Missionary work, like that of the early nineteenth century, was typically very paternalistic, and did not help Māori to identify with Christianity for themselves. From the 1880s to the 1910s, missionaries to the Māori received minimal support from the European churches, and many were forced to abandon their work. Only the Māori spiritual awakening under Rātana awoke Europeans to the spiritual needs of Māori society.

From the 1950s a movement of Māori into the towns created new challenges and opportunities. The United Maori Mission, along with the Methodist and Presbyterian churches, began opening hostels for Māori young people in the cities. The Anglican Church was very aware of the large numbers of Māori coming to Auckland and how few of them (an estimated 1000 out of 21,700 by 1963) were affiliated with the church.[67] Evangelicals tried hard to convert Māori and encourage their participation, but sometimes Māori gained the sense that they were second-class citizens. Māori did not put the same priority on church membership as Pākehā did (faced with competing loyalties to family). As late as the 1980s, congregations did not understand the different ways in which Māori community operated.[68] Not until the Pentecostal movement and the Destiny Church in the 2000s did Māori again become the centre of a major spiritual movement.

Churches irregularly felt the need of special services in order to stir up faith and life. Catholics drew on the Redemptorist Fathers to revive commitment to the church and its sacraments. In Whangarei every couple of years visiting priests would hold services throughout the parish, culminating with an attempt to get all to say their confessions and attend a great Eucharistic procession and service.[69] There were also significant Anglican missions, including those of the Rev. Charles Bodington and G. E. Mason, who were brought out from England by the Bishop of Auckland in 1885 with the aim of 'recalling to their allegiance to Him those who have become negligent of their duty as Christians'.[70] The High Church tone of this Anglican mission contrasted with the evangelical tone of the 'Keswick' evangelist George Grubb, who came in 1890 and 1892. He focused on the Nelson Diocese, which was becoming more markedly evangelical as other dioceses slowly became 'higher' in their ritual.[71] The Mission of Help in 1910 was an Anglican mission authorised by most of the bishops, which sought to improve lay Anglican levels of devotion. Some of the missioners actively promoted a greater range of High Church practices.[72]

Visiting speakers were also welcomed by a new type of Protestant, best called 'revivalists'. From the 1870s these preachers, who used 'altar calls' to stir people's emotions, became common. In their view there was a spiritual cycle which at its low point was reflected in declining faith and few conversions. At this point only a revival could help. Huge efforts by church members and dramatic messages from a visiting preacher might then renew the church, revive hope and lead to conversions.

Churches often combined for evangelistic efforts. Protestant evangelism at its best was non-denominational. In 1872 the Rev. Andrew Stobo of Invercargill, after a survey of the world which concluded that only one-third was even vaguely Christian, argued that evangelical Christians were a tiny proportion, and so:

> In the view of such a disproportion it was of the utmost importance that the forces should be disposed to the best advantage, and that could only be attained

by a systematic and cordial co-operation between the various evangelical denominations. He would desire to see a confederation of all the evangelical churches in the world for this object, and the co-operation so attained might ultimately end in incorporation. In foreign missions this was especially needed.[73]

Massive efforts went into cooperative church missions. Although critics labelled them as Bible bangers and profit-taking hucksters, these missions satisfied a very deep instinct to transform the country by public evangelism.[74]

Revivalism was often popular with Baptists and evangelical churches, although others were bothered by the exuberance and disorder inherent in it.[75] Revivalism was a communal experience, as Geoff Troughton showed in his study of the revival in Wanganui in 1875.[76] If the whole community was whipped up into emotional fervour and sensed a spiritual crisis, then the impact extended far beyond regular churchgoers. The preachers sometimes had a tarnished life history (and perhaps this kind of faith encouraged those with colourful backgrounds to become preachers), but they brought together a rich amalgam of Protestants in experiences that reshaped the forces in rough settler communities.[77]

In the countryside the term 'bush Baptist' was sometimes used to refer to the way in which fervent groups of lay people separated from the main churches and joined the Brethren or other smaller churches. A working-class version of revivalism was the secret of the success of the Salvation Army.[78] This pattern particularly attracted young people, who were more open to a wave of emotion, but it also revived flagging zeal in colonists who sensed that church life in the colony was tougher and less integral to the community.

Methodists quickly adopted this style of preaching, given their history. Thus, in 1865 Durham Street Wesleyan Chapel in Christchurch and Pitt Street Wesleyan Chapel in Auckland were enthralled by the great campaign of Bishop 'California' Taylor of Africa, a colourful American Methodist who made his name as a preacher in the Californian gold rushes.[79]

Many Methodist preachers aspired to be recognised as evangelists. It is interesting to look at how revivalistic evangelism flavoured Methodism by sampling what happened in the cavernous Durham Street chapel. Some of the preachers were local. Joseph Berry and Alfred Fitchett were local Wesleyan ministers whose preaching at Durham Street in June 1875 led 110 converts to be 'placed on trial for membership' (or as we might say, sent to training classes before becoming members). Two other local ministers, William Gillam and William Baumber, held revival services in the same place in 1881, resulting in 200 conversions. Mrs Joan Scott held special meetings in Durham Street in 1885, while the preaching of Matthew Burnett, the gospel temperance advocate, in 1886 produced 40 penitents. In the same year the Wesleyan Connexion commissioned Joseph Smalley to hold evangelistic meetings throughout the country, and his meetings filled every seat at Durham Street.

There were united evangelistic meetings in August 1887; a Mr Coad held a 10-day mission at Durham Street in December 1889 where 80 sought fuller blessing, and many Sunday school children professed Christian conversion. In July 1891 Mark Guy Pearse, an English non-denominational evangelist, spoke at the church in the course of his New Zealand tour. In 1895 the Rev. Thomas Cook arrived from England, and in February 1895 his meetings at Durham Street produced 300 converts. In March 1897 the Rev. David O'Donnell preached at Durham Street and there were 70 converts and 50 claimants to full salvation, the Methodist doctrine of Christian perfection. After a long gap, when the cycle seemed to have been broken, Val Trigge, the Australian Methodist evangelist, conducted a mission in 1913 and again in 1918. So for 50 years the church in effect lurched from revival to revival with many a struggle in between.

The meetings were very different from the sedate world of respectable Wesleyan services, for they were characterised by simple emotional preaching, shouts of hallelujah and loud amens, then the shuffling of penitents to the front of the church in the altar call. Notably, in some of these crusades there are no precise numbers, and probably there was no altar call.[80] Some ministers adopted this style of preaching for themselves, although a more formal preaching style was more characteristic of large Methodist churches. Methodism, however, felt the need regularly to return to its roots, prompted usually by lay voices concerned that the denomination was drifting.

In later years the revival preaching focused on the conversion of children in the Sunday school. In August 1915 Decision Day was introduced, when Sunday school students were invited to join the church; 24 did so at Durham Street, then took the sacrament that evening. There was a widespread view that such preaching was tolerable for children but not adults.

In the twentieth century, mass revival meetings were conducted across New Zealand by the Americans Dr Reuben Torrey and Charles Alexander in 1903, and Dr Chapman and Charles Alexander in 1912; by Billy Graham in 1959 and 1969, and by Leighton Ford and Luis Palau in 1987.[81] In 1959, as a result of the Billy Graham's Crusade in Lancaster Park, there were 60 'decisions for Christ' from people associated with the Durham Street church, along with the thousands across New Zealand. By then the impulse for Methodist revivalism was in decline and the denomination strongly opposed the National Council of Churches sponsoring another visit by Billy Graham.

In order to get an audience, the smaller denominations threw significant energy into publicity. Newspaper advertising often contained the name of the preacher and, for the Protestant churches, often the subject of the sermon. (When the Baptist Church in Kaiapoi announced in a pamphlet that the Sunday night topic that week was going to be 'the three men in Kaiapoi who will be in hell' a large congregation came, eager to hear if the Methodist, Presbyterian and Anglican ministers — or some other erring citizens — were going to be named.)[82] In the 1950s until the 1970s, the new denominations began pouring a significant proportion of their budgets into newspaper advertising, although sometimes the size of the advertisement was in inverse proportion to the loyal congregation.

The arrival of the Salvation Army had a large stimulus on the evangelistic efforts of others. Some more activist Wesleyan evangelists moved to the Salvation Army.[83] City mission services also worked very hard to recreate the equivalent of the British Pleasant Sunday Afternoons, which sought to combine social and religious activities. The efforts of the churches were huge, but in the long run much of this was wasted. An unusually honest Methodist minister explained frankly that while it was perfectly easy for a visiting evangelist to attract outsiders, if you were not Gypsy Smith you had enough problems in retaining the adherence of the partially converted congregation. He cited a local minister who had told him when he first arrived from Britain that 'The work of the Church here is not extensive, but intensive.'[84] Smart words!

The colourful or ingenious or exotic often attracted audiences in New Zealand, but this does not mean that these methods produced converts. Visiting speakers from other parts of the colony or abroad were an attraction. It is sufficient to observe that in the life of the local church the outside evangelistic speaker produced an upsurge of activity and a significant increase in numbers.

I**N THE NINETEENTH AND** early twentieth centuries there was far more variety in the pattern of church services than is now the case. Each little community wanted church services and provided either a small church or another place — a large drawing room, a woolshed, a hall — for services when they could be provided. These were often arranged by the community, and various denominations provided preachers for them. So one district would have monthly services, others fortnightly, and, following the rather limited roads in the colony, preachers would hold services right through the day from Sunday morning to evening, and sometimes on another day of the week.

So 'church' was one part of the fabric of the settler community, and providing it, at some time or other, was an obligation for the settlers. Denominations were urged by their members to send ministers or lay preachers, and the next step might be the building of a church for them. The initiative largely lay with members of the local community. Only rarely did denominations hold services if there was no local sponsor. Denomination was not the source of community; community already existed.

Perhaps most of these services were conducted by lay preachers or local preachers of one form or another — in the case of Anglicans, lay readers were licensed by the bishop, and provided for many of the services in country districts. Methodist lay preachers were listed on circuit-preaching plans and some of them conducted services in different communities every week. Presbyterians pioneered a system of home missionaries, who were employed by the denomination on an annual contract to visit settlers in the 'backblocks' and hold services. These preachers were not ordained. A superintendent ensured that they were sent to any places where there was potential for a church to grow.[85] Home missionaries took on a tough role. A key qualification was willingness, since a minimal payment might be all they would receive. Transport was the major need. The local preachers rode horses or cycled to small congregations in the backblocks or the poorer suburbs.[86] Services consisted of hymns, prayers and sermons, and the lay preacher took it all, choosing the hymns and acting as precentor (setting the note for the unaccompanied singing) or playing the harmonium as well as preaching.

The quality of the lay preaching left much to be desired, but beggars could not be choosers. One Methodist minister warned lay people about sending people to sleep by overlong sermons on subjects about which they knew nothing.[87] Anglican lay preachers were supposed to read homilies published by the church. Sometimes the scheduled preacher did not arrive. Haddon Dixon from Bunnythorpe in the Manawatū recalled what took place there:

> when it got past 11 and no preacher had turned up, the two local preachers in the congregation, Dad and 'Jimmy' Fowler sprang into action. They took it in turns. One Sunday, Dad would hurriedly pick some hymns and then get the service under way. In the meantime, Jimmy would duck into the vestry and tried to get a few thoughts together for a sermon. Next time it happened they would reverse the roles . . . I sometimes wonder whether their experience was one of the reasons why Irwin Fowler and I became ordained ministers.[88]

The churches may well have hoped for high levels of lay activism in New Zealand and it was necessary if the church was to grow, but in general they were disappointed. The Anglican Church in particular struggled to convert traditionally passive Anglicans into participants, even though the 1857 constitution of the church created a house of laity with similar powers to the houses of clergy and bishops. In 1880 there was an attempt by the Christchurch Diocese to establish a 'Church Work Society' to encourage lay interest in the needs of the diocese. Archdeacon Harper (son of the bishop) commented that the problem was 'a want of zeal. The cure for this was to stimulate the supineness of individuals into active life, and then maintain the newly roused activity.'[89] The Church Work Society thought that work among the labouring classes, prisoners and seamen might best be done by laymen. Bishop Churchill Julius, the second Anglican Bishop of Christchurch, grimly observed at his welcome in Timaru in 1890 that more than half of the laity did not join in the responses in the liturgy. He insisted that clergy should be accepted as men among men, implying that the church usually appealed only to women.[90]

If this sounded a particular Anglican problem, there were also complaints about this from Methodists, where it might seem more exceptional. For example, this comment came from a leader of the Wesleyan church in Gore in 1890: 'A minister was not a machine to convert souls by magic. He required assistance from his congregation, all of whom should be energetic and work. Don't be lazy said the speaker.'[91] At the same gathering, the Rev. William Baumber commented that:

> There were the grumblers: he compared these to the rolling thunder among surrounding hills — it was always growling and rumbling but never locating itself with a loud report directly overhead. Far more harm was done in that way than by direct attacks. There were also the languid people who would not do anything; also there were the people who dashed energetically into a matter and then let it drop. Others again were sick in the pocket and with these the three-penny piece was the sacred coin it was dedicated to the church.[92]

The Māori churches were from the late nineteenth century either part of the Māori mission of the churches or sometimes branches of European parishes. These small churches attracted devoted loyalty, especially from the females in the Māori communities. One Māori woman recalled creeping past the Catholic church where her uncle was in attendance to make it to St Matthew, Oruanui (near Taupō), loving the Sunday school and the little lesson books that they received. The vicar of Taupō ceased to hold services in the church in the late 1980s, but as the Rev. (later Bishop) George Connor restored the spiritual values of the community in the 1990s and the Māori community rejuvenated, they re-embraced the tiny church and restored it with love.[93]

Gradually in the 1960s and 1970s, as Māori became a significant part of urban congregations, Europeans became more used to singing Māori hymns, although sometimes they were reluctant to use the Māori language. The New Zealand Prayerbook, produced by the Anglican Church in 1989, made the use of Māori a regular part of the liturgy, and the Māori Lord's Prayer, hymns and greetings have since then often been used in worship.

'Family service' is a term that seems to have been used at first as a description of an occasional non-denominational service for Sunday school children, which was held before the main morning service in many Protestant churches. It was seen as a way to lift attendance at a time when the evening gospel service was in decline; letters were sent to Sunday school parents to get them to attend.[94] Many Anglican churches found this a more accessible form of service for people who had little familiarity with the church.[95]

As early as 1933 a 'United Family Service' was held in Hastings at the conclusion of a Protestant churches crusade.[96] Experiments with a family service, usually including some singing or performances by Sunday school children, became more common in the 1950s as congregations became conscious of their tenuous relationships with people who had occasionally attended regular services. The Methodist tradition of the Youth Sunday also sometimes involved a family service as well as 'declaration day' for the children and Bible class members (a service often avoided by other church members).[97]

There were discussions about ways to minister to the family at the 1937 Oxford Conference on Life and Work, a very important English conference that brought together representatives of churches throughout the world.[98] Mothers' Day began to be observed by New Zealand churches in the 1940s, and Avondale Methodist Church held a family service in 1945 when girls from the church or its Sunday school brought their mothers, who were welcomed with bunches of flowers.[99]

By the late 1940s a number of Anglican churches began holding regular Family Service in place of Matins either four times a year or once a month (usually the first Sunday of the month).[100] Low Church Anglicans thought that children should not attend Communion services; the Rev. Terrence Loten of Takapau in Central Hawke's Bay complained vigorously of 'the simplified non-liturgical, home-made family services which are prevalent' and insisted that the Communion service could convey far more to children through its symbolism. (He did not advocate children taking Communion.)[101] A lively discussion indicated clerical support for children attending Communion, for 'we relegate the youngsters to drab, study Sunday schools and feed them on dry bread'.

On the whole laity preferred non-liturgical family services.[102] These were quite different from regular services, although people were expected to kneel for prayers, and mothers had to be encouraged to bring young children and sit towards the back of the church.[103] One unsympathetic observer called them 'rather sad affairs, as many of our children seem to be orphans and most of the rest fatherless', but at their best they drew a large attendance of parents.[104]

Children's Eucharists were advocated by Anglican High Church leaders as early as 1910.[105] A campaign developed in the 1950s for the family service to include Holy Communion, and in 1953 a children's Eucharist was held at St Paul's Church Symonds Street on a Saturday morning which assembled people from several more High Church parishes of Auckland.[106] John Pittman, vicar of Holy Trinity Ōtāhuhu, went further and insisted that parish Communion at 9.30 should be the main service of the day.[107] His trenchant criticisms of Sunday schools as Nonconformist institutions that did not nurture Catholic Christianity speak volumes about a changing, spiky tone in Auckland Anglicanism in the 1950s under the very formal and High Church Bishop John Simkin. (It was also a rather disdainful way for an Anglican to speak of other Protestants when there was no established church and therefore could be no Nonconformists.)

A 9.30 a.m. Family Eucharist was advocated by Bishop Alwyn Warren of Christchurch in his 1954 Synod address (made more pertinent, as he noted, by the Mazengarb Report on Moral Delinquency, which was provoked by teenage misdemeanours in Lower Hutt) as an attempt by the Anglican Church to give more recognition to children.[108] Other churches also experimented with family services, as Sunday school declined in the 1960s. These services would begin with a section for all (usually including a children's talk), then the children went to their Sunday school classes, returning when the service was complete.

In the days when roughly 30 per cent of the community went to church, many who attended were there in body but not in the heart. One correspondent to an Auckland paper in 1887 accused the young of 'flirting and giggling' in church. Some advocated that ministers should caution the miscreants from the pulpit, but this was a risky procedure, for an annoyed group of young people was not likely to return.[109] It was better to make services more interesting, and indeed, although people of the day were cautious about saying this, more entertaining. The great Baptist preacher Frank Boreham, for example, thoughtfully sought to ensure that the tone of services was positive, and not to curb natural exuberance.[110]

Within the church world in the twentieth century, various positive methods of increasing and retaining membership were tried. A key approach was to change the culture of church life. An early advocate of this was the notorious Howard Elliott, a Baptist minister and founder of the Protestant Political Association in World War I, who argued for advertising, signs, pamphlets, and an Americanised approach to publicity.[111]

A hot debate began to emerge once the first religious films were produced in the 1910s. Some argued that the church needed to recognise the secular queue for the movies, even proposing the replacement of sermons with movies.[112] Colin Scrimgeour, the young man brought to the Auckland Methodist Social Service Mission during the Depression (where he became famous for his strong support of the unemployed), used movies, including *King of Kings*, to attract his huge congregation. He made a film called *On the Friendly Road*, and could attract 4000 people to services with an overflow almost as large, but first the church and then the city council banned these movies, and as a result attendance at his theatre services shrank from 1500 to 100.[113]

Anglicans were hard-pressed to incorporate entertainment in their services. Jasper Calder, the roguish city missioner in the interwar years, was not beyond deriding 'Anglican stodginess' and called for a little more warmth in services.[114] Anglicans on the whole failed to find ways to do this.

Change was forced upon the churches very rapidly in the 1960s. One striking example of this is patterns of dress for worship. Many Protestant clergy began to don a white cassock-alb — a kind of poncho also popular among Catholic and Anglican clergy — along with a preaching stole or scarf that could reflect the church season. Other clergy in subsequent years preferred civilian dress, with the suit, and in recent years casual dress, becoming common.[115] In Protestant worship the lack of prescribed liturgical robes facilitated this movement. It also happened among laity in all congregations. In the 1940s Anglican women were told that they were not expected to wear hats to worship. Then ties ceased to be worn. In effect the church ceased to be a public space but rather more private and intimate, where smart casual clothing was acceptable. At the same time, the leaders of worship and preachers in more evangelical denominations also began to abandon formal dress codes. So the style of church life altered, affecting the style of preaching, the liturgy, the prayers and the way people related. Several factors shaped this.

THE DRAMATIC DECISIONS OF the Second Vatican Council of the Catholic Church in the 1960s radically altered the experience of worship for Catholics. A book about this change in New Zealand is entitled *It Changed Overnight!*[116] Actually this is not quite true.

In June 1967 Catholic churches were introduced to congregational singing and lay reading of the epistle of the day.[117] Then in 1970 generations of history were abandoned as the English Mass was introduced. Some felt that a dull prosaic plainness had replaced the rich elaboration of the old Mass. A priest had to walk up and down the aisles of Nelson's Catholic church encouraging the congregation to sing out loud.[118] In the long term there are still examples of the Latin Mass, and they appear to be popular with new ordinands, while the lack of New Zealand-born priests means that Indian, Vietnamese and Filipino priests have brought their more traditional forms of Catholicism to New Zealand. But Catholic congregations appear to have embraced the new service, notwithstanding the complaints heard when the text was revised.

In 1966 the Anglican Church introduced its own New Zealand Liturgy, which was issued again in revised form in 1970. The early response to this service was not enthusiastic. At All Saints, Wanganui East, it was introduced on 20 November 1966, and 'not everyone appreciated the new form of service'. A key feature of the service was a greater level of congregational responses, and allowing for laity to be the readers for the epistle and the gospel. Also, with the permission of the bishop, laity could be licensed to dispense the chalice, and at All Saints three lay readers were soon given permission.[119] In Warkworth, a cautious vestry finally conceded in 1976, after much pressure, that the new liturgy could be used but only on alternate Sundays.[120]

To this day, despite some convergences, there are perceived differences in the tone of prayer and sometimes in the language used in the different churches. Anglican prayer is more formal. The composition of the prayer of the day (still called the collect) still seems to be regarded as a skill to be acquired in Anglican circles. In contrast, rambling Pentecostal prayers commonly speak to 'Father', 'Jesus' and 'Spirit' alternately. Somewhere between the two are those in most churches for whom intimacy and informality in prayer have become acceptable, and there have undoubtedly been changes in the tone of praying in recent years.

Traditionally, each community had its own codes, and these made outsiders feel unsure of themselves during the service. Catholic genuflecting was intimidating to others.[121] Anglican services seemed to have a lot of standing, sitting and kneeling; Pentecostals waved their arms in the air. Each act made outsiders unsure of the accepted code of conduct. But as the sense of denominational loyalty dropped drastically from the 1970s, there was a growing resistance to different denominational modes of worship. Anglican and Catholic priests were especially aware of those who struggled with their form of worship. There was increasingly a standard Protestant form of worship, and denominations had to exert themselves to defend their own traditions.

Some denominational traditions were revived when the Pasifika community arrived in New Zealand from the 1950s. In the Congregational churches, which were the first to experience the wave of new arrivals, Samoans, Cook Islanders and Niueans crowded in, and eventually Samoan and Rarotongan services were added. A Congregationalist historian was struck by how old-fashioned their expectations were: 'The men in white shirts and dark suits, the ladies wearing long dresses, high-piled hair and all with hats, vigorously singing hymns to Sankey and Moody refrains [nineteenth-century revivalists with their own hymn style], seemed very much at home in the

Victorian church . . . While the European services were outwardly almost identical, the Island-language services provided an inward satisfaction unobtainable elsewhere.'[122]

Pasifika people brought their own rich traditions of White Sunday, of lavish dress, of public collections, of tight communities. Aspects of this have been very significant, especially for Methodists and some Presbyterian churches, where Pasifika people are a majority or a significant minority.

From the 1960s the emphasis in services fell on congregational participation. Both the renewal in liturgy provoked by the Second Vatican Council of the Catholic Church and the charismatic movement within Protestantism, which expected that everyone would be filled with the Spirit, encouraged this. Now it seemed as though church should give everyone the opportunity to speak. The language of worship suggested that it was supposed to provide therapy to those who attended. A number of churches experimented with reorienting the church to face a side wall or long wall so that the 'stage' could accommodate a huge cast of participants in worship, a large music team, and a 'flatter' sense, where the pastor was not elevated. This change was made in many churches of all denominations; Pukekohe Catholic Church and the Glen Eden Baptist Church, for example, took this step.[123]

Styles of worship became a matter of great tension in Baptist churches in the 1980s,

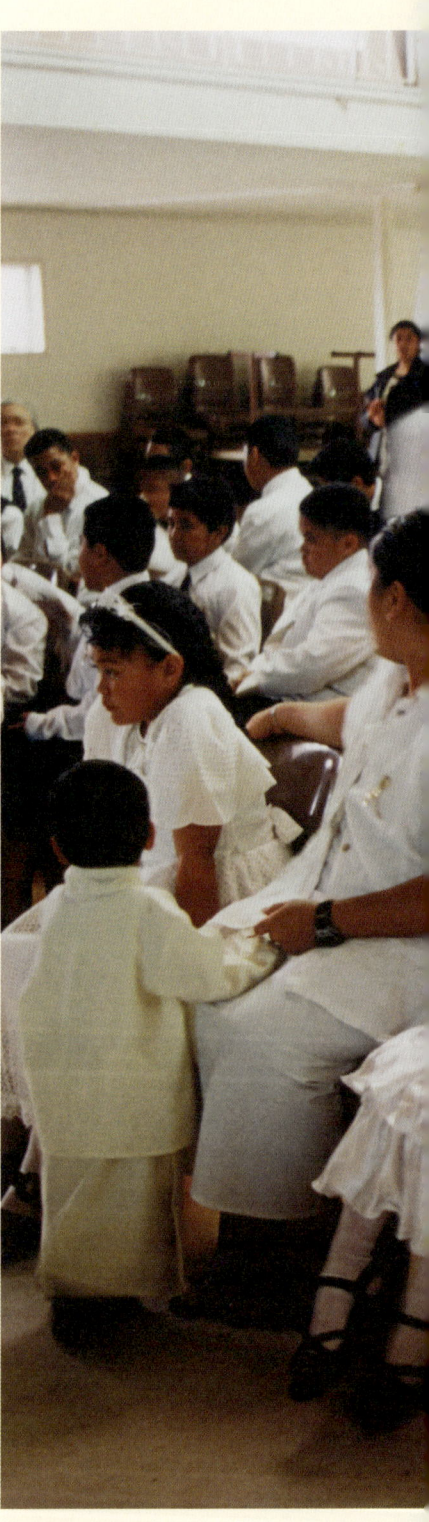

Glenn Jowitt's photograph of White Sunday celebrations at the Congregational Christian Church of Samoa, Grey Lynn, Auckland. MUSEUM OF NEW ZEALAND TE PAPA TONGAREWA. REF: O.041142

emulating the American pattern of 'culture wars'. So Glen Eden Baptist Church was tugged and pulled by various forces, and its pastors struggled to manage this 'cauldron of diversity'. As the local mayor commented to Ian Brown when he was appointed pastor of Glen Eden in 1979, it was easier to be appointed mayor than to be called as a pastor. Worship styles generally needed to be varied to accommodate these strains, with new services, traditional services, healing services, services with and without drums, with drums muffled or at full force.[124]

This pattern did not only apply to Baptists, but also to many evangelical churches. At first there were high levels of informality, and in some respects the flavour was a little like a continuous revival. But no church could maintain this without becoming exhausted. Gradually a new pattern developed where the worship was led by a music team (sometimes with several teams in the one church). Baptist churches often appointed a music director, who coordinated a group of teams with a wide variety of instruments and skills. It was often recognised that there needed to be a more conventional service incorporating at least some hymns and fewer drums, especially for older members. This usually took place at 9 a.m., followed by the more 'full-on' service at 11 a.m., although this balance varied significantly.[125]

The modern mega-church service by Pentecostal and other denominations is not a great deal different from the revival services of the past, except in the matter of scale. However, there is now far more emphasis on visual appearance rather than on sound. In the modern mega-church a high level of energy goes into the choreography of the church services; these are highly professional and polished performances. Loud amplification prevents any risk of congregational interruptions.

At Spreydon Baptist Church, which sought to balance serious Bible exposition with meaningful contemporary worship, the church felt the pressure of trite and repetitive worship as one of its most constant battles and experimented with every style that could be found throughout the world.[126] One very striking aspect is the free-flow keyboard playing accompanying the speaker, and the constant changing images. But in the careful build-up of emotional intensity in the music, the very long sermon, the absence of a Bible reading and the drawn-out altar calls, in which people come to the front to make a commitment to Christ, there is very little that is new.

Patterns have changed greatly in the past 150 years. Fundamentally, this reflects the movement of the church service from the inherited part of ethnic culture — be it Māori, English, Scottish or Pasifika — to a style that blends aspects of various traditions, and is shaped above all by the contemporary television show. Styles of church always reflect the ways in which public events are held in the wider society, as the rapid changes in the past few years strikingly illustrate.

The Last Mass conducted by a Marist at Tua Marina, in the Marlborough Sounds, the birthplace of the notable Catholic poet Eileen Duggan. The priest is Fr Dalton Campbell SM. The January 1957 photograph by B. G. Donachie of Blenheim shows the robes and atmosphere of the pre-Vatican church. MARIST ARCHIVES

The Music and Words of Faith

Previous The Salvation Army Band at the Palmerston North Citadel in the 1940s. The Salvation Army's Blood and Fire flag hangs at the back and the penitents' pew is below the pulpit. IAN MATHESON CITY ARCHIVES

AS A BOY I used to be fascinated by the way, when people from an Exclusive Brethren background turned up in our semi-exclusive assembly, they cleared their throats before speaking. It was a particular artificial cough, an announcement to others that they were about to speak (since, in theory, no one speaker is arranged in advance in a Brethren assembly). The only other place I have heard this throat-clearing method is on the marae, with its similarly democratic system of participation.

The use of the voice both for singing and speaking (and even the distinction between them) is profoundly shaped by culture. Methods and mannerisms of public speaking and singing reflect acquired styles and forms. By the time it reached New Zealand, Christianity had very well-developed language of faith expressed in its creeds and confessions, and because of the creedal and scriptural character of the faith the right tone was a matter of significance. The musical forms of harmony, for example, had a very long ecclesiastical tradition, and religious music was still a key form of Western music in the nineteenth century.

As far as speaking was concerned, there was a preaching voice and a liturgical voice — the two more sharply distinguished in the Catholic Church, where the liturgy was in Latin. The low voice of the liturgist or precentor was very different from the tone and volume required to carry the sermon out into the congregation in those days before electronic amplification. There is a rich literature on this subject, and in recent years historians like Mark Noll have given much attention to these issues.[1] The New Zealand story has a few interesting variations.

Biblical texts lay at the heart of the Protestant mission. This began with the compelling power of the stories of the Old and New Testaments translated, however roughly, by the missionaries. Māori catechists then took those words and put them into vivid renditions.

From the mid-1820s the Rev. William Williams, brother of Henry and himself also a CMS missionary with a Cambridge degree, led a translation team, which met quarterly in Paihia after the CMS committee meeting. Individuals each prepared a text, which others then scrutinised and sought to correct. It is not clear when Māori began to participate in the team. The Rev. William Yate, a missionary who arrived in 1828, was entrusted with taking the first texts to New South Wales to see them through the press in 1830, and the little booklets thus produced were used in the schools, but not distributed.[2]

The view that the scripture had a magical power was an attraction for Māori in the mid-1830s. While reflecting the CMS view of the authority of scripture, it was also a consequence of the experiences of sickness in a Māori community exposed to the European influenza virus. Linking the European immunity from illness to the magic of their book was part of the Māori attempt to understand the inner world of the missionary. Māori were accustomed to prophetic words, and the scripture seemed similar, although this was not how the missionaries explained it. Thus Māori culture became, at least briefly, intensely literal in its use of the Bible. This absorption later showed itself in the way Wiremu Tāmihana Te Waharoa quoted Old Testament scripture to justify the anointing of a Māori king, and in other Māori movements.

Expressing Christian ideas in Māori phrases raised complex issues because the thoughts were European and translation did not necessarily place them into te ao Māori (the Māori world). As early as 1814 phrase books were attempting to express ideas about God in the Māori language, in which the word Atua is used for God.

Jehovah is the name of the great Atua	Iehovah! ta ingoa no ta Atua Nue
God is the name of the great Atua	God! ta ingoa no ta Atua Nue
Lord is the name of the great Atua	Lord! ta ingoa no ta Atua Nue
Jesus Christ is the name of the Son of the great Atua	Iesus Christ! ta ingoa no ta tamoneke no ta Atua Nue
God loved the world, He gave His Son for me	Karoha ta tungata katoa, God, eta tungata to nomi ena ta tamoneke ke ou
Great is the love of Jesus Christ for all men	Kanue ta aroha na Iesus Christ, ka nue ta aroha ke tatungata kotoa
Who is the Son of God?	Owhi ta tamoneke no God?
Jesus Christ is the Son of God	Iesus Christ ta tamoneke no God
God hears the conversation of us men	Karungho God, karungho ta na koraro tatoo
Good is the word of God	Kapi ta koraro no God
God is love, He is not soon angry	Karoha mi God, kioure addide viva
Jesus Christ is love, He came to save the souls of us men	Karoha mi Iesus Christ, e ta iremi ra ke aoura na whidooano tattoo.[3]

The decision on what Māori word should be used for the name of God was not straightforward, since 'Atua' and 'God' were uncomfortable equivalents.[4] Eventually, however, it was decided to use 'Atua' as scriptural translations proceeded apace in the 1820s, and the church liturgy, too, was translated and a prayer book produced.

A hymn book may also have been issued in 1830 but no copy has ever been seen, so *Ko te Pukapuka Inoinga, me nga karakia hakarameta, me era ritenga hoki o te Hahi o Ingarani*, produced in 1833, is the first extant of Māori liturgical text. It contains morning and evening prayer, prayers not for the royal family but for the Māori chiefs, a form of communion and a form of baptism, and 27 hymns.[5] Even so, one may see that the language is still consciously translated or even transliterated. The focus lay on good translations of scripture, with the New Testament complete in 1837. There was a very long delay until the Old Testament was issued in 1868. That text became a sacred book in a way that the Authorised Version or King James Version of 1611 was viewed in the English world. Later, much-needed revisions of the translation were resisted by Māori.[6]

Māori culture was inevitably oral in character, and language, tone and style are marks of status and role, far more so than in European society. Observing speeches at pōwhiri, the missionaries were very struck by the mastery of tone that chiefs could achieve:

> Titore then mounted a little eminence upon the beach, and commenced his brother's welcome, with a song peculiarly melancholy, but at the same time singularly attractive; during the time of his singing, he walked with a slow and solemn pace along the brow of the little hill; when, suddenly coming to a conclusion, he addressed the strangers, and in a very pleasant way continued to speak to them for more than an hour. His action was perfectly natural, and consequently very graceful: his voice was loud, but beautifully modulated; and his language copious and flowery: I was much interested in the whole, which certainly was the most romantic scene which I ever witnessed.[7]

Traditional Māori music was chanted, and the University of Canterbury scholar Margaret Orbell has greatly enriched our understanding by showing how music and words were combined. Tunes did not use the Western scale or harmonies, and often seemed like dirges to missionary observers.[8]

During the 1830s, Māori began to sing hymns in their own way. Initially Māori listened carefully to missionaries singing,[9] and the missionaries listened to Māori singing and dancing. Māori then heard visiting Tahitian sailors singing Christian hymns.[10] Wesleyan and CMS accounts show Māori reciting and singing with the missionaries by 1823,[11] and some were fond of hymns by 1827.[12] There was still an element of imitation in this:

> Last night, after our Evening Service, I overheard my Boys singing a Hymn in their own house; after which, one of them read a portion of St. Matthew, which we have translated; and concluded with the Lord's Prayer. The Boy, who conducted this Service, wrote to me the following question, upon his slate —

'How is it, that we continue to pray according to your instructions, and yet our hearts are not changed?'[13]

In 1833, when Henry Williams visited a potential site for a mission station in Thames, his party were astonished to find that Ngāti Maru not only knew the liturgical responses but also sang the hymns with them.[14] It seems likely that people taken captive in the Bay of Islands prior to this had taught the tunes to the iwi. This music was not always tuneful, according to Williams: 'Our singing a strange mixture, could scarcely preserve anything like a time from such a confusion of notes, as we had almost every one the human voice was capable of.'[15] By the 1830s there are hints that the style of singing by the mission converts was becoming more typical of Māori traditional forms, with a hint of chanting in it.[16] Māori singing of hymns was very slow, with a drawn-out tempo at the end. Māori were so attached to hymn singing that one group in Thames persisted while a group of four Europeans sang 'Old King Cole'.[17] Family prayers became common among the converts, and included hymns.[18]

The repertoire of hymns gradually grew. Natural words and colloquial expressions were the essence of a successful hymn, and the CMS was alleged to have borrowed words from a haka calling for utu, or revenge.[19] The missionaries translated their favourite hymns, and 'Ka mahue Ihipa/ Te kainga o te he', a translation of Thomas Kelly's 'From Egypt lately come', with aspirations of the pilgrimage to Canaan, was popular in 1833 (and is suggestive of how Māori came to view themselves as Israel). The sixth hymn in the Māori hymnal, another favourite, was 'Homai e Ihu he ngakau, kia rongo atu ai'. This appears to be Johann Lavater's 'Oh Jesus Christ grow thou in me'.[20] Thirty-five hymns were found in the 1837 service book, and 42 in the smaller edition in 1839. The Wesleyan service book of 1839 contained 30 hymns.

The first separate hymn book appeared in 1844, and William Colenso, the missionary printer who was later transferred to Hawke's Bay, produced a set of hymns for his congregation in 1847. An enlarged hymn book of 52 hymns was produced in 1850, with later editions in 1860 through to 1883. Various editions of this continued to be produced in later years. By 1861 the Wesleyan hymn book had 107 hymns.[21] The availability of a Māori-language hymnal was helpful for missionaries, but Māori did not require it for they committed the hymns to memory; practising the words became an important part of Māori culture, a favourite occupation on the strict Sabbath.[22] A popular early hymn was 'Matiu's Hymn', a translation of 'O God of Heaven whose power benign' by Henry Williams's son Edward. In 1878 Māori complained of their small repertoire of hymns, and Edward Williams was commissioned to produce a larger collection.[23]

Catholic liturgy was thought by Anglicans to mimic Māori tradition, as William

Williams remarked when Catholics sat through his service and then he through theirs: 'A very small book was then produced, from which was said and sung a most miserable ditty, quite after the manner of the old New Zealand songs.'[24]

Few if any of the most popular Māori hymns come from this first generation. 'Tama Ngakau Marie' ('Son of a peaceful heart') has no known translator, but it is a translation of George Rundle Prynne's children's hymn 'Jesus meek and gentle', written in 1856, which appeared in *Hymns Ancient and Modern* in 1861. It made its name through use by the Māori Battalion in World War II and appeared for the first time for general use in *With One Voice*, the ecumenical hymn book issued in 1982.[25]

While popular education in England largely came through Sunday school or the 'dame schools' run by poor women, and so the language of the kind of people who predominated among the settlers was peppered with scriptural phrases, their relationship to their sacred book was not what the missionaries had led Māori to anticipate. The age of cheap printing meant that most settlers had a Bible stowed away in their luggage, but settler culture in the 1850s and 1860s was not particularly interested in the Bible and its themes. Methodism and the Sunday school movement helped to inspire trade unions and cooperative movements in England, and many New Zealand settlers came from such backgrounds. Yet there are few reports of scriptural debates among lay settlers in the colony. Only in Otago was the external culture soaked in biblical language. Instead there was a lot of vocal criticism of 'Bible bangers', and biblical arguments were viewed with some suspicion in wider society.

Huge family Bibles were not found in the trunks of many settlers because that format of Bible was not published at the time, but by the late 1890s these were popular purchases judging by the numbers to be found in second-hand bookshops or prized as family heirlooms.

IT IS HARD TO conceive today of a church service without music, and for music one may usually read 'hymns', although that depends on the church. Many modern churches probably have only the occasional hymn in their repertoire, as contemporary Christian songs have become their standard choice. The debate between hymns and modern songs is a mild one compared to the huge debate that took place in the nineteenth-century Protestant world over the singing of hymns.

A bold essay in a nineteenth-century New Zealand Christian magazine urged people to sing Christian hymns 'to relieve the weariness of a long attention; to make the mind more cheerful and composed; and to endear the offices of religion'.[26] Yet for many people of the time, hymns were a poor substitute for the biblical remedy to a sad heart, the Book of Psalms. Scriptural words were held to be the appropriate words to sing (just as in the Catholic musical repertoire it was the musical settings of the Mass that changed, not the texts). By the time the first settlers arrived in New Zealand, modern hymns were gaining popularity with many people. They were sung in Methodist, Congregational and Baptist churches, but not in most Anglican services. They were a matter of great debate in the various types of Presbyterian church, and a battle was fought out by New Zealand Scots, as in other Presbyterian countries, over the singing of hymns.

This was not a specifically Scottish controversy, since the debate about using non-scriptural words in the worship of God raised issues for a wide variety of reformed Protestants. Scots had a strong singing culture, and they had a psalter, which used a metrical system — very different from the Anglican chants of the psalms. Various revisions, especially the new version issued in 1696 by Nahum Tate and Nicholas Brady, improved the literary quality of the translation of the psalms, but change came slowly in the face of congregational conservatism.[27] Hymns distressed many Presbyterians, including one elder who complained that God could not be properly praised with words that 'may seem pure scripture truth, yet may be displeasing to him'.[28]

Presbyterians in the northern part of New Zealand were the first to adopt the singing of hymns, and as a result the Presbyterians of the south refused to form a united church with them. The Otago Presbyterians were linked to the Free Church in Scotland, and as opinions in that church shifted in favour of a hymn book, Dunedin Presbyterians became more open to change, while rural people in Otago were resistant. Knox Church in Dunedin introduced *Psalms and Hymns for Divine Worship* in 1873.[29] The English Presbyterian hymnal was sent down to presbyteries for consideration, although others waited for a Scottish book.[30] Psalms remained a distinctive feature of Presbyterian worship for the next hundred years.

In the Anglican service no provision was made for hymns and so they were sung before and after the liturgy was read. Some clergy disapproved of hymns. One Anglican confessed to 'a secret pleasure in hearing a hymn break down. It is bad at the best; trashy verse, and lumbering music an intrusion, moreover, upon the service, more especially if suffered to usurp the place of the anthem.'[31] The chanting of psalms was prescribed in the liturgy, and so in the early years at St Michael's and St John's in Christchurch psalms were chanted successfully, while congregational hymn singing struggled.[32]

Other Protestants had gradually added hymns to their metrical psalter, and Isaac Watts's hymns written in the eighteenth century were much loved. These hymns framed devotional life in the terms of evangelical experience of the grace of God. They furnished memorable words and phrases for personal religious experience.

They were influenced to some extent by the tradition of sober and plain Dissenting language, and in many ways reinforced biblical idioms. The words of 'When I survey the wondrous cross', 'Joy to the world' and 'Jesus shall reign where'er the sun' remain in use by churches where many other hymns have been forgotten.[33]

Hymn singing had developed massively in England and the English-speaking countries in the late eighteenth and early nineteenth centuries as a result of the Wesleyan Methodist movement. Most of our familiar repertoire of 'old hymns' comes from this era. A New Zealand newspaper of 1856 printed a chapter from Latrobe's *Music of the Church*, which was an influential defence of hymn singing.[34] New Zealand settlers did sing, and hymn singing was certainly part of that culture. It was probably the most widespread form of devotional practice.[35] Communities obviously enjoyed singing, sang in their own homes, purchased musical instruments, and enjoyed it when hymns were sung at church.

A few hymns were written by local poets, including an Easter hymn written and printed by one of New Zealand's earliest poets, Robert Croudace Joplin of Auckland, at Easter 1847.[36] James George Deck, founder of the Brethren in New Zealand, set up home in Motueka in 1852 and continued to compose devotional hymns for the Brethren style of non-liturgical communion, in which any male could ask the community to sing a hymn (always slow and unaccompanied) that expressed the sense of union with Christ around the central communion table. Deck held gatherings for the 'saints' of the district, and they enjoyed the close community:

> Their 'mouths were opened wide', and filled by Him
> Who hears and answers prayer, whose praise they sing:
> They blessed His holy Name with one accord,
> To heaven on high their joyful anthems soared:
> With earnest hearts again the knee they bow
> Oh what a privilege by Jesus given![37]

In accounts of significant early church services the hymns were often listed, including 'Thou who hast in Zion laid' at the laying of the foundation of a Wesleyan chapel, 'Jesus shall reign' at the formation of the Bible Society[38] and at missionary meetings, and 'All hail the power of Jesus' name' at the formation of the first Evangelical Alliance.[39] Perhaps the most familiar hymn in those days was an Anglican favourite, Thomas Tallis's evening hymn 'All praise to you my God this night', which often served as the text for people's bedtime prayer. Similarly, Bishop Ken's 'Awake my soul and with the sun' seems to have been a very popular hymn with settlers. Two hymns by Isaac Watts, 'Salvation oh the joyful sound' and 'Come let us join our cheerful songs', also seem to have been popular. Others are less well-known to us now, including Watts's 'Before Jehovah's awful throne'. All these were very familiar hymns from the English repertoire, music that to some extent overcame denominational and other divides. Congregational hymns were not part of the Catholic Mass, but were performed by choir and organ, and some gained great popularity, including hymns to Mary and the Irish favourite 'Faith of our Fathers'.

Hymn books proliferated in the nineteenth century, all influenced by the eighteenth-century Dissenting and Methodist traditions. Wesleyans often owned copies of the *Methodist Hymn Book*, but a new supplement was issued from England in 1877 and a new hymn book with a much wider range of choice in 1904.[40] The *Baptist Hymnal* was used in Nelson.[41] Brethren slowly adopted the *Light and Love* hymn book, while Exclusives stayed with the *Little Flock* hymn book.

Anglican hymn books came more slowly because hymns were not traditionally part of the service, but in 1861 the Diocese of New Zealand (excluding the Christchurch Diocese, which was less sympathetic to the proposal) invited clergyman and doctor Arthur Purchas to prepare a New Zealand hymnal, which was then sent back to England for publication by the great religious publisher of the day, William Collins.[42] The hymn

St Mary's Pro-Cathedral choir, Parnell, Auckland, in 1900. Since women were not traditionally in Anglican cathedral choirs, they were not permitted to wear robes, instead adopting striking costumes. NEW ZEALAND MAGAZINE, SEPTEMBER 1900. AUCKLAND ANGLICAN DIOCESAN ARCHIVES

book contained the words to 222 hymns and 14 doxologies (verses of blessing used at the end of services). Analysing the first 30 hymns in that book, there is a focus on the church year, while classic evangelical hymns (including Wesley's 'All hail the power' and Newton's 'Amazing Grace') do not appear in the book, although there are three seasonal hymns by Charles Wesley. Seventeen of the 30 are found in the modern New Zealand hymn book *With One Voice*.[43]

This hymn book was widely distributed and even the Presbyterian General Assembly discussed its virtues when considering what book to adopt.[44] Unfortunately for the local publication, *Hymns Ancient and Modern* was issued in 1861 and it was a little larger, cheaper, better produced and could claim an authentic Church of England provenance compared to the *New Zealand Hymnal*. There were ferocious criticisms of the *New Zealand Hymnal* at the Christchurch Synod in 1866 as 'poorly compiled, badly printed, and expensive'.[45] Some even preferred the military chaplain's hymn book.[46] The controversy led to complaints from Anglicans about divergences between congregations, and of the expense of purchasing two books. Today, of course, few people would dream of taking their own hymn book to church.[47]

THE NORMAL PROTESTANT WAY of singing was that a precentor 'lined out' the hymns, singing each line before the congregation sang it. The effect was awkward and, as some complained, it meant that hymns were sung very slowly.[48] Training a congregation and providing them with tonic solfa books (using the doh-ray-me notation) helped some, and the Rev. John Crump taught Wesleyan congregations up and down the country this simple way to learn a tune.[49] Some highly valued precentors claimed that musical accompaniment would make a congregation lazy, more inclined to listen and less inclined to sing.[50] But precentors were notorious for starting a hymn so that it went too high or too low for most voices.

The debate over the use of organs spread widely across the Protestant churches. There was a lively debate in the first Methodist magazine in 1870, which provoked a rousing editorial in favour of organs and how they improved the quality of singing.[51] At the Baptist Church in Christchurch, the debate was prompted by the offer of the loan of an instrument in 1866, but the church declined the offer, not purchasing its first harmonium until 1873.[52]

In practice the debates over instruments and over hymns were interconnected. After all, the argument in favour of psalms rather then hymns was that 'the psalms, being sound and inspired, can only furnish this real and refreshing intercourse'.[53] Exactly the same argument could be used against organs, but in both cases the argument relied on Old Testament texts that were dubiously applied to the Christian church.

Organs were originally only installed in cathedrals. Parish church music in England was largely provided by a village band. So the development of a small portable reed organ — the harmonium — in 1840 was a very convenient development for the New Zealand churches. These 'American organs', as they are sometimes called in reports of the time, assisted in the adoption of hymn singing, as the hymn repertoire moved away from standard metres and thus expanded the range of tunes. Ira D. Sankey had made the harmonium popular when he sang his lilting and sentimental sacred songs from one during the American evangelist Dwight Moody's revival meetings. According to some stories, at least one Anglican minister carried a portable harmonium with him to his services in the Pukekohe area, for even the thin, reedy sounds conjured up a religious memory.[54]

Once they had decided to sing hymns, Presbyterian parishes typically decided to purchase a harmonium. It was fortunately a modest investment. At Queenstown Presbyterian Church the precentor promptly resigned when hymns were introduced, and an organ and organist were necessary. The Queenstown church committee in its minutes noted cryptically 'that Miss Jessie Reid be thanked for taking the instrument in hand'. In the 1890s the first harmonium was replaced with another for £30.[55]

The sound in harmoniums was produced as air moved over reeds, while pipe organs pumped air through pipes, and so were capable of ejecting far more air and making far louder sounds. Pipe organs go back to the Classical age.

Before leaving for New Zealand, Bishop Selwyn purchased for £270 a small Avery cabinet organ originally built in 1779. This, the oldest organ in Australasia, he subsequently passed on to the first St Paul's Church (since demolished) on Emily Place, Auckland, in 1859, and it was used for the processional and recessional at the beginning and end of the service. In 1898 it was sold to the Ponsonby Baptist Church for £98, and it has now been restored to its original charm.[56] Other than the expense, Anglicans and Catholics had no objections to the use of these instruments, new though they were to parish churches, and Bishop Cowie, the Auckland successor to Bishop Selwyn, was enthusiastic about them.[57] In Christchurch, St Michael and All Angels had an organ installed by an Italian organ-master and the result was a much warmer tone than the harmonium, which became very popular with performers.[58]

Back in the United Kingdom there had been a split in the Leeds Wesleyan Chapel in 1827 over the installation of a pipe organ, but thereafter they were the mark of a fashionable chapel. So seven years after the Durham Street Chapel was opened in Christchurch in 1865, a pipe organ was ordered to replace the harmonium, at a cost of £602; this organ was replaced in 1909 at a cost of £1854 (of which £1000 came from a single donation). A new console was installed in 1945, and in 1946 collections began towards a £1761 rebuild.[59] (Replacing a harmonium with a pipe organ was not cheap — and pipe organs never cease being expensive.) Trinity Church in Dunedin and St Alban's Wesleyan church in Christchurch both paid £200 for a pipe organ, and figures over £500 were increasingly common.[60]

The first pipe organs were simple cabinet organs, whereas the later fashion was for large instruments with very large pipes independent of the keyboard. The placement of the organ was much debated for theological and aesthetic reasons, and larger organs required significant building alterations. Pipe organs seemed to have a resale value.[61] The first organ at St Michael and All Angels was subsequently sold to the East Belt Wesleyan Church in Christchurch, which in turn sold it to Rangiora Wesleyan congregation in 1906 for £70. They in turn wanted a grander instrument when they moved into their new church in 1952, so the organ was sold to the Opawa Methodist Church.[62] The organ at All Saints Palmerston North was reinstalled at the Cuba Street Methodist Church at a total cost of £572, the money entirely raised by the choir.[63] Churches often purchased a small cabinet organ and later sold it, replacing it with a larger instrument. The best-known New Zealand maker was George Croft & Co. of Auckland.

The organ at the Pitt Street Methodist Church cost £568 in 1878, and was replaced in 1911 by an instrument costing £2500. One-fifth of this was paid by George Winstone, a member of the family that established the Winstone construction and building materials company (for organs were status symbols very suitable for endowments). At the same time the organ was moved from the back to the front of the church, reflecting a growing emphasis of the place of music in the service.[64] Organs were constantly being adapted and altered, with new stops added and old keyboards remodelled. Anglican churches spent much more, and this remains the case, with the recent installation of massive pipe organs costing up to a million dollars in St Matthew-in-the-City and Holy Trinity Cathedral in Auckland.

For Presbyterians the issue proved more divisive. In the typical Presbyterian church the precentor was a crucial agent of the congregation (rather than the ministerial staff), and at some prestigious churches he (for it was always a male) was paid for his services.[65] At its inaugural assembly in 1862 the newly formed national denomination permitted use of organs as a result of a petition from the Napier congregation under the Rev. Peter Barclay, who was the moderator of the assembly. As a result the churches in Otago refused to participate in the national denomination, forming their own synod.[66]

St Paul's in Christchurch was the first Presbyterian church to use a harmonium, in 1867.[67] In 1876 the Otago Synod was pressured into a further debate over the issue and finally allowed congregational discretion in the matter so long as there was substantial local agreement in favour.[68] The forward-thinking Knox Church in Dunedin voted in 1882 to install an organ after a vote in 1880 was indecisive. The organ was built in England and installed in 1884 at a cost of £1800, radically transforming the experience of worship.[69] By the twentieth century these hesitations were largely forgotten except in Brethren congregations, but the cost of running and maintaining a pipe organ remained a major problem. [70]

CHOIRS IN THE MODERN style were unknown in the parish churches in England until the mid-nineteenth century; instead a village band sat in the gallery. Formal church choirs of boys and men were used in English cathedrals, and they were increasingly used in parish churches during the nineteenth century. Anglican and Catholic choirs were permitted to sing anthems, and Anglicans enjoyed choral settings of Evensong; Catholic settings of the Eucharist could draw from the Classical repertoire.

From the outset choirs were popular in colonial society, for this was one of the easiest self-made entertainments. A sacred harmonic society was formed in Auckland in 1849.[71] There was some opposition to secular choirs singing sacred music; Baptists criticised the Auckland Choral Society when it announced its repertoire in 1858.[72] An early church choir was at St John's Church in Christchurch, which was probably the first church in the colony to introduce a choral service with anthems, intoned responses and processions. In the 1870s St Michael's in Christchurch became renowned for its choir.[73]

In other churches the role of the choir was mostly to accompany congregational singing, and solo singing was thought inappropriate. The Primitive Methodist Church in Wellington received compliments for its choir in 1857, when the *Wellington Independent* reported: 'Everything in the Church ought to be well done, we ought to have the best sermons, the best singing, and the best of everything and he hoped others would take the hint from the gratification he, and he was sure he might add in common with others, derived from the vocal ability displayed this night.'[74]

Choirs could assist with congregational singing, but they also wanted to perform in their own right, and this produced sharp differences of opinion. Knox Presbyterian Church had a distinguished choir, with up to 445 voices, and a choir like that expected to sing anthems.[75] The Thames Presbyterian Church was divided 40 votes to 40 on whether anthems should be permitted, although the minister, the Rev James Hill, used his casting vote in favour of them.[76] The choir was intended to add dignity to the service, although the distinctive *esprit de corps* within it could have the opposite effect; the choir of the Primitive Methodist Church in Timaru was told by the church trust in 1877 'to conduct themselves with propriety during divine service'.[77]

Choirs were also able to show their skills at the tea-meetings and the soirées which filled the weekends. Choirs developed ambitious musical repertoires, soloists sang classical masterpieces, and harmoniums were wheeled out to provide musical accompaniment.[78] Renditions of the 'Hallelujah Chorus' seemed de rigueur for all choirs. Some choirs had humbler ambitions, and struggled to find suitable music. Many years later the Rev. Edward Coulthard took the bold step of stopping the choir at Warkworth from singing a curiously secular Easter anthem about April mornings and lambs.[79]

Marie Peters, the historian of St Michael's in Christchurch, has suggested that the Victorian love of ornateness became reflected in more elaborate church services. This does not seem to have occurred in all denominations, but in the Catholic and Anglican churches it was very striking. In Catholicism by the 1870s, the sung anthem was common in the more formal morning service, and the ancient hymn by St Ambrose, '*Te Deum*', was often sung.[80] By the 1880s city churches were beginning to become more ambitious in their musical repertoire; St Mary of the Angels in Wellington was a model for this.

Catholic services for the great festivals of Christmas and Easter were especially magnificent. In 1866, midnight Mass in Nelson included music by Mozart, Van Bree and Webbe, Novello's setting of 'Adeste Fidelis', concluded with a voluntary of Handel's 'Hallelujah Chorus', and also included solo items by the choirmaster and a duet by two women in the choir. The church was so full by 10.30 that many had to stand outside to listen, and the crowd included many non-Catholics.[81] (This was before the musical rules introduced by Pius X in 1903, which restricted music from interfering with the flow of the Mass.)

Anglican churches were permitted an anthem in Matins, and the Anglo-Catholic movement led to a spread of 'cathedral services' to New Zealand, in which parts of the service were intoned and others were sung. Intoning the service was generally disliked by ordinary Anglicans, but was admired by the musical elite. When Ebenezer Bailey, minister of St John's in Christchurch in the 1870s, used performances of oratorios in the church during the week he became the subject of complaints to the bishop because he had departed from the approved services — and it's a sign of the conservatism of colonial Anglicanism that Bishop Harper indicated that the approval of the General Synod was needed for such departures from protocol.[82]

The opening of ChristChurch Cathedral in 1881 marked an important milestone for New Zealand choirs, for the Cathedral Grammar School was established at the same time to train 24 boy choristers under the former choirmaster and organist of St Michael's Church. The school struggled and in 1894 became the lower school of Christ's College, but in 1923 it became independent again. Two great organists and

Above The Maori Methodist Mission Waiata Choir in 1932. The choir's tours through Pākehā Methodist churches financed the Methodist mission, and they dressed up with patu and poi to attract interest. Paipera Tapu is te reo Māori for Holy Bible. ALEXANDER TURNBULL LIBRARY. REF: PACOLL-0240-01

Below St Peter's Onehunga choir, Auckland, about 1952–55. The vicar is Rev. A. R. Anderson. AUCKLAND ANGLICAN DIOCESAN ARCHIVES.

choirmasters dominate its story: Dr John Bradshaw, from 1902 until 1937, when he fell out with the dean,[83] and Charles Foster Browne, who succeeded him from 1938 to 1976 and was for a while headmaster of the school.[84] David T. Childs (1941–1999) took his place as choirmaster until 1998, and subsequently Lennox Willett and Brian Law have held this honoured position.[85] Boy choirs proved difficult to establish and maintain elsewhere, and Auckland attempts to emulate the ChristChurch example failed.

Choirs formalised church music. Many Anglican bishops saw them as a helpful way to improve the standards of congregational life; there was much praise for those who could improve the order of services.[86] The Anglican vision for choirs was undoubtedly to raise the tone, figuratively as well as literally.

Church music must, however, be viewed across a wider front than this narrow Anglican world. Music was a symbol of intellectual cultivation, and Justice Christopher Richmond, the Nelson Unitarian and leading intellectual in early colonial life, in an address to the YMCA in Dunedin in 1863, acknowledged that Protestants were instinctively suspicious of fine arts because of their role in Catholic worship. He called for the redemption of things beautiful. 'True, at present men in the colony were necessarily much occupied with utilitarian pursuits; but he hoped the time was not far distant when public provision would be made for the cultivation of arts.'[87]

The goal of church musicians was to inculcate a more traditional and better-quality religiosity into New Zealanders. Church music directors were often associated with secular choirs as well. In Christchurch, by the 1960s Robert Field-Dodgson's Royal Christchurch Music Society stood on one side and Vic Peters' Harmonic Society, with its strong links with non-Anglican churches, on the other, and there were theological and social differences at stake. Anglican ministers feared that popular religion would inhibit attendance at the better class of church service and thus undercut the maturing of New Zealand society. They longed to reproduce the traditions of the English cathedral in New Zealand parish churches.

The robing of choirs in surplices, with mortar boards on their heads, was also part of the cathedral tradition — presumably because they succeeded monastic choirs — and this became one of the most nonsensical features of the late-nineteenth-century choir. The St Michael's choir was one of the first to wear robes, from the 1870s.[88] Robing a choir was often coupled with High Church aspirations, and the Rev. Cecil Watson at St Paul's Symonds Street in Auckland caused outrage with his plan to exclude women from his robed choir in 1912.[89] Gradually other denominations copied this pattern of robing. In 1953 the 75-member choir of Durham Street Methodist Church in Christchurch, including the women members, were provided with gowns and mortar boards, to the delight of the congregation.[90] In 1960 the Knox Church choir in Dunedin was decked out in robes for the one-hundredth anniversary of the church.[91]

Cathedral and other noted church choirs became a force in their own right and expected the church to give priority to their interests.[92] The composer and conductor Thomas Vernon Griffiths (1894–1985) was the son of an Anglican priest and came to New Zealand in 1926 to escape family criticism after his conversion to Catholicism. He was a highly regarded musical educator, although it was not until 1942 that he became professor of music at Canterbury University College. His involvement in church choirs and compositions was significant, for he was a vehement defender of traditional musical style.[93] Peter Godfrey, born in 1922, came to New Zealand in 1958 as a lecturer in music at Auckland University College, but also served from 1958 to 1974 as the director of music at the cathedral. From 1983 to 1989 he was director at St Paul's Cathedral in Wellington. He was more open to musical experimentation, and for this reason he is sometimes called 'the father of New Zealand choral music', for the cathedral continues to be a platform for wide influence.[94]

The place given to choir and organist in Anglican worship set up the potential for rivalry between choirmaster or organist and clergyman, and such disputes were legendary. At Dunedin Cathedral the director of music, Raymond White, was dismissed in 1998.[95] His successor was also dismissed. Similarly, in Auckland there was a struggle between Michael O'Connor, the dean at the newly enlarged Holy Trinity Cathedral, and Indra Hughes, musical director, and the choir, and in 2000 choir and director left and formed the highly regarded independent Musica Sacra.[96]

These stories could be repeated many times over at the parish level with devastating consequences. In 1981, for example, such circumstances turned the once prosperous Epsom Presbyterian Church into a very weak church.[97]

THERE WAS A VERY different tradition of revival hymns in New Zealand, drawn from a more popular musical world, in which less-educated laity were suspicious of formal music. The flattened class structure of New Zealand and the casualness of the society meant that a more informal religiosity had a powerful appeal.[98]

So at more or less the same time as choral services emerged, the evangelical hymnal gained new popularity as Ira D. Sankey introduced a new range of hymns written for the harmonium. As early as 1874, a Methodist Sunday school anniversary in Motueka was enhanced by hymns from the *American Sacred Songster*.[99] In 1875 Moody first published a little booklet of 30 songs, filled with hymns by Philip Bliss

The choir of St Mary's Pro-Cathedral, Parnell, Auckland, at an Advent carol service in 1959. By this time many churches held an annual 'Nine lessons and carols' service before Christmas, modelled on the practice of King's College, Cambridge. The image was featured on the cover of the *Auckland Weekly News*. The splendid wooden Gothic interior of one of the finest of Mountfort's churches was well suited to this theatrical display. AUCKLAND ANGLICAN DIOCESAN ARCHIVES

and Fanny Crosby, which eventually grew into Sankey's *Sacred Songs and Solos*, with 1200 hymns.[100] Even the first edition of the book was widely used in the colony.

By 1880 performances of Sankey's songs were often a highlight of social gatherings, and they were much used in evening services.[101] The hymns were sentimental and dramatic; they told stories and stimulated a surge of emotions, and supposedly appealed particularly to women. This troubled those Protestants who placed an emphasis on the rationality of worship. The revivalists defended their services: 'Shall Satan have all the force of the sensational element . . . and the friends of Jesus be debarred from using it in trying to rescue men from the jaws of hell?', wrote a Methodist.[102] The Salvation Army made this repertoire very popular in working-class circles, where brass bands were all the rage.

John Kent has shown how this pattern of culture became very popular in the British context in the late nineteenth century.[103] The intensity of the drama and emotion of songs like 'There were ninety and nine' was accentuated by the accompaniment on the harmonium. Brethren revival meetings used the *Old Revival Hymn Book*. Frank Bullen, the renowned writer of sea stories, visited New Zealand in the 1880s and was struck by the tone in the Port Chalmers Sailors Rest, where Alexander Falconer led the singers from the Garrison Hall: 'I heard singing . . . A burst of melody, floating on the evening air brought me up all standing. It was so sweet, so unearthly.'[104]

High Church and revivalist hymns were direct competitors. In the words of the Rev. James Paterson, Congregationalist minister of Wellington, in 1869:

> the energy of a congregation might be measured by their mode of singing. No matter how beautiful the grandest cathedral music might be, yet if confined to choral services, and performances by choirs, to the exclusion of the congregation, it was to his mind very far inferior to the singing he had heard in Mr Spurgeon's tabernacle, where four thousand people sang heartily together, although many of them probably sang dreadfully out of tune.[105]

This sense of congregational participation was the essence of non-liturgical worship. The freedom to choose favourite songs, the link between singing at home accompanied by piano or harmonium and singing at church, the concept of a fellowship defined by faith, commitment and sacrifice, made these churches distinct. But Methodists did not all like the new music. One Methodist correspondent confessed: 'It is perhaps a relief to some to know that the brethren still adhere to the sober hymns of Wesley, and do not tempt rebellious flesh by indulging in a jig-like song of Sankey's.'[106]

Providing music for strangers to church was seen as a problem by some Anglicans.

In 1886 Arthur Purchas, editor of the *New Zealand Hymn Book*, composed a hymn for the Auckland Anglican mission led by Charles Bodington and G. E. Mason, 'Return, O wanderer, to thy home', which found its way into the 1889 supplement of *Hymns Ancient and Modern* (although the first verse is by Dr Thomas Hastings and in the later edition of *Ancient and Modern* Purchas's words were replaced by Hastings' text).[107]

The Pasifika musical tradition has kept traditional church music alive in recent years. The slow, drawn-out style of hymn singing in the Pacific involved large choirs, and choir night remains a feature of the Pasifika churches. Huge choir competitions, including children's competitions organised by the Sunday School Union, and women's and men's choirs, have been very active. Out of these choirs have come noted opera singers such as Jonathan Lemalu and Benson Wilson, and many contemporary musicians have also come from the same background.

In the twentieth century the revivalist repertoire rapidly evolved. Sankey's *Songs and Solos* provided choir settings for the songs. *Redemption Songs*, the Pickering & Inglis British collection (1900), with 1000 hymns, was used by Brethren, Baptists and others in their evening 'gospel services'. The English Scripture Union's *Golden Bells* (1890) was widely used in children's services.

The musical frontier was shaped by visiting evangelists. When the American evangelist Reuben Torrey visited with the gospel singer Charles M. Alexander in 1902, Alexander's hymns were introduced to New Zealand audiences. Robert Harkness met Torrey and Alexander in Bendigo during that visit, and in Dunedin he dedicated his life to proclaiming the gospel. He accompanied Torrey and Alexander from 1902 to 1916, and then when Torrey retired and Alexander teamed up with another evangelist, Wilbur Chapman, he accompanied them. *Truth*, the populist newspaper, expressed its scorn for Chapman's 'little red book of ranting tunes and badly-composed verse', but at 1s 3d it was within the reach of many.[108]

The Harkness Music Company of Pasadena, California, became a key publisher of gospel music.[109] Other evangelists also had musical signatures. When French Oliver of Kansas preached in New Zealand in 1919, he brought with him *Songs of Deliverance*, which included in its 260 songs a new range of music.[110] The songbooks of Tom Rees, the postwar English evangelist, were available in New Zealand, and when Billy Graham visited in 1959, *Billy Graham Crusade Songs*, with 74 hymns and songs chosen by his musical director Cliff Barrows and soloist George Beverly Shea, was very widely circulated.[111]

Pentecostals and Salvationists had their own versions of revival music. The *Redemption Hymnal*, published by the Elim Publishing House of England in 1951, was widely used in New Zealand.[112] Inevitably, although the revivalist range was well represented, some songs and some emendations reflected the particular doctrines popular in these groups. The Salvation Army had a very strong tradition of brass bands, which has interconnected with the strong Scottish and working-class traditions of bands in this country, and their touring bands attracted crowds all over New Zealand. The bandmaster Henry Goffin was also appointed Wellington city's bandmaster in 1914. By 1934 there were 900 bandsmen in the Salvation Army in New Zealand, whereas there were only 470 songsters.[113]

By the 1950s rising standards of musical and general education meant that the churches bred on revivalist music were aware of its deficiencies. So there came about an attempt to improve musical standards. While the Inter-Varsity Press hymnbook, *Christian Worship*, made little impact, *Hymns of Faith*, the Scripture Union book of 1964, was widely used by more open Brethren assemblies. Youth singing often used the chorus books of the British Children's Special Service Mission, but was revolutionised by *Youth Praise*, published in 1966 by the evangelical Anglican Church Pastoral Aid Society in England. In some respects *Mission Praise* has come to occupy that place in England in recent years, but this has had little impact in New Zealand.

By the twentieth century the various denominations were revising their hymn books. There was a convergence in the content of these books, and English and American editors were influenced by rubrics from bodies like the Royal School of Church Music.

In New Zealand several other factors were significant. Sunday school unions had long issued hymn books, and these were widely used in the Sunday schools. Prayers and hymns, although excluded from primary schools, were a normal part of the secular secondary school assembly. Schools had their own hymns and songs, often put together into a hymn book. Often music teachers were also church musicians in their private time (for example, Vic Ellena, my teacher at Burnside High School, was also organist and choirmaster at St Barnabas at Fendalton).

Another influence was the *Radio Hymn Book*, one of several ecumenical and semi-official productions; these also included the *Forces Service Book* issued in World War II, which abbreviated versions of the Anglican and Presbyterian communion liturgies. The Central Committee on Broadcasting felt the need of a book of hymns for people listening to broadcast church services, so that those at home could sing along with what they heard. Supported with funding from publisher A. H. Reed, who was deeply interested in the project, this hymn book was issued in 1961.[114]

There was discussion at the time about preparing a New Zealand or Australasian book for all the churches, and this project got under way in Australia in 1968 despite not attracting support in New Zealand.[115] It finally emerged as *The Australian Hymn Book*, issued in 1976, with Protestant and Catholic editions. At that time the New Zealand Hymnbook Trust, consisting of Anglicans, Baptists, Methodists,

Presbyterians and Associated Churches of Christ, saw an opportunity for a New Zealand supplement and this was published as *With One Voice* in 1982. The revised edition of the Australian book, *Together in Song*, published in 1999, is very little used in New Zealand, for these days hymns and music change so much that service sheets or video projection is more practical.

M OST OF THE CONGREGATIONS that wanted pipe organs had them by the middle of the twentieth century, but the costs of repairs were high. The South Island Organ Company was dedicated to the endless task of refreshing organs, but there were very few new commissions. Three of the company's workers were killed in the second Christchurch earthquake in 2011 while they were repairing the organ of the Durham Street Methodist Church, which had been damaged in the first quake. A few Baptist churches and even the Open Brethren Elizabeth Street Chapel in Wellington installed pipe organs, but their favoured music called for different accompaniment.[116] There was scope for an 'off the shelf' solution, for example the Melodia pipe organ, a Dutch brand that was franchised in New Zealand by Petrus Matla, an immigrant who arrived in 1953, and found the existing organ builders uninterested in the needs of smaller churches. The Melodia, at a price of £2000, was widely installed in Mormon chapels and in some small churches, for example in St John's Methodist Church in Levin in 1955.[117]

Another alternative was available: the Hammond electronic organ. First manufactured in 1935, it flourished over the next 40 years because of the range of tones and the soft tremolo produced by the Leslie speaker. A significant share of Hammond sales were to churches that were hesitant about the huge expense of pipe organs, but tired of pedalling harmoniums. In New Zealand, Hammond organs were aggressively marketed by Chas Begg & Co., installed in St Stephen's Shirley and in Epiphany Church in Newton in 1938, and then in Mornington Presbyterian Church in July 1939.[118] Beggs regularly advertised the installations that were taking place: in 1961 two Anglican, four Presbyterian, two Methodist, one Baptist, two Brethren, two Catholic, one Church of Christ and one Apostolic church installed the organs.[119] Small churches such as St Columba Presbyterian Church, Ōtūmoetai, appreciated the Hammond tones.

Other competitors in the business won church clients, including the Minshall organ at Ngaio Methodist and the Conn Caprice organ at Ngaio Presbyterian, which was later moved to Ngaio Union Church.[120] A pipe organ may have had cachet, but a Hammond was regarded as modern. The Hammond organ received its ultimate endorsement when it was used in the Billy Graham crusade in 1959. Opawa Baptist

Sisters of Compassion at the St Joseph Relief Centre in Wellington sing, accompanied by their new Japanese electronic organ, on 24 December 1984. The gentleman in the back had just delivered the new organ, which had been donated to replace their 80-year-old harmonium. ALEXANDER TURNBULL LIBRARY. REF: EP/1984/6088/15-F

Church of Christchurch, which had just erected a large A-frame church, paid $2000 for an organ (financed by weekly donations of 20 cents each by the congregation) and lent it to the Crusade Committee, which installed it in the centre of Lancaster Park for the week of the crusade. When it returned, Opawa Baptist used it in combination with a piano, a choir and solo singers. This was ideal background music during altar calls in the evening service, a miniature version of what happened at the crusade.[121]

By the 1980s the Hammond and its competitors were in decline, as the soft tones were disdained by the younger generation. Instead guitars and a wide range of other instruments began to be used. Evangelical churches were somewhat cautious about allowing these on Sunday morning, but permitted them in their more informal evening service. The advent of the family service also loosened the attachment to traditional instruments. By 1982 Hawera Baptist had acknowledged, 'we are glad of the musical team support in two cornets, two violins, a cello, a flute and two or three guitars'.[122]

In the years after World War II musical styles changed rapidly, influenced by American show music (for example, of Rodgers and Hammerstein) and electronic sound reproduction. This reshaped styles of speaking and singing. Elim choruses and Singspiration, the American music company founded by John W. Peterson, were leaders in this field in the 1950s and 1960s. Gradually the 'chorus', the short song influenced by modern secular styles, and capable of repetition, came to be acceptable in church services. At Opawa Baptist Church choruses were introduced into worship in 1967, with the words written out on cards and held up as they were sung.[123] The advent of the overhead projector and then the video projector enabled the repertoire to be greatly expanded.

Recorded music (for example, from Maranatha Music, a branch of the Calvary Chapels, linked to the Jesus Movement in the United States) spread awareness of new music. Popular rock music stimulated a vast number of home bands, and church people were not immune to such music making. By 1967 even the Brethren, renowned for their conservatism, accepted that the new styles of music could arouse spiritual interest.[124] Catholic music radically changed with the institution of the new English Mass. Some of the early hymns were very weak, such as those using the tune 'Michael Row the Boat Ashore', but later a rich range of chants and songs was introduced through a plethora of songbooks.

The new singing revolution has strong New Zealand roots in David and Dale Garrett, a husband and wife duo with connections to Wellington Brethren, who had been singing together since 1962 and moved to Auckland in 1967. They began to attend fellowship meetings in the home of Wyn Fountain in east Auckland, at which various people received a charismatic blessing, including Archdeacon Ken

Prebble of St Paul's Anglican Church in Symonds Street and Bill Subritzky, the lawyer and property developer. Fountain invited the Garretts to lead the singing at the fellowship meetings and they then produced a 45-rpm extended play record of the music written for these occasions, called *Scripture in Song*.[125]

The first song was 'Blessed be the Lord God the God of Israel', composed by David Garrett's sister, Shirley Powell; like traditional Presbyterians, these early charismatics wanted to focus on singing the psalms. Other songs included 'A New Commandment', 'For Thou Art Great', 'God is Not a Man' and 'Thou Art Worthy'.[126] Wyn Fountain's sons, Warren and Jeff Fountain, trained David Garrett to play the guitar better, and a new movement in music was under way. The informality of guitars was the key to the music. A second record, *Thou Art Worthy*, came in 1970 and included 14 songs; two records, *Prepare the Way*, followed in 1972. In 1971 a booklet was produced called *Scripture in Song*, with 28 songs in its 16 pages, adding to the repertoire 'Thy Loving Kindness' and 'His Banner Over Me Is Love'; *Songs of Praise*, a book of lyrics, was issued in 1971. The support of Loren Cunningham, head of the American charismatic organisation Youth with a Mission, who was visiting New Zealand, assisted.

In 1977 three other New Zealand musicians, Brent Chambers, John Olding and Graham Kelly, became contributors to *All Thy Works Shall Praise Thee*, with 25 songs including 'From the Rising of the Sun' and 'He Is Exalted'. By 1979 a decent music score was produced, entitled *Songs of Praise, Book One*. In 1981 a second volume, *Songs of the Kingdom*, was issued, and the American song 'Majesty' took first place, reflecting a broadening beyond the New Zealand origins of the movement. In the 1980s the Garretts were music leaders at Valley Road Baptist Church in Auckland.[127]

This was simple, singable music with an intense sense of an imperative to claim the promises of power taken from the Old Testament's more militant side, and 'spiritualised'. The best known of all these songs, 'This Is the Day', was written by Les Garrett, who was born in Matamata in 1943; his career as an evangelist was largely in Australia,[128] although the music of this song is described as a 'Fiji Island Folk Melody'. Such songs were above all 'worship music': music with the simple downbeat rhythms that touched emotions and united people in a common vision, rather than challenging them.

In the 1970s the Assembly of God in Queen Street, Auckland, whose meetings were transferred to the town hall after it grew rapidly, led the way in musical innovation. Its emphasis on prophetic trends led to a 'time of worship' in which Pentecostal hymns, choruses and the new scriptural songs were blended together into a stream of musical worship and 'singing in the spirit'. In 1976 Bruce McGrail became its musical director, then, after that congregation imploded, he served as musical director of the Auckland City Elim congregation from 1985 to 1994. These two congregations in succession were very influential, although alongside them were the softer sounds of the St Paul's Musical Singers at St Paul's, Symonds Street, Auckland, and the Valley Road Baptist Church singing group.

Increasingly young people in local churches demanded to sing the same sort of music. David Wood has described the anguish of Tawa Baptist Church, which had a distinguished musical tradition led until 1972 by Roy Kennerley, who encouraged choirs, musicians and composers such as Shona Murray, and installed a pipe organ in the church. This congregation was able to produce a Christian musical, *Saultalk*, which was widely performed. But by 2000 all of this had been replaced by a youthful but very professional band, amplified music and much less congregational singing.[129] The story could be paralleled in many evangelical congregations.

The changing styles of Christian music have been reflected in significant institutions. Youth for Christ (YFC) rallies had sponsored musical groups since the 1950s, and by the 1970s their Capital Teen Convention at Queen's Birthday Weekend was a hugely popular Christian musical event. Out of it came the YFC musical group sent around schools every year, the Certain Sounds. From 1989 to 1991 a Christian Music Festival was held at Ōtaki. From 1992 to 2014 Mark de Jong, who had been a member of the Certain Sounds in 1978, ran the Parachute music festival, first in Waikanae and later in the Waikato, attracting a crowd of up 27,000.[130]

De Jong was also the senior pastor of the CLC or Christian Life Church (later Life Church) in Auckland, and increasingly the needs of mega-churches and the focus on music within them led to the establishment of Christian schools of music. The participatory style of scripture in song was replaced by a very professional sound produced by teams of musicians. The music of Sydney Hillsong church and college exerted a very strong influence from the mid-1990s. New Zealand Christian music colleges included the Excel School of Performing Arts established in 1994 in Auckland, and music degrees were offered by Vision College in Hamilton (part of the Apostolic Church) and the Elim Ministry Training College in Auckland.

Striking numbers of Māori and Pasifika people were attracted to this training, although there was little interest in theological study. In both Australia and New Zealand, Pacific people have played an increasing role in the musicianship in Pentecostal churches and have made an impact on the secular music scene as well. The Christian musical training has been significant for such popular musicians as Adeaze, Stan Walker and Brooke Fraser. Overall the role of gospel music is very significant in the New Zealand popular music world. Of course some musicians tired of this music, and there was a significant group of folk musicians who wanted to move beyond worship music to music with meaning, including Derek Lind and Guy Wishart. But their audience was largely gathered on weeknights rather than Sundays.

NEW ZEALAND'S CONTRIBUTION TO music in the church world was much wider than just the scripture in song tradition. After many generations of New Zealand congregations singing about snow at Christmas, a revolution in Christian thinking began in the 1960s.[131] A number of New Zealand hymns sought to translate scripture into the contemporary New Zealand context. One of the earliest was Willow or Katherine Faith Macky's 'Not on a Snowy Night: Te Harinui'. This remarkable invocation of an antipodean Christmas was written in 1957 and first performed by an Australian choir in 1959; it was recorded on Kiwi Records in 1964 on the 150th anniversary of the sermon at Rangihoua.[132] The blending of Māori and European in folk-style format was characteristic, and was praised by the Māori opera singer Inia Te Wiata.

There was an obvious desire to provide contemporary words and music for the denominational churches, and for those who despised the musical simplicities of *Scripture in Song*. The result was *Alleluia Aotearoa*, the New Zealand Hymnbook Trust's contribution, published in 1993. The leading hymn writer was Colin Gibson, a Methodist, born in 1933, who taught at the University of Otago for 42 years and also served as organist at Mornington Methodist Church in Dunedin.[133] His delightful hymn 'He Came Singing Love', written in 1972 for a TVNZ competition, was later included in *With One Voice*. His other popular hymn, 'Where the Road Runs Out', was written in 1976 to commemorate the Mornington Methodist Church's centenary. From the 1980s the work of the New Zealand Hymnbook Trust led to a fine group of additional hymn writers.

Shirley Murray was the most prolific of the New Zealand composers of hymns. Born in Invercargill in 1931, a Methodist, in 1954 she married John Stewart Murray, who was later moderator of the Presbyterian Church. Her books include *In Every Corner Sing* (1992), *Every Day in Your Spirit* (1996) and *Faith Makes the Song* (2003). She became a member of the New Zealand Order of Merit in 2001, received a Litt. D. from the University of Otago, and recognition by the Hymn Society of US and Canada.[134] Her husband was minister of the prominent liberal Presbyterian church, St Andrew's on the Terrace in Wellington, from 1975 to 1993. Shirley Murray's hymns rework Christian themes.[135] 'Loving Spirit, Loving Spirit', written in 1986, is an excellent example of this.

Another significant composer was Bill (William Livingstone) Wallace, born in Christchurch in 1933, who was deeply influenced by the Student Christian Movement. He served as a Methodist minister from 1961 until 1995. His superb hymn 'Deep in the Human Heart' was written in 1977 for a combined Methodist-Presbyterian celebration. Wallace helped select hymns for the television programme *Praise Be*, and he is also a sculptor and stained-glass designer, seeking to reinterpret faith and sense its mystery.[136] His hymn 'We Are an Easter People' suggests values of Easter which may be extracted from traditional theology, for as he said, 'It is my firm belief that through recovering the awareness of the mystery of God we will move to a deeper level of faith.'[137]

Other hymn writers included Jocelyn Marshall née Crabtree, another Methodist.[138] Catholic writers include Sister Cecil Sheehy and Fr John Weir, the interpreter of James Baxter. Joy Cowley, the well-known New Zealand children's story writer, also has written hymns.

In 1973 Christian Advance Ministries issued a cassette, LP record and guitar chord book, *Songs for Prayer and Praise*, edited by Ray Muller.[139] By 1977 the huge success of the Queen Street Assembly of God led to a recording and a songbook, *Promise of Things to Come*, edited by Bruce McGrail and Bonnie Low, and a songbook for young people edited by Bruce McGrail.[140]

The English charismatic movement was much more open to creativity than the New Zealand movement and this helped to inspire a new generation of musicians. One of the most popular of these songs has a New Zealand provenance: Richard Gillard's 'Brother Let Me Be Your Servant'. Now amended to 'Brother Sister Let Me Serve You', the song has worn well. Its author was an English migrant as a boy and wrote the song for the 1978 album *Scripture in Song*.[141] He was a member of the Anglican charismatic congregation at St Paul's, Symonds Street, where he helped to found the St Paul's Singers, who performed contemporary music not choral anthems. Brent Chambers, born in Napier in 1948, wrote 'Be Exalted O God Among the Nations' and a song with a Jewish lilt, 'In the Presence of Your People'. His songs appeared in the 1977 edition of *Scripture in Song*.[142]

Guy Jansen, a well-known leader of school music and founder of the National Youth Choir, provided considerable leadership in this blending of popular and contemporary with his Celebration Singers in Christchurch and Festival Singers in Wellington.[143] *Servant Songs*, edited by Jansen and Felicia Edgecombe, was published in 1987.[144] He was also the editor of the New Zealand supplement in *With One Voice*. Peter Godfrey at Auckland Cathedral was an important influence on Rosemary Russell (born 1953), who was from an Anglican clergy family although she became a member of Titahi Bay Community Church alongside Felicia Edgecombe.[145] From 1987 David Dell made an independent reputation for preparing songbooks. His *New Zealand Praise* (1988) was published by the New Zealand Christian Resource Trust of Hastings.[146] Dell became Baptist minister of Rimutaka in 1992.

At a great music festival in the Durham Street Wesleyan Church in June 1872, the Rev. Alfred Fitchett expounded on his view that music was a critical instrument of culture, that 'Music [has] a high mission — one of the highest in fact — by bringing man into accord and harmony with the great artist — God Himself.'[147] The church and the Christian tradition have been and remain key stimuli for music, both serious and popular. Sometimes the music was highly sentimental, or lacked much originality, but congregations were unlikely to be comfortable with challenging music styles.[148]

All church music has been shaped by particular styles, and this chapter has deliberately sought to highlight the very divergent styles that have merged in a Christian context. In America the debate over styles of church music has been described as a culture war. In New Zealand there are sharp differences between churches. Today only the cathedrals and a small number of local congregations are able to maintain a choir and include anthems in their services, and many use some contemporary hymns; churches often have one or two hymns using the organ, but their other music is a blend of contemporary music; and the larger evangelical churches have bands who lead a very strong musical focus with limited congregational participation. Sometimes churches have both contemporary and more traditional services. In a smaller society very different approaches have been forced to coexist, and this unusual amalgam is a strong feature of the New Zealand scene.

A LTHOUGH NEW ZEALAND HAD no state church, it did have a state Bible, the King James Bible, which, as the cover said, was 'authorised to be read in churches' and was the recognised book on which to swear oaths. The Bible Society ensured the widespread availability of Bibles, and from 1960 Gideon Bibles were placed in hotel rooms, thus the text of the Authorised Version remained available.[149] Scripture memorisation was much aided by this agreed standard text, however awkward the authorised version was in places. Sunday schools encouraged children to remember verses and even whole chapters, and texts like Psalm 23 were very well known.

Only in the fundamentalist sects and in the theological colleges was the accuracy of the Bible translation ever discussed. In New Zealand it was the Brethren who were the most obvious fundamentalist sect. Brethren viewed the Authorised Version as an inspired translation, and joined in the polemical Protestant defence of it. A few other translations were circulated in the Protestant world, but not until the translation prepared by Scot James Moffat in 1926 did a contemporary version achieve widespread appeal. In the Catholic world, the *Douai-Rheims Bible* of the seventeenth century was used in public readings and in school classes.

Then came the *New English Bible*, which sold many copies in New Zealand when it was issued as a New Testament by Oxford and Cambridge University presses in 1961, and as a whole Bible in 1970. (The *American Revised Standard Version* of 1952 was little distributed in New Zealand.) Meanwhile the evangelical world began to be captured by a series of translations and paraphrases, beginning with John Phillips's work, and followed by the hugely popular *Living Letters* and other parts leading to the *Living Bible*, translated by Kenneth Taylor and published in 1971. For a period Bible translations became the staple product of Christian bookshops. *Good News for Modern Man* (1966), followed by the *Today's English Version* or *Good News Bible* in 1976, were written deliberately in a simpler English. The *New International Version* was produced by the New York Bible Society as a New Testament in 1973 and a whole Bible in 1978. It is notable that American English was displacing that of Great Britain as the dominant form of the language. New Zealand played little part in Bible translation except for Murray Harris's contribution as a translator of the Books of Colossians and Ephesians in the *New International Version*.[150]

For a while there was furious debate about these new translations, led by Frederick Channing of the sectarian Bible Presbyterian Church, and some churches insisted that only the Authorised Version could be used for public readings.[151] In the United States this is still a formidable movement, but in New Zealand such sectarian dictates gave way in the rush to be contemporary.

The choir and vicar of Holy Trinity Church, Fitzroy, New Plymouth, in 1972. This is the oldest church in Taranaki and was opened in 1845. It was designed by Frederick Thatcher for Bishop Selwyn, and much altered in 1872 and 1888. Note the painting of the Last Supper behind the altar. SWAINSON / WOODS COLLECTION, PUKE ARIKI AND DISTRICT LIBRARIES

Clergy Culture

Previous The new vicarage at All Saint's, Ponsonby, Auckland, being dedicated in July 1954. The elderly Bishop Simkin leads the vicar Lionel Beere and the curate John Brokenshire. This building was designed by Richard Toy, and the old vicarage behind it was then demolished and the new church, also designed by Toy, was erected where it had stood. The vicarage was demolished and replaced by three townhouses in 2005.
AUCKLAND WAR MEMORIAL MUSEUM. REF: PH-NEG-H1278

From the earliest times, churches appointed clergy, initially bishops, but gradually the church imitated the structure of the Roman Empire, appointing deacons. In some respects clergy defined a denomination, and were defined by it. Their ordination made them representatives of divine authority. Although Protestants largely rejected the notion of 'apostolic succession', which Catholics believed gave them authority directly from Christ and St Peter, clergy were always the critical leaders in the church. They were not merely the appointed official, but priest standing between the congregation and God, and pastor, the therapist who was the healer of souls.

Aside from the ritual role, the clergyman was directed to be the spiritual leader of the community. This role might be partly shared with the elders in the Presbyterian context, but never abrogated on account of youth or inexperience. This presented challenges for both congregation and clergy. This chapter seeks to explore how spiritual leadership functioned.

The first clergy in New Zealand began as missionaries, and this forever coloured their subsequent ministries. The Church Missionary Society had employed lay people partly because it was unable to recruit clergy in sufficient numbers, but also because their initial duties were to 'civilise the natives' rather than lead a church. Nevertheless, its members made a priority of recruiting clergy, whom they believed were required to lead the church. In those days ordination by a bishop could be quite informal, carried out by the bishop in his chapel after examination. Some CMS agents arrived ordained, others sought ordination in England or from Bishop Selwyn after his arrival. Often missionaries were not natural leaders and exercised rather heavy-handed authority in their little spheres, struggling when local rangatira overrode them.

The CMS clergy were largely out of step with the settler church, with its very different priorities and constituency. In the 1860s, during the land wars, they were forced to leave their Māori flocks. A few, like Thomas Grace, later returned. Others, like William Williams, Robert Maunsell and Octavius Hadfield, achieved high rank in the church, but on the whole there was little continuity between the settler church and the missionary church.

Methodist missionaries were ordained by being commissioned by the Methodist Conference. After 1840 these missionaries acquired responsibility for European congregations as well as their Māori converts. Some, like James Buller, were popular with European congregations, but for others it was an uncomfortable transition.

Catholic clergy were ordained by the bishop, and Jean-Baptiste Pompallier therefore came with an expectation of exercising authority. He soon discovered that the Marist priests were reluctant to accept his authority because of their loyalty to their order. In 1848 the Diocese of Wellington (which covered the southern half of the North Island and all the South Island) was created for them, and so they were removed from Pompallier's Auckland Diocese and from their Māori flocks. Many of them ended up serving parishes of settlers. Because the Marists were largely French, there were some strains when they sought to work with the Irish who increasingly dominated Catholic congregations.

In the 1840s and 1850s the CMS in London developed a series of principles under which the 'native' church should become self-sustaining in its ministry and finances, but these ideals were difficult to implement in the face of European settlement of New Zealand. Anglican ordination was in two steps, first to the diaconate and then to the priesthood. Just two Māori were ordained in the 1850s, and another 15 in the 1860s, half of them by Selwyn and the others by the missionary bishop William Williams. Most of these ordinations were only to the diaconate, and only one of the candidates was trained at St John's College.[1] Eventually Williams set up a college to train Māori clergy at Te Rau in Gisborne.

The Māori clergy who were ordained were hugely esteemed within their communities. For example, Hakaraia Pahewa, who trained at Te Rau from 1889, became curate and then vicar of Te Kaha (stretching from Ōpōtiki to East Cape) in 1895, and he remained vicar until 1939. He was fiercely loyal to the local community of Te Whānau ā Apanui and Te Whānau a Te Ehutu. He was one of the group of Māori clergy who attended the Waiapu Synod (the proceedings of which had originally been conducted in Māori), yet he lived in a Māori world and firmly defended a very traditional moral code.[2] The Māori clergy were, however, rarely treated as equals by others in the Anglican Church, and experienced many hardships within it.

Some early clergy who ministered to Europeans came out as chaplains on migrant boats. The migrant ship exposed their lives to close scrutiny. Some were thought pathetic by those who observed them on the boats; James Edward Fitzgerald, the early Canterbury settler who was never at a loss for a word, criticised them as 'the fellows in the pothouse and a shame and disgrace to us all'.[3]

New Zealand scholar Kathy Orr-Nimmo found that the Oxbridge-trained colonial clergy soon ceased to dominate the Canterbury church.[4] While all denominations sought to recruit clergy from the United Kingdom, there were many opportunities for clergy to serve overseas at the time, so it was essential also to recruit and train clergy locally. Bishops on visits to England or, in the Catholic case, Ireland, went looking for clergy. They also had commissaries, who searched for and checked the suitability of offers. Thus Bishop Neligan, the third Anglican Bishop of Auckland, returned from England in 1909 with five clergy and three school teachers.[5]

During the later nineteenth century many Baptists wrote to the great English

Baptist pastor and educator, Charles Haddon Spurgeon, asking him to identify a pastor from students at his college. In 1876 the Christchurch Baptist congregation wrote to him that 'the church would prefer a gentleman somewhat advanced in years . . . single, if possible'. Spurgeon obliged with a 24-year-old who was recently married,[6] but at least he sent someone, and his judgement was good in picking quality suitable for the colonial pastorate.

Ministry was seen as a very special vocation. This was evident in the debate surrounding the exemption of the clergy from conscription in World War I.[7] While some of the arguments were pragmatic, focused on the need for pastors to offer comfort to the bereaved at home, it was also argued that the role of clergy was incompatible with warlike sentiments — yet large numbers of those in training to become clergy enlisted as soldiers, so clearly they did not feel this.

Clergy were expected to have a calling from God. While this was individual, the church recognised it through ordination. Bishops and church committees at congregational and national level struggled to discern the validity of the call. Sometimes they got it badly wrong. The greater problem was the lack of people offering. Bishop Cowie, the long-serving Anglican Bishop of Auckland, expressed the problem thus:

> For the efficient pastoral care of our country congregations we want clergymen endowed with gifts of mind and body such as are not commonly found in combination with those rarer graces of the spirit, that are rightly considered of paramount importance in all who would be wholesome examples to the flock of Christ . . . it is well for us to realise the fact that for those country districts in which hardness has to be endured by the clergyman, and in which a stout heart is essential, we shall have to train our own pastors from among our own sons.[8]

From the mid-nineteenth century, the numbers offering to be clergy did not keep up with the creation of new parishes as the population grew. In the 1870s Bishop Harper suggested that part-time deacons might need to be used. Over the next 60 years the problem grew worse as the flow of overseas clergy dried up, and a crisis emerged after World War II. In 1949 the General Synod was given a blunt report on this, which argued that the Anglican training of priests was inadequate, comparing it unfavourably with the training received by Presbyterians, Baptists and Catholics, but also arguing that the conditions of the Anglican priesthood had little to attract vocations.[9] The Rev. C. H. Arnold argued that the wars and the Depression years had profoundly affected the number of those willing to volunteer, but the trends were there long before the Depression.[10]

Some clergy and bishops inspired young men to consider a clerical life. Bishop William Simkin, at Auckland from 1940 to 1960, was famous for inviting newly confirmed young men to consider this vocation, and the Low Churchman the Rev. William Orange at the Sumner parish, near Christchurch, had a similar impact on a group of 'orange pips' in the 1930s.

There is much in common between the patterns of Catholic expectations of their priests and those of Protestants, but there are obvious and striking differences as well. A celibate clergy was bound to have different notions of calling and different expectations.

THE DESIRE FOR AN educated ministry was largely a product of the Reformation of the sixteenth century in both the Protestant and Catholic churches. Presbyterian clergy inevitably had a university degree, but the degree did not train them to be ministers. The Council of Trent required Catholic priests to attend seminaries. Other denominations were slow to follow suit. From the nineteenth century, appropriate education was expected of professional people throughout the Western world, and professional values reshaped understandings of the calling to ministry. The New Zealand churches were aware that this was a wise expectation, but providing it posed challenges.

Colonial training was rather scrappy and undemanding; it prepared people for the colonial church. Bishop Harper, the first Anglican Bishop of Christchurch, created an upper department of Christ's College to provide a modicum of training for potential clergy. The training at St John's College established by Selwyn in Auckland in the 1840s had a very inconsistent history, and the Anglican Church suffered all the disadvantages of dioceses inclined to set up their own local colleges. Gradually, in the early twentieth century, the college gained more students, although Nelson and Christchurch were cautious about the theology of sundry wardens.[11]

Methodist ministers often had their training cut short because of urgent needs in the circuits (the Methodist equivalent of parishes), so they needed to keep studying during their probationary years.[12] Presbyterians put a high priority on an educated ministry at the theological hall in Dunedin, and they were stricter than others in seeking an academic training — the Presbytery of Otago even rejected the former premier and erudite Congregationalist Thomas Forsaith in their insistence that a minister should read Greek and Hebrew.[13] No wonder that the church had to resort to untrained home missionaries to fill rural vacancies, and that some ordinands struggled with its academic expectations.

Holy Cross College, the place of training for New Zealand secular priests (those who did not belong to an order like the Marists), was established at Mosgiel by the Diocese of Dunedin in 1900 and for 97 years supplied priests (other than Marists) to the New Zealand dioceses.[14] The training was long and rigid, but little focused on the challenges of priesthood. Training for the Marist order was long and drawn-out. From 1924, candidates went first to the Novitiate House at Highden near Palmerston North, and then to Greenmeadows Scholisticate (which had originally been founded in 1890); priests served six months in their first placement, and usually worked as teams in parishes.[15] In 1998 Marist and secular training was combined into one programme based at the Good Shepherd College in Auckland.

The New Zealand seminaries were like monastic institutions. Allan Davidson's history of St John's College, where Anglican priests (and later also Methodist ministers) were trained, indicates that the college, on the site chosen by Bishop Selwyn in the 1840s, was particularly inclined to the monastic under wardens with a High Church flavour. Similarly, Susan Thompson, who wrote a very detailed account of Methodist theological training, has shown the tight rules imposed on Methodist trainees. The Theological Hall for Presbyterians in Dunedin was set in the academic environment of Knox College. In all the main Protestant colleges, married people were not accepted for training and single people were not permitted to get married while in training.

The Presbyterian *Book of Order*, while it did not exclude married ordinands, was emphatic that 'students preparing for the ministry be forbidden to marry during their course of study'.[16] Anglican regulations from 1898 did not permit clergy to marry in the first three years of their ministry, and ordinands were required to get the permission of the warden to become married.[17] The Methodist Church placed trainees on probation for the first three years, during which they were required to be single — and single men cost much less for a parish or circuit.[18] These regulations were not unlike the restrictions on all university students, but they also reflected old traditions that ministry was a calling. The first choice was to become a clergyman, and family responsibilities should not modify this. Any woman who married a clergyman needed to accept her lot willingly.

From the 1930s, attitudes began to change. In this decade a few Methodist students became engaged while studying, and were subject to much teasing. In 1943 the first married students were accepted for training by the Methodists, who were more acutely short of ministers, but they were not housed in the college. In 1958 they were fully admitted, after women were approved for the ministry.[19] By 1960 the Presbyterian regulations had become a little more permissive, to the extent that candidates could seek approval to become engaged, but marriage was still extremely rare.[20]

Anglicans allowed married students but required them to live in St John's College for their last year; the first married people's flats were built at St John's in 1961. Wives were, from 1968, encouraged to attend some classes at the college. In 1975 the Warden of St John's reported that the presence of wives and children had transformed the community.[21] By the 1980s a second route to ordination for married people was opened through non-residential diocesan training programmes, which was associated with the decision to admit women into their ranks.

The choice to be a minister was not a route to wealth. Presbyterians had a reputation of paying best, but even their clergy were often discontented, and increases in stipends could awaken sharp disagreements. (Average stipends in 1870 were reported to be £197 per annum, well below what a labourer would be paid, although doubtless the provision of a manse helped.) Parishes of all denominations constantly fell behind the denominational guidelines for stipends. Ministers in country parishes experienced much the same variations in income as their parishioners.[22] In an impassioned address to the conference in 1908, the Methodist president for the year, William Slade, complained that clergy were receiving a mere £200 per year when many lawyers and merchants were receiving £1000 or £2000 a year.[23] On the other hand, the much-respected Rev. Donald Stuart of Knox Church in Dunedin told the Otago Synod in 1870 that many ministers were not sufficiently active to deserve much reward from their hard-working parishioners.[24]

Successful ministers were sometimes generously rewarded. The small but elite Trinity Congregational Church in Christchurch persuaded its distinguished minister, William Habens, to forgo supplementing his income by teaching with an offer of £50 more per year above its base of £300. Habens was insulted, commenting, 'The services of a Christian pastor are not properly the subject of bargain and sale.'[25]

Anglican stipends were poor. Congregations had to achieve financial stability to become independent parishes and one measure of this was their ability to pay clergy. Anglicans reserved the Easter offering as a free-will offering to the vicar, but few achieved prosperity that way.[26] When in 1910 the unpopular vicar of Inglewood was not given the offerings by the church wardens he proceeded to denounce them from the pulpit.[27] In the 1940s the expected stipend was £385 per annum, as well as a vicarage. Most congregations were unable to achieve this secure provision and remained at the status of parochial districts with no right to have a say in the appointment of their minister.[28] Anglican vicars were paid by the vestry, and this gave them power to hold the clergyman to ransom if they disliked his actions. Only in 1964 did the Diocese of Auckland centralise the payment of clergy, fixing vicars' stipends at £750 per annum and those of curates, the assistant clergy, at £550.[29] Once this was established, it was far easier to monitor stipends and conditions.

Catholic clergy received a modest living allowance, but parishes had to pay the costs of a housekeeper unless a volunteer was available for this work.[30] This meant that the provision of Catholic clergy was less inhibited by costs and more shaped by their availability, and until the 1960s the Catholic priesthood was highly respected by parishioners.

Despite the relatively low financial rewards, there was no real equivalent in New Zealand of the 'poor curates' of the English church, doomed to a pittance and to no permanent employment because they could look nowhere for patronage. The reforms in the New Zealand church and the shortage of clergy meant that curacy was strictly a stepping stone to being priested and appointed as a vicar.[31]

IN THE EARLY YEARS the life of clergy was tough. Parishioners lived far apart. James Cowan, the famous journalist of the early twentieth century, recalled two Catholic priests, Fathers John Golden (for many years parish priest in Pukekohe) and Francis A. Luck (brother of Bishop Luck of Auckland), and their genial ways, and the rough and ready Rev. Henry Edward Newton, vicar of Ross in Westland from 1901 to 1907. But not all were the same:

> An up-country clergyman's work, in pioneer times, at any rate, called for men of tough physique; and it was not for the weakling. There was a Presbyterian minister, a young man who had come out from Edinburgh for the sake of his lungs. A contrast to his country-weather flock, that pale, ascetic, lean-bodied scholar, with the great dark eyes and the thin black beard; he looked a man of another world. His spirit burned too ardently for that frail frame. The rough horseback travelling, the solitary life in that little manse in the fern in the bend of the foggy river, was not the cure for his trouble. The robust climate carried him off.[32]

How were people to be attracted to such a vocation? In his address at the Fifth General Synod of the Church of England in New Zealand in 1871, Selwyn's successor as Primate of the New Zealand Anglican Church, Henry Harper, pondered whether in the absence of clergy, lay readers or part-time deacons could take their place.[33]

Ministers were often viewed as surplus to pioneer society. They were the odd-job men for the parish.[34] Bishop Julius, second Anglican Bishop of Christchurch, sensed this, urging the loss of 'their mannerisms, their peculiarities, and to get rid of all those little finicking ways which very often separated a minister from his parishioners and made him neither fish nor fowl nor good red herring'.[35]

In a way, ministry in pioneer society was very like ministering in a working-class environment, and as difficult. As a Primitive Methodist minister in Thames acknowledged in 1880, 'Many people were of opinion, which was fallacious, that a minister had a rosy time of it. If ministers liked they could have a very sunny billet by running with the tide, but their consciences never permitted them to relax their efforts to win souls for Christ.'[36] In 1882 the Rev. George Monro, of St Luke's Presbyterian Church in Remuera, was lashed in the newspaper by a correspondent after he had criticised the residents. Heavy sarcasm suggested that ministers were lax:

> The ministers have quite enough to do in getting up sermons for the people on Sundays and lots of reading up &c., for I am sure it must take some deep study to get up the sermons we hear in some of our churches. I would suggest if they have any spare time, to take gentle exercise in the daytime, and take great care in the evening to keep within doors and in the immediate neighbourhood of a good fire.[37]

Clergy in rural communities faced many obstacles.[38] Some were relatively isolated, and support from parishioners might be hard to find. Alan Mulgan, literary editor of two newspapers and brother of the more famous John Mulgan, wrote a graphic account of country clergy in the early years of the twentieth century:

> In rusty black the aging vicar smiles,
> Priest of a flock that straggles thirty miles.
> Riding at call to funeral or feast,
> Judge of disputes involving man or beast.
> Stifling regret, outfacing household fear,
> Six mouths, two hundred doubtful pounds a year.
> Long since the Church said: 'there's a call to bless
> For youth and strength out in the wilderness.'
> And then forgot him; city churches need
> Men of bright learning, dropping polished seed
> From rich safe store, draped with a famous hood.
> Rough road apprenticeship of course is good,
> But can be waived for grace and eloquence.
> And so the shepherd mends his long weak fence,
> Rising on dusty duty year by year;
> Preaches a simple gospel, hope not fear;
> Runs a few cows; takes prizes for his beans;
> Conserves the school committee's scanty means;

> Arranges concerts in the little hall,
> Goodbye, The Holy City, On the Ball.
> Glad now and then to rub his rusty learning
> And help some young and raw ambition burning
> to leave the muddy routine, early, late,
> And wear the white clean livery of the State.
> And if he wishes Colin could be sent
> To school in town, or hard conditions bent
> To bring the budding Nancy, chilled by duty,
> A petal from the great world's rose of beauty;
> Or sighs to see his youth-deserted wife
> Mother and servant, curate too for life,
> Screw up her strength to meet the sharper thrust
> Of circumstance — brighter in roadside dust
> May blossom his reward than the fine flower
> That scents the cushioned rooms of place and power.[39]

These extremities can be exaggerated. A high proportion of clergy were based in the towns even if they had to also hold services in country churches. The struggles were mostly associated with new congregations, for many parishes had makeshift parsonages and inadequate churches. It was not a life to suit a sedate clergyman, and the most effective clergy were rarely sedate.

There was a lively correspondence in the *Otago Daily Times* in 1929 about the failure of ministers. There were criticisms that ministers chose words that sounded good to parishioners rather than offering what they needed to hear, that they were intellectual snobs, lacking in energy and slow to get out of bed and work for the kingdom of God.[40]

Catholic clerical patterns were significantly different. Clergy had no wife to connect them to women parishioners, and they often mixed far more with the men of the parish than Protestant clergy. Catholic attitudes to alcohol and entertainments provided some acceptable recreations for priests, and the drinking, gambling priest enhanced his reputation with the Irish men and families who were the staple of parishes.

Catholic priests were in no way accountable to their parish, and so priestly eccentricities and extravagances, while often well known (sometimes because the Presbytery housekeeper was a gossip), were accepted and even celebrated. Catholics did not subscribe to a puritan code, and so some of these misdemeanours were simply a source of amusement. After the 1960s priests were given extensive scope.

One parish history included among its priests Fr James Gavin, the black-singleted Monsignor who loved carpentry and built a boat for his retirement during his last parish appointment. Fr Kevin Keen, the owner of a Lincoln Continental and then a De Lorean, and Fr Patrick McAleese, the priest who won Lotto and was devoted in orchid growing, were legendary in the parish.[41]

Clergy were as interested as any in public issues. By law clergy of the state Church of England were not allowed to hold secular office, but these rules did not apply in New Zealand. Clergy of any denomination could and did enter Parliament. Matthew Green, a Church of Christ minister, served as Member of the House of Representatives for Dunedin East for one term, between 1881 to 1884, before returning to the ministry. Leonard Isitt, a Methodist minister ordained in 1879, was secretary of the New Zealand Alliance from 1900 and Liberal MP for Christchurch from 1911 to 1925.

Among Labour MPs there have been several members of the clergy. Clyde Carr was a minister of the Congregational Church from 1915 and Labour member for Timaru from 1928; Arnold Nordmeyer was a Presbyterian minister from 1925 and Labour MP for Ōamaru from 1935 to 1969; and Russell Marshall was a Methodist minister from 1960 and MP for Wanganui from 1972 to 1990. Other notables in the Labour Party included the third Labour Prime Minister, Walter Nash, who had been secretary to the Church of England Men's Society, and John Archer, Baptist minister and president of the Labour Party, who stood four times for Parliament and served in the Legislative Council from 1937 to 1949. Although religious views compelled many to engage in political activity, sometimes the public was unsure that they wanted to be represented by a clergyman.

S OME NEW ZEALANDERS REGARDED the clergy as having the easiest of jobs, and in an age of greater differentiation of professions and definition of tasks, for a professional there was irritation at clergy who regarded their duties as just leading the Sunday services. But clergy also played a number of recognised roles in the community; to the clergy were reserved the roles of baptism, marriage and burials. These were very large responsibilities, and they meant that the church was integral to the life cycle of all New Zealanders.

At first there was a limited choice of ministers available to baptise children. In the first two years of the Port Nicholson settlement, the only minister was John Macfarlane from the Church of Scotland, who baptised people whatever their denomination.[42] Anglicans were rather more particular about who baptised them, and in the 1840s Bishop Selwyn upset Wesleyans by devaluing their baptism as a sacrament.[43] Settlers often travelled a significant distance to baptise their children. In the 1860s and 1870s Presbyterians from Clevedon walked 13 kilometres to Papakura to have their children baptised by the legendary minister Thomas Norrie, who also travelled as far as Te Awamutu baptising and holding services.[44] Baptism was probably seen as much as an act of registration as of admission to the church. Such views remained standard for many years. The Plunket Society in 1946 took this view in its book *Mothercraft*.[45] The doctrine that baptism ensured the child of salvation — baptismal regeneration, as it was called — was hotly resisted by many Anglicans and went against much Protestant theology.[46]

From the 1950s churches began to realise that families vaguely linked to the church were no longer bringing their children for baptism.[47] This was an early indication that the church had ceased to have a standard place in the life cycle of the nation.

Clergy also conducted weddings, which in the nineteenth century were often held in the bride's home on a Wednesday.[48] Consequently, weddings were relatively independent of regular congregational life. Anglican weddings were conducted in the church. There were differences of opinion as to whether the vicar should charge a fee for a wedding. In the Christchurch Anglican Diocese the bishop viewed marriage as a sacrament that should be provided free of charge, but the costs of the organist and the verger, who cared for the church property, needed to be met. Popular Christchurch wedding venues, such as St Mary's Merivale and St Barnabas Fendalton, felt justified in charging fees since conducting weddings for people not from the parish took up a great deal of the vicar's time; charging for these services provided recompense and enabled him to supplement his income.[49]

Funerals were another of the clergy's responsibilities. No event brought the community together as much as a funeral. The undertaker and the minister worked hand in hand to organise the farewell to the person, but alongside the choice of singable hymns lay the duty of ministering to the grieving family. Finding the right words, which sometimes had to carefully navigate around delicate issues and also provide solace, was a skill, and there was little warning as to when a minister would be called on to do this. (The custom of long eulogies by friends and family was unheard of until relatively recently.)[50]

Catholic clergy were also responsible for the confessional. This was a matter of high suspicion to Protestants, but it meant that priests knew a great deal about the misdemeanours of their parishioners and had exceptional opportunities for pastoral care of them, albeit at the same time carrying the burden of knowledge.

Helping those in need was a long-standing role of the clergy. In Britain clergy helped to administer the poor laws and most Charitable Aid Boards, which provided modest assistance to those who were judged deserving, had clergy members. Providing assistance to the poor remained a duty of the clergy, and people in need would often knock on the vicarage or manse door seeking assistance. There were occasional complaints that Protestant clergy were miserly, while Catholic priests had a better reputation, resting on their understanding of the Irish poor,[51] but in 1914 Herbert Walter Bull was brought to court in Auckland for having defrauded 12 Auckland clergy of different denominations with a hard-luck story about being an immigrant unable to find work. He had netted £1 per cheated clergyman.[52]

Clergy were also parish visitors. In England Richard Baxter, the seventeenth-century Nonconformist minister of Kidderminster, had exalted this as the highest privilege of the clergyman, and in the nineteenth century this was seen as the best way to regain working-class support. Thus Charles Kingsley, the pioneer of the English Christian Socialists, was famous for his ability to enter the homes of the poor. Settlers certainly expected clergy to have a pastoral ministry bringing support to the needy, and in all denominations there was concern when clergy did not treat this as a serious responsibility.[53] Catholic clergy were expected to be 'at the bedside of the sick and dying administering to their depressed spirits the consolations which our Holy Faith alone can supply'.[54] In the early years visitation from house to house was an endurance test. There was a story that Catholics in the backblocks of Canterbury would have a cabbage tree cut back to indicate that priests were welcome.

The visit of the bishop was a particularly significant event. When Bishop Redwood, who had just been appointed Catholic Bishop of Wellington, visited Lower Hutt in 1875 a triumphal arch was erected at the gate of the church.[55] Confirmations and other events were held during episcopal visits. When Redwood visited Takaka in 1876, the Protestant community joined in a grand welcoming dinner.[56]

Special pastoral calls were occasioned by funerals and the personal and financial troubles that were common in settler life. The quality of visitation in working-class areas was critical for the church.[57] In colonial society the funeral was sometimes a moment in which the high hopes and prospects of settlers suddenly dissolved, leaving the bereft family in a crisis. Settlers were often very mobile and communities much less solid than we imagine in retrospect, so the skills of clergy were on show before the whole community.

Pastoral visits were quite significant in isolated local communities. When Fr Petitjean first visited Otago in 1855, his slow horseback trips to the 90 Catholics in the province, often many miles apart, took a great deal of time. He would often perform baptisms during these visits. Similarly, Fr Moreau, who succeeded him, was legendary for his pastoral exertions: 'No matter in what part of the back country his services were required or what dangers he had to face in the shape of wild mountain tracks or dangerous rivers to cross unbridged, nothing would deter him from doing his duty, and attending to those in need of his services.'[58]

Above Māori Anglican clergy at East Cape in 1900. The names on the back of the photograph indicate that the first right in the back row was Rev. Mohi Turei, who was ordained in 1864 and was a great Ngāti Porou leader and carver. His mana shows the strength of the ordained clergy in the Waiapu diocese, where synod proceedings were conducted in Māori in the early years. ALEXANDER TURNBULL LIBRARY. REF: 1/2-022632-F

Below Bishop Wally Averill opens the new Kaitaia cemetery in the 1920s. The Revs Hector Hawkins, Claud Brown and Alfred Drake are seated on the left. The bishop's car is behind. ALEXANDER TURNBULL LIBRARY. REF: 1/1-006303-G

Country clergy travelled huge distances by horse. The Presbyterian parish of Frankton was forced to hire a horse and trap, and in 1910 they decided to buy a buggy for £45 and a horse for £20.[59] The Anglican parish of Warkworth was constantly struggling with hopeless horses, and the need to stable them.[60] Imagine the travails of Fr Morkane, newly ordained and sent for two years as assistant priest in Lawrence in 1910 and therefore obliged to travel every fortnight to Tuapeka, Roxburgh and Millers Flat, distances of some 73 kilometres now followed by the popular Clutha Gold Trail.[61] Clergy in such parishes needed to be fit and enterprising.

The provision of a horse was the responsibility of the parish. Buggies seemed to be optional, but were seen as more respectable. Early in the twentieth century the bicycle became standard in the towns, but it was not much use in country parishes. At first motorcars were too expensive for parishes, and so the clergy continued to use horse and trap.[62] By the 1920s parishes felt the need to provide a car. The cost occasioned some head-scratching by boards of managers, since denominations had not yet established rules for this.

In the early years cars were purchased by people with a knowledge of technical details; clergy were presumed not to have this knowledge. There is more than a whiff of contempt in one story of a clergyman being taken through the Oropi Gorge at Pyes Pa in the Bay of Plenty when the car got bogged; the minister sat in the car when he should have been out pushing.[63] The occasional clergyman made great use of a motorbike, but eventually this was thought not becoming of a professional man.

The quality of the pastoral visit determined whether or not a minister or priest was loved, and this was what they aspired to, but many a minister struggled to maintain these visits and found them painful events.[64] As social divides grew, the challenge increased. Maurice Andrew, an intellectual who later became a theological lecturer, in an acute analysis of his own awkwardness as Presbyterian minister of Ngaio in 1959 indicated that 'some people thought I was cold', and 'some men had the habit of half turning away from me as though I reminded them of something unpleasant'.[65]

Clergy did not necessarily have a prescribed uniform when out visiting. Catholic clergy wore the soutane, a cassock that went down to the ankles.[66] Anglican clergy wore white cravats and frock coats. Few Anglican clergy wore cassocks in the street, whereas in England Anglo-Catholics preferred to dress in this way. It was one mark of the extremism of Cecil Cherrington, first Bishop of the Waikato from 1926 to 1950, that he expected clergy to wear their cassocks at meetings of the synod of the Anglican Diocese of Waikato.[67]

The back-to-front clergy collar was introduced as clerical wear about the time of the foundation of colonial New Zealand. It was initially used by ministers of the

Church of Scotland and slowly became adopted by almost all other denominations, Protestant and Catholic (although the latter were the slowest to adopt it). The white collar generally went with a black shirt, and the intention was to provide appropriate clergy dress out of the context of church ritual. Some disliked this as the clergy style. *Truth* in 1930 praised a Gisborne clergyman who dressed in 'a Van Heusen collar, four-in-hand tie, doggy cardigan, and a rakish felt hat' and lauded him for his broadness, tolerance and his ability to demonstrate that 'a parson can be a perfectly good mixer'.[68] Clerical garb set the clergy apart even in normal life, and that was not always respected.

As this pattern became expected, fraudsters adopted the dress in order to exploit the religiously gullible. John Frederick Amos in Christchurch, in 1934; Ivan Bicknell (alias Rev. or Professor James Cameron) in Thames in 1937; and most spectacularly 'the Rev' George Samuel Thomson in Christchurch in 1938 all used the back-to-front collar to gain money. In the last case, 'Rev' Thomson claimed to have been ordained by the Liberal Catholic Church in Melbourne. He was charged with reading horoscopes for two police witnesses, work that he described as 'hack work', preferring to be a metaphysician.[69]

T HE CLERGYMAN AND HIS wife were intended to be a model couple, and with children a model family. A barbed reprint in a Methodist paper in 1889 shows that already the itinerant Methodist clergy wife was troubled by accusations that she had failed to live up to the devotion and thrift of her predecessor.[70] There were so many meetings to attend, organisations to chair, and kindnesses to be shown to people in need. The wife administered much of the hospitality of the parish, and was the eyes and ears of her husband. In the Anglican church the good bishop's wife served not only as a model in the community but as a further model to the clergy wives, chairing key organisations and ensuring that appropriate hospitality was offered at Bishopscourt.[71]

The wife had at least chosen to marry a clergyman. The children had no such choice, and badly behaved children of clergy could be a public embarrassment to them, and especially to the clergy wife. It seems to have been a commonplace that parsons' kids *were* badly behaved. It cannot have been easy to have the behaviour of the children of the parsonage discussed by the parishioners. It was essentially their identity that put them under this spotlight, fuelling discussions of hypocrisy in the clergy. For their part, parsons' children often in later life reflected positively and negatively on this exposure.[72]

As late as 1974 Bishop Gowing, Anglican Bishop of Auckland, noted with approval that clergy wives were great supporters of their husbands.[73] By then, in fact, the role of the clergy wife was changing. Thrown into confusion by the advent of female clergy, it was also the experience of some clergy wives that the only way to escape their menial spousal duties and supplement their husband's meagre stipend was to seek employment. Today it is not unknown for the clergy spouse to have no particular interest or involvement in the church.

The provision of a vicarage (Anglican), manse (Presbyterian or other Protestant) or presbytery (Catholic) was a requirement for the establishment of a parish.[74] These dwellings took many forms, and the character of the house seems to have often been a determining factor in the decision of a minister (and his wife) to move parish, especially in the Presbyterian system. The right manse meant a lot to a minister's family; 'we thought we were "in heaven",' said one son of the manse when he saw the fine house and its garden at Epsom Presbyterian Church.[75] One parsonage was located so close to the local Chinatown on the West Coast that the family became alarmed at the fireworks at the time of Chinese New Year.[76]

Increasingly, specifications were laid down as to the dimensions of the vicarage or manse. Four bedrooms, separate bathrooms for visitors and for family, and a study with a separate entrance were some of the requirements.[77] In the vicarage an extra bedroom was required for the visit of the bishop. There was a notice in the lounge of one manse, warning visitors not to stay too long.

The manse or vicarage was a hub of social activity superintended by the clergy wife, and parishes greatly approved when they became open homes, hosting young people and needy people. But hospitality could go too far. When Frederick Hart, vicar of Warkworth, invited the poor 'on the tramp' north from the city of Auckland during the Depression years to doss down in the vicarage, and allowed the overflow to sleep on the vestry floor, the vestrymen became alarmed.[78]

Clergy were temporary residents, and in the Methodist Church and the Salvation Army they moved frequently. Consequently the parsonage was expected to be furnished so that the minister's removal expenses could be minimised. Ministers were expected to pack up and move at a set time of the year, and they had to bear part of the burden if they moved in less than three years. The house came with furniture and even bed linen, but clergy were responsible for replacing breakages in the parsonage.[79] One minister's wife recalled to me that another spouse hid the old pots in the gooseberry bushes in 1960 so that her successor would not have to endure them.

In the 1970s the Methodist rule changed, firstly to exclude bed linen, then later in the decade the furniture in their parsonage was assigned to the incumbent clergyman. A board of equalisation was appointed to value the furniture and ensure that each clergyman had no less than $200 or more than $500 worth of furniture. This was a crucial step in recognising that the clergy had their own tastes and values, and were in fact no longer part of a single profession with shared professional values. The next stage was for clergy to live in their own houses, and today in most denominations clergy receive a housing allowance equivalent to renting in their suburb, which helps with the cost of the mortgage.

Salvation Army regulations for officers were brutally ungenerous. Unmarried officers were to be provided with two rooms, a front room and a bedroom, and the specified furniture included a narrow bed, two seats and a couch, a clock and blinds. Married officers were provided with a house, and every item of furniture was specified, including the number of sheets, pieces of cutlery (six of each), dusters, curtains and buckets. When they were due to move, they had to account for all these items.[80]

In the Protestant churches the provision of a manse was only made for a married minister. Methodism, for example, sharply differentiated between the probationer minister who was single, and the minister in what was known as 'full connexion', who was expected to be married. In Woodville, a single man was greatly desired in 1885 so that money could be spent on the church not on a parsonage.[81]

The Catholic presbytery might be assumed to be somewhat like the Methodist parsonage, but this misapprehends the power relationships between the priests and the parish. While occasionally the priest would be placed in a boarding house, bishops regarded this as highly unsuitable and parishes were expected to give priority to the presbytery. This was often a substantial dwelling adjacent to the church, where the parish priest reigned supreme, cared for by a housekeeper. Curates (and most parishes had more than one priest) also lived in the same residence, not always comfortably if their personal style differed from that of the parish priest. In Ashburton, the parish priest in 1907 insisted that the need for a presbytery was greater than the need for a new church (he described the old presbytery as 'a cottage in which it would have been difficult to swing the proverbial cat'). He soon raised the £3772 needed for the presbytery, and used the surplus money as the beginning of a fund for a new church.[82]

Meanwhile the women religious were organised in a convent, and this was usually far meaner and more run-down than the presbytery, since the nuns had far less opportunity to campaign for financial support. It was not uncommon for the old presbytery to be converted into the convent. In Ashburton that same cottage, which was far from the school, was passed on to the sisters by the priest, and they had to resort to praying to St Joseph that if he would remedy their situation they would erect a statue of him.[83]

Given their status as moral exemplars, clergy found it difficult to have a leisured

life. Perhaps it was to their advantage if they enjoyed the sports popular in the community. For example, when in 1910 Fr Quinn left the Hastings parish after three years, the Hawke's Bay Cricket Association wrote in appreciation of his services in the parish cricket club.[84] But sometimes clergy (especially Anglicans) preferred to keep a distance from their parishioners when off-duty.

Monday became the clergy day off. But what were they to do on that day? Entertainment with other clergy — golf or the like — was the simplest option. Some loved greyhound racing, and a witty reporter observing a clergyman without his collar on sarcastically commented that the same man who had denounced the greyhounds in his Sunday night service was an avid enthusiast out of sight of his congregation.[85]

Sometimes clergy became broken down in health, and a wise parish would then urge them to take a break. So Dr Stuart was sent to England by the Knox Church deacons and also given a break in Queenstown when he grew unwell; his medical adviser, the redoubtable James Copland, stepped into the pulpit in his place.[86]

THE PROCESSES FOR CLERGY changing parishes differed between denominations. Catholic priests were mostly accredited by their religious order (the largest of which was the Marists) and in this

Rev. John Wilkinson, vicar of St Aidan's Anglican Church, Remuera from 1919 to 1925, and his family on the steps of the vicarage. SIR GEORGE GREY SPECIAL COLLECTIONS, AUCKLAND LIBRARIES, 2-4920

CLERGY CULTURE 187

case the bishop needed to negotiate with the order and arrange the transfer with the respective parishes. In the early years, Marist priests stayed in their parishes for lengthy periods, but later a rule of a maximum stay of six years was imposed; even a strongly worded plea from the Timaru parishioners in 1920 to keep Dean Tubman was unable to sway Dean Holley in his imposition of the rules of the order.[87]

Protestant parishes were always consulted about the move. In the Anglican Church the bishop would facilitate the transfers, but financially stable parishes (although not the parochial districts) were able to dominate the appointment committee. The great majority of Anglican clergy remained within the one diocese. Salvationists were transferred every two years; Methodists every three years, by the stationing committee of the conference. Increasingly complex matches were tried to place people into appropriate parishes, with a good deal of private consultation that sometimes gave parishes the person they wanted. Finally in 1893 the Methodist rule was changed to every five years.[88]

Presbyterians and Congregational churches invited clergy to 'preach with a view' before the congregation voted to extend a call. In this process, a happy match often led to a very long incumbency unless the clergyman grew lazy or tired. Younger men often started their careers as single men in a country parish, where extensive itineration between churches might be required. Highly regarded clergy, like Donald Stuart at Knox Church in Dunedin, could remain in one parish for their whole ministry, in Stuart's case from 1860 until his death in 1894. City parishes often had high expectations and this could lead to a complete breakdown of relationships for relatively minor misdemeanours.

There was often a very close-knit relationship between pastor and congregation.[89] Leaving a congregation was often a painful event; the farewells could be very emotional, with great grief manifested on all sides. Congregational churches happy with their pastor often resorted to pleading, complaining to the rival congregation or offering an increase of salary.[90] At retirement, a former clergyman was expected (although not required) to move to another parish; if he remained, his successor had little chance of success.

Sometimes conflict resulted in resignation from the ministry. The larger denominations had a greater range of options for those who failed in one parish, and bishops sought positions for misplaced ministers and priests (although New Zealand had none of the easy sinecures that the English church contained). Some grew irritated and changed denomination, especially from smaller and more prescriptive to larger and broader denominations. A notable example was Alfred Fitchett, a highly acclaimed Wesleyan minister who resigned from the denomination in 1879 in disgust after criticism of his sympathetic advocacy of evolution. He became a well-respected Anglican minister and dean of the cathedral in Dunedin, and his son became the third Bishop of Dunedin.

There are other examples that illustrate the challenges. Fred L. Frost, who had been a Wesleyan minister, was ordained an Anglican in the Diocese of Waiapu. After eight years as a minister at Taradale he stood for Labour in New Plymouth in the 1935 parliamentary election, winning the seat in 1938. Quite a few people felt a calling to ministry but were mismatched with the denomination they grew up in. A calling to ministry was in essence a calling recognised by a known community, so it was natural to seek ordination in the church of one's childhood. If they left, they were likely to face the loss of their erstwhile friends.

Quite frequently a vicar or minister had a spectacular falling out with his congregation. In 1876 Henry Edwards at St Michael's in Christchurch was protected by Bishop Harper when he got offside with the vestry but, faced with a mass resignation of all parish officers, he had no alternative than to resign.[91] When the vicar of Devonport fell out with his congregation in 1899 over suspicions that he was expecting candidates for confirmation to come to him for confession, the vestry refused to pay his stipend, and he was forced to become an army chaplain.[92] Liturgical or theological innovation often caused division; such events were entertaining to outsiders and troubling to denominational officials. The Presbyterian *Book of Order* laid down meticulous but slow processes to deal with such situations. The Anglican or Catholic bishop could extract an unpopular clergyman more swiftly, although their usual approach was to support clergy. Members of Congregational and Baptist churches sometimes took sides, resulting in struggles for control of the church. Sometimes the only solution was a split in the congregation.

Denominations were strict in disciplining badly behaved clergy. The New Zealand churches showed little of the tolerance of misdemeanours of the lax church world of Britain in the eighteenth century. In a church that was perpetually short of funds, parishioners were not forgiving. Bishop Selwyn withdrew the licence from the missionary William Colenso when his adultery was discovered in 1852, and it was not restored until 1889. It is worth noting that in the nineteenth and early twentieth centuries teacher conduct was also heavily regulated in New Zealand, and so were clergy.

Retirement was difficult. Clergy lived in vicarages or manses all their working lives, and had relatively little opportunity to save; in a property-owning democracy they were potentially facing poverty on retirement. The Methodist Superannuation Fund (originally called the fund for worn-out preachers) was one of the earlier superannuation schemes to be established.

The General Synod of the Anglican Church sought to solve the problem at its first meeting in 1859, but no national scheme was ever established.[93] Individual dioceses instead created their own schemes. The Auckland Diocese established a scheme in 1888 that included a sick fund and a widows' fund, and it slowly became fiscally stable, but the base of investors was very small.[94] Smaller churches like the Primitive Methodists struggled to get buy-in from congregations in New Zealand.[95] Following the government's introduction of the universal superannuation in 1938 clergy schemes in some cases sought exemption, or ways to incorporate the two schemes.[96]

In the postwar years, the Methodist Church set up a Home Acquirement Fund into which ministers subscribed at a modest rate when they were first ordained, and as funds became available it was intended to help them into homes.[97] Some church retirement villages gave priority to ministers. The *Book of Order* was constantly amended by the Presbyterian General Assembly to clarify the Beneficiary Fund Regulations.

Meanwhile Catholic priests retired to homes run by their orders, and were constantly called upon to lead services when no other priest was available. The same was also true of retired Protestant ministers.

New migrants brought different patterns with them. The most striking of these was the model brought by the Pasifika clergy — Methodist, Congregationalist and others — who were by definition nobles, while their congregations were New Zealand reproductions of Pasifika village communities. Within these communities the status of the minister was high, and they were supported with frequent gifts of food and money.

Within the Catholic world this expectation was also evident among the Indian clergy, who were frequent imports in the face of the decline in Pākehā vocations after the 1970s. They were not used to the pragmatic approach of New Zealand priests. Pasifika priests were placed with their own people, but Asian priests generally served in integrated parishes, and the divergence between the expectations of clergy and congregations has sometimes been striking.

OVERALL, HOW LARGE A group were the clergy? The 1921 census indicates that 484 women and 1807 men were employed by the church in religious work (including 394 Anglicans, 413 Presbyterians, 311 Catholics and 238 Methodists).[98] In 1936 there were 2241 male religious workers, including 436 Anglicans, 421 Presbyterians and 535 Catholics. Such a list would include those who were not ordained, and exclude some who had secular employment.

The lists of officiating ministers licensed to conduct wedding ceremonies had 1641 names in 1921, which had risen to 1928 names in 1936. There was one Anglican

Above Bishop Thomas O'Shea, centre, wearing a biretta (cap), with his clergy (mostly members of the Society of Mary) at St Joseph's Church in Buckle Street, Wellington, where he also served as priest in the 1930s. He was appointed in 1913 to succeed the elderly Francis Redwood as archbishop of the Catholic Archdiocese of Wellington, although he did not take control until Redwood died in 1935, at the age of 96. O'Shea was called 'Little Arch' on account of his size.
ALEXANDER TURNBULL LIBRARY. REF: EP-0705-1/2-G

Below Clergy and bishops at the consecration of the coadjutor Bishop Hugh O'Neill of Dunedin by Archbishop O'Shea in Wellington in 1943. O'Neill retired just three years later, perhaps discontented with the diocesan bishop, James Whyte (the tall figure on the left). To Whyte's left are O'Shea, Bishop O'Neill and Bishop Liston.
SIR GEORGE GREY SPECIAL COLLECTIONS, AUCKLAND LIBRARIES, AWNS-19430407-14-3

minister to every 1075 nominal Anglicans in 1906, and one to 1289 Anglicans in 1936. For Presbyterians, the second largest group with 428 ministers, the ratio declined in these years from one minister to 775 adherents to one minister to 859 adherents. Most other denominations had a much lower and improving ratio of ministers to adherents. Catholics, with 359 priests in 1936, had one priest to every 544 Catholics, compared to one to 647 in 1906. Methodists, with 297 ministers, had improved from one minister to 511 adherents, to one minister to 407 adherents. The ratios were one minister to between 200 and 300 adherents for the smaller denominations, and among Salvationists the 109 registered officers produced a ratio of one to 116 adherents.[99] In 1947 the Anglican ratio was one minister for every 1246 Anglicans.[100]

The general view of the denominational offices was that there were not nearly enough clergy in New Zealand if the church was to minister to all its nominal adherents.[101] The precarious funding of denominations surely argued against any massive increase in the number of ministers and priests, but since clergy were paid by parishes, denominations were not concerned about this. The idea that the community needed a set proportion of clergy, as it needed lawyers and doctors, now seems somewhat optimistic. In colonial and post-colonial society, however, clergy had responsibilities, not so much as ministers of congregations but as those who conducted baptisms, marriages and funerals.

In England, Anglican clergy were often funded by historic endowments. The major lack of clergy there was in the towns. It was very different in New Zealand, with its thinly populated country districts.[102] Nevertheless, the Anglicans and Presbyterians divided the whole country into parishes and sought to supply them, although they were dependent on unordained lay readers, home missionaries and others.

In 1871 the Anglican primate (the archbishop) advocated the use of lay readers to meet the need, but this raised the issue of the appropriate role of lay people.[103] The Presbyterian Church solved the problem of the backblocks by appointing home missionaries from 1862 and set up a very active department to administer them. This innovative and economic solution employed a mobile team of minimally educated religious agents, who aimed to provide monthly coverage of services and support in the backblocks. They were centrally administered by the church's Home Mission Department based in Wellington.[104] Other denominations followed suit.

From the 1960s ecumenical cooperation reduced the need for country clergy, while the ordination of non-stipendiary clergy empowered local congregations. This, along with the decline in the number of total adherents, dramatically improved the ratio of Anglican ministers to adherents. By 2006 there was one ordained person for every 361 Anglicans.[105]

Striking new patterns of ministry emerged in the late twentieth century, directly influenced by changes in the international scene. The clergy have ceased to be the officiants of the community. Infant baptisms are less commonly requested, and charismatic ministers from traditional churches have often been cautious about administering infant baptism, long the symbolic difference between congregational churches and parish churches.[106] Meanwhile many couples chose to delay marriage, and legislative changes have made it easy for private officiants to celebrate weddings, while gradually funerals, too, have become secular events.

The staffing of congregations varies greatly. A Presbyterian scholar, Margaret Galt, has classified the religious bodies by types using information reported to Charities New Zealand. This shows that in Wellington independent churches have 25 per cent of the congregations, 30 per cent of the staff and 40 per cent of the income. Anglicans have about 12 per cent of the congregations, 25 per cent of the staff and 15 per cent of the income. The rest are in a grim situation.

In the Pentecostal world, the status of the pastor was greatly elevated. Apostolic and authoritarian notions of leadership were put in place, although along with this went a rapid system of demotion if the pastor was not sufficiently successful. The pastor usually had no more than a basic Bible school training. The focus was sometimes on management and leadership skills.

American mega-church pastoral styles had a powerful influence on the ways in which pastors from many of the proliferating variety of churches developed. For while the mainstream churches faded, new churches flourished, and their success hinged on the style of the pastor as a manager of the Sunday service, which was carefully 'curated' and took enormous degrees of energy and sophisticated musical and other apparatus. Increasingly powerful and authoritarian pastors predominated in independent Protestant churches, sometimes directly influenced by 'apostolic' notions of authority, which proceeded from top to bottom, in contrast to traditional Protestant ideas of authority which was congregationally based. These authority structures gave great respect to the pastors. Congregational members who did not like it simply left. Pastors viewed the church assets as effectively their private property. The result could be very inspirational, as long as you were in tune with the pastor.

The pastor's wife rose in status in these congregations, but this was in effect as a photogenic foil to her husband. In some respects this was no more than a modification of the old role of clergy wife, updated and plastered on billboards. A notable example of this is Hannah Tamaki at Lake City Church (which grew into Destiny Church), whose skills were neatly complementary to those of her husband.[107]

Certainly some of the new churches are sceptical of these trends and have moved towards a community focus. Lifepoint Assembly of God Church in Wellington, Glen Eden Baptist Church and others have focused on community-oriented evangelism and practical community work. A number of Elim Pentecostal churches have employed community pastors.[108]

Other evangelical Protestants have been placed under pressure by these trends. Staffing numbers in some Baptist churches grew significantly as congregations developed a slick style of Sunday service. Commonly the staffing was headed by a senior pastor, while youth, children's and music pastors came and went. Sometimes these congregations also developed community ministries, often struggling to keep their congregations in the transition. Presbyterian and Baptist churches experimented with both possibilities. Salvationists had a community tradition, but not always the pastors who could envision congregations. Even the Brethren, so resolutely opposed to pastors, employed some who sought to adopt the pattern of strong leadership, but then discovered that elders were very reluctant to surrender control.[109]

By the 1970s the vision of a clerical vocation went into rapid decline in the main Protestant denominations. The average age of people coming forward to serve as clergy rose rapidly. This was very problematic for training. Candidates were already spiritually formed when they came. Would they want to undertake a three-year training programme? Was it practical for the church to provide this? How did one train for this kind of ministry? Increasingly ministry has become defined as a job. The role of the spouse has changed hugely, too. Male spouses and gay spouses presented other variations to the pattern, which again changed expectations. Clergy careers, like many other careers, no longer seem set as life vocations. Ministries frequently hit turbulent waters, and ministers are more inclined to give up. As early as the 1990s, Baptist ministries often lasted as little as three years.[110]

As the finances of Anglican, Presbyterian and Methodist parishes have declined, so churches have sought part-time ministers. Such ministries are often less enduring given that ministers have to supplement their incomes from other sources, and congregations and clergy struggle to define expectations. The results are striking, especially in Christchurch following the 2011 earthquake. A Presbyterian minister in Christchurch commented to me about the Alpine Presbytery, which was created in 2014 and covers Canterbury and the West Coast: 'As at [July] 2016 Alpine Presbytery covers 61 parishes. Of these: 21 have full-time ministry — 34 per cent; 4 have part-time ministry — 7 per cent; 12 have Ministry Settlement Boards working in them — 20 per cent; 18 have Interim Moderators in them — 30 per cent.'[111]

An Anglican minister reported on the instability in the Christchurch Diocese and many other denominations:

> When I moved here 9 years ago I was in the Riccarton Avonhead area and in that time every church represented at the 'Ministers Fraternal' has changed leader at

least once. In the Anglican Diocese a significant number of the stipended clergy are in temporary roles (by my count more than one-third). I am not sure that all this instability bodes well for the future of the church. It takes a long time for Church leaders and congregations to grow to trust one another and to be able to give attention to more than just surviving week to week.[112]

There is a similar situation on the North Shore of Auckland, where a period of long-settled ministries has been replaced by a period of unstable ministries, with the risk that a church traumatised by a ministerial crisis can quickly exhaust its members.

This is one extreme. At the other extreme sits the Catholic Church, where there are very few new European priests, and where those who come forward with priestly vocations often subscribe to a romantic view of the older style of Catholic priest and want to use the Latin Mass. Ever since the abandonment of clerical garb, the status of priests had dropped; parishes are likely to have little sympathy with this. Vacant positions are filled by migrants or by elderly priests who maintain the Mass but are unable to provide much pastoral care. So in this respect one of the key components of church life has profoundly shifted, changing the assumptions of past generations.

Convictions of the Faithful

Previous Bishop Arthur Winnington-Ingram of London visited New Zealand in March 1927 for the Empire Settlement Mission. He is shown here with the Auckland Diocesan Immigration Committee at the back of St Matthew's Church. The front row of clergy were leaders of the Auckland diocese, along with the visiting bishop in the biretta. They include Richard Godfrey of the Melanesian Mission; Wiremu Keretene; George MacMurray, who was the Vicar-General; Bishop Wally Averill; Grant Cowan, vicar of St Matthew's; Hector Hawkins, archdeacon in the north; J. Gordon Bell, vicar of Holy Sepulchre; and George Cruickshank, vicar of St Mark's. AUCKLAND ANGLICAN DIOCESAN ARCHIVES

SOME RELIGIONS ARE IN essence private and personal in character. Christianity certainly has an intense personal side to it. Catholicism has a long tradition of inviting its members to 'enter a religious life', by joining a religious order. Protestantism is often interpreted as an adaptation of Christianity to an age of individual identity and effort. Churches with a Reformation heritage expected that each member would live a life of faith and obedience. The evangelical revival of the eighteenth and nineteenth centuries called for personal conversion and advocated a life of dedication within the world, or missionary service. Private prayer and devotions were highly valued by churches, and over the past two centuries the forms of these devotions have changed significantly.[1]

This chapter explores the values of the religious culture, and the ways in which people within the churches expressed their religiosity. Such attitudes were themselves shaped by a cultural and community context. The passionate commitments of lay Christians need to be understood as they developed, and they need to be interpreted within a cultural context. Such views were rarely profoundly theological. There were, however, real differences between Anglicans, other mainstream Protestants, Protestants from smaller churches and Catholics, and these were deeply interwoven into the cultures of faith. They focused partly on beliefs, partly on individual behaviour, and partly on moral codes.

The significant change in the tone of contemporary Christianity has obscured our understanding of the late Victorian and early twentieth-century churches. Today the pattern of Christian behaviour has tended very much to homogeneity, and there is a strong emphasis in the community and among Christians of non-judgementalism. This was not the style of Christians before the 1960s. During the period from 1880 to 1940, in particular, churches and their members energetically and vociferously moralised about the failings of their society.

These phenomena cannot be comprehended without understanding the evangelistic tone of most Christians in the nineteenth and twentieth centuries. The loud voices were intended to bring people and society to repentance and to faith. Our twenty-first-century ears hear these voices as very loud and rude. We should remember, however, that society as a whole was previously very judgemental. The churches believed that they had a designated role in society as the voice of morality and propriety. Exactly what they chose to condemn was up to them, but we do not understand the cultures of faith unless we hear the voice of accusation.

The tones gradually altered over the two centuries, and different parts of the church spoke with their own particular emphases. The loudest and most judgemental voices came from parts of the religious community that were less recognised as mainstream culture. These smaller churches were more naturally inclined to withdraw from society, but many felt sufficient connection to express their concerns about social and moral standards. The Catholic Church was shaped from the 1860s by the 'Syllabus of Errors' in which Pope Pius IX denounced the errors of modern secular society, and not until the Second Vatican Council a century later was this outlook abandoned. The Anglican Church, which counted nearly half the population of New Zealand as its nominal adherents, was much less inclined to strive for a pure Christian culture. It tolerated a high level of disconnection by nominal Anglicans. Anglicans often stood back from the Christian campaigns to reform society, and hoped that this would make them more attractive to their nominal members.

At the opposite extreme, the Salvation Army presented itself as the people's church, with music and practices that appealed to the working class. But it was surprisingly sectarian, exclusive, doctrinally separate from most other Christian groups, and prepared to exploit its acceptability to the New Zealand Army at the cost of good relations with other churches.

The CMS was very different from mainstream Anglicanism. Shaped within the evangelical movement of England, which sought to challenge the lax religiosity of the period, it promoted a tight moral code. Missionaries insisted that Māori show evidence of moral transformation before being baptised. There were further tests for admission to Communion. Although the CMS theology focused on grace, in practice it had a strong emphasis on self-improvement.

From his Ahuriri station near Napier, William Colenso issued a list of 12 prohibitions imposed upon those who wished to take Communion, which included not working on the Sabbath, no card-playing, limited commercial relationships with Europeans, and no drinking of rum, riding for pleasure or oppressing the vulnerable.[2] Ironically, Colenso's own morality failed these tests when he was found to have fathered a child by a Māori woman in his mission; as a result, his licence as a priest was revoked.

Māori parishes remained more conservative, and Māori priests constantly surveyed their flocks for misdemeanours. Similarly, Wesleyan Methodist and other denominations maintained a boundary between truly moral members and the fringe adherents who had not fully been admitted into the church.

Private devotions and religious behaviour underlay many of the cultural themes. These devotional practices had been disrupted by migration; the migrant ship was an unsympathetic place in which to say one's prayers. Lady Mary Anne Barker, who wrote about her life in Canterbury from 1865 to 1868, noted that this became worse in the early days of the new settlement: 'It is really melancholy to see the different ways in which God's name and service is slighted in the [New] World. On the ship there were only a few who seemed to think anything beyond

Me penei ano, e koe. Tirohia tau mahi me tau wakahaere, e rite ana ranei ki ta te wakapono? A, e kite koe, kua he tetahi wahi, hiahia ranei, kupu ranei, mahi ranei, na, me tangi mo tau hara, me waki atu hoki ki te Atua, kia u hoki te ngakau ki te mahi i te pai amuri ake nei. A ki te mea kua kino koe ki te tangata, me hohou ta korua rongo, me wakautu hoki, kaua e kaiponuhia kia rite ra ano te utu. Na, ki te pena koe, tahuri mai, wakarongo ki tenei kupu pai a Hoani, *"Ki te hara tetahi, he Kai-Inoi to tatou kei te Matua, ko Ihu te Karaiti tika; a ko Ia te wakamarietanga mo a tatou hara."* 1 Hoani, 2. 1.

Tirohia hoki, e koe, ta Matiu, 11., r. 28, 29.

E ta, kia kite koe, he mea te Hapa Tapu nei na te Atua; he mea wakahari i te tangata e kai tika ana, he mea wakamate hoki ki te tangata ekore e tika te kai. Koia ahau ka wakahau nei i a koe, kia waka-arohia e koe i tenei takiwa te nui o tenei mea tapu, a kia rapu koe, kia wawa iho ki roto ki tou hine-ngaro ki tou ngakau; kaua ano hoki e mahi hia-nga, e pera me te hunga e tinihanga ana ki te Atua; engari kia tika. Kia pai ai tau haere mai ki tenei Hakari.

Tirohia, e koe, 1 Koriniti, 11., r. 28, 29, 30, 31.

TUKUA TENEI TANGATA KI ROTO,

Na te Koreneho.

A class ticket for Māori issued in 1847. Methodist class tickets were used to admit to the class meeting and to Communion. William Colenso of the Church Missionary Society issued an equivalent which entitled a person to take Communion, thereby acting more strictly than was usual for Anglicans. Both sides of the card are shown. HAWKE'S BAY MUSEUMS TRUST, RUAWHARO TĀ-Ū-RANGI, 22320

the form and here there is no care at all.'[3] The early years in the colonies were also unsympathetic to religious practices.

The devout person said their prayers and had other devotional practices. For most ordinary Christians a few simple prayers on waking up and especially when going to bed were at the heart of their devotional life. Most of these prayers were learned in childhood, at Sunday school and from the mother. The rosary for Catholics, the Lord's Prayer for Protestants, and other simple blessings were very well known. Devout Protestant families would also have devotions at the family meal table. While there were important differences between the practices of Catholics and Protestants, Anglicans were very similar to other Protestants, although they generally used the Book of Common Prayer to guide their devotions, and many families probably brought a copy with them to the colony.

At the heart of Protestantism in the nineteenth century lay an emphasis on redemption, the cycle of sin and forgiveness. This theology, and Protestant devotional practices, was reinforced by the revivalism of the late nineteenth century. It was a simple theology of the fear of Hell, the hope of Heaven and the forgiveness in the cross.[4] Some reacted against this emphasis. Maurice Gee's novel *Plumb* reflects this, with its semi-biographical account of Gee's grandfather, James Chapple, who left the Presbyterian Church in 1910, finding himself 'no longer nourished by a penitential religion'.[5]

In the late nineteenth century, the availability of cheap Bibles and changing views of conversion and personal spirituality led to the emergence of organisations that aimed to inculcate a personal calendar into the spirituality of ordinary believers. Scripture Union and the Bible Reading Fellowship both worked for what became called 'the quiet time', a private time of Bible reading and prayer in which God spoke directly to the person, especially focusing on teaching the habit to children. Scripture Union became very active in New Zealand after 1930, and 39,000 people were using its Bible reading material at its height in 1962.[6]

Sales of the Bible rose significantly after World War II as new translations became available, yet indications in Bible Society surveys, especially from the 1990s, were that biblical literacy had declined sharply.[7] Whether this means that the disciplines of prayer had also declined we do not know.

Strikingly, the penitential pattern of Christianity became less characteristic of mainstream Protestantism in the later twentieth century, with much more emphasis on divine goodness, God's love and peace. Within the charismatic world, celebration and a search for spiritual benefits became characteristic.

Catholic devotion changed radically in the nineteenth century, and the impact of this on Irish Catholics was particularly marked. Emmet Larkin's account of the devotional revolution notes that the lax levels of Catholic practice in the eighteenth century were radically changed through the influence of Archbishop Paul Cullen. As a result, Irish Catholics increased their level of church attendance and confession, and developed devotion to the Sacred Heart, praying the rosary and joining confraternities. Certainly New Zealand Catholicism demonstrated all these features, and levels of practice rose strikingly during the first hundred years of the church in New Zealand.[8]

THE CHURCHES TO A lesser or greater degree felt the need to define who was in and who was out. In order to create a sense of belonging it was necessary to clarify who was straying. For Anglicans and Catholics, and to a lesser extent for other Protestants, the boundaries of the church were defined by the sacraments. Baptism was for most the rite of passage into the world. Certificates of baptism were carefully preserved. The tradition of an annotated family Bible began first with entries in the old Bible, but increasingly grand Bibles were purchased and dates were entered for crucial events.

The churches struggled to control and discipline their members. Excommunication was sometimes used to punish immoral behaviour, particularly sex outside of marriage; other behaviour was harder to control. Churches resorted to private admonitions. A few more sectarian churches publicly denounced erring members, but mostly they preferred to admonish the congregation in general terms.

Villagers in traditional England used ducking pools, tin-canning and other practices to shame the immoral. The church urged people to act properly, but beyond this, lay behaviour was often ignored. The English ecclesiastical courts governing immoral behaviour had become inactive in the early nineteenth century, and the Anglican Church in New Zealand did not seek to revive them or find an equivalent. It went against their outlook that the church needed to speak to all, saints and sinners.

A characteristic part of Anglican spirituality (although by no means restricted to Anglicans) was a deep reverence for the monarchy and the United Kingdom, even though the colonists now lived far from it. During services Anglicans prayed for the monarch, and they regarded the faith and example of the monarch as an inspiration to Britons everywhere. The monarch's religion and devotion to family life made a religious patina very natural in the later nineteenth century and through most of the twentieth century (with the exception of the reigns of Edward VII and Edward VIII).

Anglicans consequently tended to regard the official acts of state as divinely ordained. They showed deep respect for those who acted heroically on behalf of Britain. The laying up of regimental colours in churches seems to reflect a state church, but it is a reflection of the residual attitudes within New Zealand Anglicanism, as, for example, in the military flags that hang in St Mary's in New Plymouth, and hung in ChristChurch Cathedral before the 2011 earthquake. All churches in wartime saw loyalty as a religious duty, and most churches ended services with the singing of the national anthem. Still, New Zealand churches, Anglican or otherwise, rarely displayed the national flag within the church, unlike churches in the United States.

The churches expected the state for its part to be righteous, and this was why they joined in political campaigns. Protestants urged prayer for the wellbeing of the nation when it was threatened. When, following the hanging of three Fenians in Manchester, there was an outburst of public excitement across Australasia, the churches played a key role in this. Every denomination including Catholics held special services, with crowds of attendees who enthusiastically sang the national anthem.[9]

On civic occasions, the older tradition of separate denominational services began to wane. During the South African War, when the citizens of Wanganui gathered to farewell its men of the Third Contingent, a joint service 'of a purely undenominational character' was held at the racecourse, led by Anglican, Presbyterian, Wesleyan and Baptist ministers. The sermons and hymns on that day, with their view of service as sacrifice, and the empire as an instrument of God, were a practice run for the religious response at the outset of World War I.[10] The Great War (as it was termed) helped to shape a united community committed to service and sacrifice, and it led to the modern Anzac Day service in which Christian symbols have been selectively used and modified into a commemoration of the virtues of nationalism. Today the nation is viewed as our fundamental community, in which rugby victories and America's Cup wins are seen as shared triumphs. Now, however, there is little room for traditional religion in the formula.

In the late nineteenth century, church and state worked together on this enterprise. The Anglican Primate, Bishop Julius, commented along these lines at the farewell in the Domain in Auckland for troops on the way to the Boer War:

> To settle racial antagonisms by an appeal to arms is undeniably contrary to the spirit of Christianity; but it is equally undeniable that, without the power and will to resist aggression, a Christian Empire cannot in these days carry out its mission in the world. Never was a greater mission bestowed on any nation than that of our own Empire at the present time. The influence of English-speaking people extends to every part of the inhabited globe. Our language is spoken in all lands, on all seas. Our soldiers and sailors and our merchants identify British citizenship with justice and freedom. It is the mission of our race, entrusted

to us by Almighty God, to spread abroad among all peoples the love of justice and freedom and brotherhood. If the day ever comes when the Empire shall be indifferent to the spreading abroad of these principles, or shall shrink from the cost — in blood and money — that its high mission involves, the decline and fall of the Empire will have begun. To maintain the position of influence for good now held by our race, all the subjects of Queen Victoria seem to be willing to do what they can. A man cannot do more for any cause than to be willing to lay down his life on its behalf.[11]

The church was keen to shape the community response to military crises. For example, when news arrived of the Relief of Mafeking during the South African War the Invercargill harvest festival was postponed and replaced by a service of commemoration.[12] The churches had a formal role in Anzac Day services in the early years, and were sometimes entrusted with the organisation of the music and seating.[13] This aspect changed when these services became the responsibility of the Returned Services' Association. In the postwar period the RSA shaped these civic events and their evocative rituals, and chose the clergymen it considered suitable.[14]

With regard to mission and missionaries, the church preferred to focus on work further afield. Overseas missionaries had a special status in the church. Women missionaries were encouraged to speak in church about their experiences, even though other women were obliged to remain silent. Support for missionary endeavour united and preoccupied churches. International awareness grew rapidly in the twentieth century, often shaped by newspaper reports and influenced by imperial alliances and international preoccupations.

Mission played a changing role in the culture of the churches of New Zealand over a long period. Missionary endeavour gradually developed a huge appeal. The roots of this lay in the nineteenth century. In a fascinating new year sermon, the Rev. William Morley, then minister of Pitt Street Methodist Church in Auckland, surveyed the glories of the previous 50 years. He thought that the greatest glory of the churches was the vast increase of Christian mission, but lamented that, 'if the Church had been thoroughly in earnest, for every one there had been ten such men — and that there has not been may well humble us'.[15]

By the 1930s leaders of the Methodist Church sensed that a compelling missionary interest mobilised sentiment and commitment in a remarkable way.[16] Other churches felt the same. These missionary aspirations inspired an elite within the churches. Those with the greatest zeal went out to serve the churches in many places throughout the world in a range of social, medical, educational and evangelistic activities. Others poured energy into raising support for those missionaries, and in particular women members found this an area that inspired their creativity.

Anglicans and some other Protestants often happily embraced all positive religious forces in the community, and for this reason Freemasons in full regalia sometimes had church parades. This relationship provoked sharp disagreements within the churches. Catholics banned membership of the Freemasons, although the Hibernians seem like a Catholic equivalent.

Protestants were sharply divided. Freemasonry attracted many of the leading business and professional men in the cities, and Freemasonry was quasi-religious. Consequently Freemasons liked to hold church parades dressed in their aprons, and some churches had very strong Masonic connections, which often came out in the desire that there be Masonic dedications of new buildings. The first St Mary's in Timaru was consecrated with Masonic rituals.[17] The fine building of Hawera Methodist Church still has two columns that appear to be Masonic symbols.[18] Balclutha Wesleyan Church also commenced with such ceremonies in 1880.[19] When the Remuera Masonic Lodge was built in 1880 across the road from St Mark's Anglican Church the service of consecration started in the church and proceeded to the lodge, so intertwined was the membership.[20] Dunedin

The Palmerston North Methodist Mutual Improvement Society in 1889. A very popular society, which was open to both men and women (although only men are apparent in this picture), it provided debating, discussion and the exploration of improving educational topics.
PALMERSTON NORTH LIBRARIES AND COMMUNITY SERVICES

Anglican Cathedral included Masonic ritual in the laying of its foundation stone in 1915.[21] St Matthew's Anglican Church in Auckland planned a Masonic ceremony to precede its dedication service in 1905 but this was banned by Bishop Neligan.[22]

This sympathy to Freemasonry continued through much of the twentieth century. The Bible Society General Secretary in the interwar years used Masonic networks to find members of his executive.[23] Dean John Rymer of Auckland Anglican Cathedral in the 1970s was probably the last prominent Freemason minister. Other Protestants circulated anti-Freemason literature, and the Rev. Richard Colegrove denounced Freemasonry at the 1979 Auckland Synod.[24] By then, membership of Freemasonry was in deep decline and the issue lost its relevance.

CATHOLIC MORAL CONTROLS OPERATED differently from those of Protestants. The Catholic emphasis, deeply ingrained in its members, was around the defence of the church and its reputation. Catholics took pride in their schools and they defended their priests and nuns from secular criticism. In 1876 Bishop Patrick Moran of Dunedin brought a libel case against the *Evening Star*, which had reprinted a claim that a former priest had married a Dunedin nun, and fiercely defended Catholic hostility to Freemasonry.[25]

Lay Catholic experience was increasingly shaped by membership of the 'sodalities' and other societies. In effect every parishioner belonged to at least one of these, and was supposed to attend weekly meetings and appear in regalia at the appropriate monthly Mass. For men there were the Holy Name Society, the Knights of the Southern Cross and the Hibernians; for women the Sacred Heart sodality and the Catholic Women's League; for girls the Children of Mary, and for boys the honour of being an altar boy.[26] The levels of attendance grew significantly in the early twentieth century.

Catholics took pride in their Irishness but, as the scholar Chris van der Krogt has argued, they did not form a separate world; they traded and interacted with Protestants and were very angry when their schools were excluded from sporting competitions with state schools. Catholics were therefore happiest when they could be distinctive in their religion but relate inconspicuously with Protestants in other aspects of their lives.[27] In the 1960s they campaigned against abortion in alliance with conservative Protestants, but they had always been active in politics with an eye to Irish and working-class causes.

The Protestant moral framework is often conceived as essentially moralistic and restrictive, but other aspects of Protestant values were just as important. Many Protestants had been shaped by the evangelical awakening. For such church members the moment of conversion was a shared value.[28] Evangelical Protestants were shaped by the doctrine of grace, and the experience of conversion, and this infused their hymns and preaching. The conversion narrative was hugely respected.

These Protestants could hardy comprehend Catholic sacramental theology. As early as the 1890s denominational leaders were uncomfortable with the narrowness of this conception of theology, and in the 1930s Colin Scrimgeour argued for a non-doctrinal religiosity. Within the Presbyterian and Methodist churches, many laity were suspicious of fundamentalist styles of religious belief long before Professor Lloyd Geering, principal of the Presbyterian Theological Hall, gained a strong body of support among educated laity in the 1960s for his suggestion that the resurrection needed to be understood in figurative terms.

Evangelicals were enormously active in nineteenth-century England, and an evangelical tone characterised most lay religious actions before 1960. Other forms of conservative Protestantism (for example, Presbyterian Calvinism) tended to become more evangelical in the dominion. This evangelicalism became increasingly combative in the twentieth century, defending the authorised version and six-day creationism, and fighting rearguard actions against any attempt to change doctrinal statements and denominational traditions. Thus they were very like High Church Anglicans and conservative Catholics, the very people whom they regarded most suspiciously. Meanwhile liberal Protestants backed internationalist and anti-racist causes with as much vigour and in similar ways to those who backed conservative causes.

Smaller denominations were inevitably more sectarian, despite the intense dislike with which outsiders viewed this. The weekly Auckland paper *Observer* treated such people with contempt but also with pity: 'The average public accuser who moves between his own home and his little bethel, who sees nothing, lacks sympathy, tact and humanity, and who condemns a whole community on poisonous hearsay evidence is a special kind of blight, not particularly dangerous, because no one takes him seriously . . .'[29] So evangelicals had a similar public reputation to Catholics for narrow bigotry.

By the twentieth century the hot issues were often biblical infallibility and evolution. A huge public lecture was held in Auckland in 1929 to attack the views of the Anglican modernist Henry Major, who was on a return visit to his New Zealand homeland.[30] The heart of the issue was the approach of 'Higher Criticism' to the Bible as a work that needed to be viewed as shaped by human ideas rather than as the words of God. The same issue provoked very sharp debates in Methodism and in Presbyterianism.[31] There was a huge level of popular conviction in the absolute truth of the words of scripture, but there was also an educated lay elite suspicious of literalism.

One debate that gained fresh energy in the twentieth century was the controversy over Darwinism. In the nineteenth century, as the Otago University scholar John Stenhouse has argued, only a small minority of people within the church rejected the doctrine outright. The most noted debate took place in Dunedin in 1876 when the Wesleyan preacher Alfred Fitchett was refused membership of the YMCA for his support of the Darwinist doctrine.[32] The debate became sharper in the early twentieth century as the fundamentalist view of scripture became more clearly defined.[33] This was in effect an aspect of the debate over the truth of scripture, but crusaders like Baptist medical missionary Dr William Pettit and D. S. Milne's anti-evolutionary society also used it to criticise the school curriculum.[34]

These are all striking illustrations of the intellectual discomfort of traditional Christianity in the twentieth century. In effect, conservative Christians were increasingly askew of contemporary views and values, for example, on sexuality, on science and on what was broadly called 'secular humanism'. The contemporary church debates on homosexuality and on science have a long history.[35]

CRUCIAL TO THE CULTURE of Victorian Christianity was subscription to a moral code that shaped behaviour and taboos. From the very earliest days of Christianity in New Zealand, churches reinforced this code. When, for example, the missionaries discovered the sexual infidelities of Thomas Kendall and his wife, they were swift to shun them.

John Bluck and others have argued that an abiding legacy of New Zealand's Protestant background is its sour puritanism.[36] The so-called puritans were a significant part of the religious scene in a range of churches. Someone reflecting on a particular style of Brethren leader in the early twentieth century recollected, 'You could almost perceive puffs of sulphurous smoke from their nostrils.'[37] Such views were widespread. Country communities were conservative, and disapproval of divorce was strong (and the marriage of the monarch to a divorced woman unthinkable). On the other hand, rates of premarital sex were high. The churches learned ways to overlook 'shotgun weddings', as they were termed.[38]

The general community viewed such attitudes as hypocrisy. The popular newspaper *Truth* declared, 'The Methodist business man is at heart a humbug, a sordid shekel snarer, and a sweater of the worst possible type, who would run his own mother in harness if he thought he could show a profit on her.'[39] Catholics were contemptuous of the puritan outlook. While Catholic moral outrage could be intense on matters of personal ethics, they were relaxed about styles of leisure and drinking. Protestants would have been horrified if they attended the bazaar held by

Whangarei's Catholic parish in 1898 and saw one of the parishioners disguised as a gypsy fortune-teller reading palms.[40]

Evangelical churches felt a great obligation to restrain the 'flesh', for the body was perceived to be the greatest threat to Christian values. The enemy lay within, in the subtle pressures that undermined the faith and standing of individual members of the church. Here lay the most profound and difficult struggles. The personal aspect of religion is clearly intertwined with the social, and faith was expected to be reflected in personal and bodily behaviour.

Sexual misdemeanours were the greatest concern, perhaps because in New Zealand there was a certain laxness towards misdemeanours prior to marriage. As Sarah Dalton notes in her analysis, men were thought to have natural sexual impulses, which needed an outlet, whereas women were expected to remain content.[41] The church strongly opposed the Contagious Diseases Acts, but also objected to colonial prostitution.[42] The evangelical churches were concerned that women could so easily lose their innocence and purity, and become hardened to good advice.[43] Colonial males operated on a code that emphasised control of the body and contact between bodies. Protestant church codes added to this the middle-class rules in which formalities needed to be observed. The kiss between women was a distinctive feature of the sectarian community, but there was nothing like this between men. The mainstream churches limited expression of sociability to the handshake, which implied that church members were not closely related to each other. The bodily functions were hidden away. There was no toilet in church buildings erected before the 1950s.

Masturbation and sexual experience outside of marriage was the ultimate defilement of the body, and churches were very uncomfortable with such issues.[44] The shyness on the topic may explain why sexual abusers in churches were often undetected. Often references to such issues were so vague that it is difficult to be sure of the subject, or whether prostitution was the issue.[45] Addresses on masturbation were occasionally given to young men, for example by Henry Varley, Joseph Berry and John Hosking, in the nineteenth-century cities.[46] When Dr William Pettit was employed to lecture to troops heading to World War I he was explicit in his warnings of the risk of venereal disease if they resorted to prostitutes.[47]

There were many ways in which the body of the believer was supposed to reflect their faith in God. A favourite text in the evangelical world was that one's body is a temple of the Holy Spirit. The obligation to maintain personal self-discipline was powerful.

One concern was smoking. This was a very popular social activity in the community, and missionaries often used tobacco as a way to buy the attention of Māori. Many a Catholic priest was a heavy smoker. But smoking was strongly associated with drinking, and this affected its reputation.[48] From the 1880s Wesleyan speakers regularly condemned smoking, and there were firm statements at the 1878 and 1879 conferences.[49] (It should be remembered that Robert Stout, the noted freethinker and politician, also condemned it in his newspaper, the *Echo*.)[50] When the prominent minister Joseph Smalley spoke at conference in answer to a temperance delegation, he noted that all candidates for the ministry were asked if they smoked, and he suggested that two-thirds did not. Voices from the floor forced him twice to raise his estimate, first to three-quarters and finally to nine-tenths.[51]

The Women's Christian Temperance Union expressed deep concern at reports that boys of just 14 years old were smoking, and during the war the union was troubled by reports of cigarettes being sent to the front and women smoking at home.[52] Evangelicals were passionate on the issue, and felt that others were soft on the subject.[53] There was particular concern when women smoked, which seemed more outrageous (and more common after World War I).[54] By the 1960s churches were uncomfortable with the puritan condemnation of smoking, but by then medical evidence of its risks had emerged.[55]

Another example of immoral behaviour was gambling. The Presbyterian Church was strongest in its opposition, and urged the state to stand firm against pressures from the racing fraternity to loosen controls. Young people were frequently exhorted to eschew gambling.[56] The heart of the concern was that people could not be trusted to act responsibly — that young people would be so caught up with the lure of winning that they would not know how to stop and thus cast savings and home priorities to the wind. Again their criticisms provoked cries of hypocrisy and inconsistency. For example, when the Dunedin Presbytery criticised the racing industry in 1929 it was accused of using one of its parishes to show movies of questionable morals.[57]

The lips were also important — profanities were a high disgrace. The fear was that corrupt language effectively defiled the body from within, making it coarse and comfortable with bad behaviour of other kinds. The churches thus were renowned for a series of negatives, urging young men to disavow drinking, smoking, cursing and swearing, and going to the movies.[58]

THE ISSUE OF DRINKING and temperance is profoundly linked with this view of the defilement of the body. For while it is not within the scope of this book to explore the political campaign for prohibition, the temperance movement arose from the definition of sin as a kind of pollution. So temperance became a profound movement within the churches, shaping and sharpening their culture and life for many years. Within the larger Protestant churches some sought for a broader theology in which personal change was less important than the transformation of society. The prohibition movement had a vision for personal and social transformation in which pollution would be replaced with purity.

Malton Murray, the eloquent General Secretary of the New Zealand Alliance in the 1930s, saw the political task as being to convince the masses that 'there is neither economic, social nor moral salvation to be found in the continuance of the liquor traffic'.[59] While the political campaigners had to be careful not to demand moral reform, it was hard to keep such language out of the discussion. Biblical analogies were constantly evoked in prohibitionist meetings.[60] Here is an example from an impeccable fundamentalist source in 1926: 'Is it not time — it is time — it is long overdue — when the common sense of the community will declare this thing shall not be and no longer shall we tolerate this sacrifice of our sons and daughters to the Moloch of drink.'[61] The thick language of religiosity made little sense to those from other backgrounds, but its aim was to convince the converted that the uphill struggle was worth it. Temperance flourished on lurid stories of 'spirit-maddened men and gin-sodden women'.[62]

In 1896 the Congregational Union declared the last Sunday in November should be temperance Sunday, in order to get support from the churches.[63] Malton Murray sought to inspire Christians in the belief that 'the cumulative effect of the work of hundreds or even thousands of small groups conscientiously working will prove a moral, spiritual and material force that the traffic cannot withstand . . . The premonitions of a great awakening are thrilling through the land.'[64] Churches were in fact relatively loath to spend too much time on the issue in services.

Temperance mobilised an enormous number of church people into crusading mode, including children and women but also adult men, although men were less willing to be activists given that they were resistant to the temperance message.[65] Women aspired to get men to take the pledge, but the cause seemed hopeless without legislation.[66] So prohibitionists mingled personal effort, evangelism and moral and political reform. Altogether the work was a high and holy aspiration.

Wowser culture was naïve in both its methods and its goals. The teetotal movement was more like a club or a cult than a church, with aims to purify society by symbolic pledges. It became a popular political movement that attracted a huge number of people into democratic politics who previously had felt excluded — and this applies to men as well as women. It was also a movement of health reform, or of self-conscious modernisation of social structures. It was a gendered movement in the way it gave agency to women who were otherwise disempowered.[67] It was also deeply rooted in a religious culture, and those who, like the Stouts, were not religious campaigners, had to endure a great deal of evangelical sermonising.[68] As a religious culture, it expanded the zone of church life, taking clergy and congregations into common spaces where Protestant culture and life were renewed and redirected. Arguably it was more a religious culture in New Zealand than in some other places, because of the strength of the churches that supported it.

Church culture directly intersected with wider culture in the temperance movement. In New Zealand, from the early days temperance had a loose affiliation to the churches, with early total-abstainer societies mostly located in the churches.[69] Temperance advocates also emphasised that it was a scientific health reform.[70]

Many forces were tangled up in this campaign, which expressed simultaneously in contradictory ways the desire to convert people, the desire to reform society, and the desire for the church to be an instrument of good. In the process the temperance campaigners grew very frustrated with the churches, suggesting that it was much easier to do Christian good outside the churches than within, where so much energy was wasted on procedures.[71]

In practice temperance work was primarily directed towards the young, who were invited to take the pledge in Sunday schools and join 'bands of hope', church clubs for those who had taken the pledge. Members of the bands of hope grew massively in the late 1880s. The Temperance Committee of the Wesleyan Church felt the need to keep temperance organisations under the control of the local church, 'because we think that by these means we can maintain a better oversight of our people, especially the young and guarantee the correctness of their teaching and associations'.[72] Temperance sometimes drew people and their energies into its own organisations, like the Good Templars and the Women's Christian Temperance Union (WCTU).

In 1869 the West Taieri Total Abstinence Society convinced the Rev. William Gillies and his Presbyterian Session of Elders that they needed to become abstainers so that the church could be active in the matter.[73] Some people in that and other congregations were uncomfortable. They felt coerced.[74] It was one thing to get the young people to join bands of hope but quite another to pressure an adult congregation. The Good Templars tried to urge churches to preach on temperance.[75] The persuasion of Mrs Mary Leavitt, who came from America in 1885 to urge the creation of a branch of the WCTU, transformed the movement and made it more acceptable.

The test of denominational commitment was their willingness to use unfermented wine in Communion, thus purifying the churches so that they could be involved in the sacred mission. As early as 1856 the new Nelson Methodist Church had debated the issue, and experimented with using two cups in order to test opinions.[76] By 1888 most Protestant denominations were under pressure to change, and this led to the use of individual cups from about 1900.⁷⁷ In the late 1890s the Wesleyan Church and the Congregational Union both resolved that liquor sellers could not be office holders in the church.⁷⁸ Only the Primitive Methodists and the Salvation Army ever made the pledge a condition of membership, but the Wesleyan Temperance Committee was proud to be able to tell the 1887 conference that all Wesleyan ministers and probationers and nine-tenths of members were teetotallers.⁷⁹

A distinctive aspect of the Christian temperance movement was the Blue Ribbon campaign. In 1884 T. W. Glover, from the United Kingdom Alliance, visited New Zealand for an extensive campaign, and in 1885 his colleague Richard Booth came for a shorter tour. Booth collected 10,000 pledges, and 20,000 people agreed to wear the blue ribbon.⁸⁰ This gospel temperance preaching highlighted the religious aspect. A New Zealand Methodist minister, Leonard Isitt, also held temperance missions in churches of various denominations.⁸¹ Some prohibition campaigners disliked what was known as 'Blue Ribbonism'. Secular temperance campaigners were annoyed at the religious tone it gave to temperance.⁸² The Blue Ribboners thought that evangelism with temperance thrown in was a powerful combination.⁸³ In the later 1870s Fr Patrick Hennebery addressed many Catholic parishes, calling for men to abandon the booze and return to the church.

A number of church leaders had grave doubts about the call to take the pledge. Some fundamentalists opposed it, including the evangelist Charles Hinman, who was convinced that it gave men improvement without redemption.⁸⁴ Most Anglican and Catholic clergy were very cautious. Not all were as rude as the Rev. Vicesimus Lush, vicar of Thames, who when asked to preach a temperance sermon chose as his text Ecclesiasticus 31:28 on the virtues of wine.⁸⁵ Many feared that the church was engaging in moralism rather than religion, and that this was a secularisation of the church's message.

After World War I the church campaign for prohibition rapidly collapsed, although the commitment to temperance remained. In 1949 the Methodist Conference polled its representatives and found that 1147 were in favour of continuing a prohibition stance, while 212, mostly younger delegates, wanted it abandoned.⁸⁶ Yet it took another 30 years for the churches to admit that many of their members had no qualms about imbibing.

It would be wrong to view the prohibition movement as a gigantic distraction for the churches. As the campaign became more political, it forced many conservative and inward-looking church people to focus on society as a whole. The editor of the prohibitionist magazine the *Vanguard*, W. H. Judkins, believed it was a movement that inclined many otherwise conservative people towards social reform, which the church failed to embrace at its peril:

the church must lay hold of this great modern movement and turn it in the right direction . . . The masses must move or be enslaved, and the church must direct them so that they move in the right direction. To this end it must try to solve economic problems, but from the standpoint of Jesus Christ, to save men wholly, completely, in the sense in which He desired their salvation. Economic conditions will not be altered till the church alters them by wise legislation; but side by side with that must go the preaching of the Gospel of Salvation. To me, this social reform movement is a religious movement.[87]

This merging of the social with the religious was a significant result of the prohibition campaign. Congregationalists without any hesitation identified the drink traffic as 'one of the greatest obstacles to the extension of the kingdom of God on earth'.[88]

The next step for some of these campaigners was to broaden their attempt to elevate society and to campaign for improvement in the conditions of the poor, not just remove their temptations. For men like Walter Nash, the organiser of the Church of England Men's Society and later Labour politician, and the Baptist minister and president of the Labour Party, John Archer, socialism was profoundly Christian. There is a direct trajectory between the prohibitionists and Labour Party members who responded to the debates of the 1970s with strong support for nuclear bans and Māori aspirations, and reacted to the racism of the rugby union's relationships with South Africa. They would regard temperance as appallingly moralising and individualistic, but modern Christian political actions are in continuity with the temperance campaign. All share a passionate moralism and the belief that politics ought to focus on improving the values of the world.

There were, however, conservative themes in the prohibition movement, focusing on the defence of the family. Prohibitionists worried about what was good for the families of the nation, while a later generation of campaigners regarded the feminist movement as a threat to family life. Anne Morrow's 'Save Our Families' campaign in the late 1970s mobilised Pentecostals as political objectors. Again that mobilisation was sometimes more important than the concerns that motivated it. A member of Save Our Families might by now be a passionate greenie or a campaigner for homosexual marriage — although probably in a different church.

So this moralising culture remained although it evolved in its approaches and targets. There were also variations between denominations. Religious campaigners had much in common, whether their cause was divorce law, or unsought pregnancies, or sexuality. In each case they felt that the church needed to speak out on current debates. Although different groups engaged in different disputes, eruptions of concern were natural within the Christian community.

A parade through the streets of Wellington by Catholics attending the Eucharistic Congress held February 1940 to help celebrate the hundredth anniversary of modern New Zealand. Notice the orders of nuns in white. EVENING POST, 5 FEBRUARY 1940, ALEXANDER TURNBULL LIBRARY

It is easy to say that the churches ought to be more accepting, more loving or kinder. From the first centuries of church history, churches voiced moral concerns and defined 'canon law' against immoral acts, for they were constitutionally inclined to build fences, to frame definitions of wrong-doing. Individual Christians and congregations were at risk of straying, and the church, which learned through scripture, wanted definite answers to modern questions as well.

TODAY ON THE WHOLE the church operates indoors, located in private spaces, and even its appearances in public places do not suggest that it is a public institution. Certainly there are occasional crusades in public arenas, street appearances and arresting billboards, but the public space is largely occupied by commercial organisations, and by political banners at election time. Annual Santa parades, for example, very rarely have any religious content or contributors.

Such was not the case over the first century of the churches in New Zealand. Frequently the Salvation Army aroused both ire and enthusiasm by street preaching. Still there were other places where the church could not be found. When Dr Stuart of Knox Church in Dunedin visited the goldfields in the late 1860s and saw the lack of religious provision for the miners, he was horrified that there was no church extension fund to support a missionary. He was soon able to mobilise energy from his huge congregation to fund James McCosh Smith's evangelistic work.[89]

By the 1930s some churches were eager to put Christianity out on the streets in the face of the prevailing secular atmosphere. On Good Friday small processions of witness walked silently through the streets of Auckland, organised by the Church Union (a High Church body).[90] The Salvation Army organised an Easter sunrise service on Mount Eden in 1935, imitating services held at the Hollywood Bowl in Los Angeles from about 1919.[91] In Wellington from 1939 to 1941 an interdenominational service was held on Mount Victoria and another was begun on Mount Eden in Auckland.[92] This reflected an ecumenical era as the main Protestant churches sought to work together, and the national broadcasting of major religious events worked in favour of the service. Attendances could reach 3000 — large enough to warrant special traffic arrangements. A 60-foot-high white cross was placed on Mount Victoria as a sign of Easter. These services were significant events, but there was some desecration of the Easter cross in 1945 and attendance slowly faded in the 1950s.[93] Today it is very unusual to see street preachers except in South Auckland.

The streets were occupied again during the Jesus Revolution of the 1970s. Youth activists joined with others in 1972 to hold loud marches for Jesus, and there were marches for righteousness down the main streets of many cities. The crowds were large and jubilant, even though the message was a strange admixture of conservative protest and public zeal.[94] Both themes have recurred in various public events over the years.

In 2005, when Destiny Church took to the streets with its 'Enough is Enough' campaign, there was palpable outrage and even fear, despite the long history of religious displays and protests.[95] Other Pentecostal churches were cautious about being linked with the negative exposure that it produced for them. Destiny clearly reckoned that all publicity is good publicity, and it has since been stalked by the media. As Greta Bond has argued, these public performances by Destiny and others demonstrate their understanding of society and how it is to be changed.[96] The subsequent anti-smacking public protests in 2008 were similarly divisive.

There is another model, however, in the 1998 Hīkoi of Hope. This long march was initiated by the Tikanga Māori group in the General Synod of the Anglican Church, and drew widespread support from churches and secular people as it made its way through the country towards Wellington. Although its actual demands were somewhat diffuse, it did remind the government of the day that church groups were concerned about the social needs of the country. It paved the way for an agreement made with the Labour Government, and continued since, for regular meetings between church leaders and key government ministers.[97]

Corpus Christi processions, of expositions of the Blessed Sacrament, and of sacramental devotion were revived by twentieth-century Catholicism. Generally these annual processions travelled from convent to church, reciting prayers on the way, but did not stray onto the secular streets.

It was the Eucharistic congresses that revived the medieval tradition of parading on the streets.[98] At one of the first such congresses in London, in 1908, there had been a brutal dispute with the Liberal Government, which refused to allow the procession through the city.[99]

In February 1921 the Catholic Church in Dunedin celebrated its fiftieth jubilee with a long progression from the cathedral to the priory gardens, with the children from the Catholic schools, the Hibernians, and the Children of Mary in white veils, and the Blessed Sacrament paraded with roses thrown in front of it.[100] The visual display showed how much the Catholic vision differed from the rational format of Protestant events. However, the procession may not have strayed into the Protestant streets.

Bishop Liston certainly carried a monstrance with the Blessed Sacrament down St Benedict's Street and around the local streets of Newton Gully in Auckland at the time of a Marist Fathers mission in 1923, but stayed well away from Queen Street.[101] During the Catholic centennial ceremonies in Wellington in 1938 the Eucharistic display was taken into the streets, but St Stephen's Presbyterian Church in Lower Hutt encouraged a denominational protest against this 'act of idolatry' and asked the city council to ban it.[102]

Today, religious content in the media is largely confined to specifically Christian radio and television stations, and it would be easy to forget the critical role the churches played in the development of radio broadcasting. The emergence of radio stations was associated with the various city missions, since at first they were rarely seen as commercial propositions. The story of Colin Scrimgeour and 1ZB is well known, but there are many others, for example the Radio Church of the Helping Hand, begun in 1933 as 4ZM and then transferred to 4ZD.[103] Radio broadcasts significantly extended the impact of the churches, although Anglicans were slower than others to realise the importance of having a radio presence.[104] The broadcasting of their services gave churches the opportunity to reflect on what the service sought to achieve. It also forced tight attention to timing and balance.

An astonishing range of churches participated in these services, carefully supervised by the Central Religious Advisory Committee. Denominations carefully worked out their own procedures.[105] The Rev. Charles Harrison was appointed director of religious broadcasting, and there was a subsequent increase in professionalisation of the area. One of the best-known religious broadcasters was the vicar of Fendalton, Bob Lowe, who was also a polished cricket commentator. Most others were unwilling to hand responsibility over to a small group of experts, because all denominations wanted to be heard.[106]

Gradually the radio and television producers withdrew from the expense of live church services, partly as a result of the replacement of regional programming by national programming. What little religious content was left was either studio-based or carefully edited to produce the perfect effect rather than the coughs and splutters of the broadcast event. This distressed churches, but seemed more to the taste of regular listeners who were not churchgoers.[107] Doubtless the church services had appealed more to regular churchgoers who were unable to attend.

The state broadcaster slowly reduced the time allocated to religious broadcasting, and virtually the only religious television it provided was a programme of hymns. Meanwhile television stations sold time in the early morning to religious entrepreneurs. Most of them were from overseas, but Destiny Church made its name through purchased television time. The law from the 1980s allowed for private religious stations, the most notable of which was the Rhema group,[108] although

Adventist groups provided relays of American religious broadcasting. It is a strange circumstance when the public good aspect is lost completely to the cheque book.

The media often seems to think that the only news from churches these days is offensive behaviour. Whether it is Destiny Church or the ChristChurch Cathedral rebuilding, there is little sympathy for religion in the media.[109] It is well for any study of the convictions of the churches to conclude by recognising that these convictions have often generated strong public reactions.

If today churches are often far less strident, there is no lack of issues on which Christian opinions diverge from mainstream values. Perhaps at some time churches may recover both the imagination and the self-confidence to express themselves.

The Money in the Bag

Previous St George's in Thames, the church built in fine kauri for Rev. Vicesimus Lush in 1872 during the prosperous years of the Thames gold rush. It remains largely unaltered. This black and white photograph, *Church of England, Tararu (Thames) South Wall and Entrance*, taken by John Fields in 1973, conveys the sensuousness of its rough-hewn wooden details. AUCKLAND ART GALLERY TOI O TĀMAKI, GIFT OF THE ARTIST, 1976

SOMETIMES THE CHURCH SEEMS obsessed with money, and sometimes the level of the financial demands on church members is quite extreme. But over the years the churches in New Zealand were voluntary bodies that built the physical churches, staffed them, held a full programme of services, and met the needs of the community. They provided as much as churches in the United Kingdom, which had the legacy of hundreds of years of activity. The churches drew heavily on social capital, but there were bills to be paid, and this chapter focuses on that cash nexus.

The churches were not able to be unworldly about money. In the debate over the emergence of capitalism, the great sociologist Max Weber suggested that the 'ideal type' of Protestant was a proto-capitalist, whose approach to money was very different from that of Catholics. He argued that saving and accumulation was highly valued by Protestants, reflecting their notion that lay people as well as priests had a vocation. There is some evidence of such attitudes among New Zealand Protestants. Protestant culture stressed the importance of saving and urged people not to place value on possessions. Lay behaviour did not necessarily conform to type, though. Methodists (whom John Wesley had exhorted to 'earn all you can, save all you can, give all you can') were accused in a pamphlet in 1880 of being rather mean.[1] Lay miserliness towards the payment of clergy seems to demonstrate this.[2] Catholic communities were much poorer and had very different attitudes towards saving and sharing.

Churches have never charged for admission to services, but most church services in New Zealand have included a collection of some description. It formed a ritual all of its own, whether taken up in a bag or on a plate, and at the end of the service or as the bread and wine were prepared at Communion.

The colonial congregation faced many financial demands. The established Church of England only held collections for special needs or collected alms for the poor, but more than this was necessary in New Zealand, for the church had virtually no endowments. David Bruce, an eminent Presbyterian minister in Auckland between 1853 and 1889, thought that typical members of colonial congregations gave 3d, the smallest silver coin they could find in their pocket when the collection was taken up, but this was better than the coppers of Scottish congregations.[3] One report from 1900 analysed a large collection as including 652 threepences, 190 sixpences, 108 coppers, 50 shillings, one half-crown and two florins.[4] Another observer claimed that he watched 22 people as the collection plate went around, and all but one person gave less than 6d.[5]

The lack of giving could be discouraging. The preacher at the Wellington Anglican Diocesan Synod in 1928 lamented: 'Many clergy ordained with high hopes and burning enthusiasm for the Kingdom of God grow discouraged with the passing of years ... they deliberately faced a life of constant duty and of small material rewards, but from the outset they have found themselves oppressed by problems of Church Finance, forced to spend precious time in dubious and semi-worldly ways of raising funds to pay their own stipends.'[6]

Needs simply had to be met, and what New Zealand settlers did in their private lives, they did in their churches. They borrowed money. Debt enabled the churches to get under way, but as a result it was a major issue for the churches. Many settlers lived with debt for long periods, and so did their churches, but as for individuals the result could be crippling for congregations. When St James' Church became the second central Auckland Presbyterian congregation in 1865, it built an elaborate church at a cost of £3336. There was a debt of £1500 when the church opened and the interest was £200 per annum. By 1872 the debt remained at £750, with an annual interest bill of £75 (at an interest rate of 10 per cent).[7] In Christchurch, St Michael's, the first Anglican church, struggled with debt despite some very generous donors, and other churches in the city scarcely broke even.[8] The most typical interest rate in the nineteenth century was 8 per cent, and the effects of this could be very tough if the debt was not quickly cleared, especially during the very hard years of the Long Depression in the 1880s and early 1890s.

Catholic parishes faced additional challenges. Although there were parish committees to assist, in effect the priest was answerable to no one in the parish. He could incur debts with minimal local awareness. In Ashburton, Fr Edmund Coffey took some pride in the fact that just one year after his ordination and arrival from Ireland he had managed to erect a convent and a school. Unfortunately these were the grim days of the 1880s and he had muddled his personal finances and parish finances, taking out personal loans using the parish property as security. As a result the parish petitioned the bishop for his removal, accusing him of incompetence.[9] They remained responsible for the debt.

Debts were a major issue in wider society, and the whole colony operated on debt. The Rev. James Paterson told a Wellington meeting that 'It was a bad thing for an individual to be in debt, a bad thing for a family and a bad thing, nay, it was a shame to a Christian congregation.'[10] Frank Isitt, the Wesleyan minister and temperance campaigner, and brother of the politician Leonard Isitt, once told a soirée that he would rather a church was left unpainted than with a debt over it (although the debt in question was a mere £17).[11] The problem was that members could exit the congregation whenever they chose, leaving remaining members saddled with the debt. Yet the activities made necessary to pay the debt kept people loyal to the congregation. As a speaker told the Primitive Methodist Conference in

1910, a church in debt was a hard-working and aggressive church, and an overdraft at the bank was therefore a good thing.[12] Denominations in the end had to take responsibility because of the shame they incurred if the congregation defaulted, but they rarely had a legal responsibility.

Most property was held by local trusts, except for the Methodists, where there was a strong commitment to a denominational property trust. No denomination or diocese defaulted on its debts, but the Auckland Catholic Diocese came close, and during the Depression of the 1930s many parishes had to be bailed out. For example, the Akaroa Anglican parish ended up owing some £84 to the diocesan office.[13] The Whangarei Catholic parish was taken to court by Thomas Campbell, the father of the priest responsible for the building of the brick church in 1928, who had lent his son — or, he alleged, the diocese — £3500 towards the new church, without any formal documentation. The court tried to encourage arbitration, but found for the diocese and the parish and left the father acutely aware of the persuasiveness of his ordained son.[14]

Finances sometimes predominated over all other congregational concerns in the minds of local lay church officials. A clergyman in 1900 supposedly saw a woman reading the church's annual balance sheet during his sermon, took a huff and refused to continue.[15] Reading church reports, it almost seems as though the moment the debt was cleared, the vestry or management committee would authorise a building extension or replacement.

Church finances were always marginal: churches always spent to the level of their income, if not beyond it. An advance — the building of a new church or Sunday school hall, or the division of a circuit or parish into two — could put significant pressure on the budget. Thus, for example, there was a struggle when Pahiatua was separated from the Woodville Free Methodist Circuit to become an independent circuit in 1894, and the resultant financial pressures made union with the Wesleyan Methodists in the area very desirable when it happened in 1895.[16]

THE GREATEST CHALLENGE, UNDOUBTEDLY, was financing the construction of buildings. Dr Stuart, the first minister of Knox Church in Dunedin, recalled the opposition to the rebuilding of the church in 1872: 'the enemy met us at every turn. "You will never build that church; you'll never get in half your subscriptions; you won't get a shilling from the Synod; the bazaar will be a failure." However, all the evil prophecies came to nought.'[17] A major factor in this was Stuart's own skill as a fundraiser.

Many churches were built in the late nineteenth century, and there was a degree of competition for funds. Communities were proud when church buildings were erected, and would usually contribute towards the construction of churches of other denominations, including Protestants to Catholics and Catholics to Protestants. Individual gifts were generally small, however, for New Zealand had very few pious rich. Few churches were paid off by the time they were finished, and congregations literally borrowed on their future. The construction was often curtailed or plans altered on the run in order to keep costs down. Many a church abandoned the proposed bell tower or vestibule in order to reduce the budget. Builders were often generous, and congregational labour often assisted when prices rose. Many of those early buildings remain in use, although much modified, for renovations are always cheaper than new beginnings.

Maintaining the church was a further expense, given that many buildings were simple and roughly constructed. Since these buildings were almost all wooden, they were at serious risk from fires. Fires certainly did damage or level more than a few buildings in the late nineteenth century, making insurance an important factor. The annual insurance bill combined with the interest on loans created significant pressures on congregations, and made denominations very nervous, since generally they did not control the loans but risked reputations if the congregation defaulted.

In medieval England the church exacted a tithe of one-tenth of the harvest, but this was gradually commuted into a monetary payment which inflation steadily reduced. In New Zealand typically the word 'tithe' was used in a very vague way by Anglican preachers.[18] Some Protestant churches taught tithing, but it was regarded as a quite extreme request, and the Bible Society banned the use of the phrase from its pamphlets.[19] In some Presbyterian, Baptist and evangelical churches the giving of 10 per cent of income to God was taught, and churches where this was upheld rarely had any financial problems, but it was too demanding a level for most.

In urban England the standard source of church income was pew rents, and most New Zealand churches resorted to this for a period. Respectable citizens showed their denominational affiliation by renting a pew in the appropriate church (whether or not they attended) and pew rents were the most regular source of income for the main Protestant churches. The fashionable churches found this a more stable source of rent than free-will offerings, and they provided a steady regular income despite fluctuations in congregational attendance.

Wesleyans, too, depended on pew rents. The large Durham Street Wesleyan Church in Christchurch struggled with debt over a very long period, and the pew rentals were collected quarterly by the caretaker (who received a 5 per cent cut of the takings). The rentals brought in £147 per year, the largest item of regular income.[20] Although seats in the gallery were made free in 1914, there was a strong vote against

Above Church of England fête in Cambridge, Waikato, in 1885. Cambridge was Anglican heartland, and those attending are very fashionably dressed and stand around a maypole. SIR GEORGE GREY SPECIAL COLLECTIONS, AUCKLAND LIBRARIES, 4-8732

Below Mrs Joseph Palmer opens a sale of work in the church hall of St Michael and All Angels Anglican Church in Christchurch in 1905. At this time, the church was at the height of its respectability. CHRISTCHURCH CITY LIBRARIES. REF: PHOTOCD 6, IMG0002

the abolition of rentals in 1939 and they were only abolished in 1944.[21] Pitt Street Methodist Church in central Auckland collected £170 from pew rents every year (some 25 per cent of the annual income).[22] Catholic churches also rented seats, in the case of Blenheim adopting Fr Hennebery's system (which seems to have involved lists of families in the parish and whether they had paid) in 1879.[23] Even country churches used rents. In Frankton Presbyterian parish in Central Otago a pew cost 20 shillings per year, or five shillings for a single seat,[24] a fairly standard price throughout New Zealand.

Pew rents were widely criticised by church reformers in England and in the colonies. Bishop Selwyn was a reformer who was opposed to this way of funding the church, but he was unable to deter any of the main Anglican churches from introducing pew rents. The original vision for the Canterbury settlement had included the reform of church finances, including the elimination of pew rents, so outrage was high when St Michael's, the first church in the city, introduced rents in its early years. There were further complaints when pew rents were proposed as a means to raise funds to pay for the cathedral.[25] Officials at St Michael's responded that rents shamed people into coming to church to be seen in 'their seats', although they agreed to make the north aisle free.[26]

The campaign to abolish pew rents rumbled on for nearly a century, long after it should have ended. Church treasurers were cautious about surrendering a steady income for an unknown free-will income, and it is interesting that it was Methodist churches, which supposedly sought working-class congregations, that were slowest to abandon them. Anglican publications frequently criticised the system, but parishes felt financially entrapped.[27] The Auckland Diocese finally voted against charging for pews in 1917, and the Wellington Diocese in 1919.[28]

Churches in towns felt forced to rent their seats out. One criticism of pew rents was that pew renters were determined to keep other people out of their seats, but showed no concern for the wellbeing of the building as a whole, and were hostile to plans to expand the seating capacity of the church. Renters were also inclined to think that they had paid their share towards the church and need give no more.

One solution was to provide free seats for those who could not afford to pay. While churches wanted to maximise their rentals, free seats were essential if the church was to welcome the poor. Sometimes the gallery was reserved as unappropriated, 'and would be inviting to some who were unwilling to place themselves too conspicuously in contrast to the well-dressed people'.[29] The quality of these 'free and unappropriated seats' was hotly debated, especially as seats to which visitors were directed. Rented pews were usually declared open for any late arrivals at one or two minutes before the hour of the service, but woe betide the person who sat in someone's pew if the renter then arrived late. Hostility to pew rents ran deep in working-class communities, and it coloured their view of the church as an organisation that wanted their thruppence.[30]

BY FAR THE MAJORITY of fundraising for the church was done by women members; in fact, congregations of almost all denominations were dependent on their ladies' guilds. These guilds accepted the financial responsibilities and challenges identified by male vestries or diaconal courts.

For example, at Queenstown in 1897, the Presbyterian Elders' Session decided that the church needed to be reroofed immediately, and agreed to call on the ladies 'to make arrangements in connection with the enlargement of the church'. The same happened when the church decided to provide the minister with a car.[31] Men decided, but women raised the money. This called for delicate diplomacy on the part of the vestry or deacons' court. For example, at All Saints in Foxton in about 1891 the vestry encouraged the Ladies' Guild to raise money for their project of a Sunday school room, and then decided that it would be smarter to ask the women how they wanted to use the money.[32]

Because ladies' guilds formed the committed heart of the church, sometimes the guild virtually took responsibility for the care of branch Sunday school or church buildings.[33] They may have had other functions, but above all they raised money. As the Greytown Methodist circuit acknowledged, 'without the women, much of the Christian service could not have been accomplished'.[34]

Many church activities with other ostensible purposes had a financial goal. The range of events included bazaars and fairs, lectures and concerts, some of which required massive organisation. Fairs were significant community events, with the potential to raise money from people who had no other connection with the church. While fairs were popular in the community, they sometimes revealed a crass side of the church.[35] Huge arrangements were required to gather in the goods, set people to making jam, gathering produce, and then setting up, pricing goods and presiding at the sundry stalls. Fairs could raise up to £2000, and this made a huge difference in most parishes.[36] Sometimes the range of items collected up for sale at the fair was surprising. Anglican ladies at Warkworth in 1879 gathered items including a wedding cake, a pig and a washing machine along with the usual food items.[37]

The church sometimes undermined its own message in the way it raised money. Often, many stalls in the fair involved some sort of lucky chance or other form of gambling. At All Saints, Foxton, around 1900, a huge bazaar organised to lift the debt was set up as an oriental scene, and it was highly successful, raising some £500.

One part of the success was the use of little sweepstakes and chocolate wheels, but when the vicar arrived he promptly banned them. The moment he went home the sweepstake resumed.[38] After all, the objective was to raise money.

Catholics were less troubled by gambling than Protestants, or indeed by the sale of alcohol. St Brigid's Church in Anderson's Bay, Dunedin, was funded in the 1950s by numerous raffles of domestic goods, but the most successful (although totally illegal) raffles were of alcohol and stakes in horse races (despite the TAB). Art union ticket books were posted out unsolicited to every Irish name in the phone books. Female parishioners kept watch while the men gambled in the presbytery, and prior to outdoor fêtes a statue of St Joseph was erected so that prayers could be said for a fine day.[39]

Most Catholic churches resorted to a weekly housie session in order to raise more money. Some went further. In Timaru a priest persuaded the Altar Society to take out insurance on his life to benefit the parish to the extent of £500, and this proved a handy contribution to the building fund on his death in 1898.[40] In 1910 the junior priest at Timaru raised money for the new basilica of St Mary's by every means at his disposal, and a great bazaar raised £1800. When a young lad asked whether he could leave the Mass during the sermon, he was told he should not. 'But supposing the priest was preaching about a bazaar,' was the boy's cheeky riposte, presumably reflecting family concerns.[41] In Whangarei in 1951, sympathetic men were invited to gambling nights to raise money, but the sessions were kept secret on account of disapproval from some parishioners (and perhaps because they were of dubious legality).[42]

Presbyterian churches similarly became dependent on sales and soirées and fairs as a source of additional funds. Stricter Presbyterians disliked the implications of socialising with the world and viewed fairs as offensive and compromising ways to raise money, making the church dependent on the sponsorship of outsiders. This is why such events were rarely held by Congregationalist and Baptist churches.

These fairs and similar events were an important part of community life, and a significant part of the lives of the women who organised them. In 1956, when many Anglican churches took part in a major fundraising campaign, Warkworth parish was promised that no other fundraising would be required and the church stall was banned. However, its women organisers complained so vigorously that the stall was reinstated.[43]

SOME CHURCHES HAD OTHER ways of levying their congregations. Methodism in England depended on the penny-a-week from the weekly classes to which members belonged, but those classes were very weak in New Zealand and in the Pitt Street congregation they contributed just £181 out of £1232 in annual income.[44] Most churches, including Anglicans, made collections part of every service, not just for special appeals. Regular collections were more successful among Methodists, Congregationalists and Baptists because these churches had never looked to the state for support.

Another option was an annual pledge from members. Presbyterian churches had a sustentation fund to support the ministry and members made formal commitments to it before a minister was appointed.[45] Pledges were very important. The Rev. Charles Connor quoted an Aberdeen scholar when explaining to the Presbyterians of Popotunoa (the earlier name for Clinton, in South Otago) why it was thought good to get pledges: 'Ask a man for £1 6s, and he will stare you in the face and say, "I cannot afford it you ask an impossibility." Ask the same man for 6d a week, and he will blush and say, "Well, I cannot refuse that I give that to my newsboy every week. I must give you more than that, for I spend far more on my whiskey and my pipe."'[46]

Churches needed a system to collect these pledges. Given there was no tax rebate for donations until 1961, congregational members had few inducements to give, but church treasurers valued such a scheme so that they could prepare a budget. Church leaders began to advocate the envelope system in the late nineteenth century. This operated through members pledging a certain annual figure to the church treasurer, and then paying it off in an envelope that bore the unique number assigned to them. This enabled churches to have some kind of realistic annual budget, which previously had only been available from the despised pew rents, and it enabled members to be receipted for their gifts.

High hopes were held out for this method, but the secrecy unnerved some church treasurers. The treasurer of Durham Street Wesleyan Church in Christchurch advocated it in 1877 and 1880, but it was not adopted at this time.[47] The Masterton Methodist treasurer, A. H. Daniell (a prominent businessman in the town), reported in 1911 that 41 subscribers had pledged £35.2.0 for the quarter.[48] St Mary's Anglican Church in New Plymouth pushed the scheme in 1910 and gained 62 subscribers after a year, who contributed £40.[49] At St David's Presbyterian Church in Khyber Pass Road, Auckland, it was adopted in 1909, and led to an increase in offerings by 34 per cent. However, there remained a certain amount of caution about pledging money before it had been earned, and about the loss of privacy in giving, and at St David's the number of pledgers dropped from 260 to 70 in the next four years.

The organisation of the envelope system improved with the adoption of the 'Duplex Envelope System' advocated by American writers (for example, Samuel Stein in *A Guide to Church Finance*, published in 1920) in which subscribers received two pockets in the one envelope and therefore could divide their gift between two funds.[50] When the 'weekly free-will offering' system was adopted at St David's in 1922, it was almost certainly the duplex system.[51] It had reached the Akaroa Anglicans by 1932.[52] Catholic churches were slower off the mark, but increasingly used it, facilitating designated gifts for schools.[53]

The churches' treasurers were probably no help when it came to raising money, for the skills of a responsible treasurer were usually quite different from those of a fundraiser. Presenting an annual budget or a deficit does not necessarily inspire people to give.

Special collections on particular occasions were one method of raising money. Among Catholics the Redemptorist Fathers (an order noted for their skills as preachers) were respected for their ability to motivate Catholics to increase their giving.[54] Some Protestant ministers were equally effective. J. M. Saunders, the Welsh minister of St David's in Auckland (1912–19), opposed pew rents, bazaars and sales of work and insisted that the church should depend financially only on the free-will offerings of

The Grand Loyalty Dinner held at the Auckland Town Hall for St Jude's church, Avondale, in 1956 as part of the Wells Campaign. The photograph shows the women who played a crucial role in encouraging people to attend the function and make their pledges.
AUCKLAND ANGLICAN DIOCESAN ARCHIVES

congregations, and his eloquent advocacy was very effective. He placed a special focus on collections at the huge Harvest Festival and Sunday school anniversary services, where the church could receive up to £700 in a single offering.[55] This was a precursor to the giant 'love offerings' of the mega-churches in recent years.

Few congregations had such an eloquent Welsh preacher. The Anglican Board of Missions commented in 1940 that 'the whole church needs terse, tense, direct and emphatic direction on giving'.[56] Churches were on the search for ways and means.

The Wells Organisation, founded by a Colonel Wells in the United States, had established a branch in Australia and was invited to run fundraising in New Zealand in the 1950s. This had a staggering effect on church finances. Its fundraisers went house to house canvassing local members of the denomination, and ended with a Great Loyalty Dinner at which members were invited to make a pledge, following the example of the organising committee, who had been chosen on the basis of their willingness to make a generous gift. The Auckland Anglican Diocese used the organisation in 1955 in order to finance the cathedral, and then used it to help parish projects. Thus at Warkworth, a country parish, with 500 Anglican families but only 26 regular communicants, a target of £20,000 was set, including a commitment to give to the cathedral. Seven parishioners underwrote the costs of £2500, and a typewriter and duplicator were bought because of the level of communication required, although Warkworth held a lunch rather than a loyalty dinner.[57]

Noel Derbyshire, priest, accountant and scholar, has analysed the increase in parochial income that resulted from these efforts, and estimates that incomes grew up to fourfold through the use of the Wells Organisation.[58] The tone of these events was designed to reinforce that the church was truly a community organisation valuable to all. Soon Presbyterians and Methodists approached Wells, although they already had their own schemes. The New Life Campaign of the Presbyterians was rather more theologically based and reached across the whole denomination.

By 1960 the churches had new financial needs and they approached Wells again. This time, using the same people, the results were disappointing. Denominations and dioceses resorted to engaging their own fundraisers, but although the overheads were lower, so were the results. In some Catholic parishes an imitative scheme, called Planned Giving, launched in 1965. This involved visiting every home and inviting the people to a formal dinner at which they made their pledges. The Nelson parish raised £50,790 by these means.[59] From 1963 the government allowed church people to claim up to £25 as a deduction from income tax, so churches needed to devise schemes (and the envelope system suited this) to issue annual receipts.[60] In subsequent years the level of donations that could be claimed rose, and there is now no limit.

Paul Reeves (the future Archbishop and Governor-General) selling goods at a fair at St Matthew's, Auckland, in the early 1980s. AUCKLAND ANGLICAN DIOCESAN ARCHIVES

HISTORICALLY THE EVANGELICAL CHURCHES had been small and poor, while the Presbyterian and Anglican churches were able to command large sums, especially for building projects. A change took place from the 1950s. The rapid expansion of evangelical congregations from the 1920s was made possible by very dedicated giving. Other institutions looked with awe at the levels of Brethren giving (although the expenses of these congregations were very low, with no employed pastor).

From the 1970s the Pentecostal churches gained a reputation for the huge collections they could raise for specific projects. The Pentecostal dollar became a new symbol of generosity, although it was mostly used to pay for staff and buildings at the mega-churches. Destiny Church gained a reputation for the supposedly extravagant lifestyle of its leaders, funded by generous donations from the relatively poor congregation, but many other Pentecostal churches were just as guilty.[61] Another example was the giving of Pasifika churches, which became notorious for the ways in which they announced donations from the pulpit, and accepted donations that had been financed from personal loans.[62]

The alternative to the envelope system today is the automatic payment. Indeed, when collection plates or bags go round, they sometimes yield virtually nothing in our increasingly cashless world. Mega-churches have installed money machines in their foyers in order to facilitate giving. Finance apps are obviously the next step as giving adapts to new circumstances.

Churches have always struggled financially, and as a new style of church emerged, with large building complexes and many staff, the overheads were high. Meanwhile the older church traditions have a huge portfolio of properties, but their income is increasingly drawn from rentals rather than congregational donations. The Christchurch earthquake has made more acute the very different experiences of church finances. In the 1990s the British company Ansvar became an important insurer of New Zealand churches, but the Christchurch earthquakes had such a huge impact on the company that it subsequently withdrew from the New Zealand market.[63] Churches have as a result faced a significant increase in fixed costs, and many have also been required to undertake earthquake strengthening. Financial issues remain an important test of the church's viability.

Above The St Thomas's church bazaar in Riddiford Street, Wellington, in August 1898. The parochial district had been established in 1896. The bazaar featured yet another maypole. ALEXANDER TURNBULL LIBRARY. REF: PA1-O-289-425

Below A loyalty dinner for St Jude's, Avondale, held at the warehouse of the Apple and Pear Marketing Board in Henderson, Auckland, in 1956 as part of the Wells Campaign. The vicar, H. G. Boniface, and the dean's wife, Mrs Monteith, accompany Bishop Simkin, whose wife was evidently not available. AUCKLAND ANGLICAN DIOCESAN ARCHIVES

A Sociable Religion

Previous A Sunday school picnic at Ngāruawāhia in the 1880s, the children in their best clothes and the Waikato River in the background. Photograph by Daniel Manders Beere. ALEXANDER TURNBULL LIBRARY. REF: 1/2-096156-G

I N AN IMPASSIONED SERMON at the opening of the alterations to St Paul's Church in Hamilton on 21 June 1914, the President of the Methodist Conference, the Rev. Samuel Serpell, warned the newly united Methodists of Hamilton that the church was always tempted to lose its commission as a man-saving and woman-saving institution and become just a social club.[1] This chapter explores this 'temptation', which was an overwhelming tendency within New Zealand churches. Sociability in this context means in the first instance the ways in which members of religious communities socialised with each other, but also the extent to which these communities mixed with secular community and people from other religious communities. Thus conviviality reflects broader issues of intimacy on the one hand and boundary-setting on the other. Understanding this aspect of church life illuminates many aspects of the operation of churches within their communities.

For there were boundaries to this sociability, boundaries that were set by the denominations. In many country districts, a shared community church was the first religious institution, but eventually denominations separated themselves out. Sometimes there were intense disputes between them. It is necessary to explore the boundaries in order to understand the sociability.

When the Wesleyan missionaries arrived in New Zealand in the early 1820s they worked closely with the CMS, living initially in the CMS settlement until they were able to commence their own work at Whangaroa, a few miles north. The Whangaroa mission station had to be evacuated after local Māori attacked it in 1827, and at this point the Wesleyans were welcomed back to the Anglican station. As equal participants in the Evangelical Revival, the two missions believed in the fellowship of all who were truly converted, and the division between the saved and the unsaved.

In England, however, denominational identity strengthened in the period between 1790 and 1850.[2] In New Zealand friction developed between the missions in the 1830s, and they negotiated a comity agreement, which identified separate mission fields for each denomination. Further tensions emerged with the appearance of the Catholic missionaries in 1838 and the arrival of the Anglican Bishop Selwyn in 1841. As we have already seen, Selwyn had a strong sense of denominational integrity and a low view of Wesleyan ordination. The Wesleyan missionaries grieved to see 'the enemy of Souls to triumph in the divisions, & infirmities of the heralds of the Cross'.[3]

The tension between the Catholic and Protestant missionaries was more profound. It drew on deep theological tensions, in which each side castigated the other as satanic. Tensions between Catholics and Protestants in Ireland heightened the sensitivity of British Protestants, and since the Catholic missionaries were French, tensions between Britain and France exacerbated the situation. Māori were not beyond playing off both parties to their own advantage.

Different religions also reflected different cultures and ethnicities. The Catholic Church, and the Presbyterians, too, assisted the minority cultures of Britain, the Irish and the Scots, in preserving their identities in the face of the overwhelming English majority. The most dramatic example of this occurred at the opening of the first Catholic church in Westport on St Patrick's Day in 1868. A morning mock funeral procession for the Manchester Fenian martyrs preceded the opening, then there was a late-afternoon Fenian protest, then a wedding in the church at night.[4] Irish Catholicism throughout the British Empire had an inevitable political dimension. Irish partisanship was a key element in Catholic churches, and in Presbyterian churches there was sometimes an Ulster flavour, although they were predominantly Scottish.

One hundred years later the cultural distinctiveness of these two denominations remained. When Presbyterian services were begun in Ngaio, Wellington, in 1945, for people who had previously had no local church of their own, the first congregational meeting ended with the 50 people present linking hands and singing that great Scottish song, 'Auld Lang Syne'.[5] There are other examples where ethnicity and culture have worked in tandem with religion. Tensions between Scandinavians and Germans meant that there was no united Lutheran church in New Zealand until 1958. Similarly, small ethnic minorities of Italians crowded the Catholic church in Island Bay in Wellington, and Greeks built the Orthodox church by the Basin Reserve. In more recent years, Pacific Islanders have used the church to simulate their island world, splitting into Methodist and Congregational affiliations. Koreans, too, have used Presbyterian, Methodist and Catholic churches to create a place of their own in New Zealand.

THE BOUNDARIES OF THE churches were most evident between Catholics and Protestants. The Catholic Church was shaped by the authority of priest, of bishop and of the Vatican. Priests needed to be sure that communicants had been baptised, and sometimes challenged them as they appeared at the altar. Priests became adept at recognising who were Catholics, and in practice this was culturally rather than sacramentally defined. The parish had less autonomous life than a Protestant congregation, since little responsibility was entrusted to the local laity. Catholics moved freely from one parish to another, attending Mass wherever it was convenient. They were united by a common culture. The *Tablet*, the Catholic weekly newspaper, was full of secular content, particularly sporting news and politics in Ireland. The Catholic Church took a strong interest in Irish issues, and was slow to support other ethnic cultures.

The Catholic experience of church was quite different from the characteristic Protestant one. Laity did not participate much in the Latin Mass. The Mass was familiar yet obscure, and generally parishioners were expected to supply their own Mass books. There was a sharp boundary between clergy and laity, for celibacy set both priests and nuns apart in a separate sphere, and sometimes priests only socialised with other priests and this was even more true of nuns.

The boundaries of the Catholic Church were explicit in the case of marriage. Marriage to a Protestant could not take place at the altar, and this removed its sacramental quality. The Catholic partner was required to make pledges that the children would be raised Catholic. Priests thus assumed the right to supervise family behaviour, and sometimes these rules were harshly enforced. Fr John Broomfield, a Mill Hill Father with an unusual Irish background, tried to ban a girl from marrying a non-Catholic, and although Fr Van Dijk, his superior, received permission for the marriage to go ahead, the church in Tauranga was left locked, forcing guests to enter through the sacristy door.[6] In many other cases, however, despite the promises, the commitment of the mixed-marriage family weakened. Another example was the rules prohibiting cremation, which meant that any Catholic wishing to be cremated would be denied a Requiem Mass.

Anti-Catholic rhetoric was common in Protestant churches before World War II. A stream of tracts were published on the subject. The Baptists Alfred North and his son John North were contributors to the genre, but the sharpest pen was that of the Rev. John Dickson, a Northern Irish Presbyterian. The literature invariably contrasted the Protestant understanding of grace with the Catholic belief that God worked among humans through the sacraments. Attacks on specific Catholics were regarded as unseemly, however. The visit of the pastor Charles Chiniquy, a former priest, in 1879 dismayed Protestants because his language verged on the lewd. Similarly, although the slurs on Catholics by Howard Elliott of Mount Eden Baptist Church in 1917 had much initial appeal as people looked for culprits in the wartime environment, in the long term they lost him friends within the community.

Although the Protestant–Catholic rift was the largest boundary in the church, there were other tensions between Protestants. Some Presbyterians were suspicious of the theology of other Protestants. Charles Connor, the Presbyterian minister at Ōamaru, was a Northern Irish Presbyterian. He preached against the Brethren and Catholics, and even battled the local Wesleyan minister. In one notorious case Connor furiously attacked a Wesleyan sheep station owner who would not allow him direct access to Presbyterians on the farm.[7] This contentious approach did not go down well in tight communities. Presbyterianism did often react to what it saw as theological error, but there was also an eirenic trend in that church. Donald Stuart, the first minister of

Knox Church in Dunedin, welcomed people from various denominations and criticised 'the spirit of bigotry and exclusiveness'. Stuart's church prospered precisely because of this open-hearted and expansive attitude.[8]

Among Baptists the issue of closed versus open Communion was a contentious issue decided by congregational constitutions. The first Baptist church in New Zealand was 'closed Communion', so only those who had been baptised as believers by immersion could sit down for Communion. In the friendly Protestant world of Christchurch, the majority of the founders of the Baptist Church wanted it to be open Communion, and their first two pastors, Decimus Dolamore and James Thornton, both ceased to be ministers of the church partly because the congregation would not change its stance on this matter.[9]

Protestant churches thus had exclusive tendencies, but they were also aware that boundaries between them were porous. Protestants believed that the true church was invisible, so no one church could fully express it. Protestants were also very conscious that many of their adherents were not regularly involved in church life; nominal Christianity counted for very little in the eyes of most Protestants. Churches focused on retaining current members and recruiting new ones, encouraging a certain degree of competition as well as cooperation.

Churches had various methods to re-engage

A dinner in the schoolroom of St Luke's, Masterton, in the 1920s, held to raise money for the electrification of the hall. The principal Methodists, including Frederick Daniell, are present. MASTERTON DISTRICT LIBRARY ARCHIVE, 04-166/64

nominal members.[10] Anglicans sought to use Easter and Christmas celebrations, while Presbyterians sent their elders out on pastoral visits. For most Protestants the Sunday school anniversary and other public events were helpful means to renew contact with adults, since almost everyone recognised the value of religion for children.

ROUGHLY 40 PER CENT of the population for the first 100 years of European New Zealand saw themselves as Anglicans, and the Anglican Church provided baptisms, weddings and funerals for them. This kind of Anglicanism was very vague, and since it was no longer the state church, it was necessary to define what an Anglican was. In 1857 a constitutional conference called by Bishop Selwyn defined Anglicans as those who had by voluntary compact entered the church, benefitted from its sacraments, and come under its authority.[11] There was much debate in the 1850s over the criteria for membership of the church. Were baptism and confirmation both required?[12] People chose to be part of the church, but many Anglicans had not yet opted in. When Bishop Julius addressed a local society, the Churchmen's Club, on his arrival in Christchurch in 1890, he urged the club to avoid any stigma of narrowness and accept all Anglicans as members. But the result was that its members were scarcely able to distinguish themselves from outsiders, and the club faded away.[13]

Anglicans were cautious of other Protestants. Bishop Selwyn believed that Anglicans retained the Catholic heritage of the church which others had lost. Vicesimus Lush told a Wesleyan woman who visited him in Howick that he would not refuse her attendance at the church, but that she should not take Communion. She reported to others that he had said, 'I had rather admit a heathen or a Roman Catholic to the Communion than a Wesleyan.' Although Lush insisted that he harboured no grudges against Dissenters, the story remained wedged in the memory of Methodists, many of whom regarded themselves as loosely part of the Church of England.[14]

The Anglican Rev. Algernon Gifford arrived in Ōamaru before the first Presbyterian minister, and so at first his services were attended by Presbyterians. When a Presbyterian congregation was established he was invited to chair its soirées, but declined when they were held in the church.[15] Anglicans like Gifford were careful to preserve their status and reputation. In Wanganui an Anglican clergyman insisted that he would not address a Wesleyan as 'the reverend', at some cost to his public reputation.[16]

The most striking example of Anglican snobbery was when the Rev. Edward

Lingard at St Luke's Christchurch forbade his organist to play at the St Alban's Methodist soirée. Even his vestry felt that this attitude was wrong. His position was that of the English High Churchman who did not want to identify with other Protestants. For many years Anglican clergy took this stance.

Such words and actions were often confusing to others. Bishop Nevill in Dunedin was firmly High Church in his outlook, but he aspired to 'a real and manifest union of the Church of God on earth'.[17] Bishop Julius, who was much more generous in spirit, provoked the irritation of other church leaders when he chose an ecumenical occasion to define the distinction between Anglicans and others.[18] Evangelical and Low Church Anglicans viewed the Anglican Church as just the English form of Protestantism, and at the celebration after George Grubb's mission of 1890 the Bishop of Nelson invited all present to share in Communion.[19] But Nelson was exceptional.

The narrow attitude of many High Church Anglicans waned in the postwar years. In 1964 the Anglican Church decided to participate in church union discussions, but still sought concessions from others in the face of their High Church members, requesting that an ordained Anglican be present whenever Anglicans received Communion. Bishop Gowing of Auckland was very supportive of ecumenism but insisted that Anglicans not be placed in compromising positions at ecumenical gatherings.[20] Only in 1970 did the General Synod rule that inter-communion was permissible in certain circumstances.[21]

Recent Anglican theological thinking is much less institutional than in the past.[22] There is an increasing congregationalism in evidence. Many Anglicans feel their primary loyalty to their home parish, perhaps not knowing what they will encounter if they visit another parish. In practice they have become much more like other Protestants.

Peter Barclay, the first minister of Napier's Presbyterian church, felt that Anglicans in New Zealand were closer to Presbyterians than in the United Kingdom, because both churches in New Zealand were regulated by synods.[23] Nevertheless, the majority of Anglicans voted against church union in 1964, and in recent years have put little energy into cooperation with others.

If denominations were sometimes at loggerheads, at times tensions exploded within local congregations, and this was infinitely more painful, and could result in schism. In general this was rare in the episcopal churches, although tensions between High and Low Church Anglicans have occasionally occurred, and in 1901 this led to a division of the Takapuna Anglican Church. Congregational splits were more common in smaller Protestant communities, for each Protestant had the right of private judgement and disputants had no higher authority or arbitrator to settle the matter. Thus, Timaru Baptist Church was suspended from the Baptist Union in 1884, and its minister lost his denominational credentials on account of his views about eternal Hell.[24] In the same town Samuel Buchanan led a schism of the Primitive Methodist Church in 1903, when his role as minister was terminated, and half the members formed the Star of Hope Mission in Bank Street, which survived for some three years.[25]

Presbyterians had a long tradition of schism over such issues as organs, singing of hymns and similar matters. Brethren experienced schism over attitudes to divorce and to bankruptcy. Many other examples could be cited. Internal dynamics often fuelled congregational disputes. In a voluntary body, it was difficult to challenge the quality or character of someone's contribution, and petty struggles for control could get out of hand. The minister, as the one employed person, might for various reasons link up with one faction rather than riding above the conflict. Unless help came from outside, local congregations could be torn apart by the infighting.

Schisms of this kind were significant indications of the amount invested in the church by many lay members. They were very painful and devastating for friendships, for families and for the reputations of churches. Finances were immediately affected. Sometimes loans and debts were dishonoured and the church had to be sold. In other cases, the schismatics immediately sought to raise money to erect a new church. Individuals in the Timaru Primitive Methodist Chapel hastily made up the loss in the church accounts after the 1903 schism, but at a high personal cost.[26]

These denominational and congregational tensions are an indication that church mattered immensely to some members, inclining them to breach the rules of civility in colonial society. They also show that the church hoped to be the centre of community for its members.

Community is a very ambiguous word. These days it is used in two quite contradictory ways in connection with the local congregations. On the one hand, the church usually seeks to identify with the local community, to live in it, minister to it, even convert it, but on the other hand the church is often described as a community in itself, an autonomous family of believers. These two usages reflect the analysis of the two types of community by the early-twentieth-century German sociologist Ferdinand Tönnies. He described the traditional community as a *gemeinschaft*, a face-to-face society. This was a society in which the individual was governed by familial and village rules, from which there was no escape except by leaving the place.

Tönnies' model goes some way towards explaining traditional society. He argued that modern society was *gesellschaft*, the anonymous society, in which most of our formal relationships are as individuals. So he suggested that we go to one place for work, we are taxpayers, we are voters, and we make choices as to whether we link up with any church, leisure venue or other roles and venues. Tönnies argued that in the modern world community is something we opt into, and the family is itself reshaped by individual choice.[26A]

The settlers in colonial New Zealand had in many cases come from rural communities in which *gemeinschaft* still existed, and in some ways the rural communities of New Zealand were also like this. But New Zealand towns had high levels of mobility, so the church often offered a form of *gesellschaft*, the community that you *choose* to belong to. In the early colonial years in New Zealand the community combined to organise churches that were not seen as exclusive to any denomination. Various denominations provided services in the church, but while they provided clergy or missionaries, the congregation did not particularly belong to any denomination.[27] In subsequent years as the community became more modern, the congregation became more denominational, but it cultivated the aspect of a community, through its socialising.

In early years, the church in New Zealand was an accepted part of the community (although not the centre of it — that was reserved for the school), and the community was important to most people. Locals would meet one another in the church, but also in the school, the pub and on the streets. Kathleen Hawkins captured the tone of services in a country district where there was a monthly service in the school classroom:

> And maybe, e'er they reach the home hearth-side
> But little of the preacher's talk remains
> And yet somehow it seems a kindlier air
> Breathes through the home throughout the coming day,
> That mother, fretted with the household care
> Bears patiently with mankind's vexing ways
> That worries press less hardly upon Dad,
> That young folk keep their discontents well-hid
> And all, in secret heart are dumbly glad
> They've kept 'Church Sunday' as their fathers did.[28]

Changing relationships between the local community, the denominational community, the congregational community and the broader church community are observable over the past two centuries.

In the period from 1900 to 1920 many local communities built halls, some of them secular and others of them church halls. After that, communities had many more opportunities to socialise. Church halls therefore tell their own stories. At St John's Northcote, in Auckland, a large hall was added in 1907 which served the

Above Stallholders at the Northcote Anglican Church fair, held in 1904 in the Gladstone Hall, on the corner of Onewa Road, on Auckland's North Shore. Present are members of the Hunt, Pengelly, McClymont and Evans families. Each stall was themed, in this case including gypsies, milkmaids and Americans. SIR GEORGE GREY SPECIAL COLLECTIONS, AUCKLAND LIBRARIES, NZG-19041210-40-5

Below The Baptist Sunday school of Mosgiel in 1913, when the famous preacher Frank Boreham was minister. They stand outside the oddly crenelated church; their numbers demonstrate Boreham's success in attracting teenagers. BAPTIST CHURCHES OF TASMANIA

community well in subsequent years. Placed slightly forward of the church, it was much used for social events and community dances. At the Levin Methodist Church the Century Hall, erected in 1900, was used for social events as well as for the Sunday school, and increasingly for services as well. As the church became inadequate, the hall was used for most services, and as the biggest social hall between Wellington and Palmerston North it was also used for horticultural shows, political meetings, wedding breakfasts and the annual meeting of the dairy factory.[29] However, the halls of some churches were not permitted to be used for dancing. In the postwar era, especially under the New Life Movement in the Presbyterian Church in the 1950s, the first step was to build a hall, not a church.

Secular socialisation did not appeal to all church folk. The settlers worked hard and played hard. Playing hard meant a lot of booze, it meant racing and gambling and regattas. The annual provincial regattas (which began when the provinces were created) and Agricultural and Pastoral shows (mostly commencing in the 1860s) were popular occasions for community leisure. Most churchgoing folk also participated in these events, but the alcohol at them, the male domination, and the crudity of them distressed the pious types of the Protestant churches. The 'fête', and its associations with gambling, drinking and fortune-telling, caused fear in the hearts of the pious editors of the *New Zealand Evangelist* in 1850.[30] As we have seen, the issue of sports on a Sunday did not trouble Anglicans or Catholics, but it did trouble other Protestants.

Sabbatarians debated the issue of 'private leisure' on a Sunday. Sunday picnics were often condemned, especially a notorious case during the Duke of York's visit in 1893.[31] Fishing excursions were criticised by churchmen.[32] Although this gave some churches a reputation as killjoys, they often sponsored alternative and free Sunday leisure. Sacred concerts by donation were acceptable, so long as admission was not charged.[33] The Salvation Army band was popular, but the Rev. Richard Coffey, vicar of St Mark's in Wellington from 1879, criticised other bands playing in the Basin Reserve (opposite his church), and in Dunedin such bands were banned in 1885.[34]

Churches had their own reasons for providing for congregational entertainment. Sunday services were too formal to provide much community support. Churches were constantly urged to make newcomers welcome, and to support existing parishioners. The church also sought to meet the intellectual needs of its members, so it was logical for them to hold additional events on other days of the week. This took various forms. Self-improvement was a significant goal of many such church activities. In the nineteenth century, many churches had mutual improvement societies focusing on self-discipline, cultivation and rational knowledge. By the 1930s, Catholic parishes had copied the Protestant pattern, with a range of social, educational and sporting groups, and separate Catholic services on Anzac Day.

Churches also frequently sponsored educational lectures. The ulterior motive was usually fundraising. For a modest fee, members of the community could attend lectures in churches on an amazing variety of themes virtually every week of the year. In 1863 St Michael's in Christchurch founded a church institute, which held lectures for a shilling, which raised money for church needs. Lectures from the vicar or visitors and musical performances were the common fare. The clergy were the educated elite in the nineteenth century and well placed to meet the demand for popular education, but they were not the only performers. Missionaries and other travellers from exotic lands got the best audiences.

The range of topics was extremely broad. Popular science, reports from foreign places, political commentaries and readings of popular literature were all included. The lectures were also an opportunity to present theological arguments. Lectures on Protestant and Catholic values were common.

With the arrival of movies in 1896, secular entertainment completely outclassed church-based entertainment. 'These picture shows are a real opposition, and one we never had to contend with in years past,' wrote Fr Le Menant des Chesnais to Bishop Grimes of Christchurch in 1905.[35] Subsequent church social events became focused on church members and people interested in joining the congregation. A large congregation like St David's Khyber Pass Road in Auckland, which had up to 800 members, could attract significant numbers to its community events, but they had little appeal beyond the church.

Sociability cultivated a spirit of generosity in the community. Church people were not richly endowed with material possessions. Leisure activities provided by the church helped it to retain significant links with its community. The Oddfellows organisations complemented the churches in the practical insurance they provided to respectable poor migrants.[36]

Most churches encouraged members to find a religiously compatible husband or wife, and events such as soirées, which attracted a wider network to the local church, helped in this. By and large white settlers in New Zealand chose their spouses for themselves, but families preferred the partner to be found within the local community or the relationships of the wider denomination. For Catholics and for members of some of the 'stronger' forms of religion, marrying within the faith was seen as vital.

The Caversham Project has tracked the details of many thousands of people in South Dunedin in the period from 1890 to 1940, and its data shows the denominational backgrounds of many marriages. It can be seen that 201 of the 317 offspring (63 per cent) were married in the same denomination as their parents (or had a registry-office

Above The children of St Christopher's Sunday school, in Redwoodtown, Blenheim, are taken by traction engine to the annual Sunday school picnic at Taylor's Pass in about 1908. Scholars went free but other children paid sixpence for their two meals and another sixpence for the traction engine ride. Obviously one or two cycled in preference. FROM BYTHELL, J. M. THE GOLDEN JUBILEE OF ST. CHRISTOPHER'S SUNDAY SCHOOL REDWOODTOWN 1909-1959 WITH AN ACCOUNT OF THE YEARS 1905-1908. BLENHEIM, THE VESTRY, 1959

Below A Salvation Army dinner laid out at the Linwood Citadel in Fitzgerald Avenue, Christchurch, about 1910. Linwood was a working-class district, and this is the main church rearranged for the Saturday night function, which was very popular with the local poor. ALEXANDER TURNBULL LIBRARY. REF: 1/1-026395-G

wedding like their parents). The highest percentage was among Catholics, where 86 per cent of children were married Catholic. In the case of Anglican, Presbyterian and registry-office weddings the percentage was between 63 and 67 per cent of marriages — so in roughly two out of three cases the offspring was married in the same religion as the parents. The percentages were much lower for the smaller denominations.

So there was quite a high level of cross-denominational change between generations — more than a third of people — although it was lowest for Catholics and highest for smaller groups in the absence of sufficient marriage partners. This evidence shows that Protestants were a united community in this period, and the difficulties facing small denominations as autonomous communities, in comparison with the larger denominations.[37] There was so much socialising and intermarriage between members of all churches that church practices became more alike. When intermarriage occurred it was the custom for women to change to the denomination of their husband, and very often the wife would be more faithful to the new church than her husband.

By the early twentieth century the Easter Bible class camp was a key opportunity to choose a potential marriage partner. Although they were single-sex camps, at crucial points in the large Easter camps the men's and women's camps joined together. These very large camps were intended to exhort young people to live as Christians, but they were also very important in linking them into a denominational community. Hundreds of young men or young women were at each regional camp, and so they certainly multiplied the social contacts of many people, especially in the days before compulsory education was raised to the age of 15.[38] The Student Christian Movement, established in 1896, and its evangelical rival, the Inter-Varsity Fellowship founded in 1935, introduced university students into a wider social sphere beyond their denomination.

THE PURITANISM OF THE Protestant tradition meant that leisure in general was somewhat problematic. 'But the question will be put, what amusements would you recommend?' wrote one author in 1850.

> You denounce horse racing, theatre, gambling, balls; if you take away all these, what would you substitute? We frankly acknowledge that the subject of Christian amusements is one of considerable difficulty, and one to which the Christian public would do well to pay more attention. Amusements are one of the last strongholds in which Satan entrenches himself in Christian communities . . .

> All experience proves that the simple, soothing and cheery entertainments that individuals and families can provide for themselves are immeasurably more satisfying than the boisterous, exciting amusements that can be obtained only a few times a year.[39]

One hundred years later, 'the racecourse, the theatre, the dance hall, the billiard room, the card-table, gambling and the pernicious novel' were still attacked by evangelists as 'worldly'.[40] Catholics, too, had their version of this concern; for example, a father who expressed horror that 'the boarding-house apple, the painted, powdered, cocktail drinking and cigarette smoking girl is far more sought after than the happy but decorous Catholic girl'.[41] It was not uncommon for 'sacred concerts' to compete with vaudeville, but the tone was very different.[42]

Boxing Day and New Year's Day picnics were sometimes sponsored by the church, but the greatest outdoor event in the church calendar was the annual Sunday school picnic. This was an immensely popular occasion in the community. The Sunday school picnic attracted all the Sunday school children (even irregular attendees) and often their families. A sportsground or domain would be booked and transport to it arranged. Various summer sports were organised in different corners of the domain, including cricket, football, rounders and tug of war. Families might bring their own picnic lunch, but food would be provided for children, and boiled water would be provided for tea. After various races came the climactic moment of the lolly scramble, sometimes including 'the lolly man', in which a volunteer wearing a coat with bags of sweets sewn into it would be mauled by children seeking to rip the bags off him. Often such events ended with a sing-song of hymns.[43]

These picnics could be huge. At Motueka in 1874 the Wesleyans' Sunday school anniversary picnic was held on Good Friday (for Methodists in those days ignored 'Holy Week'), and 250 people came to the picnic and the public tea that followed.[44] In Auckland, 1400 people went by steamer to their destination in East Tāmaki for the Baptist Tabernacle's Boxing Day picnic in 1890, which also included an informal welcome to the new pastor.[45] St Michael's in Christchurch took the children by train to Lyttelton and hired a steamer to take them out on Lyttelton Harbour. In Tauranga, New Year's Day was the day when all observed their Sunday school picnics, so the Presbyterians and Anglicans went to Mount Maunganui, and the Catholics and Wesleyans to Ōtūmoetai. Massive preparations were required, with teams going early to light fires for boiling billies and to set out tables. In 1890 appalling weather disrupted the journey to the sites, with seasickness, torn dresses and upset women.[46]

These picnics continued through the first 60 years of the twentieth century, with some changes. Some secular bodies and a few churches began to hold their picnics

A Sunday school picnic at Zabell's Paddocks, near Carterton in the Wairarapa, in 1934. The adults are handing out food and the children hold cups of drink. MASTERTON DISTRICT LIBRARY ARCHIVE, 06-133/26

on a Sunday.[47] Graham Barnett, Dean of Waikato from 1927 to 1932, regarded this trend as symptomatic of the moral collapse of modern society.[48] Even in 1963 there were protests when Waikari Presbyterian Church held its picnic on the sacred day.[49] The other major organisers of picnics were large businesses, and the working class found that day far more convenient.[50]

The other great social event organised by churches in the nineteenth century was the mid-winter Saturday night soirée or tea meeting. The soirée was, as one speaker explained at the Whangarei Presbyterian Church in 1869, 'calculated to foster and promote intimacy and good feeling among the settlers. Although nominally denominational, the interest taken in them is not by any means confined to the body towards whose funds the proceeds are applied. They are attended promiscuously by all classes, and the friendliness and good feeling which pervade the assembly testify to the usefulness of the institution...'[51]

We know a great deal about these events because secular newspapers, short of copy, often described them in detail. One wet night in Invercargill in 1869, the soirée completely lifted the mood: 'what with the cheery chink of china, the aroma of the steaming tea, the profusion of rich cake, the delicious looking fruit, the other nice things, the blooming looks and gay dresses of the ladies, and the generally felt though unexpressed sympathetic cordiality of a happy crowd, the aspect of comfort within presented a strong and pleasing contrast to that of misery and mire without'.[52]

Thus at the soirée the church entertained the community. Churches sought to attract the largest possible crowds, and extract money from them by offering food and entertainment. Sumptuous displays of food were characteristic of New Zealand communities and congregations, both in town and countryside. The tea meeting displayed this very publicly. Generally one woman took charge of providing food for each table. The food was served in the first half-hour. This description of the annual soirée organised by St Paul's Presbyterian Church in Ōamaru in 1868 is a vintage of the style:

> Ample provision was made in the way of creature comforts, the tables being loaded with fruit, cake and other good things in such profusion as would have been ample to satisfy ten times the number of persons that could possibly be got into the hall. The building was thronged, there not being a single spare seat, and indeed some had to content themselves with mere standing room. Tables were furnished by the following ladies Mrs Connor, Mrs Hassell, Mrs Hall, Mrs Fleming, Mrs Hedley, Mrs M'Aulay, Mrs Young, Mrs Kerr, Miss Scott, and valuable contributions were given by Messrs M'Master, Gilchrist, King, Booth Brother, Morton, and many others... The proceedings were opened by praise

and prayer and after due attention has been paid to the tea and etceteras, the clatter of cups and spoons, and the hum of merry voices were hushed, and all present joined in the singing of a hymn. The Rev. Chairman then addressed the meeting . . .[53]

Sometimes others took responsibility for the food, and at the previously mentioned meeting at St Paul's Wesleyan Church in Invercargill in 1869, the bachelors prepared the tables, supervised by the women of the congregation.[54] Salvation Army tea meetings were simpler but more frequent, for they were intended to entice people to services. Working-class people seem to have often looked forward to 'a proper Salvation Army tea'.[55]

The meeting that followed the meal was generally interspersed with speeches, choir items, and sometimes a collection for church funds. The options on Saturday evening in the nineteenth century were mostly home-grown, and tea meetings competed with dances in popularity. Tea meetings lost secular support in the twentieth century. By then, churches were hard-pressed to sell tickets, and they became much more modest in-house affairs for members of local congregations.

The structure of Catholic sociability was somewhat different from that of Protestants. The parish sponsored a wide range of activities, some of them with no particular religious focus, although the priest was always the honoured guest at these occasions. This was the Catholic Church acting as an Irish community centre, and keeping Catholics from contamination by the Protestant world, following the urging of Pope Pius IX's strictures against contemporary society. Nevertheless, Catholics also welcomed opportunities when Protestants availed themselves of Catholic community fundraising events.

Public socialising was not the only aspect of the church community. A wide range of church activities required volunteer labour. Commitment meant volunteering to help, since the clergy were not expected to undertake menial tasks. Many people were required to run the Sunday school. Weekly rosters of church members were required to keep the church and its grounds clean and tidy. Flowers had to be replaced every Sunday. At least once a year (usually before a key public occasion, whether Christmas, Sunday school anniversary, or a wedding) a working bee would be held. The men of the congregation would tidy the grounds, and the women would spring-clean the church.[56] The event would end with a large morning tea.

The first use of the term 'working bee' that I can find was when members were called in to assist the rebuilding of a fence around the Wesleyan church in Wanganui in 1872, thus saving money, and developing good feelings between members.[57] Churches with a strong and active community also cut the costs of building projects massively by harnessing their membership. However, such projects needed to be short and sharp if the congregation was not to become exhausted and resentments build up. Glenfield Methodist Church was erected in a single day in 1915 by a carefully planned combination of volunteers and prepared material.[58]

RELIGIOUS GROUPS ALSO HOSTED a range of clubs and interest groups. The YMCA was the first such society, introduced to New Zealand in 1855 by Richard Shalders, a prominent Auckland Baptist layman, and for its first hundred years it blended social, sporting and devotional activities. Subsequently, local congregations also sponsored a range of organisations that encouraged a more committed sociability that was at once ethnic, political, social and religious. Such clubs were less important in the Protestant world where secular organisations — Freemasons, friendly societies and the like — flourished alongside congregations. Nevertheless each church had a wide range of literary and debating clubs, often indicative of the particular interests of the clergyman of the time, and often designed to retain links with the community. There were also temperance bodies for young people and adults. Most days of the week every corner of the church was in use by these parish organisations.

The Catholic parish organised itself into smaller units, the parish organisations called sodalities. Such communities, membership of which was strictly limited to Catholics, provided centres of sociability outside of the family. These many groups — the Holy Name Society, the Hibernian Society, the Children of Mary, the St Vincent de Paul Society, the Sacred Heart sodality — the earliest formed in the 1880s, the latest in the 1950s, held weekly meetings and a monthly Mass. Such groups brought together the natural peer groups within the parish, and kept them linked to the parish community. Each had its own distinctive uniform, which would be worn at the weekly meeting and at the monthly Mass.

Most of these groups were for women and children. There were two main groups for men. The Holy Name Society, first established in New Zealand in 1926, campaigned for Catholic interests in wider society.[59] The Hibernian Society was not a sodality as such, for it operated beyond the parish, but it was a Catholic equivalent of the Oddfellows Lodge, organising welfare payments for needy members, on strictly Catholic principles, and it was an alternative to the Fenians. The organisation was very significant in welding Catholic and Irish values together.[60] It was established in New Zealand in December 1869 when F. H. Byrne from the Ballarat society toured the West Coast goldfields and organised seven branches.[61]

By 1875 the Hibernian Society had spread widely, with its lodge-like green sashes and uniforms for the officers, and a good deal of dancing, drinking and socialisation. It also aimed to build up the church and, as explained during the address at the combined ordination of Bishops Whyte and Liston in 1920: 'Catholic young men who join our ranks insure themselves against want in times of sickness, old age, and distress, while at the same time, being in a thoroughly Catholic organisation, working with the approval and under the aegis of the Church, they are protected against many of the pitfalls to faith and morals which beset their path through life.'[62]

These organisations went into decline in the period after World War II, as their approach of order and hierarchy ceased to have wide appeal, and there was less need of their social insurance schemes.

DENOMINATIONS WERE HIGHLY IMPORTANT in the development of sociability. New arrivals, especially in towns, gravitated to their own denomination; here they were likely to find themselves absorbed into an existing network. It gave them a community, business contacts, and so on. Within smaller churches, members supported each other, and employers often offered positions to workers attending their church.[63] It encouraged them not to forget their Christian commitment as settlers. At that Wesleyan tea meeting in Invercargill in 1869 the local Presbyterian minister, Andrew Stobo, 'confessed to a strong love, or partiality for his own church, and believed it right that everyone should be attached to, and have a preference for some particular denomination, such a preference was to be praised rather than deprecated, as those who had no preference were generally rather indifferent to religion altogether, than simply liberal in their views, as they would have us believe'.[64]

Every denomination inculcated a sense of internal loyalty. Given the level of cross-denominational marriage in New Zealand, and the degree of mobility among settlers, congregations and denominations had to work to retain membership. Narrow denominational bigotry was much criticised, and many settlers were more interested in the quality of the church than its claim on existing loyalties.[65]

In the early part of the twentieth century Anglicans began to feel that their church required warmer sociability, lest it be undermined by other denominations. In 1930, Auckland Anglicans held a rally focusing on social services, which was choreographed by that great impresario Jasper Calder, the first City Missioner of Auckland. Ceremony and performance were emphasised. The event was held in the town hall, complete with an organ performance, choirs in robes and with banners, and with addresses that emphasised enjoyment and fellowship. Anglicans always hoped that traditional English rituals would create a feeling of belonging. But more than this was required. Jasper Calder's sermon included the remark that, 'The corporate life of the Church would be very much improved if the congregations, as well as the clergy, could only overcome a fault which was commonly described as Anglican stodginess.' He felt the church would flourish more 'if a little more warmth could be infused into the ordinary occasions of religious activity'.[66]

Another example was when the Rev. Joseph Feron, when vicar of St Matthew's in St Albans, Christchurch, between 1931 and 1937, attempted to revive the tradition of the clipping of the church, the practice of parishioners surrounding the church on a festival day and holding hands, looking outwards.[67] The revival of forgotten Anglican traditions appealed to some, and the approach continued to be successful at least in prosperous congregations like that of St Barnabas in Fendalton, Christchurch.

Still the overwhelming tone was one of cooperation. In the nineteenth century, most Protestants joined in each other's social events. Andrew Stobo, in that Invercargill event previously cited, went on to comment that 'he thought that all small, petty jealousies should be discarded, and that all should unite as one man in the great work of the church, the regeneration of the world'.[68] At social events the choirs of Presbyterians, Wesleyans and Anglicans could sing together.

Commentators looked on approvingly: 'It is evident, from many signs of the time, that the days of hard uncompromising cast iron creeds and formularies are fast passing away, and that a spirit is being developed in the churches braver, warmer, softer, more simple, more genial . . .'[69] At the Wellington Congregational Church soirée, the local Presbyterian minister, James Paterson, commented that the need for 'catholic intercourse' was much greater in a young country where the churches were so undeveloped.[70]

Non-Anglican Protestants (those called Dissenters in England) socialised together more than others. The Albertland Nonconformist settlement, which was launched in 1862 to commemorate 300 years since the Nonconformist Protestants were driven out of the Church of England, was intended to be built on a combined chapel led by the Rev. Samuel Edger. Actually the settlement failed disastrously, for its setting on the Kaipara Harbour was effectively a mudflat, and few of the settlers were willing to live in undefended country during the land wars. Yet Edger continued to advocate non-denominational Christianity in his chapel in Auckland, and the Congregationalists of Maungaturoto, the Wesleyans at Paparoa and the Baptists of Matakohe each supported the others' churches.[71]

The Presbyterian Church raised the issue of a union of denominations in 1902, and discussions developed between the world wars and progressed from 1951. The organisational church union movement is not the focus here, especially as the union never took place. At the local level, the first union parish was created by the Presbyterians and Methodists at Raglan in 1943, and in the new suburbs of Wainuiomata (1945), Johnsonville (1970) and Tawa (1972) in Wellington. In the 1960s, some Anglican dioceses began to participate in the creation of cooperating parishes, although some of these ventures were not sustained. In the countryside, as the population dropped, the churches explored amalgamation. These days two-thirds of Methodists are part of union or cooperating parishes (although it is more like one-third of Methodist members). The proportions are smaller for Presbyterians, and Anglicans have consciously withdrawn from most such relationships. At the local level, congregations soon decided how to work together, but struggled with the need to satisfy their sponsoring denominations.[72]

These cooperating ventures were difficult because the customs and protocols of denominations were different. Moreover, the networks of each denomination were inevitably separate. Union congregations worked best if they ignored all their denominational links and focused on the local community. The Wainuiomata union broadened to include Anglicans in 1965, but the existence of two buildings led denominational attitudes to survive. As a former minister noted, it was 'a parish which at times seemed intent on pulling itself apart by sections taking action without full thought for the total parish', as Anglicans demanded their ways of running services while Methodists and Presbyterians refused to concede.[73] The Anglican Church eventually withdrew, and the Presbyterians and Methodists became part of a larger Hutt Valley Cooperating Parish in 1995. Meanwhile the number of other denominations in the area multiplied.

In the nineteenth century, non-denominational churches were able to connect with a broad spectrum of their community. By the late twentieth century, the churches had mostly lost that connection, as the church became less mainstream in society. The trend was evident at least from the interwar years. T. Z. Koo, the Chinese Christian leader who visited New Zealand for the Student Christian Movement in 1931, noted the growth of labour activism and urged New Zealanders to find a spirituality that did not exaggerate differences with the people around, noting that 'if we attempted to carry out the teachings of Christ in the Church we would be given the cold shoulder'.[74]

Within the Christian community, links increased across denominational boundaries. The Student Christian Movement created a profound link between people of many liberal Protestant churches from 1900 to 1970, while the evangelical community included people from a wide range of very small churches. The charismatic movement in the Anglican, Presbyterian and Catholic churches in the 1970s created another network. Catholics in particular developed networks that were outside regular diocesan supervision. The visit of the American charismatic

Above A Bible class picnic on Labour Day in 1941. At the instigation of the Christian Youth Council, 300 members of various Wellington Bible classes went by train to Takapu Road Station in Tawa, and then climbed the Belmont hill to Lower Hutt. ALEXANDER TURNBULL LIBRARY. EVENING POST, 29 OCTOBER 1941

Below The Cub pack at the front of the Anglican congregation at Titirangi, which met in the Soldiers Memorial Church, opened in 1924. The photograph was taken in 1956. PAROCHIAL DISTRICT OF NEW LYNN (WELLS CAMPAIGN CANVASS BOOKLET), AUCKLAND, 1956

leader Bob Mumford in 1969 led to the formation of groups like the Light of Christ Covenant Community in Nelson and the Lamb of God community in Christchurch, which survived with little episcopal supervision.[75]

Charismatic Christians received little sympathy from Protestant denominational leaders, and charismatic churches came close to seceding. In the late 1970s a complaint was sent to the Bishop of Auckland about the charismatic vicar of the Pukekohe Anglican Church, who was discouraging nominal Anglicans from being married in the church or being candidates for confirmation.[76] Similarly, the charismatic movement at Hornby Presbyterian Church in Christchurch was frustrated with Presbyterian views on baptism and spirituality, and a group seceded to form a branch of the Elim Church.[77] These sorts of churches had a very strong sense of community.

IN SOME RESPECTS THE charismatic movement was the result of people seeking a style of church life that was less formal and more spontaneous. Historically church services had been public events, so people dressed up, looked their best and were on their best behaviour. The colonial churches had a minimal foyer, suitable for a coat and hat rack and nothing else. There was no morning tea after nineteenth-century church services. People did not attend church to socialise.

Church socialisation took place separate from services. Evening events like choir practices commonly ended with supper, often with cakes or scones provided. Sometimes after the Sunday evening service the minister's house was opened to guests. Supper was sometimes used to attract the working class to evening services (following English patterns).[78] In the 1970s, 'coffee times' were introduced after evening services.[79]

Morning tea was not offered after services. The women who would have been expected to bake the scones and serve the tea were, in fact, hard at work at home until just before the service preparing the weekly Sunday roast, the major meal of the week. It was not until the 1950s that morning tea seems to have been provided, initially for young people after Bible class and before the 11 a.m. service. Hamilton Central Baptist Church began to serve morning tea before the service in mid-1964. In the same year, Hanover Street Baptist Church in Dunedin began using its teenagers to serve morning tea after Sunday school and before the church service as they raised money for an overseas trip.[80]

When family services were begun (as discussed in Chapter 3), morning tea or lunch were provided so as to develop 'a deeper sense of togetherness'.[81] At St David's in Auckland, under the Rev. Owen Baragwanath, the numbers attending by 1963 warranted holding two Sunday morning services, with a family-focused service at 9.30, from which the children would depart to Sunday school. So a cup of coffee was provided after the service as parents waited for their children to leave their Sunday school classes.[82] In Baptist churches a new pattern emerged of a service of family worship, followed by morning tea and then an adult Bible hour. This occurred at Taita Baptist from 1973, followed by Wellington Central Baptist Church in 1979, and many other churches subsequently.[83] The morning tea also became important as some growing churches were forced to hold two Sunday morning services and they wanted to ensure some links between the two congregations.

Anglican morning teas aimed to make newcomers feel welcome. As the parish Communion became the central service, the commencement was adjusted to 10 or 10.30 a.m., specifically so that it could be followed by morning tea.

Changing social habits, including the decline of the Sunday roast, helped to reshape the pattern of worship. By the late 1980s most Baptist churches, like many others, had mostly reduced to one service at 10 a.m. followed by morning tea.[84] Amidst these changes, food symbolised the increasing emphasis on socialising within the congregation. One Baptist woman mused on ways in which the (more recent) New Zealand ideas of potluck and progressive dinners and barbecues, as well as the more traditional morning tea and supper, could make church life more attractive.[85]

As family patterns continued to change, another factor was the broader trend away from inviting people into the home. Churches realised that the one chance to incorporate parishioners into the church community was after the service. Eventually churches were modified to provide space for morning tea. (Colonial people would have abhorred the idea of bringing food into the sacred space.) Increasingly, people selected the church to attend on the basis of its perceived friendliness. In the nineteenth century a friendly church community might have been seen as inquisitive and invasive, but today the coffee is part of the religion.

Morning tea has steadily gone upmarket in some New Zealand churches, as the emergence of a coffee culture has forced improvements in their style and quality. The mega-churches have become known for the quality of their coffee. City Impact Church at Northcross in Auckland, for example, has a commercial café in its foyer. It is striking how the names of churches now signal this. Traditionally names of churches defined or hinted at the denomination, for example, Knox, or Wesley, or St Patrick's or St George's. In recent years the newer churches have dropped denominational labels, and call themselves 'Christian Fellowship' or 'Community Church', or a brand name like 'Life' or 'The Street'.

An early example of the search for sociability was the use of annual 'family camps'. Denominational campsites, which were initially created to be used for tenting camps for uniformed movements, Bible classes and youth groups, were converted into family campsites with better accommodation. For 20 years the Family Camp became an annual event for many churches, enabling families to get to know each other close at hand. By the 1990s, however, few families were able to be absent together for a whole weekend, and the practice faded out. Another example was the development of small home-based groups within the church during the 1970s. 'Home groups' or 'fellowship groups' became very popular, reflecting the desire of isolated people for supportive relationships.

At the heart of these trends lay a growing tendency to describe the church as a family. This language was rare before the 1950s, perhaps because the family itself was so strong a unit in New Zealand. In the age of the baby boom, family language became very strong throughout the community. Dean Gibson of Waiapu hammered home the point in a church newsletter in 1949. Complaining of how people absented themselves from some events, he insisted, '. . . cultivate and show the family Spirit. So we will have a healthy and happy parish, and from this a healthy and happy diocese and church.'[86]

Another indication of the new environment was a change in church newsletters. I own copies of the newsletters of the Church of the Holy Sepulchre in Auckland from the 1870s, which provided monthly information on services to that scattered parish, along with a lavish British-produced insert of 24 pages of Sunday reading (including stories with a moral, sermons, poems and lithographs).[87] This pattern was probably quite common, for St Mary's Merivale had a monthly newsletter from 1909, supported by local advertising.[88]

Changes in printing in the latter part of the twentieth century had dramatic effects on newsletters. Churches and schools installed Bandas, Gestetners and Xeroxes, and produced weekly bulletins circulating news to parishioners. The Catholic parish of Tainui began a three-monthly newsletter in April 1968, delivered to letter boxes, but then introduced a weekly bulletin at Mass every Sunday from June 1971. Computers, cheaper printers and email distribution lists have continued to facilitate the distribution of congregational news.[89]

At the same time as these changes were taking place, advertising declined as the church ceased to be a doorway to a local market and local shops became part of national chains. The members of the local congregation knew each other better, but the church was less part of the broader community. Some secular newspapers had a regular church column before the 1970s, but thereafter churches struggled to profile themselves in the local community. The contemporary move away from printed media has offered opportunities in sophisticated electronic media that some churches have taken up very skilfully, but others lack the resources to use them.

CATHOLIC PATTERNS OF SOCIALISING probably changed more than in other denominations. In Catholic parishes, like Protestant, it became evident that religious socialising had lost ground. After the Second Vatican Council of the 1960s all the parish sodalities, including the Holy Name Society and the Children of Mary, faded away. The Hibernians went into decline.[90] The coercion of the priest was challenged, and as a result many aspects of parish loyalty collapsed. Catholic parishes became much more like Protestant congregations, voluntary communities in which members chose how far their participation would go. The church sought to remain distinct from the other denominations. Conscious of the high number of marriages between Catholics and Protestants (which reflected the increase in secular socialising) the church was much criticised for its strict rules on intermarriage. From 1969 the Catholic bishops began to reshape their outlook on ecumenism, and slowly the regulations on mixed marriage were amended.[91]

As society became more individualistic, churches had to provide more room for choice. The church ceased to be so formal. As in broader society, people became freer in expressing their emotions. The Pentecostal movement introduced the hug in a manner not previously seen in churches. People clapped to music, raised their hands in worship, and expected to express their feelings.

People also became much freer in abandoning conventional religious behaviour. Since the 1980s it has become more common even for people who are themselves religious to say that their children have no religion until they 'make up their own mind'; thus religion becomes like a favourite colour or food, far less integral to identity, but related to self-presentation. Meanwhile, people in the wider world try out relationships, and there are now dating apps that target church members. The venue for marriage is no longer a measure of very much; a church may be chosen simply because it is pretty, just like any other attractive setting. Divorce procedures, once rare among those within the church world, have gradually loosened. In the early 1970s Anglicans for the first time allowed the marriage of divorced people, but only through the bishop's office. In the first year of this practice the Auckland Diocese reported 185 applications, and approved all but eight of them.[92] Figures for Catholic annulments are not available, but they are likely to be high.

Responding to these changes has become a major preoccupation for churches. A very perceptive Brethren elder once commented to me that many members of congregations demand that the church provide activities and support to make up for failures in their social lives, even when the need is irrelevant to their spirituality. His suggestion was to let people organise these things for themselves. Few churches can afford to be so bold, but only the mega-churches are able to meet the varied needs thrown up in contemporary society.

It may be that the emphasis on church as community reflects a decline that has taken place in recent years in the individual aspect of Christianity. Christian involvement seems to come today in surges rather than consistent habits. Private Bible reading appears to have dropped dramatically from the patterns of 50 years ago, for regular Bible readers now make up just 21 per cent of church attendees.[93] In the Catholic Church, saying the rosary would also appear to have declined.

Yet the Christian tradition is that worship is not just an individual act, the quiet visit to a temple at a time of particular need. The congregation worships as a community. Does the bond of socialisation facilitate that worship? Is it possible to distinguish one from the other? Do the new migrants who come to church to practise their English find there a doorway to awakening a religious sense? Certainly contemporary churches seem to assume that traffic between the two is for the benefit of both.

The sociability of faith is a reflection of a range of needs and pressures, from commercial emphases on styles of socialisation to the nature of church events in the lives of people. Religion is not just sociability, but sociability has always been important to the Christian churches.

Above The Sunday school at St Thomas's, New Lynn, Auckland, in 1956. It clearly overwhelmed the space available for it. A new hall was finally opened in 1961. PAROCHIAL DISTRICT OF NEW LYNN (WELLS CAMPAIGN CANVASS BOOKLET), AUCKLAND, 1956

Below The Catholic Women's League's float at the procession celebrating Upper Hutt attaining city status on 28 May 1966. The motto of the League — Faith and Service — is set in a floral display. Photograph by Revelle Jackson. UPPER HUTT CITY LIBRARY

The Gendered Church

Previous The wives of the Anglican bishops in the 1860s. From left: Emily Harper, Jane Williams (seated), Sarah Selwyn, Caroline Abraham and her son Charlie. Bishops' wives were responsible for diocesan hospitality and social service.
ALEXANDER TURNBULL LIBRARY. REF: 1/2-053363-F

GENDER CAN HARDLY BE overlooked as an aspect of culture in the churches. It has permeated all aspects of the life of the churches and has been profoundly accepted as an intrinsic aspect of their character. In a country as strongly gendered as New Zealand, the church needed to be strictly coded. That role has changed profoundly over the years. From the 1970s a radical movement transformed the churches as it transformed many other parts of society, and perhaps even more, since it attacked a clearly articulated ideology. This subject has been very intensively researched by students over the past two decades.

Growing up in one of the most gendered of all denominations, I inherited all those traditions, as well as coming from a large family of boys, and I had few problems at first with the teachings of Paul. So I took a long time to understand the subtleties of gender. Applying a cultural lens has clarified my perspective. Women were critical to the success of the New Zealand church from the outset, and yet their role was nowhere else so tightly circumscribed. To understand this, we must explore a set of cultural assumptions that now sound very strange.

The norms of the missionary movement were rather different from those of the churches they came from. Women were not initially accepted as suitable on their own for missionary work. Then Marianne Coldham, who married the early CMS missionary Henry Williams, and Jane Nelson, who married his brother and fellow missionary William Williams, insisted that they be accepted by the CMS as missionaries in their own right.[1]

In practice their opportunities were curtailed by their responsibility to maintain a missionary home, but they did find opportunities for school teaching and getting alongside Māori girls. Later a number of single women missionaries joined the CMS, including Dorcas Baker who served with Alfred N. Brown at Tauranga from 1839 to 1847; Hannah Hart, who was sent to help in the school in Paihia but drowned in 1829 when the ship she was on sank en route; Mary Ann Williams, who took her place at Paihia in 1831 and married another missionary, James Preece, in 1833; and Maria Coldham, sister of Marianne, who from 1832 to 1835 helped in the school in Paihia until she married John Morgan. Most of the single women missionaries came as sisters of existing missionaries and became teachers at their mission stations, which gave the mission inroads into Māori households.

There is also the striking case of Elizabeth Fairburn, daughter of one of the first missionaries, who had a powerful sense of vocation, which overrode her arranged marriage to the missionary printer William Colenso in 1843 and its subsequent collapse. She gave long and remarkable service in correcting the drafts of the Māori Bible and with the Melanesian Mission. As Cathy Ross, a student of CMS missionaries, has written, she was certainly more than a wife.[2]

Historian Angela Wanhalla has shown that 'native women' were viewed as an enticement to the male missionaries, yet those missionaries were anxious to conduct the ceremonies when 'Pakeha Maori' married their Māori wives.[3] After the marital difficulties of Thomas Kendall and accusations of homosexual acts by William Yate (after which his sister Sarah abandoned her vocation), missionaries needed a strong marriage. Little wonder that some early female missionaries were so resilient.

The missionary vision included concern about gender issues. Missionary supporters in England were aroused by the fate of widows in India, whose responsibility to immolate themselves when their husbands were cremated was seen as one of the most pernicious aspects of Hinduism. The 'Zenana' missions were those that reached out specifically to women, and later New Zealanders strongly supported them.[4] There were concerns about the lives of indigenous women in New Zealand, for the wife of Ruatara committed suicide after his death and other women gashed themselves on the death of their husbands.[5] Missionaries made it their business to rescue women at risk.[6] They also taught that Māori converts should abandon polygamy.[7]

G ENDER IS CULTURALLY SHAPED. Māori notions of female propriety did not require them to be delicate, instead requiring most to undertake manual labour. Women were expected to show aroha, love, family obligation and care for whānau and community.[8] Some were ngā wāhine toa, strong women — women holding together the framework and values of the society. Māori grandmothers played a critical role in the preservation of the church. Grandmothers kept values alive, and made up for men who might be absent doing rough work as shearers or shepherds, or serving in the Māori Battalion during World War II.[9] After the war, the Maori Women's Welfare League inspired and directed women to take initiatives to protect their communities. The churches and their welfare organisations used many of the same women and knew their skills. Māori men, however, were not comfortable with women too engaged outside the marae.

The male Māori Catholic clergy were a small but influential part of Māori society, but Māori women were not generally encouraged to join religious orders. One who did was Hoki or Peata, niece of Rewa, the great leader of Ngāpuhi in the 1830s, who professed as a Sister of the Holy Family in 1863.[10] There were only a few subsequent Māori nuns. When Anglicans debated the ordination of women, Māori were generally opposed.[11] Numia Tomoana, a Māori Anglican priest and chaplain, in an interesting survey of Māori women ordained after 1977, observed that they faced intense hostility from male clergy.[12] Diana Tana was ordained by the Methodist

Church in 1975, and Puti Murray was ordained to the Anglican priesthood in 1978, but these pioneers ministered initially in Pākehā contexts.[13]

The dominance of males in nineteenth-century New Zealand was not as great as in Australia, but still significant. At the extreme in 1861, at the beginning of the goldrush years, there were only 620 women to every 1000 men in the colony. By 1901 this imbalance had improved to 903 women to 1000 men. Nevertheless, there was a significant group of men among the first generation of settlers who never married, and a higher proportion of widowers than today. The proportion of married or widowed men among the over-45s was 768 per 1000 in 1896, which is very low. These factors awoke concern about their wellbeing in old age, and the Liberal Government enacted the Old Age Pension to address the situation. By 1966 the proportion of married people among those over 45 was 831 per 1000. In contrast, almost all women in New Zealand were married in the nineteenth century, and the proportion of single women consistently declined until 1961.

The church sought to minister to both genders. There were no religious equivalents of the code that women should not enter the public bar. All worshipped together (although James Pinfold reported that in his first Wesleyan circuit of Upper Thames, or Coromandel, in 1881 only men attended one of his churches, and when the first woman arrived she was such a curiosity that the stares of men forced her to retreat.)[14] Families sat together in almost all churches, which also made the male loners a little uncomfortable.

In a well-known article the Auckland historian Raewyn Dalziel argued that the Victorian domestic ideal was somewhat modified in New Zealand because of the heavy work required of women settlers.[15] Yet women's work was regulated by gender rules. The home was seen by church leaders as the sacred sphere of women, and religious authority was cited to endorse this ideal. In a sermon given to young women in 1872 the Rev. James Buller, Wesleyan missionary and minister, insisted that the sacred role of women was to be home-makers.[16] When the Anglican Mothers' Union was founded in 1886, its listed 'objects' focused on children and the sacredness of marriage.[17] The watchword of the Women's Christian Temperance Union, which commenced New Zealand activities in 1885, was 'For God, for Home, and Humanity'.[18] The domestic ideal was attacked by some women in the 1890s, but support for it revived in the early twentieth century.

The Victorian domestic ideal became more prevalent in New Zealand as colonial society matured. In a debate on women's role in Auckland in 1871, the Bible was repeatedly cited.[19] Admittedly, colonial advocates modified the British middle-class vision of feminine delicacy. An article in the Methodist *Christian Observer* in 1870 praised 'the wife of noble character' of Proverbs 31, rejecting 'dainty' Victorian expectations. The author complained that: 'Some seem to be of the opinion that she ought not to be expected to lift anything heavier than pins and needles, and never more than a cotton reel; and that if she faints in a crowd, or sinks down on a sofa with the slightest exertion, she is only giving evidence of her distinctive womanly characteristics.'

Yet although the author considered women strong enough to survive the 'stern demands of an unsympathising world', the article also urged women to marry husbands to whom they could safely submit and trust.[20] An editorial in a later issue of the same magazine suggested that the colonial woman needed to be Martha — active, working, with a high view of domestic duties — and it therefore reproved enthusiasm for clothing as immoral. A woman replied to this editorial, insisting that 'I have not learnt that women are vainer than men,' but she felt obliged to deny that she was a champion of women's rights.[21]

Behind this was a stereotypical vision of women's spirituality. Female spirituality was understood to be passive, although women were also urged to prayer and action. Women's prayer meetings were often praised in the nineteenth century as models of spiritual zeal.[22] The church deployed two languages: one of advance, war, engagement, militancy, which might be termed a masculine language; the other a language of suffering and service, and this was largely a female language. Women were the symbol of good values and religiosity. A daybook compiled during World War I included the poem 'Sisterhood of Service' by the American poet Margaret E. Sangster. The words seem to have been changed to reflect the number of women who served in the New Zealand Baptists' mission:

> In sisterhood of service
> Dear master may we be
> Consecrated members
> Working, serving thee.
> Our aim to spread thy gospel
> To people of East Bengal
> Our prayer, that they may know thee
> As Saviour & Lord of all.[23]

Women were devoted servants, and so the characteristic virtues of women were supposed to be their patience and endurance.[24] They also felt responsibility for the purification of society.[25] Women were placed on a pedestal as responsible for great social reforms, but the pedestal inhibited them from actual participation. The editor of the *New Zealand Methodist Times* praised women, 'Oh, you queens, you queens,' in an exhortation that women would swing the vote in the 1922 prohibition poll, but he did not encourage them into actual engagement.[26] Because women were weaker, they deserved protection by men. Church leaders consistently demanded that women deserved special treatment.

MARRIED WOMEN IN THEIR home base had a status and authority that enabled them to treat unmarried women and young men as incomplete. Women drew on the authority of their husbands. The view of the congregation as a 'family' implied that there were gender patterns in the church and different roles for men and women. Elderly women could be 'mothers in Israel'. Perhaps this thinking still exists in the way the church is viewed today, although the family now seems much more casually structured. Sarah Dalton has argued in a fine thesis that the temperance movement encouraged women to develop a maternal protective vision.[27]

The colonial pattern of the hard-working wife with few or no servants subtly changed the Victorian ideal of the woman in the home. Women learned to be strong and determined, and challenged the demure image of Victorian women. In 1866, the small Methodist City Mission in Auckland began to hold a mothers' meeting on a Monday at 2 p.m., where respectable working-class women could offer their services to middle-class church women, in a kind of labour market.[28]

Despite these changes, the vision of the ideal woman was still very maternal. The good Catholic mother was praised for protecting the home from defiling influences such as improper reading matter.[29] Mothers' Unions (with the vicar's wife presiding at the parish branch and the bishop's wife at diocesan level) began in the Anglican parishes from 1886, and the wife of the Governor, Lord Glasgow, helped these bodies to develop rapidly in the 1890s.[30] They affiliated to the English organisation, so a Mothers' Union Dominion Council was not formed until 1926. The League of Mothers meanwhile flourished in other Protestant churches.

Movements of 'scientific motherhood', eugenics and race purity, and above all the Plunket Society, founded in 1907, portrayed the ideal woman as domestic in her outlook, giving her all to her children.

A different kind of morality was demanded of women than of men, and the code had become more restrictive by the early twentieth century, especially for respectable women. Unrespectable women preserved their freedoms. A marvellous short story by the Methodist minister and prohibitionist the Rev. James Cocker, published in 1918, tells the story of a young Kiwi soldier from a good Methodist background, who on going to war broke his teetotal pledge at Sling Camp in Britain, and then got engaged to a working-class woman with no religious background. She came out to New Zealand to marry him, and all went well until he discovered that she smoked. The husband was a smoker, of course, but, as he explained, his body was more able to cope with cigarettes than hers. Her next step was drinking whisky. Happily, when they were both converted she instantly gave up both vices and discovered a life of purity and marital bliss.[31]

Many women connived at their own exclusion from public participation in the church. Gender stereotypes were limited in the first church services, for they were held in homes, open spaces and undenominational chapels, but denominational churches immediately adopted existing rules. Consider the case of the fascinating Brethren pioneer Catharine Squires, née Dewe, from an Anglican background, who with her husband lived in an unchurched part of Southland. She became leader of a Brethren assembly and, having resisted the local Presbyterian minister because of his willingness to take up a collection from the unconverted, she established preaching in 'the temple', her front parlour. From 1883 to 1896 she was a powerful influence, and her husband simply the back-up.[32] But when they retired to Invercargill, she kept silent in services at the gospel hall.

So while women often were the strongest supporters of the building of churches,[33] those buildings became public or even sacred space with their own restrictive gender codes. Women continued to take responsibility for the care and furnishing of the church, but their role changed on Sunday. The church was a place one dressed up to go to; there, one behaved properly. Women were expected to show their modesty in the church service, for at such a formal event roles were tightly segregated.

Hats were profoundly important for all churches as a symbol of submission and modesty. As early as 1870 preachers were complaining that women dressed too fashionably in church.[34] Catholic women wore hats or a handkerchief, and a nice story from a Catholic context where one woman criticised another — 'You with your fancy window dressing on your hat and you only ever put threepence on the plate' — shows some of the status hinted at by the hat.[35] Among the Brethren hats were even more important, some insisting that outsiders should be furnished with hats if they visited the church.[36] Hats were also a potent class symbol when combined with white gloves when at church.[37] (St Paul said nothing about gloves, demonstrating that the underlying issue was the formality expected in a public space.) Women in church were almost always 'the ladies', and church women guarded their status even more than men did.

These rules were linked to a wider concern over inappropriate dress. At least one nineteenth-century Methodist editor made fierce criticisms of 'dress among Christians', largely focusing on women.[38]

There were rules for men as well. They were expected to remove their hats in church, and at an early Salvation Army meeting there was a showdown with the young men who chose not to comply.[39] Most men wore a suit and tie to church, and many respectable working-class men owned suits that were solely used on Sunday. Boys were expected to wear a tie. Church dress was very different from their garb for work or play.

STRONG AND DETERMINED WOMEN still found some opportunities. At various times, male leadership failed, and then very often women stepped forward, as Methodist circuit stewards, for example.[40]

Women were treated as housekeepers for the real leaders of the church. Among their major responsibilities were the church cleaning, catering, picnics, and floral displays. Catering was important, and gave women a key role in shaping the framework for sociability. 'Ladies a plate please' was uniform in society and church. Some fundraising was also dominated by women, through fairs, sales of work, flower shows, bring and buys, and sewing.

Church music offered only limited opportunities for women. English Anglican cathedral choirs were made up of men and boys. The early New Zealand church choirs had women members, but the moment the choir was robed, women had to be hidden away, since there was no precedent for robes for women. Similarly women were also often organists, but could not appear to lead the music (or be robed).[41] At St Mark's Remuera, women were excluded from the choir. At St Mary's Merivale they were still enrolled in the choir (and were far more consistent in their attendance than men), but they were seated in the front rows of the church, not in the choir stalls. It remained like this until at least 1934.[42] Only in the postwar period did most Anglican choirs agree to dress women in similar robes and mortar boards to the male choristers, recognising that their voices were needed.

Lay women were sometimes more dedicated to the church than any man, ordained or not. Consider the case of Mrs Jane Dickie née Smith (who died about 1928). Her focus was a longing for a revival in the Mataura area. Her obituary indicates her great faith and prayer, commenting that 'those who were privileged to listen to Mrs Dickie in public prayer felt the definiteness and reality of her petitions', as well as her sense of love and sympathy towards the sick, her assistance to her husband, who was for some time a home missionary of the Presbyterian Church, her huge Sunday school class of senior girls and her work for temperance through the Band of Hope.[43] The obituaries of the many such women usually give them the honorific biblical phrase of being 'mothers in Israel'. Such praise recognised Mrs Dickie's ministry to the community as a whole, not just her backroom domestic support of her husband. Modest assistance was an important female duty. In the Catlins, in south Otago, William McKenzie's mother urged her son to invite preachers who brought revival to the district in 1885.[44]

In exceptional circumstances women were allowed to speak in church. Mrs Leavitt, from the American Women's Christian Temperance Union, spoke widely in the Protestant churches of New Zealand, much to the surprise of onlookers.[45] Mrs Margaret Hampson was very widely used from 1881 to 1884 as an evangelist throughout the same churches.[46] Mrs Joan Scott, a Christchurch Wesleyan, held revival meetings in Wesleyan churches up and down the country in the 1880s and 1890s. The striking eloquence of these women enabled them to break the rules, although that did not stop complaints against Joan Scott from some who opposed women speaking in churches.[47]

Smaller denominations stood to benefit most from allowing a wider ministry by women, and for this reason such denominations were obliged to decide where they stood on the issue. The Primitive Methodists and the Salvation Army increased their impact through their effective use of their women members. The Primitive Methodists were the first denomination that placed women preachers on their preaching plan. The denomination acknowledged Mrs P. W. Jones of Greendale, whose preaching engagements included the Phillipstown Sunday school anniversary in Christchurch and at the original New Plymouth church; Mrs J. L. Wright of Wellington; Mrs Douglas, the temperance speaker, and Mrs Linton of the Manawatu, and Miss Lefanu and Mrs Kerr of Auckland.[48]

The Salvation Army provided a new deal for women, and its women officers had a significant profile. Nevertheless, as observers noted at the time, the militancy of the army rhetoric had a particular appeal to men, rather than women. In the Catlins revival, the initial religious groundswell came when two female Salvation Army officers spoke at cottage meetings. 'The people used to come from miles around to hear those earnest spirit-filled lasses,' commented a local historian.[49] However, even co-founder Mrs Catherine Booth, formidable in her power to direct the movement alongside her husband, was not able to create an organisation of complete equality save by the force of her personality.[50] After her death in 1890 the opportunities for Salvationist women increasingly depended on the status of their husbands. This reflected a broader decline in female opportunities in the dominion after 1900.

Most New Zealand congregations had boards or vestries and congregational meetings, but women were rarely permitted to make contributions in these forums. In its founding Articles of Faith and Rules, adopted on 14 June 1842, Woodward Street Congregational Church in Wellington required that 'No female members be allowed

Above The Temperance Ladies' Brass Band of Auckland in the 1910s. The identity of this band is unclear; no reports of its performances have been found, although there was a Temperance Guards Brass Band. ALEXANDER TURNBULL LIBRARY. REF: 1/2-000336-G

Below The ladies of the New Lynn Anglican parish meeting with Mrs Isherwood, the vicar's wife (unidentified), in the vicarage to plan for the Wells Campaign, 1956. PAROCHIAL DISTRICT OF NEW LYNN (WELLS CAMPAIGN CANVASS BOOKLET), AUCKLAND, 1956

to speak in the Church, only to vote according to the command of Scripture.'[51] This was consistent with wider patterns in society. Women were not permitted to speak at the annual meetings of the Ladies Benevolent Association in the 1870s, even though they managed the society themselves.[52]

At the time of the debate over the women's franchise, there was discussion in many churches as to whether women should speak in church meetings. The Congregationalists were the first to lift the ruling against female representation at the annual church conference in 1891.[53] The reluctance to make this concession is evident at the national level, but most congregations were even more reluctant. The former premier Sir John Hall was a member of St Mary's Merivale at the time of the enfranchisement of women in 1893 and he ensured that the parish debated the issue, and a further debate took place in 1911. However, both the vicar of the day and his successor argued that it was a bad idea because women were driven by instincts rather than reason, and because if they came to church meetings in the same numbers that they came to church, they would outnumber men.[54]

In all institutions, roles were defined for each gender. Men chaired committees, even if women were permitted to play other roles in the organisation. Men were always responsible for finances. Women's role in church activities outside of services included caring for the needy

The ladies of St Peter's Anglican Church, Onehunga, Auckland, in the 1940s. The women of this working-class suburb appear to have been photographed with their children at nearby Jellicoe Park. AUCKLAND ANGLICAN DIOCESAN ARCHIVES

through very extensive charitable work (although men controlled the funds and directed the charity), providing informal pastoral care and educating children. Sunday schools were a key organisation in most churches, and a Christchurch writer, Ruth Fry, demonstrated in her study of Methodist women that this was the main public role occupied predominantly by women.[55] Women provided voluntary labour as collectors for such charities as the Bible Society and the Leprosy Mission, and in this they proved far more skilled and successful than men.[56]

There was a hierarchy among church women. The minister's wife wielded considerable influence, but she had in return to fulfil a series of expectations. A skilled woman was a massive support to her pastor husband. She could be much more enterprising and operate well beyond the ladylike role assigned to the English vicar's wife.[57] In 1889 the Methodist newspaper reprinted a grim account of the frustrations of a minister's wife who was constantly reminded by the congregation of her predecessor's skills.[58] The wife of the minister was the classic example of the helpmeet, modelling the submissive role of the Christian woman.[59] As late as the 1950s the brochures of the Wells fundraising organisation presented a very stereotyped role of the vicar's wife, providing loving but silent support for her husband and hospitality for the parish.[60] The wives of bishops had a more important role, and historians have shown that it required great skill to be supportive of the bishop, a hostess to the clergy and the synod, and taking the lead in social agencies and benevolence.[61]

The temperance movement upset the gender roles but had surprisingly little impact on the culture of churches. When Christadelphianism (a sectarian split from the Churches of Christ) commenced in New Zealand in the 1890s it had a significant appeal to women, including some who had been active in the WCTU. This sect, while eager to teach women the scriptures, and allowing them some part in its leadership, taught emphatically that women could not speak in public meetings. The result was that some erstwhile supporters left, but at least one became silent because of her new convictions.[62]

THERE WAS WARM SUPPORT for women's education among church people, to judge by the applause when Major John Richardson, a former superintendent of Otago Province, spoke on the subject in Knox Church, Dunedin in 1870, but this education was expected to be very practical.[63] The churches sponsored girls' schools, and had clear views about their curriculum.[64] They did not expect the schools to advocate equality, and many expected daughters to be brought up more strictly than boys.

The large congregations in the cities sometimes devolved social service roles to women. Thus the Knox Church deacons court gave responsibility to their Ladies' Association for the distribution of assistance to the poor in 1879, providing either food or homemade clothing and advising the poor in their homes.[65]

Above all, women provided practical care for people in and beyond the congregation. Although the minister was in theory the person responsible for pastoral care, women's networks became very quickly aware of families where illness or bereavements meant that they needed childcare, meals or other practical support. This aspect of the church community is impossible to measure, but at the funerals of women members, tributes were given that show the levels of generosity and care so necessary in immigrant communities.

The story of Suzanne Aubert (Sister Mary Joseph) shows that women were particularly welcome in the post-colonial Māori communities. Protestant missionaries among Māori included a significant group of women, many of whom began with no knowledge of Māori culture; the scholar Margaret Tennant has shown this in her analysis of the role of deaconesses among Māori.[66] Sister Dorothy Pointon, a Methodist, had a tough background in the settler world, but she was shaken by her experience in the Māori community. She was sent without any guidance to work with Māori at Te Kūiti in 1938, and caused offence when she appeared at the Ngāruawāhia regatta, as a white woman. She was sent to vacuum the lounge for Princess Te Puea.[67] European women may have been welcome, but they had to learn not to threaten the prestige of iwi leaders. Women deaconesses in the Māori branch of the Presbyterian Church were displaced by ordained Māori men after World War II.[68]

The greatest contribution of New Zealand women was to missions throughout the world. In the late Victorian era, when women became acceptable as missionaries, there was a flood of vocations. A very significant group of single women were sent to places all over the world, sometimes facing astonishing risks. New Zealand contributed a very interesting range of missionary women to overseas missions, including women in the Bolivian Indian Mission, the China Inland Mission and the New Zealand Church Missionary Association.

Missionary interest was unevenly distributed. From the small community of Ōwaka, for example, Annie Morton went to India with the Poona and Village Mission in 1897 and again in 1903, and Mary A. Bradfield went to India with the Baptist Mission in 1918.[69] A significant proportion of the missionaries from that most male-dominated of churches, the Open Brethren, were women. The same was true for almost all denominations. Hugh Morrison, the Otago scholar, has produced a very detailed list of missionaries, which suggests that New Zealand may have had one of the highest levels of missionary volunteers in the world, and that single women contributed significantly to these figures.[70]

Strong women sensed an opportunity to use their gifts on the mission field, and some were nudged into missionary service. There they could be heroic, could organise men and preach, but when they returned to New Zealand to report their adventures only the women were invited to hear them. Brethren had the tightest restrictions on women but many missionary volunteers. One writer did not want women to write missionary reports in the denominational magazine, which seemed, as the editor pointed out, a bit rough, considering that the men had failed to volunteer as missionaries.[71] There was even a case in the Brethren where men listened from behind a curtain to a missionary talk from an eloquent sister just back from overseas.

In the 1921 census, the distribution of women employed in religion was quite out of proportion to their numbers in society. Among the 484 women were 58 Anglicans, 47 Presbyterians, 140 Catholics, 26 Methodists, 12 Baptists, 153 Salvationists and 10 Brethren. Catholics and particularly Salvationists were significantly over-represented. In addition, it seems likely that many of those employed in charitable work and in education may have been nuns.[72] This is borne out by the less detailed 1926 census numbers for women in employment, which combined the figures for social welfare and religion. Employed Catholic women in this list numbered 1369 (compared to 319 Anglicans, 207 Presbyterians, 61 Methodists and 249 Salvationists).[73] The total of 2347 was 1.8 per cent of the 129,812 women employed in the dominion.

The culture of Catholicism was utterly different for women than for most Protestants. Mary Betz has traced the way in which Catholic women's images and concepts of God have been shaped by the New Zealand environment.[74] Catholic working-class homes were sometimes as rough as any working-class home when alcohol was abused, but young women from such a background could be and were called to a religious vocation. Most of the orders active in New Zealand had been formed by very strong visionaries and purposeful figures, although mostly the pioneers were not based in New Zealand. The founders of religious orders often wielded power even when the authorities opposed them. Mother Celia Maher, who brought the first Sisters of Mercy to New Zealand in 1850, and Sister Mary Joseph Aubert, who came to New Zealand in 1860, both came from superior backgrounds.

Sister Aubert fell out with bishops, changed diocese and changed locations until her Daughters of Our Lady of Compassion were set up with all that they could possibly need. Her case is doubly interesting because she frequently irritated the church authorities (including her original order), but could count on the unwavering support of the Māori and working-class communities she ministered to. In the process she became adept at finding male supporters who were then expected to back the order. These men did not need to be Catholics — she was very happy to use

Protestant premiers. Her lively interactions with politicians are a reminder that the colonial community was not misogynistic in essence.

The Catholic religious orders carried out a vast amount of ministry in the most squalid and harsh of conditions. They also earned the support of the Catholic hierarchy by their willingness to teach in Catholic schools, where the nun was an all-powerful figure. In Waihī, for example, one particularly tough nun in the 1950s intimidated students, and left a rather unfortunate view of the church:

> Sister Mary Perpetua was an extremely elderly nun who should have been retired years before, but due to the shortage of teaching staff she had been sent to Waihi as a replacement teacher. Sister Perpetua has the distinction of being the only nun to ever make me cry while I was at St Joseph's. It was at the time of the change from ink-filled fountain pens to the new 'biro' type of pen . . . My biro had run out of ink and Stephen Sale and myself attempted to suck some red ink up into the tube of the biro and then replace the head. This was done during a morning Christian lecture by one of the priests. Naturally enough our system of refilling the biro didn't work and I had red ink on my face and hands from trying. When Sister Perpetua re-entered the classroom at the end of the lesson she took one look at my face and hands and dragged me by the ear out to the front of the class where she then broke several rulers over me, she then moved on to a triangular ruler however that also broke after a while. Finally she seized a length of one inch dowel which had served as the blackboard pointer. I was then dragged out into the corridor and beaten mercilessly on the back and legs by Sister Perpetua for several minutes until finally she had exhausted herself. I was a mass of bruises for many days afterwards and the memory lasted a lifetime. I mention this beating simply because it happened and was a part of that period in history.[75]

To this astonishing story, told in a history of St Joseph's school, the editor appended a note: 'unfortunately a common memory for many'. Part of the explanation for this approach probably lies in the utter frustration of elderly women in charge of huge classes, and allowed no respite in the business of supporting the educational aspirations of the bishops. So whether or not they wanted this, they became the teachers of Catholic children, all their ministry focused on this episcopal priority.

The women's religious orders had a rich internal life, though their convents were often inadequate and their work was often taken for granted. Only the Dominicans were enclosed in New Zealand, so in most cases they were kept hard at work. The world within the enclosure was full of love, care, and a fair share of infighting and grasping for positions.[76] Spirituality within the religious orders was very formal and ritualised. There have been many fine histories of religious orders in recent decades, and these have illuminated the inner spirituality of these orders, and the way they manifested in particular styles of service and prayer.[77]

In England, evangelical churches and agencies like the London City Mission had employed middle-class women to enter the homes of the poor and instruct them. These Bible women were rare in New Zealand, although Knox Church in Dunedin did employ Mrs Welsh from 1885 to 1888 to visit the poor, the aged and the sick and to identify worthy recipients of congregational benevolence. When she moved to South Africa, these responsibilities were taken over by the church's Ladies' Association.[78]

At the end of the nineteenth century many more churches began to appreciate the need for deaconesses. Drawing on the Catholic Church, the Salvation Army, and the Anglican religious orders, as well as overseas missions, Protestant churches began to appreciate the ministry of women. For example, by 1893 a secular newspaper was urging that deaconesses were needed in Christchurch.[79] So when Rutherford Waddell, minister of St Andrew's in South Dunedin, employed the Australian Christabel Duncan in the poor community around the church in Walker Street her work soon became a model for a new order of ministry in the church.[80]

While the concept had been pioneered by Waddell in the Presbyterian Church, there were many overseas precedents, mostly arising from the new religious orders formed from the Oxford Movement and in the Salvation Army.[81] When the Presbyterian Church formalised the role it cited the example provided by the China Inland Mission, the Poona Village Mission and the Salvation Army. So long as the deaconesses were trained, the synod was positive about the idea.[82] Soon the title was also approved by the Methodist Church. The Baptist Church was cautious about following this example.[83] Protestant deaconesses often worked primarily among the sick and the poor when they served in the Pākehā world and they were very poorly paid; their role had much less glamorous associations than overseas missionary work.

The ministry of women was mostly within rather than outside the church. The role was a tough one precisely because women in diaconal ministry were expected to be the housewives of the church, doing anything that was thrown at them. Margaret Tennant has illustrated this in her moving account of a Methodist deaconess, Sister Eleanor Dobby, "'Sometimes when my heart was sad with snubs and coldness'".[84] These were middle-class women reaching out to people with a deep sense of compassion.

Deaconesses met with approval because they were symbolically submissive, and it was precisely because of this that Anglican deaconesses sought to be priests.[85] There was a high demand for their work in the parishes. Yet in a survey of 40 deaconesses serving in the Presbyterian Church a prominent minister, Ian Fraser, noted that while they were permitted to conduct services and baptisms, only in the Māori mission did they have the status of elders, although they performed duties normally reserved for elders in Pākehā congregations. Although in a few cases they attended the meetings of the parish board of managers, they were excluded from virtually all other forums. Thus women ministering in the Pākehā mainstream church exercised less leadership than missionary or Māori deaconesses.[86] Pākehā men kept women from competing with themselves in the local context but let them loose on the world stage!

The Anglican Church did not create an order of deaconesses until 1964.[87] The Anglican women's orders established in Christchurch in 1893 (the Community of the Sacred Name) and in Auckland in 1894 (the Order of the Good Shepherd) sat uncomfortably between Protestant deaconesses and Catholic nuns.[88] The members of the Community of the Sacred Name in Christchurch included the remarkable Sybilla Maude, known as Nurse Maude, who was the founder of district nursing in New Zealand. The vision of a revival of women's religious orders was a fruit of the Anglo-Catholic revival in England. Auckland and Christchurch dioceses had Anglo-Catholic parishes, and the two orders were associated with these specific parishes, but were also supported by the local bishops. The support did not extend much further, leaving them with an inadequate basis of support.

High Church parishes had a narrow view of women's ministry. When, in 1912, St Paul's Church in Auckland, like St Michael's in Christchurch, introduced ritualistic reforms and vestments it also excluded women from the church choir.[89] Altar boys were introduced, but not altar girls. The Ladies' Guild at St Michael's mutated into a sacramental guild.[90] The Anglican nuns were a poor and marginalised part of the church, and their work with the poor was heroic and sacrificial.

THE IMAGE OF THE true New Zealand male — rough, roguish, a mate, given to few words and little self-reflection — suggests that such males would have felt uncomfortable in the New Zealand churches. This was of course a stereotype and few men fitted it exactly, but this culture thrived in the pubs of the dominion. Working-class masculinity seemed out of place in the New Zealand church. The men in the church were on the whole 'nicer' and nobler, or — to phrase it another way — more middle class than this.

Nevertheless the churches used very masculine language, using the rhetoric of battling, fighting and crusading. An Australian scholar, Anne O'Brien, has suggested that clergy in Australia were embarrassed from an early stage at the effeminacy in the self-image of the English evangelical male.[91] She commented that 'the relationship of men to the church in Australia was marked by an uneasiness which the English church did not confront in quite the same form'.[92] But the Australian bush was very different from the New Zealand dairy farm. In the shearing sheds men drank and played together, and there was little room for Christian culture there. Few places in New Zealand were like this after the 1890s. On the farm the 'cow-cocky' was generally a family man and the community recognised and respected the farmhand as a hard worker.

In towns the small number of larger factories and workshops had a collective culture of drinking, and abstemious Christian workmen distanced themselves from this rough culture. Team sports sponsored by sports clubs often had strong associations with the pub, and the wowsers sensed this. After a Springbok rugby tour in 1937 the Rev. Clarence Eaton observed 'an orgy of drinking in his neighbourhood among well-dressed, well-educated young and middle-aged men . . . Indulgence in alcoholic liquor is said to be a common feature of weekend sport. Respect for law and order is whittled away when sly-grog selling is winked at in Club-house and pavilion.'[93] Such factors operated against men identifying with the churches.

The influence of the temperance movement meant that Christian males felt somewhat excluded from the male realm. The Christian community heaped praise upon the family man who cared for and supported his wife and children. In popular male culture it seemed as though women had defined this image of manliness, so there was a dilemma for Christian men who aspired to achieve manliness.

The Anglican Church struggled most with attracting men to services. In the 1860s Bishop Julius, in essence an advocate of 'muscular Christianity', urged more action, while others observed that Anglican men were notoriously reluctant to participate audibly in services.[94] Presbyterians, too, called in 1908 for a more democratic and more robust, manly type of Christianity that would suit the working man.[95] Married Methodist women were exhorted not to humiliate men, lest they lose interest in the church and in a moral life.[96] Catholics placed strong emphasis upon integration in the sports realm, helped by the tradition of alcohol within Irish sociability. The Catholic Church was glad to acclaim those who found recognition in sports, and the Marist schools were very anxious to be included in state school sports' competitions, despite attempts to exclude them. The Catholic Church faced the same challenge not to alienate men from religion.

The clergy did not generally help the reputation of the church with men. Some were regarded as interfering legalists, especially chaplains to the 'boys' in the army. Some clergy, especially Anglican, were very far from the manly ideal, for much of their ministry was directed to women, although the 'cultured ministry' so fashionable in the United Kingdom in the later nineteenth century was rare in New Zealand. A few homosexual people were attracted into ministry who did not fit in the brave, rough new world, but this was a much more common style in England.

Bishop Neligan, retired and back in England, complained of the lack of suitable male recruits to the Melanesian mission, and remarked apropos of the English but surely also the New Zealand church:

> I cannot help saying that I think we have twenty times too many services, guilds, and addresses. The holiness and beauty of life of some of our men at home puts me, as a bishop, to shame, but I long to see some of them doing men's work instead of old women's work. Tommy can be got to Church or Sunday-school by an old lady with one leg, but the Melanesian people cannot be evangelised by an old lady . . .[97]

Occasionally the clergy were successful emissaries into this forbidden territory of tough masculine society. 'Muscular Christianity' had some appeal in the colonies. Some clergy became more comfortable with labouring men and their drinking and smoking. Rural clergy and lay home missioners had to be resourceful to have any ministry in rural districts. Jasper Calder, the first Auckland City Missioner, thrived in ministry to men, and some of the military chaplains were at ease with working-class men. Guy Thornton, the Baptist minister and chaplain, struggled against booze and prostitution in Cairo in a way that suggested his skills as a man with men.[98] Some younger clergy, particularly those of more liberal persuasions or eagerness for evangelism in the world, wanted to speak to the tough world of men, and knew the need to avoid the appearance of preciousness.

Catholic clergy were often better at connecting with men. The Redemptorist missionaries were frank and direct in their appeals for men to sort out their moral commitment. The Catholic priest who didn't drink was rather isolated in the parish,[99] and some priests drank as much as their male parishioners. They could as a result be blunt in their criticism of the moral failings of men.

The churches were fully involved in community attempts to bring mateship under control. This was a challenge — enter the wowsers! In Chapter 6 we explored temperance as an aspect of the Christian convictions within local churches. In this context we may observe the desire to civilise men and make more room for family life.

Temperance idealised the family man. The sacredness of home was intended to shame men into better behaviour. The churches were concerned for the young man, lest he reject the home and domesticity. Honour and nobility were the goals of manhood. The strongest support for prohibition came from respectable suburbs and settled farming districts, where churches were also strong.

The leading members of the Women's Christian Temperance Union were often the wives of prominent Protestant clergy. The women temperance campaigners intended to call the church back to its true duty.[100] Women saw themselves as a moral force in a necessary social campaign. Temperance women also sought to train wives and mothers to better fulfil their maternal instinct.[101] They wanted the church to show more concern about the health of society as a whole. Prominent Congregationalist Mrs Amy Daldy, the wife of the Auckland harbourmaster and a superintendent of the WCTU, expressed her opinion forcefully: 'The churches — oh the churches — can they not see that good may be done for the people outside their walls? They will learn their lesson some day after paying dearly for it. With all our vaunted progress, we are still very narrow and can have no dealings with the Samaritans.'[102]

THE CHURCHES WORRIED THAT there were few opportunities for Christian men to socialise together. Bible class movements, as we will see, addressed this issue, and sought to present a local form of muscular

The pupils and nuns at Sacred Heart Convent School in Wanganui in 1912, playing at a maypole. The nuns were the Sisters of St Joseph (known as the Black Joes, on account of their habits) and they are clearly delighted with their new convent, which opened that year on the plush St John's Hill. ALEXANDER TURNBULL LIBRARY. REF: 1/1-021229-G

Christianity. There were various attempts to create men's fellowships. The low proportion of men was most apparent in Anglican parishes. The large Anglican parish of St Mary's Merivale made various attempts to address the issue, establishing men's clubs, holding events in which they could participate, and encouraging men to dress more casually when coming to church.[103] The deficiency was a little less evident in the other Protestant churches, and inactive men also troubled Catholic parishes. The parish history of Blenheim records that many priests came to the town with the intention of getting the men cracking, but eventually gave up and concentrated their attention on more responsive beings.[104]

The Church of England Men's Society (CEMS), which influenced Walter Nash so deeply, was intended to address the need.[105] Harry Woollcombe, an emissary from the CEMS in England who made a significant impact when he toured New Zealand in 1910, explicitly urged men to join the CEMS and bluntly presented them with the choice between morality and immorality.[106] At its 1914 meeting in Dunedin the CEMS conceived its task as strengthening the church in its impact and outreach to young men.[107] But it never became very strong. By 1965 the only branch still active in the Auckland Diocese was in Howick.[108] Men's groups languished, because the committed men were too busy running the church to have time to run a men's group.

In contrast, women's organisations in the church played a crucial role in the changing role of women in the church. In Chapter 7 we observed the enormous importance of the Ladies' Guild in the operation of the churches. They were the largest single contributor to church funds over the first century of church life. In the interwar years, the Ladies' Guild raised a quarter of Upper Riccarton Methodist Church's income.[109]

In the Protestant churches, Women's Missionary Unions emerged as more women were accepted as missionaries.[110] Women who could not possibly consider being missionaries themselves threw their energies into supporting missionary work. The tone of the missionary unions was entirely different than that of the guilds. In essence, they called women into participation in religious work. They were inspired by intense prayer and passionate concern about the needs of the whole world. Missionary supporters were a new breed of activists.[111]

Soon national denominational bodies were formed: the Methodist Women's Missionary Auxiliary was founded in 1902, the Baptist Women's Missionary Union in 1903, and the national Presbyterian Women's Missionary Union in 1905.[112] The significance of such organisations was partly financial, for they funded the missions to a lesser or greater degree, raising money and sending parcels of used clothes and other supplies. These organisations were consciously created so that women could work for women.

The Missionary Unions were very active bodies in many Protestant churches. The Presbyterian Women's Missionary Union was formidable at the national level; it could mobilise virtually every parish in the country in fundraising activity and expressions of opinion, with most urban parishes running cake stalls, organising events, and providing parcels of goods for missionaries in the New Hebrides, India and China.[113]

These church bodies contributed significantly to women's identity in the nation. The WCTU had been a pioneer women's organisation at a national level, and it had encouraged the formation of the National Council of Women (NCW) in 1896. As the denominational national bodies formed, they signed up as constituent members of the NCW. Thus religious institutions had a key role at the table, and they were able to draw on their many members to support and enforce NCW concerns. This tradition remained important for 80 years. In the early 1980s Dame Miriam Dell, chair of the NCW, had served as an Anglican women's leader, and her successor, Dame Vivienne Boyd, had served a parallel role in the Baptist women's movement; the two were neighbours in Lower Hutt. The women of the church had few opportunities in church services, but they were strong, vigorous and confident in their separate sphere.

Many churches developed informal support groups for young married couples in the years after World War II. Out of this emerged a new kind of Women's Fellowship in Methodist, Presbyterian and other churches.[114] In the Auckland Anglican Diocese, for example, by 1961 there were 53 young wives groups, with 2670 members, compared to 77 Mothers' Union groups, with 2645 members.[115] Joan Beere, the wife of a prominent clergyman, led the development of the young wives groups in the Auckland Diocese.[116] In the evangelical world, women's coffee hours were popular, as well as husband and wife evenings.[117]

In these organisations women were autonomous. There were inevitably tensions and disputes within and between the various organisations, and clergy were ill advised to intervene. When Maurice Andrew, then new to parish ministry, proposed at Ngaio Presbyterian Church that the women's groups should cease to act like clubs and direct themselves towards more profound questions than flower arrangements and cake decorating, his proposals seemed like orders, and they were firmly rejected, undermining his acceptance in the parish.[118]

In the 1960s, as the Anglican Church in New Zealand agreed to permit divorced women to play a full part in church life, the Mothers' Union felt restrained by its English rules.[119] Those unhappy with the Mothers' Union created a new organisation, the Association of Anglican Women. The two very different organisations competed within the Anglican Church. These tensions were often replicated at the local level, with the women's guild group meeting on one day and the young wives group on another. By 1970 there were 29 branches of the Association of Anglican Women in the Auckland Diocese. By 1978 the Auckland Anglican Synod heard a lament about the lack of young women's groups in parishes.[120] Gradually both groups faltered, and churches replaced them with mixed fellowship groups.

In other Protestant churches, women's guilds and missionary unions began to come together. In effect, Women's Fellowships absorbed the old organisations, both Ladies' Guilds and missionary fellowships. This happened for Methodists in February 1964.[121] Similarly, Presbyterian women felt that a union of women's organisations was warranted, although the stalwarts the Presbyterian Women's Missionary Union were particularly bitter, feeling that the missionary tone would be lost in any amalgamation.[122]

The status of women in the Catholic Church calls for special attention. In a notable report written for the church in 1990, Christine Cheyne argued that the Catholic Church was sexist to its core.[123] Its lay women were expected to be silent and passive. Yet powerful women could not be completely silenced, and the history of the New Zealand Catholic Church contains many significant stories of the ways in which lay women have exercised influence. When an opportunity at last came, lay women's organisations seized the opportunity for more direct influence and involvement.

There was a massive decline in recruitment to religious orders from the 1960s, as Catholic families ceased to pressure their daughters and sons to explore a religious vocation. The Second Vatican Council urged Catholic religious orders to stand aside from the burden of teaching in the schools and rediscover their essential vision. Many histories of religious orders have described the trauma that followed as some left their orders and others were exhilarated by a new sense of mission.[124] The Sisters of Mercy, for example, forced the reshaping of church schools when the order decided that it no longer wished to focus on general education. When they abandoned their habits, many Catholics were shocked.

IN THE 1920S AND 1930s, women speakers became more common at interdenominational events, and by the 1930s Christian women were organising their own conventions. The Council of Christian Women was formed in Auckland in 1939.[125] The denominational missionary organisations held national conferences. As early as 1912 Mrs Gray of the Baptist Women's Missionary Union spoke at the annual conference, held parallel with the Baptist Union's annual conference, on 'the position women occupy in the scheme of the Christian faith and its propagation', but her talk focused on women's equality in salvation and evangelism, not church government.[126] In 1940 the Presbyterian Church held a

The front page of *Outlook* magazine celebrates the first three Presbyterian women elders, who represented their congregations at the General Assembly of the Presbyterian Church in 1957. The title above the photograph is 'The three who were there!' They are named as Mrs W. H. O. Johnston of Tokomaru Bay, Sister Margaret Hewson of Wellington and Mrs E. M. Webb of Papatoetoe. OUTLOOK, 20 NOVEMBER 1957

women's conference, including among its speakers the first deaconess, Christabel Duncan (who had in old age married the Rev. Rutherford Waddell), the Baptist missionary Mrs Annie Driver, Miss Salmond (sister of the director of Christian Education for the denomination) and Sister Anna Kirkwood.[127]

Yet such bodies had virtually no voice in the denominational synods, presbyteries and the like. One male preacher in 1937 disingenuously argued that, 'It were easy and unjust to throw the blame for the present unhappy state of things upon a too frail sisterhood newly exposed to the collision of the sexes in office.'[128] Women were sometimes allowed to comment on missionary matters since most of the missionaries were women. Baptists allowed women to be elected on to the Baptist Missionary Society executive from 1907, but not as office holders. Women were allowed to speak to a report at conference in 1912.[129] These were minimal opportunities.

The denominations meanwhile felt a responsibility for women. In 1944, the Methodist Church, conscious of the loss of clergy as chaplains, launched an urgent appeal for women workers who could act as deaconesses.[130] The same conference expressed concern at reports that American servicemen were marrying New Zealand women, and urged in a separate motion that women police be employed in Timaru.[131] As late as the 1960s, the denominational women's religious groups opposed the state's pressure for women to enter the workforce.[132]

New Zealand women were relatively slow to abandon the wearing of hats. In the 1940s the Archbishop of Canterbury told English Anglican women that they need not wear them. Although this was reported in New Zealand at the time, as late as 1961 Archdeacon Sam Woods had to defend women who did not wear hats in fashionable Merivale.[133] In 1962 they were still near-universal in Presbyterian and Methodist churches.[134] Hats were still worn by women attending weddings, funerals and the races, and by school students to and from school, so this suggests that the church remained a part of the public world. The wearing of hats vanished with little controversy in most churches in the 1970s. Far more debate surrounded the wearing of slacks to church. This was viewed as 'dressing as a man', and awakened tension in the 1980s.

Writers on the history of women's ordination note that there were several phases of the reform, and that the aspirations of women changed in a number of stages. The tone of the church changed in the process. In a 1950 survey of the Presbyterian stance on women, the Rev. Ian Fraser argued that most of the Protestant churches offered more opportunities for women than his own denomination, even including the Brethren and the Anglicans.[135]

Methodists agreed to permit women to be ordained as ministers in 1958; Presbyterians in 1964. Phyllis Guthardt in 1959 and Margaret Reid Martin in 1965 were the first female ministers. An insight into the continuing caution can be seen in a regulation adopted by Methodists that if a woman minister married, her appointment would expire unless by special permission of the conference.[136] So the reform was implemented very cautiously in its early years.

The Anglican debate over women's ordination has dominated most analyses of the issue, but this is unfair to the other churches that preceded it. We have already seen that Anglicans were very slow to adopt the role of deaconess. General Synod commenced formal discussion of women's priesthood in 1970, but there was a very convoluted process between dioceses and General Synod, and a law suit, before finally it proceeded in 1977.[137] New Zealand was seen as dangerously radical in the Anglican world by then, but the cumbersome structure of the denomination attracted more attention to its attempt to come to a decision.

The activism of the evangelical churches depended on women, although their role was heavily circumscribed by interpretations of the Bible which militated against any female role in preaching or leadership. The Brethren, who were a significant part of the evangelical community, permitted no woman to speak in the Sunday Communion service, whereas participation was encouraged from all male members. Emphatic on their biblical literalism, these churches seemed incapable of change.

Change did come, though, albeit slowly. In 1965, Averil McIntosh was allowed to be leader of the Kaka Point Children's Special Service Mission (a part of the popular evangelical organisation, Scripture Union).[138] Margaret Malcolm from the Brethren was appointed to the Scripture Union Council in 1964, but said that she felt at times like the tea lady.[139] Then in the 1980s a few Brethren churches began to change.[140] In the end the evangelical churches felt the need to be relevant and attract outsiders. In contrast to the Catholic Church of New Zealand, which could not make independent decisions, evangelical churches had always been willing to diverge from congregations in other countries.

Pentecostal women appeared much less constrained than others. Women had been very active in Pentecostalism from the beginning, and some played a pioneering role, among them the glamorous Californian evangelist Aimee Semple McPherson, who visited New Zealand in 1929. Pastors' wives played a distinctive role, which was more powerful and independent than the wives of ministers of other denominations. Anne Morrow, wife of the founder of the New Life Churches, took a very public role in the campaign to save families, and the attempt to prevent New Zealand ratifying the United Nations Convention for the Elimination of all forms of Discrimination against Women (CEDAW).[141] Yet the ministry of Pentecostal women was not recognised unless it complemented their husband's role.

A glossy magazine, *Above Rubies*, edited by Nancy Campbell, wife of a Pentecostal pastor in Palmerston North, was widely circulated in the 1970s and expressed an ardent 'complementarian' vision for women. It has continued to be published, but since 1992 the Campbells have lived first on the Gold Coast and then in Tennessee, where such views continue to have traction.[142]

Pentecostal women leaders could be glamorous yet curiously decorative figures in their churches. Life Church, one of the Auckland Pentecostal mega-churches, holds the Sistas conference every year, with content that reflects the desire of women to be independent and spiritual. Hannah Tamaki, wife of the founder of another Auckland mega-church, Destiny, which has a focus on Māori, is called 'First Lady' in the church, and plays an independent and maverick leadership role. The essential Pentecostal gender pattern is not egalitarian, but a new style of relationship that is still complementary to men.[143] The women seem more modern, highly glamorised, even sexualised, with independent voices, yet they staunchly defend complementarian theology.[144] Change is happening, but slowly. Only in 2005 were women ordained to the eldership in the Apostolic Church.[145]

Within the traditional churches, the styles of ordained ministry have changed for men and women. Today something like one-third of the ordained clergy are females. Unfortunately there are not enough full-time positions for all of them, and men still get more than their share of the stipended positions.

PASIFIKA PEOPLE BROUGHT THEIR own gender roles to New Zealand, partly shaped by the missionary churches, and the changing gender roles in New Zealand startled them. Women played an important role in the churches they founded in New Zealand, but they were never pastors or elders. The Pacific churches were patriarchal communities, especially as the church was an imitation of the traditional village life. The strong women of the church were inevitably the wives of the leading matai.[146] When Marie Ropetu, the daughter of a respected minister in Western Samoa, was ordained by the Presbyterian Church her ministry was served in European congregations.[147] Polynesian Pentecostalism began to flourish in the late 1970s, and the role of women was somewhat freer in this context, but it reflected the deep conservatism of Pacific people.

The appearance of very large concentrations of Asians in the churches of Auckland raised new and difficult issues, which were more acute here than in many other parts of the world. Again gender roles were very different in the deferential societies of the Korean Christians in particular.

In the mainstream Protestant world some of the newly ordained female clergy were very conscious of feminist issues, and in 1981 Susan Adams challenged the

Above The ladies' guild of the Dominion Road Methodist Church outside the church door in 1943. Rev. Frank Gardner Brown is the smug minister surrounded by these key supporters, including his wife Eileen on his left. Brown went from the church as a chaplain in the Middle East but was never able to return to a settled parish ministry. WHYLE, I. DOMINION: FROM GENERATION TO GENERATION: CENTENARY OF DOMINION ROAD METHODIST CHURCH, AUCKLAND, 1897–1997. AUCKLAND, PITT STREET METHODIST CHURCH, 1997

Below Women officers and supporters of the Salvation Army corps in Broadway, Palmerston North, photographed in the 1950s in the citadel's back hall. The panels on the back wall list the officers (women on the left, men on the right) who have died and been 'promoted to glory'. IAN MATHESON CITY ARCHIVES

Anglican Synod of Auckland about its masculinist language.[148] In 1984 a motion was presented to the Auckland Synod stating that rape was an abuse of power by men over women. Subsequent amendments transformed it into a motion about the beauty of sexuality.[149] Feminist theology pointed ordained women to different concepts of mission and ministry. The Women and Ministry conferences held from 1980 to 1994 invited the church to rethink its identity with a more acute understanding of gender.[150]

Pentecostals in the 1980s were abusive of what they called 'women's lib', and declared at the women's forums that they attended en masse that women enjoyed being traditional wives and mothers. This voice is no longer as apparent within the Pentecostal context, but nor is an egalitarian perspective.[151]

The boundaries of genders are muddied today. The churches have been deeply divided by massive disputes over the ordination of gay people. This has become the rallying call for conservatives in the Presbyterian and Anglican churches, with potential to provoke schisms, and it has shown how strong the Pasifika group is within Methodism. Meanwhile the transgender issue has become a major one for some families and churches. The Auckland Rainbow Church, founded in 1980 as the Auckland Community Church and meeting in the Anglican Church of St Matthew's in the central city, suggests that gay and lesbian people have not abandoned the church. The church welcomes many refugees from other churches, from Catholic to Pentecostal, who themselves feel abandoned. The argument of this chapter is that the gender culture of local churches has always reflected wider social trends, but the church has also been slow and cautious to treat genders and sexualities as equal.

Above The Presbyterian Women's Missionary Union members in Feilding in 1930. In the centre is Mrs D. R. McDonald, the president, and there are four vice presidents and a secretary and treasurer present. The Union raised support for Presbyterian missionaries in India and China. FEILDING PUBLIC LIBRARY

Below This group of women was photographed in April 1982 in the Rosehill Presbyterian Church in Papakura with their knitted work, which they had been producing for 14 years for the Save the Children Fund. FAIRFAX MEDIA, AUCKLAND LIBRARIES FOOTPRINTS, 00469

Children and Young People and Church

Previous This small Taranaki church has not been identified but James McAllister, the photographer, was from Stratford and the photograph has been dated to the 1920s.
ALEXANDER TURNBULL LIBRARY.
REF: 1/1-012538-G

CHURCHES SOUGHT RECOGNITION FOR their important role in the raising of children and young people, and devoted significant amounts of energy to this work. From the colonial period until the 1960s, roughly three-quarters of children and young people were in some sort of regular contact with the church, compared to a quarter of adults. While adults without links to a church were the norm, few young people were in this situation. For much of the nineteenth and twentieth centuries the respectable public viewed churches as supporting family life, and for young people the church was a key aspect of socialisation. Because the church was viewed as a safe place, parents entrusted their children and young people to its care for a great deal more than religious instruction. Memories of childhood shaped people's knowledge of religion, as Grace Bateman has argued in a very interesting thesis centred on people growing up in South Dunedin.[1]

Catholics often linked mothers and the church. The editor of the *Tablet*, James Kelly, who could be highly sentimental, commented on the dedication of the nuns at the grand celebrations of the Diocese of Dunedin in 1921: 'So they bring us not only Dominic's spirit but also the spirit of Ireland's Saints and Scholars, and — forget it not — the spirit of the grand Christian Irish homes in which the pioneer nuns learned the secret of holiness from that best of teachers, an Irish mother.'[2]

It is far from clear what Irish mothers had to do with the story. Yet Fr Kevin Maher evoked this connection at the Centenary of Marlborough celebrations in 1959, speaking of the pioneer women (including his own forebears): 'they reared large families, and taught and trained them, they brushed and washed them up on Sundays and packed them off to Mass; they kept the Faith! . . . Hard work was almost a creed to them . . . and their Faith was of the same quality . . . Perhaps because Mass was said [so] often in private houses . . . an intimate union between priests and people has grown up.'[3]

The family was viewed as sacred, and the mother was largely responsible for this. It was in the family that children learned the rosary, the acts of penitence and the good deeds that framed the Catholic world. In the Protestant world the family was urged to attend the 'family altar' daily, as the father led them in Bible reading and prayer. Clergy were concerned that this practice was not as common as it ought to be, and in 1927 the Presbyterian Church attempted to revive it by introducing a 'Family Altar Card', but just 2000 copies were sold. It certainly enforced the formalities of religion on those who adhered to it. In other respects, too, Protestants viewed the family as a key axis of the Christian community, equal to the local church.[4]

Children quickly learned the traditions of religion. Nell Scanlan, the Catholic novelist in the 1930s and the 1940s who wrote so compellingly of the Pencarrow dynasty in Wellington, recollected her childhood in Picton, and how when out birdnesting with her brother Dan she would thread the blown eggs through a string; she once made a rosary out of birds' eggs, in which the Our Fathers were blackbirds' eggs and the Hail Marys were sparrows' eggs.[5]

The Victorian rule that children should be seen and not heard was an iron rule in church, for a crying child brought great shame on the mother. There was some concern that the colonial church allowed children too much freedom, and the vicar of Merivale in 1872 told the members at their annual meeting that 'a proper reverence' needed to be inculcated in children, even though a superstitious awe was bad. So he urged that it was unwise to 'unduly familiarize the Church and its sacred objects to the children'.[6]

Sunday schools were vastly bigger than the churches that sponsored them. One example among many was St David's Presbyterian Church in Khyber Pass Road, Auckland, which touched its local community very significantly through a range of Sunday schools, youth organisations, clubs and classes. The Very Rev. John McKenzie was deeply involved in the youth work of St David's as a boy, and was later a distinguished missionary in China (from 1923 to 1935) and minister of various Presbyterian churches. He recalled the huge significance of the church in his life:

> How large a place St. David's filled in our lives! We grew up in the Church in a very real sense. Apart from school and work, all our interests tended to centre there. It was not just a spiritual home and centre of worship, it was also our social centre, our recreational centre and our friendship centred there too. Classes and clubs, picnics and socials, gymnasium and debating, all were there in the life of St. David's as we knew it and loved it and benefited from it.[7]

Statistics on Sunday school enrolments, which were collected by the government statistician until 1926, provide interesting insights. They show that in the country districts attendance was much higher than in the towns as a proportion of 5- to 14-year-olds. In 1871 just over 50 per cent were attending Sunday school, rising to over 60 per cent by 1881 and reaching 65 per cent in 1886, nearly 67 per cent in 1896, and 69 per cent in 1901. Nevertheless, the male attendance began to drop in this period, while the female proportion grew. The percentage of children attending dropped from 1916 but remained above 55 per cent.[8]

The striking success of the Sunday school in the nineteenth century reflected the concern of parents and the community that more should be done to protect and help children. Sunday schools were tools used both to shield and guide children. The schools and their teachers also wanted leisure alternatives tightly controlled, and viewed the rise of commercial leisure activities as a threat. They doubtless recognised that many children attended at the instigation of their parents rather than through their own choice — hence the Auckland Sunday School Union (a body to which most Sunday schools belonged) wanted the museum shut and the toffee machines locked up on Sundays.[9]

Sunday schools reflected the Victorian view that children needed a religious start to their lives. Methodism was probably the most successful denomination in mobilising its membership into Sunday schools, for initially its mission in New Zealand was predominantly directed towards children and young people. A Sunday school was integral to every Methodist church, and was open to all the children of the neighbourhood.[10] Wesley Church in Wellington had the largest Sunday school in the country, with nearly 800 students at its height in 1925. At that time, Methodism had 31,000 names on the rolls of its Sunday schools. Other denominations were very active as well.

New Zealand Sunday schools were large enterprises. Until the 1920s they were generally held on Sunday afternoons. They were run like schools, and thus extensive classroom space was needed for urban schools. Classrooms did not come cheaply. For example, St Andrew's Presbyterian Sunday school in Palmerston North had a very large building containing several rooms. St Michael's Anglican Church in Christchurch (which also ran a day school on a much smaller scale) had up to 450 regular attendees in seven classrooms (plus other spaces in the vicarage and church) with 25 teachers in the late nineteenth century.[11]

In England, Sunday schools were sometimes quite independent of the local church, and even in New Zealand some Sunday schools avoided interference by the pastor. Sometimes enthusiasts began a Sunday school without seeking any authority. Within any church there could be different members running Sunday schools in various suburbs and competing with each other for teachers. The story of St Christopher's Sunday school in Redwoodtown, Blenheim, was so lovingly commemorated by the early founders that the commencement of church services in the building was mentioned only as a casual aside.[12]

Parents were happy that their children were going to Sunday school, and some cared little as to the denominational background of the school, to the concern of the larger denominations.[13] Many of the smaller sectarian churches conducted Sunday schools in poorer suburbs and country districts, picking up children in buses and cars to take them to a hired hall.[14] All churches hoped to gain members through their Sunday schools, but there was limited evidence to show that this actually happened. Some churches began as Sunday schools, particularly in the suburbs of the towns and in the rural districts. The building rented or erected for Sunday school was the logical place in which to hold services when the district had grown.

Sunday school certainly played a role in connecting church with community. Families were grateful for the work of the schools, and parents were persuaded by children to attend special events. The Sunday school picnic and the Sunday school anniversary service, referred to earlier, were huge events. Most churches kept scaffolding or tiered seating in storage so that the Sunday school children could be seated in front of their adoring parents during the anniversary service, which was usually the largest service of the year.

Sunday schools sometimes seemed a very amateur enterprise, with little training of teachers for the task.[15] As the historian of Methodist Sunday schools, Frank Hanson, emphasises, it was a lay movement. It was organised by enthusiasts within the churches, and its ability to enlist volunteers, however raw and unscreened, shows the extent to which its vision inspired New Zealand church members.[16] Although the teachers for the schools had no preliminary training, there was a certain amount of assistance available for those who sought it. The work of the Sunday school unions and denominational endeavours turned a volunteer movement into a serious enterprise, especially in the poorer suburbs where Sunday schools were strategic outposts.

Nine classes struggle for space in the Anglican Sunday school hall in Glen Eden, Auckland, in 1956. Their teachers are all female.
PAROCHIAL DISTRICT OF NEW LYNN (WELLS CAMPAIGN CANVASS BOOKLET), AUCKLAND, 1956

Larger Sunday schools needed to be more systematic. The Dunedin educationalist David Keen, in his fine thesis on Otago Sunday schools, shows that superintendents were concerned about curriculum and teaching styles, and tried to reach the standards of state schools.[17] Keen shows that curriculum became increasingly important in the 1880s, drawing on international resources, and the schools established libraries and held annual examinations. Gradually classroom standards were raised and teacher training improved.[18] More systematic approaches to religious education led to the keeping of rolls, and the introduction of graded lessons.

Sunday school teachers had divergent opinions on the best curriculum. A. H. & A. W. Reed began as a publisher of Sunday school material, but in the end the Australian graded lessons were widely adopted by the Methodist and Presbyterian schools. There was growing recognition that the level of material provided to children needed to be at their own level. As Hugh Morrison has shown, Sunday schools increasingly allowed for children to develop an appropriate level of Christian understanding.[19]

THE PARISH SCHOOL WAS an even more vital part of the Catholic world than the Sunday school was in the Protestant world. The school took precedence over all other parish organisations, and financing it fell heavily on parishioners. At the school, Catholic children learned not just the Catechism but also the performance of Catholic rituals, such as genuflecting, clasping hands in prayer, bowing heads and respecting the sacred mysteries.[20] Within the school fervour was encouraged, and nuns laboured on the pupils' sinfulness and the need for penitence and faith.

A few Anglican parishes had schools, especially those in the Diocese of Wellington, where Octavius Hadfield, the second Bishop of Wellington, had despaired of secular schools.[21] There were also parishes with close associations with denominational and state secondary schools, and a 'croc' of pupils who had paraded in line and would sit in designated pews for the Sunday service; an example of this was the John McGlashan College students who attended First Church in Dunedin. In other parishes, children from the local orphanage were present; for example, the children from the Allen Home in Remuera were sent to Somervell Presbyterian Church.[22]

The women among the early CMS missionaries to the Māori introduced schools for infants and their mothers, and a careful study of the Paihia and Waimate North schools has shown that this was an important aspect of the CMS's 'civilising' work among the people of the north.[23] Similarly, in later years the ministry of deaconesses who worked among isolated groups in the central North Island focused on the education of children.[24] Māori teachers were also employed by the CMS and remained dedicated to the religious education of children.

Māori children frequently connected with Pākehā through Sunday school as well as day school, although most of their Sunday schools were provided by Māori women. The Rev. Wendy Scott recalled being dressed up in her best clothes by her parents and taken in a carload of Māori children on the outskirts of Whangarei to a little Baptist Sunday school where they learned a very simple evangelical gospel.[25] This pattern continued and perhaps strengthened for Māori children in the city, but in the 1970s it slowly lapsed.

Sunday school did not clash with church when it was scheduled in the afternoon. Church families also took their children to the church service at 11 a.m., and sometimes children from the community might attend as well. Churches paid little heed to the children in their midst during these services, although in later years a children's talk was often provided (which a clever minister could use to prepare the ground for his main sermon). This tradition began at Oxford Terrace Baptist in 1916.[26] A good talk could be memorable. Sixty years later, Marjorie Ayrton recalled a children's story at Auckland's Somervell Presbyterian Church in the 1930s about the starving children of China.[27]

Children were also recruited into the choir. The high pitch of the unbroken boys' voices was a traditional feature of English cathedral choirs. Cathedral Grammar School in Christchurch ensured that ChristChurch Cathedral emulated the English standard, and boys were often coerced to sing for special services in other churches. In the days before electricity was connected to churches, boys were often paid to pump the bellows for organs. There are numerous stories of organ pumpers little interested in the service and failing in their duty, leaving the organ silent for the opening bars of the hymn. Obviously church had little inherent attraction to them.[28]

The Catholic ceremonies associated with First Communion were profoundly significant for children, who were typically at a very impressionable age, under 10 years old, when this took place. The Catholic school system was so extensive that most young Catholics experienced First Communion ceremonies. For the girls it was especially memorable, for they were dressed in white, with veils, and held wreaths. There was usually a procession with torches. The event was, as the Catholic newspaper the *Tablet* noted, calculated to convey to the children 'a thorough conviction of the beauties of the ceremonies and devotions of the Catholic Church'.[29]

Confirmation was the Anglican equivalent and it, too, could be elaborate, although fewer young Anglicans were confirmed than Catholics who took first communion. Many young people from working-class backgrounds were not confirmed.[30] It may have become more common among Anglicans in the early twentieth century, and it was a significant moment for any Anglican with some involvement in church, as Grace Bateman's research indicates.[31] At All Saints in Wanganui East, a modest-sized parish, there were regularly 40 people confirmed every year. In one very large event in 1960, Bishop Baines conducted his first confirmation in Wanganui on Monday, 28 November with 40 from Wanganui East and three or four from other parishes; because of the expected crowd, each candidate was allowed just two tickets for family members to attend.[32]

Confirmation was the passage for Anglicans into full communicant membership of the church. Most of those who were confirmed came from the church school or the Bible class. In 1962, for example, 3257 young people and 829 adults were confirmed into the Anglican Diocese of Auckland.[33] The number of confirmations peaked in 1965 in the Diocese of Auckland and subsequently declined. There was a growing sense around this time that the ceremony meant little. The Youth Council of the diocese tried very hard to develop events so that young people could make their Anglicanism a reality.[34] By 1971 Anglicans were experimenting with admission to Communion on the basis of baptism, not confirmation, and this became standard in the 1980s.[35] This view that baptism was sufficient made the traditional sign of 'coming of age' largely redundant.[36]

Being 'received into membership' was the Methodist equivalent, but it lacked the sense of a milestone. Methodists belatedly adopted this emphasis, but the issue for the churches was that in fact confirmation led few people into adult membership of the church, and was in fact the last real connection with the church for many.[37]

In Baptist churches, the sign of coming of age was requesting full-immersion 'believer's baptism'. In the colonial period there was intense hostility to this rite within the community.[38] Presbyterian ministers ridiculed those who practised it, especially when their ceremonies were conducted in local rivers.[39] There was often debate over the proper form and eligibility for baptism among those with revivalist inclinations, but infant baptism had deep significance within the nominally Christian community.[40] Occasionally evangelical ministers switched sides and adopted believer's baptism, but the churches took action against such people. Baptists remained a small denomination except in the cities, and their baptisms were in effect rites of passage like confirmation.

When the main Protestant churches proposed to unite into one church in the 1950s and 1960s, the Churches of Christ, a smaller denomination that practised believer's baptism, wished to be part of the united church, so the Plan for Union provided for both believer's baptism and infant baptism. It was a simple but bold solution. It suited those who had not been baptised as infants. Others, as adherents of the charismatic movement, had experienced a rebirth of Christian faith through

Above First Communion at Our Lady of Lourdes church in Shamrock Street, in the poorer part of Palmerston North, in the 1930s. The girls with their neat veils and the boys in their white shirts and ties are in alternate rows outside the parish school. Each holds their First Communion card with a picture of Our Lady of Lourdes. The children were presented for First Communion aged about eight. IAN MATHESON CITY ARCHIVES

Below First Communion group at Addington, Christchurch, in October 1954. The Sacred Heart parish was established in 1920 in the working-class suburb and the banner seems to show Our Lady of Missions, the religious order established by Euphrasie Barbier, which took over the Sacred Heart School in 1896. V.C. BROWNE AND SON

the 'baptism of the Spirit'. They wanted to be baptised, despite the fact that they had been baptised as infants.

It was proposed at the Auckland Anglican Synod in 1983 that a blessing service might be allowed as an alternative to infant baptism, but the proposal caused outrage among traditional church people. One Anglican minister at Pukekohe, who offered believer's baptisms, decided it was time to change denomination.[41] Some evangelical Presbyterian parishes also held surreptitious full-immersion baptisms at this time (often called a ceremony of confirmation of baptismal vows) at the request of ardent young people. The high point of baptisms recorded by the Baptist churches was in 1986, when the figure reached 1817. The figure of recorded believer's baptisms has declined since then, although not as massively as infant baptisms.

SUNDAY SCHOOL WAS AIMED at children up to the age of 12, when compulsory schooling ended. The transition to adult life was uncomfortable for church as well as society. There was widespread alarm about behaviour of young lads in what we now call the teenage years, and in the nineteenth century this was identified as the larrikin problem.[42]

In 1886 youths disrupted the Wesleyan Helping Hand Mission of Freemans Bay in Auckland,

Two photographs show the long procession of Brooklyn Baptist Church Sunday school, Wellington, at some point in the pre-war years. They may be on their way to a Sunday school picnic. ALEXANDER TURNBULL LIBRARY. REF: 1/1-023002-G

which had been founded in 1885 to help the poor community in the locality.[43] This event provoked early public alarm about the issue. In a public meeting hosted by the Auckland YMCA in 1887 the Rev. Rainsford Bavin, a Wesleyan minister, presented a disturbing portrait of dissolute homes in which colonial youths ran wild and caused chaos.[44] To Bavin, larrikins were street gangs of poor youths who lacked guidance at home. Since such youths often amused themselves on a Sunday — the day when they could most conveniently get together — by throwing stones on the roofs of churches, the churches felt that it was their problem. Certainly they contributed to the problem, for sabbatarianism limited access to other leisure pursuits, and the lack of work during the depression of the 1880s made the issue worse.[45]

The churches were easy targets, but youth disrespect was directed towards all authority. In a pioneering society defiance of authority is less easily controlled. Churches took it as a criticism or a mark of their failure, and they used alarm at larrikinism to gain more support for their programmes and their remedies. Had youth been properly taught the Ten Commandments? they asked.[46] As a result of the concern, churches rethought their provision for youths.

There was some concern that the dour Sunday had turned young people away from religion. From early on organisations were established to recruit young men, but they struggled to reach their target audience. One Primitive Methodist ruefully commented that 'we want stalwart, self-reliant, honest, manly men; but this gambling spirit which is possessing our youth is detrimental to the production of such'.[47] The Young Men's Christian Association, which was founded in Auckland in 1855 and extended to other centres thereafter, was designed to reach young men living away from home.[48] In its early years it was strongly Christian. Its focus was in the central city, but it was perceived as 'Nonconformist' or non-Anglican Protestant. Its formula of providing social, biblical, sporting and study opportunities was widely acclaimed, but Anglicans were uncomfortable with it. In Christchurch Bishop Julius proposed a broader basis to the Churchmen's Club:

> There was an ideal young man who did not play billiards, did not smoke, did not know the knave from the ace, and drank nothing stronger than coffee. He had not a word to say against such young then, but the average young men that he knew of did some of these things. If they had only the ideal young men as members of their Club they would have a small but select party who would, perhaps, be very happy, but would have little or no influence on the world at large.[49]

A female equivalent of the YMCA, the Young Women's Christian Association, had a rather spiritual flavour.[50] An Anglican alternative was also formed, the Girls'

Friendly Society, which had as a goal encouraging purity of life.[51]

In the 1870s, churches established a number of organisations for young people, including temperance clubs (the Bands of Hope). Christian Endeavour, established in 1892 when its American founder Dr Francis Clark visited New Zealand, was designed to encourage devotional life for young people within the local church.[52] Even its supporters acknowledged the criticism that it had 'a tendency to generate a kind of sentimental religiousness that will evaporate in mere emotional phrases'.[53] Not exactly the remedy for larrikins! Churches needed to find better ways to provide appropriate support for the development of ordinary young people.

From the 1880s a key emphasis in the churches' youth work was on providing training. W. C. W. McDowell, at the same meeting where Bavin had alerted people to larrikinism, argued that the wayward youths needed demanding training. 'There must be some attraction and amusement ready for them, if they are to be won over to right.'[54] In an increasingly militaristic society, where conscript organisations were common, the uniformed club had a strong appeal. A range of boys' clubs were established, many of them uniformed, the uniform implying discipline. The first Brigades came in 1886. Boy Scouts came in 1908 with a strong imperial endorsement. Many scout groups used church facilities, including a small number of groups in the Catholic Church.[55] Brigades began as a mission to 'rough' boys, with the aim of 'the Advancement of Christ's Kingdom amongst boys, and the promotion of habits of Obedience, Reverence, Discipline, Self-Respect and all that tends towards a true Christian Manliness'.[56] Christian education, warning and exhortation lay at their core. They hoped to assist in the formation of mature, disciplined and self-controlled men. Such organisations emphasised activity and training rather than religious practices. They aimed to develop 'Christian manliness' as an answer to the threats of secular masculinism.

In 1909, after the government was encouraged to develop a territorial force that would be available in any future war, all boys over the age of 12 were required to be trained in cadet corps. This was in effect a nationalisation of the training of young men. The Boys' Brigades were discontinued at this point,[57] but they were re-established by Horace and Ada Grocott in Dunedin in 1923, at Caversham Baptist Church. They drew mainly on Presbyterian and Baptist support, and soon ceased to focus on poorer boys. Growing quickly, they developed a national structure, and by 1939–40 had 4200 members.[58]

The Brigades movement reached its highest level of support in 1968, with 12,523 members. By this time the sponsoring churches had some concerns at the loss of Christian links in the Brigades' programme and their failure to integrate young people into their churches.[59] The YMCA also became more focused on outdoor pursuits than on its religious mandate. Religious activities had decreasing appeal, and the leaders believed that appropriate physical activity had moral value, for the result would be positive for the whole person. Often the outdoor pursuit was seen as reforming,[60] and this developmental notion was influential on church work among youth.

There was debate about the value of team sport, which had been much beloved by the Victorians. The Brigades and Bible classes placed strong emphasis on sports such as harriers and tennis, where individual skills were developed. Although these clubs were organised on gendered lines, the girls' and boys' groups would meet on carefully chaperoned occasions. Such organisations were never wholly successful in providing a better quality of male development. The historian Tom Brooking has vividly described the contrast between Saturday night with his mates and the tame Friday programme at the Boys' Brigade and Sunday with church and Bible class in the 1950s.[61]

Marist schools and sports clubs played a similar role in the Catholic world, and several parallel evangelical organisations and activities in the interwar years adopted the approaches of the uniformed movements. The Crusader movement's camping programme emphasised the development of strength, courage and being 'really healthy', while being firmly against any compromise over alcohol and dancing, and strongly endorsing the family.[62] Among the Brethren, the Everyboys and Everygirls rallies that emerged at the end of World War II offered a less costly equivalent to the Brigades for those who could not afford the uniform.

None of these organisations was quite the equivalent of a Sunday school for teenagers, however. Churches needed a successful Sunday programme, and this need increased as secondary schooling developed about the turn of the century. Change was abroad in the approach to young people, and the churches needed to find ways to participate in it.[63]

The key figure in the development of a new approach by the churches was George Troup. In 1883 he had migrated to New Zealand from Aberdeen and began a notable career with the New Zealand railways. As he listened to colonial concern about youth, he rejected the traditional idea that children should be seen and not heard. His vision was for Sunday Bible classes with a programme that stretched into the rest of the week.

The Bible class movement was seen as the graduate arm of the Sunday school, but with a broader range of activities, both educational and leisured. The boys' Bible class that began under George Troup's inspiration in St John's Presbyterian Church in Wellington in 1888 became a national movement focusing on young people over the age of 17. These were to be 'meetings for young men conducted by young men with

Above A Bible class group from Swanson camping at Bethells Beach on the west coast of Auckland, in the 1920s. Members of the Strahan and Cutler families dominate. Bible classes held camps every year and joined in denominational Easter camps. AUCKLAND LIBRARIES, WEST AUCKLAND RESEARCH CENTRE, STRAHAN FAMILY COLLECTION, STR-P-002

Below A Māori confirmation at St Thomas's Anglican Church, Newton, Auckland (since demolished), on 1 October 1950, with John Fisher, Māori missioner and vicar. The girls' veils differ from those worn by European Anglicans at that time. Confirmation took place in one's mid-teens and was supposed to encourage people in the full life of the church. St Thomas had a High Church tradition but became closely linked to Māori hostels run by the City Mission. AUCKLAND ANGLICAN DIOCESAN ARCHIVES

a broad programme and wide sympathies'.[64] A Women's Union began in 1904, and in the 1920s the movement was extended to secondary-school pupils. Parallel unions were established by both the Methodists and the Baptists in 1904, and the Anglicans in 1921, and on occasions there were joint meetings across denominations.[65]

The groups provided excellent opportunities for socialisation, and they also ran sporting and leisure activities, although there was often some tension between Bible study and 'cheap amusements', which some justified as a means of 'holding our youth'.[66] The classes were part of a union at provincial and national levels. A key feature was the huge Easter camps, which combined fellowship, ardent evangelistic preaching and a sports programme. After World War II the Bible classes struggled to appeal to older young people, and without that age group leadership was in short supply. Consequently there was a rapid decline in the movement in the 1960s.[67]

TAKING INTO ACCOUNT THE vast range of children's and youth activities, the level of participation in church life among young people was quite high. But not all attended services, and they rarely went on to full membership and involvement in church. The dropout rate caused deep concern. There was a feeling that the Sunday school and Bible class were detached from the church, and that young people had no idea of what church was like.[68] Some advocated that children and young people should attend the first part of the church service before heading off to their own programmes.[69] Many churches adopted this approach, while some also established young worshippers' leagues.[70]

Methodists put enormous energy into youth ministries. Evangelistic services were often focused on recruiting local youth. Samuel Lawry, the Methodist President in 1913, suggested that all this evangelistic effort was largely futile and that evangelistic services should be replaced by recruitment drives for membership among the young.[71] So Methodists established a system of junior membership, in the hope that these young people would graduate into the adult church. After World War II many evangelical churches also followed this path.

Church secondary schools are discussed in the following chapter, but they only touched a limited proportion of youth within the local setting. Churches had a range of ancillary organisations, some specifically targeting young people, and others organised informally by them. These included sports organisations and debating clubs. Sometimes congregations provided sporting or athletic training facilities and activities — Beresford Street Congregational Church in Auckland was noted for this, operating three sports clubs in 1899.[72] The Bible class movement absorbed some of these organisations. While they drew in some youth from the community, they were primarily a means of tightly linking the church into society in an age of voluntarism.[73] Catholics had similar bodies to Protestants. In 1898, for example, the Ashburton Catholic parish created the Catholic Literary and Debating Society, which organised debates, plays, literary readings and generally improving activities.[74]

There was some caution about sports in the rough world of nineteenth-century New Zealand. Often sport was associated with drinking and gambling.[75] Football was often seen by the religious as a dubious feature of colonial life.[76] The teams were thought likely to influence young men in bad ways, not least during the socialising that occurred after matches.[77] James Pinfold, on his first circuit placement as a Wesleyan minister in Upper Thames, one Sunday afternoon 'found some young men playing football in a public square. By a little tact they were persuaded to cease. What might have developed into a hurtful habit was nipped in the bud.'[78] Similarly William Colenso, the former missionary, described football as 'low animal and brutalizing games'.[79]

Since Sunday was the one free day for most young people, sport was also perceived as an enticement to breach the moral law. The Bible class movement rejected this view, taking the approach that sports had to be integrated with other aspects of the programme in a 'four square' philosophy. George Troup, in a striking letter to the Presbyterian magazine the *Outlook*, insisted:

> We have always taken an interest in the healthy games which young men engage in, and have not found them hurtful to bible class work. While it is true that many young fellows allow athletics to control them, and some of our class members may even give up too much time to them, the fact still remains that the great majority derive benefit, and are not impaired spiritually. I cannot recall a single instance where athletics have been responsible for backsliding on the part of any of our members who have taken a definite stand on the side of Christ. On the other hand, I have in my mind at the present time quite a number who excelled in outdoor games and sports, and who after entering on the Christian life, have still continued their games and exercises, and even now do so.[80]

Similarly, quoting Jesus' words about salt as a purifying agent, a Methodist footballer asked a youthful audience, 'how can athletics be purified unless the salt of the earth is brought into contact with it, and how can we come into contact with athletics unless we take a lively interest in all legitimate sport?'[81] Rutherford Waddell as editor used the *Outlook* to urge young Christians to get involved in the world.

There was sometimes a generational gap between those who thought sport wrong and those who embraced it, and sometimes a denominational gap. The Presbyterian General Assembly in 1903 was very concerned about pressures on young people, while admitting the 'healthful tendencies' of sports as whole.[82] By 1910 most churches recognised the importance of supporting good sport. In 1905 the *Outlook* reprinted an extraordinary address by George McLaren, ex-president of the Rugby Football Union (RFU), in which he extolled the religiosity of sport, for 'Football should build men up, and make them fitter and better to face the greater battle of life.'[83]

Reports of Irish sports in the *Tablet* show that Catholics did not share Protestant fears that sport could undermine religion, and parish schools, especially high schools, became very prominent in team sports. The sectarian churches continued to renounce sport until well after World War II. Thomas Claude Tutty, former Army and Navy lightweight and welterweight champion, renounced boxing in 1945 when he joined the Cooneyites (a particularly sectarian church also known as the 'Two by Twos').[84]

The four-square notion of youth development, including spiritual, mental, physical and social fitness, became very influential in the colony in about 1900. Then World War I introduced team sports to many who were unfamiliar with them. Bible class sports were significant when few people attended secondary schools. Basketball was introduced to New Zealand by the Presbyterian young people's worker John Jamieson in his work with young women.[85] St Luke's Presbyterian Church in Remuera formed the first women's basketball (netball) team in the country, but it also operated a gymnasium, a cricket team and in 1913 formed a hockey team, helped by the support of the session clerk, H. B. Burnett.[86]

Tennis and badminton clubs were formed in many churches in the 1920s, at the time when tennis was becoming very popular. Many churches had enough land to create a tennis court, and these became popular community facilities. Tennis tournaments were quite a big event for Anglican youth groups in the 1950s.[87]

Sports days were a standard feature of the Saturday at Bible class camps, and intense competition built up between different Bible classes to win trophies in individual and team sports.[88] A major feature in the life of the Catholic community was the Sports Day held on St Patrick's Day (until 1955 there were public holidays for the patron saints of England, Scotland and Ireland). These festivities became increasingly elaborate. In Auckland all the Catholic schools of the city participated in a huge event. In Ashburton, with just one Catholic school, St Patrick's Day sports were a major parish event from 1898, organised by a parish committee, and much energy went into cycling races in which all the men of the parish could compete.[89]

The threat of the state taking over provision for young people was a common concern, and during World War II the government sought to coordinate youth work.[90] The advent of compulsory secondary schooling in 1940 changed the context, however.

DANCING CAUSED CONCERN AMONG many churches long after they had reconciled themselves to sport. In 1850 evangelical Protestants expressed their concern about the injury done to health, mind, morality and spirituality by balls.[91] Colonial balls and smaller dances were a popular social activity for the whole community. Some churches held them, although they were subject to criticism by puritanical neighbours if they did so.[92] Once, when a church choir held a private dance in 1883, the pastor forced the resignation of leading members as a result.[93]

Dances were seen by the evangelical world as a symptom of declining spirituality and a 'downgrade' in theology.[94] There are (possibly fictional) tales of Presbyterian halls built with sloping floors to prevent their use for dances. Catholics were very different, and the church dance was a customary event, for example to welcome a new priest.[95] Some conservative Catholics were nevertheless cautious about the wrong style of dancing, and in World War II one letter to the *Tablet* proposed a curfew for dancing after 11 p.m.[96]

In the Methodist and Presbyterian churches the development of independent-minded Bible classes, run by the young people themselves, forced the churches to reconsider their bans. In 1924, the Presbyterian General Assembly decided to continue its ban on dancing, to the outrage of secular observers.[97] Then in 1925 and in 1939 the Assembly backed down and stated that dancing was a matter of individual conscience, but criticised 'the excesses and abuses of the modern dancing craze', and stated its disapproval of dances being held in church buildings or as fundraising events.[98]

Methodists were even more cautious, and their Lawbook included a formal ban on the use of their facilities for dances. Again their Bible class movement disagreed. When the issue was referred to the denominational Welfare of the Church Committee in 1936, it recommended continuing the ban on dances in church buildings, ostensibly because they were structurally unsuitable for them, and (more honestly) because of the fear that young people would learn to dance at church and then be enticed into the dance halls. The Methodist Conference asked the committee to reconsider its approach, but it was reluctant, noting 'the grave implications of this question', and referred the matter to district synods.

Debates raged in the church and in the newspapers, and when the report came to the 1938 conference the issue became symbolic of the divide between young and old members of the church. The Welfare of the Church Committee released a grandly named Manifesto on Dancing, which declared that the issue was in the end a matter of individual conscience, but it gave a strong psychological warning of the unhealthiness of gratifying desires, and linked dancing and alcohol, urging people to spiritual transformation. The Manifesto was adopted by the conference, with the request that it be printed in the Bible class magazine, while the Lawbook of the church was tightened up so that dances might not be sponsored in the name of the Methodist Church, even when they took place off the church premises.[99]

The issue of dancing forced the churches to consider their attitudes towards leisure. In 1937 the Methodist Welfare of the Church Committee emphasised the importance of rest, and in the face of the monotony of modern work it urged the use of leisure 'for the cultivation of neglected interests'.[100] Methodists thought that young people needed leisure, but not just any leisure would do:

> Adolescence is a period of emotional stress and strain, and undoubtedly it is largely because of this tension that young people are drawn to the dance halls. We therefore consider that the Church should take up as a vital matter the whole question of meeting this adolescent need. We do not suggest that the Church should be an amusement centre for youth, but we do suggest that much could be done by the reasoned advocacy of suitable 'Outlets' provided outside the Church, e.g. — organised games, and by sympathetic instruction of the nature of adolescent problems.[101]

In the Manifesto on Dancing the committee noted that Christians could not choose leisure on the basis of its 'immediate personal pleasurability', but should rather assess how it fitted people for the kingdom of God, and how it affected other people. The committee noted that the delay of marriage in the modern era led to 'emotional strain' that only marriage could satisfy, and urged that people should find positive outlets for reducing strain, and avoid stimulants.[102]

It was doubtless this debate that led to the Presbyterian Church reaffirming its stance in 1939. Meanwhile some local Methodist circuits began quietly to permit dancing, and the Manifesto of 1938 was challenged in 1946. This time opinions had shifted. The majority noted that the dissatisfaction of young people with Bible class socials was leading them to go outside the church, and that war service had introduced many to dancing. The minority reiterated the old reasons and feared that it would lead to tensions in parishes. Ten years later the Lawbook was changed to forbid 'entertainments or amusements which conflict with the spiritual purpose for which the church was called into being or which are likely to bring reproach upon the church'.[103] Evangelicals remained conservative on the subject; some leaders were expelled from the Crusader movement because they approved of dancing.[104]

A Sister of Mercy nun teaches a large class (25 faces are visible; more are obscured) at St Patrick's School in South Dunedin in 1959. The free services of the nuns were essential for the Catholic schooling system, which was designed to avoid a godless education in the state schools.
THE EVENING STAR

SUNDAY SCHOOLS EXPERIENCED A large drop-off in attendance early in the twentieth century, and churches began to review their options. Some changed from afternoon to morning Sunday school in the 1920s. In the end others were forced to follow. Epsom Presbyterian Church experimented with this late in 1931.[105] In provincial areas like Redwoodtown in Blenheim it occurred in 1951, when the church also commenced a monthly family service.[106]

Typically, Sunday school thereafter operated at the same time as the church service. The change to the morning was especially significant for women. Sunday morning became a very busy time, requiring children to be prepared and sent to Sunday school, the meal prepared, church attended and then the great Sunday meal eaten.

A. H. Reed made his name through his bold support for switching the Sunday school to the morning, and his graded lessons were intended to ensure that the syllabus could be more effectively followed in the shorter time available. He advocated that children first attend church with their parents at 11 a.m. and then be sent out to their Sunday school classes.[107] In opposition, the Rev. Henry Ryan, a recent migrant from Ireland, complained to the Otago-Southland Methodist Synod: 'They take their children to the beaches, and we propose to alter the time of the Sunday school to the morning, which just fits into their scheme of irreligious desires and practices.'[108]

Many Baptists at this time adopted the American solution of the All Age Sunday School, which conceived of using the hour before or after the church service for educational programmes for adults as well. It was not an experiment that lasted long.[109] Gradually the Sunday school became an adjunct to the church service, after it became apparent that the separate family service divided congregations in two. At the same time secular and even church schools stopped sending pupils to church services, as religion ceased to be seen as a necessary part of childhood and youth.

In the 1960s and 1970s Bible classes were first supplemented and then replaced by youth groups. These were much more informal and casual, reflecting the cultural shift among young people. At times these youth groups in effect operated quite independent of the church, and at St John's Presbyterian Church in Wellington they almost formed a rival movement within the church.[110]

Youth groups were much debated.[111] What was the goal of all the activity among youth? Professor John McKenzie tried to tease out these issues in a series of papers to Presbyterians in 1962. He urged churches to find ways to teach religion to young people, and to bring them to a definite point of commitment.[112]

Some churches had very successful parish youth programmes in the postwar years. All Saints Wanganui ran a youth club in the 1960s, with 70 young people meeting on a Tuesday for half an hour of religious devotions followed by social activities and regular dances. The vicar apologised to the vestry that 'not all belong to our church — probably some belong to no church — but I feel that if the Club fulfils a local want, it would not be right to exclude altogether those who are not Anglicans'.[113] This was a phenomenon of the 1960s, however, and by 1970 interest in the club began to flag.

Changes in church sociability owe much to the preferences of youth. A columnist in the Presbyterian magazine was horrified in 1963 to visit a youth group and find the young people doing the foxtrot to the tune 'Just a Closer Walk with Thee'.[114] Churches often held dances in order to provide a safe environment, since they were in such demand. Anglican churches were by the 1960s a major provider of dances for younger teenagers, since schools were reluctant to provide volunteers to run these events. Even St Barnabas Anglican Church in Fendalton was forced to allow more informal music.[115]

The Anglican Youth Movement in the Diocese of Auckland devoted much of its energy to coordinating these events so that youth groups could have a dance every weekend. Each dance would have a live band, and its merits would be promoted to others. St Peter's Church in Onehunga was constantly claiming that it provided: 'Good Supper, Good Floor, Better Band'. Sometimes the supervision provided was inadequate. The Rev. Greville Goetz, vicar of St Andrew's in Epsom, cancelled dances in 1968 in the face of gatecrashers who ruined their tone.[116] Presbyterians in the eastern suburbs of Auckland reported that dances were being disrupted by demands for 'the twist', drinking, and chaotically bad behaviour, but the dances went on because they were profitable.[117]

There was a significant experimental youth programme at the Waikari Union Church, in the west of Dunedin, from 1964. It had 'club time', guest speakers, dancing, and it catered for workers and less intellectual types.[118] Such experiments troubled other Presbyterians.[119]

Meanwhile Pentecostal youth movements drew in very large groups of young people, emphasising contemporary worship music, rhythm and sociability.[120] Teen Challenge, the Pentecostal youth movement based in Taupō, Palmerston North and Wellington, sought to reach young people through music and entertainment and the frank addressing of deeper issues.[121]

Christian youth movements had moved from an educational to an entertainment focus. A key influence was Youth For Christ (YFC), which began in New Zealand in 1950. Gradually it built up and eventually it had 17 regional groups, which had monthly rallies in all the major towns and the annual Capital Teen Convention in Wellington every Queen's Birthday Weekend.[122] Ian Grant, later well-known from his

Above The Mount Cook Bible class hockey team on 10 October 1908. Before compulsory secondary schooling, Bible class sports teams were very popular. The two more formally dressed people must be the Bible class leaders. The Mount Cook congregation was a branch of St John's in Willis Street, Wellington, the home of the first Bible class. Photographed by Joseph Zachariah. MUSEUM OF NEW ZEALAND TE PAPA TONGAREWA. REF: PS.003381

Below A youth dance at St Matthew's in Masterton about 1957. Church dances were a popular way for couples to socialise in smaller communities. The dancing was traditional.
MASTERTON DISTRICT LIBRARY ARCHIVE, 04-42/22-58

television programmes of advice to parents, began as a presenter for its ministries in Wellington in the 1960s.[123] Youth groups loved these events and its approach had a widespread influence, even in churches that did not approve of its evangelicalism.

The existing Catholic youth sodalities declined in the 1950s. From this time the Catholic Youth Movement emerged as a focus for more serious young people.[124] Reginald Delargey (later Archbishop of Wellington from 1974 to 1979, and Cardinal) used it to attract thinking young people back into the ambit of the church. Its vision was of a new apostolate based on the young workers' movement that had sprung up in some countries. Similarly, the Methodists set up the Order of St Stephen, which enabled some young people to do a year of unpaid service in the community.[125] Although these movements encouraged the future elite of the church, they had little impact on the general range of young people.

Gradually a Christian youth culture emerged, with its own magazines, music and events. A music festival (modelled on the English Greenbelt festival) began at Mainstage in Ōtaki and then became the Parachute festival. At the time it ceased in 2014 Parachute was attracting more than 20,000 people, making it larger than any secular festival. Meanwhile the traditional churches were exceedingly nervous as young people denounced the Sunday service as boring.[126]

Coffee bars became the rage throughout the Western world in the 1950s. In the United Kingdom some churches used this formula to reach young people.[127] There were a few experiments with this at Houghton Valley Community Church near Island Bay in the early 1960s.[128] When Tony Hanne, a medical doctor and evangelist, moved to New Zealand in 1965 he wrote an article on coffee bars that fell on attentive ears and stimulated various experiments.[129] In Sandringham, Auckland, the Baptist church established a coffee bar in September 1965.[130] Others began doing 'coffee bar evangelism', which consisted of loitering for religious conversations in the trendy downtown coffee bars.[131] Another experiment took place in the Willow Park Christmas Camp at Eastern Beach, Auckland, in 1965–66.

In 1966, a group of young people at the Brethren Gospel Hall in Robert Street, Ellerslie, in Auckland decided to remodel their Saturday youth group into a coffee bar format, which they named Drift Inn. The leaders were John Hawkesby (later a well-known television presenter), Luke Brough (a future Pentecostal church leader, and Ray Miller (later a university lecturer in politics). The format involved candles in milk bottles, low tables, soft lighting, string across the ceiling, and an informal mix of live music and brief spoken presentations. In 1967, this was adapted into a Sunday night event, and in the absence of competition it had astounding success. Large crowds of young people attended, some of them from other church groups, but also quite a number more used to secular entertainment. A folk club in Newmarket closed down because most people preferred to attend the Drift Inn,[132] where typically 200 to 400 people a week turned up.[133] The leaders were people of remarkable skills, of course, which developed in that context, as their future careers showed; one of those who joined them was a future judge, Stan Thorburn.

The success of the Drift Inn led to widespread imitation. The Hub at the new Hillsborough Baptist Church was one of the best known. Another developed at Glen Innes Scout Hall (owned by the Presbyterian Church), which was named Living Inn. This drew a rather rougher crowd.[134] By 1969, commentators noted that 'Auckland is peppered with Sunday night coffee bars . . . churches in Hillsborough, Northcote, Blockhouse Bay, Remuera, Balmoral, Mt Albert, Howick, Papatoetoe, the Henderson area and in several others', and they also developed in the Waikato and in Napier.[135] Catholic youth also set up coffee bars, even in the rural parish of Ashburton.[136] Overall, the leadership in youth activity was transferring to the evangelicals and Pentecostals.

The Pasifika world highly valued children, and the churches had many child-focused rituals, generally adapted from the Victorian traditions of the missionaries. In recent years the only flourishing Sunday schools have been those in the Pasifika churches of South Auckland. White Sunday is a major event and a direct reflection of the world of the islands. Sometimes parents would coerce children into attending Sunday school.

Pasifika youth groups have also flourished, although they seem to have no upper age limit, inconceivable as it is for the young people to pass out of the influence of parents and grandparents. Jemima Tiatia, a Pasifika scholar, has explained some of the frustrations of those who were forced to participate against their will when they were probably much more interested in Saturday night socialising.[137] Pasifika churches often add new groups, but rarely abandon traditions when they do so.

By the 1970s, sport was increasingly emphasised as a positive community experience. Schools had become the place where most people learned to play sports. Congregational teams regularly played against other church teams. Some church teams participated in secular competitions, and in 1986 the Christchurch Inter-Church Soccer League was created, an early example of what became a very strong pattern, especially in areas where there were many Pasifika churches.[138]

In recent years church sports have been dominated by the involvement of Pasifika people. In South Auckland there is still a very active church sports league, although because of intense competition between Samoans and Tongans, in particular, church rugby games became notorious for rough play and in many cases have been stopped. In the Islands strict sabbatarianism limited opportunities for sport, but concern for young people has gradually changed attitudes.[139] In 2016, Joseph Parker went to church to celebrate becoming heavyweight champion of the world. Pasifika church leaders are troubled by a growing number of young people withdrawing from church because of its restrictions and formalities.

YOUNG PEOPLE HAVE RARELY confined themselves to local congregational organisations. From the beginning some threw their energies into national and regional organisations. The Sunday school unions were both denominational and interdenominational; by the twentieth century joint graded lessons were shared by various denominations. Among youth, the Bible class movement had a huge impact within each denomination, and Easter camps became major events. There were other organisations encountered in the schools and universities, notably the Student Christian Movement and its competitors, the Crusader movement (Scripture Union) and the Inter-Varsity Fellowship.

Churches had large visions and scope in their youth work. The national youth bodies trained an elite that eventually took its place in church and activist organisations. Some entered the ministry of the church. Others became very active in secular agencies. Inevitably, for some, careers got in the way of continued religious and charitable involvement.

This youth work was vulnerable in rapidly changing times. The advent of commercialised leisure and the weakening of the family reduced the churches' work among the young. Little remains today, when even the children of faithful adults are reluctant participants. Sunday schools are mostly little handfuls of people. The decline has been greater than in any other aspect of church life. There is today a high level of suspicion about untrained people caring for children, and police supervision makes voluntary activities for youth more difficult. Churches are not alone in struggling in these circumstances; all youth organisations have suffered. Student politics has also declined in the same period, despite institutional support. Young people are no longer interested in joining. Perhaps youth is no longer the age of religious discovery and commitment.

Status, Hierarchy and Faith

Previous Bishopscourt in Christchurch, rebuilt for the arrival of Bishop Campbell West-Watson and his family by the noted Christchurch architect Cecil Wood. Its 22 rooms were generous even for episcopal hospitality.
ALEXANDER TURNBULL LIBRARY.
REF: MNZ-0818-1/4-F

THE ROLE OF STATUS and class in religion is a rich subject. Fashions in history change, and gender and ethnicity have become more common categories of analysis in recent years. Yet awkward though it is, class and status are relevant factors in religious culture.

The churches have long used scripture to urge Christians to treat people equally, to respect one another, to sympathise with the needs of the poor, to show works of charity and benevolence. The religious voice is also a voice of order and of honour, which values moral people and good behaviour, and views cleanliness, responsibility and respectability as the outcomes of a religious life. 'The rich man in his castle, the poor man at his gate, God made them high and lowly and ordered their estate,' wrote Mrs Alexander, the Victorian children's hymn writer, in a song popular in my own Sunday school in the 1950s. These two incompatible factors coexisted in the religious mindset.

A great deal of research has explored the alienation of the working classes from the church in the nineteenth century. The pioneer social scientists saw this as a major issue, although today their assumption that church membership was a normal expectation no longer seems valid. The British census of 1851 exposed an industrial society with extremely low levels of working-class participation in the churches. New Zealand never had a strong industrial identity, and thus its class formation differed, as did the pattern of churchgoing. We would do well to use language of status rather than class in New Zealand.

Social status may also be explored within the characterisation of church and sect by H. Richard Niebuhr in his seminal writings on American religiosity in the early twentieth century.[1] Niebuhr observed a sectarian trend in religion that is particularly apparent among the less educated. His interpretation invites us to explore social differences in religious affiliation. Yet another factor was proposed in the 1960s by Bryan Wilson, the Oxford sociologist: that religious adherence would gradually decline as the mainstream of society lost any inclination to be religious, and so the religion that survived would be very sectarian and anti-secular.[2] This strong secularisation thesis has been rejected by most sociologists in recent years, but the decline in affiliation to churches is very apparent, even though there is less evidence of a decline in believing.

Definitions of class are critical in this context. Class may be viewed rigidly using economic criteria, but most current research emphasises the need to broaden the criteria and incorporate ethnic, gender and language factors. Class is only one way of looking at society, and it is more illuminating in some societies and circumstances than others. Most nineteenth-century New Zealand migrants came from Britain, which was a very class-divided society. In the new cities industrial workers were largely absent from church services. The Chartist Movement, campaigning for the rights of the poor, denounced the church as an oppressive body. Christian socialism, temperance campaigns and urban evangelism all sought to bridge the divide, but none made much impact.[3] So the earliest New Zealand settlers included some who had been alienated from the church.

Newspaper readers in nineteenth-century New Zealand were well informed about these issues, and when they saw low levels of church attendance they frequently saw it as evidence that the working class was boycotting the church. John Stenhouse, the Otago historian, has challenged this interpretation. He has argued that historians have fallen casually into a class interpretation of church that is not justified by the evidence taken as a whole. Drawing on data from the churches of Caversham and South Dunedin, Stenhouse shows detailed evidence that working-class women and children were involved in all denominations. He argues that the rate of church attendance by women and children is very different from that of working-class men, and undercuts the argument of an alienated working class. He rightly argues that working-class homes cannot be construed as godless.[4]

In the dominant denominations in New Zealand — Anglican in most places, or Presbyterian in the south — every class was represented. The smaller denominations had a more distinct social profile.[5] Some people were alienated from church, but they were drawn from a broad social range. Low attendance rates by the New Zealand poor were attributed at the time to tiredness, the weather and denominational differences, but not to class exclusion.[6]

After the 1882 church poll in Auckland, the *Observer* had some fun at the expense of the minister of St Luke's Remuera, for the district (then partly rural) was even at that time a rather desirable place of residence, yet its churchgoing rate was 241 out of 3000.[7] 'There is woe among the jam tarts of Remuera,' wrote the *Observer*'s reporter.[8] The great bulk of non-attendees were manual labourers, but they were a majority of the population of the colony, so this was bound to be the case. Similarly, an impassioned 1901 Methodist editorial lamented the failure of the churches to reach the masses, but identified the cause as the low level of dedication of Methodist people and the lack of care for people.[9] One preacher decried the impact of class tensions on the church in Britain, but applied this selectively to the colony.[10] By the 1930s there was greater recognition of the discontent of the poor with the churches and society.

New Zealand society showed evidence of some class divisions during the long depression of the 1880s (especially during the strikes of 1889–90), and in the riots and protests of the Depression of the 1930s. The sense of class division was less apparent at other times. After World War II, class language receded, and the language of elites and status now seems more useful. Today some evidence suggests that the attitude of classes to religion may have reversed, for manual labourers and the lower paid are more likely to attend church than well-paid and professional groups — although this is explicable not so much in class terms but rather as an ethnic phenomenon.

THERE WAS A HIERARCHY in the church and its clergy, but most denominations in the nineteenth century were relatively weak, and their leading clergy are not easily identified in class terms. Serving as moderator of the Presbyterian Church or president of the Methodist Conference was a matter more of honour than of responsibility. They were certainly the elite in the denomination, however. In 1902, to the outrage of some, moderatorial robes were introduced for the moderators (and past moderators) of the annual Presbyterian General Assembly, consisting of a frockcoat lined with lace, gaiters, and a high white collar,[11] and they were addressed as 'the Very Reverend'. There were prominent office-holders in each denomination, associated with head office, missions or church extension.

The Rev. (and as moderator, the Very Rev.) James Gibb came to prominence in the negotiations to unite the divided parts of the Presbyterian Church in the 1890s. He served as first moderator of the united church, and as chair of the Home Mission Committee from 1912 to 1924. Although his background was humble, he had been to university before coming to New Zealand and he was awarded an honorary doctorate by the University of Aberdeen in 1903. The Rev. William Morley, whose father was a prosperous businessman, achieved great prominence as secretary of the New Zealand Wesleyan Connexion from 1893 to 1902, and then went on to fulfil a similar role in the Methodist Church in Australia. These were ministers of great distinction, combining learning and political skill.

Gibb and Morley also served as ministers of some of the main churches of their denominations. The most prominent ministers in the Protestant denominations were those appointed to the large city churches: First Church and Knox in Dunedin; Durham Street Methodist and Oxford Terrace Baptist in Christchurch; Wesley Church and St John's in Wellington; and The Tabernacle, Pitt Street Methodist, Beresford Street Congregational and St Andrew's and St David's in Auckland. These churches sometimes recruited their ministers from abroad. They often went on to senior positions in other places, and they were well paid. The lay leaders in these congregations were usually very prosperous businessmen. But even in these congregations the elite of the churches in New Zealand were a colonial class not an aristocracy.

The Anglican and Catholic churches had a hierarchy of bishops, and a range of other titled positions — archdeacons, deans, canons and monsignors. The first bishop of any kind in New Zealand was the French Catholic, Jean-Baptiste Pompallier. The Marists who accompanied him grew increasingly irritated by his demands that priests address him as 'Your Lordship' and that his residence in the Bay of Islands (a modest house) be treated as the episcopal palace. These airs and graces (partly derived from his aristocratic background) enabled Pompallier to contract debts that became too great a burden to the infant Catholic Church.[12]

Both Catholic and Anglican bishops were appointed from overseas, in the case of Anglicans mostly from England, and they were generally from a very different social background to their clergy. The first and only Bishop of New Zealand, George Augustus Selwyn, was a visionary who reconceived the episcopate to suit the colonial and the modern world. He was also a 'muscular Christian' who made extensive visits across his vast diocese (including the Pacific), ministering, reaching out to great and small, and conducting marriages and baptisms. His friend and older colleague Bishop Harper of Christchurch was shaped by the same aspirations. Both Harper and Bishop William Cowie at Auckland quickly learned to rough it with their clergy and made long horseback journeys to meet congregations in their dioceses. They were treated with great respect. Once Harper travelled many miles with his clergyman son; when they arrived at the distant homestead his son was offered whisky as any menial rider would be, but the bishop was received into the inner sanctum of the house.[13]

By the twentieth century bishops had become more sedate and proper. They were provided with cars and drivers. Catholic bishops dressed elaborately according to rules of their order. Michael Verdon, second Catholic Bishop of Dunedin, wore a soutane laced with purple; John Grimes, first Catholic Bishop of Christchurch, went about in silks and lace; Henry Cleary, Catholic Bishop of Auckland from 1910, wore street clothes with only a little purple, while Francis Redwood, Archbishop of Wellington from 1874 until 1935, wore a shapeless cape.[14] Anglican bishops wore the white rochet and sleeveless chimere, but Moore Richard Neligan, Bishop of Auckland from 1903 to 1910, began the custom of wearing a cope, which soon became standard.

Bishops were automatically accorded a prime position in secular society. Selwyn was able to cut it with the best of colonists, for he was unmistakeably 'Lord Bishop'. Admittedly this did not appeal to everyone. Settlers in Taranaki were infuriated by Selwyn's critical comments about their greed for land, and he was quickly accused of giving himself airs.[15]

In his survey of the pre-1945 Anglican bishops, the retired priest and scholar Noel Derbyshire notes that 26 of the 31 bishops appointed before 1946 were born in England, and most had Oxford or Cambridge degrees.[16] Campbell West-Watson, for example, had been suffragan (assistant) bishop of Barrow in Furness from

Above Anglican bishops in 1890 in their very plain white rochet and black chimeres. From left: Octavius Hadfield, Andrew Suter of Nelson, Edward Stuart of Waiapu, Henry Harper of Christchurch, John Selwyn of Melanesia, William Cowie of Auckland, and Samuel Nevill of Dunedin. JACOBS, H. NEW ZEALAND: CONTAINING THE DIOCESES OF AUCKLAND, CHRISTCHURCH, DUNEDIN, NELSON, WAIAPU, WELLINGTON, AND MELANESIA. LONDON, SOCIETY FOR PROMOTING CHRISTIAN KNOWLEDGE, 1887

Below Christchurch society surrounds Rev. Wally Averill, vicar of the prestigious St Michael's in Christchurch (standing with the papers in the centre), at his farewell in 1910 following his appointment as Bishop of Waiapu. Averill went on to become bishop of Auckland and then archbishop. SIR GEORGE GREY SPECIAL COLLECTIONS, AUCKLAND LIBRARIES, AWNS-19100113-14-2

1909 to 1926 before his election to Christchurch. Another Anglican historian praises West-Watson's vision for the future of the church, but notes that it was not always appreciated because of 'his English patrician manner and his penchant for ponderous pronouncements'.[17] Herbert St Barbe Holland had been Archdeacon of Warwick before being elected Bishop of Wellington in 1936, and in 1946 he returned to ministry in England.

Only four of all the pre-war Anglican bishops were ordained in New Zealand, although 11 of them had Australasian experience. Derbyshire also notes that the five New Zealand-born bishops before 1939 (William Williams; Herbert Williams; William Fitchett; George Gerard, who served briefly in Waiapu; and George Cruikshank, whose term in the same diocese was even shorter) had all been to Oxbridge. Seven out of the 26 English-born bishops had served in New Zealand prior to their 'elevation', while three Nelson bishops had served in Australia. Presbyterian moderators were much more often New Zealand-born than were Anglican bishops in this and later periods.

Since most bishops had not served as priests in New Zealand, they assumed they would be given the status of English or Irish bishops on arrival. Harper was concerned for the prospects of his daughters before he came, but Sarah Selwyn reassured him that 'the colonists of the Canterbury settlement stand the highest in N.Z. in point of character, education and gentlemanly tone of feeling, so much so that it has been objected by the public that it is too much of a Class Settlement'.[18] Emily Harper married Barton Acland of Mount Peel Station, to Harper's relief. Harper was also anxious that his son Henry, who became an archdeacon, should move to the Timaru parish in order to mix with 'a higher and more educated class of men' than he met at his first parish on the West Coast.[19] He elsewhere commented that 'the self educated man ... will value his parson the more, if the manners of a gentleman are united in him with earnestness in his calling'.[20] Harper did little to demonstrate sympathy with the poor during the social crisis of the late 1880s and early 1890s, when unemployment was high.[21]

Bishops were addressed by people of their denomination with the title 'My Lord Bishop' or 'Your Grace'. These titles stuck in the gullets of some from other denominations, who saw it as implying that the bishops held the rank of the peerage.[22] Perhaps it was understandable that Selwyn was 'His Lordship' to the earliest Anglican parishioners,[23] but the title was also used by the first generation of bishops after World War II. Catholic bishops were often greeted with lavish ceremony.[24] When Archbishop Peter McKeefry first visited Blenheim in the 1940s, Eileen Duggan saluted him with a poem that now strikes us as sycophantic:

> We give you welcome if ever a place gave one,
> We give you honour for all here to mind
> Our great, golden province with its tawny forelands
> Rejoices to greet one so fearless and kind.[25]

The generation after World War II gradually changed their view of the status of bishops. Twenty-three of the 35 postwar Anglican bishops were born in New Zealand; 26 were ordained here, and almost all had New Zealand ministry experience.[26]

John Holland, Bishop of Polynesia, was the son of Herbert St Barbe Holland, an Oxford graduate who had served as a vicar in New Zealand.[27] The English-born bishops in the postwar years included Reginald Owen of Wellington, who had previously been headmaster of Uppingham Public School in England, and his successor Henry Baines, who had previously served as Bishop of Singapore, and preferred to be addressed as 'Lord Bishop'.[28] The lordly episcopal conventions included the wearing of gaiters (a buttoned-up covering of the lower leg, still in use by Dean Martin Sullivan of Christchurch and Bishop Eric Gowing of Auckland in the 1960s).[29]

When Gowing became bishop in 1960 his predecessor, John Simkin, left him detailed notes on how to dress properly in order to receive the respect he was due. This included, for ordinary Eucharists, amice, alb, girdle, maniple, stole, chausable and mitre (if the service was sung) and, on special occasions, tunicle and dalmatic as well, with further instructions to wear a cope over the vestments in a procession, and very detailed notes about wearing a cross. Little concession was made to the weather, apart from advice that he need not wear gloves if it was hot. These instructions went on for six pages, and today few people who do not live and breathe Anglicanism would have much idea what many of the terms mean.[30]

Change was coming. In the 1960s, after a discussion on the issue at the 1968 Lambeth Conference of all the Anglican bishops throughout the world, Norman Lesser, the Bishop of Waiapu and the Archbishop, rejected the titles 'Your Grace' and 'My Lord'.[31] Change was also on the way in the style of bishops. Allen Johnston, Bishop of Dunedin from 1953 and Waikato from 1969, was surely the most striking case, given his background as an old boy of Seddon Technical College in Auckland. Similarly Allan Pyatt, Bishop of Christchurch from 1966, was the son of a warehouseman, who did well because he excelled at sport, won a Rhodes Scholarship to Oxford, and as bishop combined geniality with informality.[32] Nevertheless, the titles were still used in General Synod minutes in 1972.[33] One opponent of church union was still using 'Your Grace' in 1968.[34] The Diocese of Polynesia continued its use long after it passed out of regular use in New Zealand.

The key symbol of the status of a bishop was the provision of a palace. Throughout the colonies Anglican bishops were provided with a Bishopscourt. They were not quite palaces, but they were also not the typical family home.

Selwyn had first lived in the Deanery, built in 1857 in stone by Frederick Thatcher. (It remains today, on the corner of St Stephens Avenue and Brighton Road.) Then in 1865 Bishopscourt on St Stephens Avenue in Parnell was completed, a handsome house with attached library; today it is a Grade One property of the Historic Places Trust, but is again in use by the Bishop of Auckland. The house's original private chapel was designed by Thatcher and built at a cost of £2000; it now serves as one of the chapels at Auckland Diocesan School for Girls.

In 1903 Bishop Neligan told the Synod that the building was unliveable.

> When I accepted nomination to the Bishopric I conveyed to you information that, in my judgment, Christianity and debt were contradictory terms. So far as I can see at present, although living is more expensive in this country than at Home, I can live out of debt until, probably, next Synod; and my general impression is: the alternatives then to be faced are, either almost doubling the Episcopal income or, with due regard to historical association and conservation of valuable sentiment, the complete reorganisation of the Bishopric Estate. I do not apprehend immediate difficulty, owing to the action of the Trust Board; but, for the sake of the Faith we believe, I am confident it is far better just simply to state: I will never willingly be in the position of a Diocesan Bishop who cannot, without getting into debt, adequately fulfil those obligations of hospitality and courtesy that a Churchman has a right to expect his Bishop to bear.[35]

So Neligan House was erected for him next door on St Stephens Avenue, but this house proved an unsuitable rabbit warren and so many years later Bishop Gowing was provided with a house in fashionable Arney Crescent. Mrs Gowing, meanwhile, saw that the wrong carpet had been laid in the house and insisted that it be torn out and replaced.[36]

In Christchurch, a large house was needed for the 14 children of Bishop Harper so Bishopscourt was built in Park Terrace in 1858. His successor Bishop Julius had eight children, but in 1917 after they were grown up he moved to Cloudesley on the Cashmere Hills while the old house was put to use as a teacher training hostel. It was destroyed by fire in 1924. A new building was designed by well-known architect Cecil Wood for Bishop West-Watson, complete with car shelter, 22 rooms, wooden panelling and the bishop's coat of arms. On seeing it West-Watson reportedly said, 'Oh no!' The rooms were used to provide hospitality for visiting clergy,[37] and it was

Above Bishop Wally Averill and Dean William Fancourt lead Henry Duke of Gloucester (the third son of George V) into St Mary's, Auckland, for the Christmas Day service in 1934, also attended by Governor-General Lord Bledisloe and Lady Bledisloe. Prince Henry had been sent on overseas trips to take him away from an affair, and was much fêted in New Zealand. SIR GEORGE GREY SPECIAL COLLECTIONS, AUCKLAND LIBRARIES, AWNS-19350102-40-3

Left The Right Rev. James Gibb, first moderator of the Presbyterian Church of New Zealand after the Synod of Otago and Southland had joined the church in 1901. His moderator's robes include lace, frock coat and gaiters. PRESBYTERIAN RESEARCH CENTRE ARCHIVES

later refurnished magnificently by Doreen Warren, the wife of Bishop Warren.

Warren's successor Allan Pyatt used this building as an open house in the 1960s, had Asian students flatting on the top floor, and during his sabbatical rented it out to the Governor-General. But its size caused some embarrassment, and the Christchurch Synod resolved in 1979 that it was 'no longer appropriate to the needs of the bishop and diocese'. It was modified in 1984 to serve as Bishopspark, an old people's home, but damage suffered in the 2011 Christchurch earthquake led to its demolition in 2015.[38]

In Wellington a site for a bishop's residence was presented by one of the members of the New Zealand Company, Algernon Tollemache, in 1859, next to the church site provided by Sir George Grey in Mulgrave Street. The property was the former home of the superintendent of Wellington Province.[39] A new and grander house was built in 1879 for Octavius Hadfield, even though he insisted that, 'I never complained of the old house, or expressed any wish for a new one.' In 1940 Bishop Herbert St Barbe Holland complained of the noise and soot emanating from the nearby railway station, so the trustees purchased 28 Eccleston Hill, overlooking Parliament and just below the Catholic cathedral, for him. The house is now used for the diocesan administration while the bishop lives in a humbler modern house behind it.[40]

In Nelson Bishop Hobhouse purchased 158 acres in 1858 for a bishop's residence and gifted it to the diocese. Bishopdale was built for his successor in 1868 and was intended to be a seminary as well as a bishop's residence. The chapel was built in 1876. A new residence was built for the fourth bishop of Nelson, William Sadlier, in 1925 at a cost of £5267, financed by the sale of much of the land. There were a series of disputes over the property in the 1970s, and in 1997 the diocese voted to sell it. The house was sold in 2001 although the original chapel still remains.[41]

In Dunedin Bishop Samuel Nevill built a huge residence in 1871 on Highgate for £3087 plus furnishing costs, far beyond the means of the diocese, which provided £2500. His intention was to provide boarding facilities for up to 50 theological students as well, although only two ever lived there. In 1878 the bishop sold the house to a bank manager, and in 1914 it became St Columba College. Nevill moved to Bishopsgrove in Leith Valley, which was even grander.[42]

Less is known about the episcopal residences (customarily called the bishop's palace) of the four historic Catholic dioceses in New Zealand. Pompallier House in Russell was in fact the printery for the mission, and the bishop did not live here. When Bishop Pompallier moved to Auckland he purchased land on what he called Mount St Mary, a name reflected in the modern identity of St Mary's Bay, and a wooden house was erected there, but the land was later sold to recoup his excessive spending. It was repurchased by his Irish successor, Bishop Croke, then the new

Benedictine Bishop, John Edmund Luck, raised money during a tour of England in 1891–92 and commissioned plans for a fine new brick house. This was designed by Peter Paul Pugin, son of the great English Gothic revival architect Augustus Pugin. The house, which opened in 1894, is beautifully ornamented, with lavish features, including a tower and water closets; it served as the bishop's house, and following additions in 1989 it has become a diocesan centre.[43]

D ENOMINATIONAL SCHOOLS ALSO CONTRIBUTED to elitism. Christ's College, founded in Christchurch in the very early days of the colony and modelled on the public schools of England, was part of the vision of creating a new class settlement and overcoming the ills of society. Wanganui Collegiate and the unbuilt Porirua College had humbler aspirations, including service to the Māori community. Auckland's King's College grew out of Kinder's Anglican school and a school at King's College, but was not established until 1896. Again the English public school was dominant in its vision.[44] A group of preparatory schools also grew up in association with these three schools. Te Aute College in Hawke's Bay sought to provide education for the elite of Māori Anglican boys. John Thornton, the headmaster from 1878, was a lay member of the cathedral chapter and the synod.[45]

The vision of these schools was educationally impressive, and they were well informed of trends in secular education. Presbyterians and Catholics also entered the same arena, though Presbyterians had initially strongly supported the state grammar schools. Members of synods remained anxious about denominational schools, because their existence made it difficult for the church to call for changes to the state curriculum, and because the schools were 'rather for the rich than for the poor', to use the words of J. M. Hogben of Thames, speaking in the 1918 Auckland Synod. W. J. Speight (the diocesan secretary) echoed him, warning of the class basis of the schools.[46]

Yet there was clearly a religious case for these schools after the exclusion of religion from the state schools. The Methodist president in 1891, the Rev. John Lewis, expressed his concern: 'Am I to send my son to be indoctrinated by sacerdotalists, who would lead him to sneer at his parents' church, and deny his father's right to administer the sacraments?'[47] Accusations of snobbery arising from attendance at such schools were a difficult issue for the rest of the church, yet pupils at Christ's or King's, or for that matter Scots or John McGlashan, formed an elite in their churches as well as in wider society.[48]

The role of girls' schools was a little different, since such schools sometimes emerged from the finishing schools of the nineteenth century, which were intended to make polite ladies of rough colonial females. Gradually, all the principal denominations established very smart girls' schools. The Anglican girls' schools had an aura of status and decorum. Miss Mary Etheldred Pulling, who founded Auckland's Diocesan School, was 'a woman of high culture and educational attainments'.[49] 'Common people,' she once commented, 'with common graces, write their names in common places.'[50] St Margaret's College in Christchurch resulted from a merger in 1935 of a girls' school founded by the Sisters of the Church in 1910 and Mrs Lohse's school, which had been taken over by Mrs Annette Laura Bowen, wife of the Rev. Croasdaile Bowen.[51]

The girls' schools left a distinctive mark on their students. Sue Kedgley, a prominent feminist during the 1970s (and later Member of Parliament), disavowed her Anglican background and education at Marsden School but, as a shrewd reporter identified, retained an intense sense of justice and goodness.[52] Nevertheless, she noted the stuffiness of the education she had received, and her unpreparedness for a world of sex and politics.

One distinctive aspect of the girls' schools was the annual ball. In the case of the Catholic schools, their aim, undoubtedly, was to ensure Catholics socialising with fellow Catholics rather than with Protestants, and thus they were an attempt to curtail the extremely high level of intermarriage.[53]

Debutante balls were important events for upper-class girls. In nineteenth-century New Zealand girls were presented to the Governor, but the Queen brought the whole procedure to an end in 1957 in England and the Governor followed suit a year later.[54] Debutante balls had become part of the world of society women in the 1930s, and Catholic churches identified their bishops as the person with the highest status in their community. The first Catholic debutante ball I have traced was held in 1930. These were large and glittering events.[55] Despite the tradition for debutantes to be introduced to royalty, Bishop Brodie felt he was an appropriate equivalent for Catholics:

> By according ecclesiastical patronage to this function, the Church wishes to offer its approval to a form of recreation calculated to exercise a helpful educational influence, a recreation with traditions closely allied to the chivalry of earlier centuries, and with the refining influence of courtesy and honour of which many of the court and national dances are so expressive. My presence on such an occasion is an indication of a wish that the young ladies presented this evening may find in their social life that true enjoyment unalloyed by any influences not in keeping with a recreation intended to be pleasing, educational,

Above One of the 28 debutantes curtsies to Bishop Liston at the annual Catholic charity ball in Auckland in May 1936. SIR GEORGE GREY SPECIAL COLLECTIONS, AUCKLAND LIBRARIES, AWNS-19360603-45-1

Below The Presentation Ball at St Mary's parish, Blenheim, in 1962. Those receiving the debutantes are Monsignor William Heavey and Fr Patrick P. Cahill SM. MARIST ARCHIVES

and refining I would crave the kind patience of our patrons to enlist sympathy and practical co-operation in that noble campaign of relief organised in response to the invitation by his Worship the Mayor.[56]

Anglicans were slower to adopt this pattern, but Anglican private schools did not lack for elitism. Marsden School began to hold debutante balls in the 1930s, where the girls were presented to Bishop Holland (although in 1941 they were presented to the British High Commissioner). These balls continued until 1972.[57] Waikato Diocesan School for Girls was an early supporter of these events, perhaps because Bishop Cherrington and his young wife liked them.[58] In the Waikato Diocese they flourished in the 1950s,[59] including a Māori debutante ball where the presentations were to Bishop Holland of Waikato and Wiremu Pānapa, the Bishop of Aotearoa.[60] Perhaps it is an indication of their conservatism that country districts in the Waikato adopted a process exactly when they had fallen out of favour elsewhere.

St Margaret's College in Christchurch was operated on strictly religious lines, and balls were frowned on there. Some Christchurch Anglican parishes held balls, however, and a Christchurch Bible Class Union debutante ball in 1939 was sponsored by St Luke's Anglican Church.[61] Other Christchurch balls were sponsored by the Bible Class Union in the 1950s. Rangi Ruru in Christchurch, highly regarded as an elite girls' school, presented its girls to the headmistress since its links were Presbyterian.[62] In 1961 in Auckland, 62 debutantes were presented to the Anglican Bishop, Eric Gowing, but by then the practice was in the process of dying out.[63] Nevertheless, the role of maintaining upper-crust social ideals had been assumed by the church when the state backed away from it.

Catholic private schools were evidence that nothing in its essence made the Catholic Church working class. The disproportion of the poor in the church came about because the church was Irish, and the Irish were the poor of the empire. Many were unpropertied and very sensitive to the power exercised by the propertied. John Stenhouse shows that the parents of the Catholic school of St Patrick in South Dunedin were second only to the Salvation Army in the proportion of their members who were manual labourers and the unskilled, and the congregation contained few large employers.[64] In Canterbury nearly 44 per cent of all Catholic bridegrooms in the nineteenth century were unskilled, the highest proportion of any denomination.[65] The family backgrounds of Catholic clergy are largely unknown, but they were often well received by the poor they ministered to.[66]

Census results confirm Stenhouse's analysis that overall the Catholic Church had an unusual proportion of working-class people. The proportion of Catholic males who were employers was so low that only the Salvation Army and Adventists had lower rates in 1921. Just 6 per cent of Catholics were employers, against an overall average of 8 per cent. The employee rate was 44 per cent, plus 2 per cent unemployed (against averages of 43 per cent and 2 per cent), while 16 per cent of Catholic women were in paid employment, compared to an average of 15 per cent. A high number of men were domestic employees. In 1926, the proportion of Catholics in farming, building, teaching and other professions was very low, and the proportion in domestic service, transport and road construction was high. In 1936 the census showed a high number of Catholics employed in licensed hotels.[67] Most Catholic churches were located in the poorer communities or on the edge of affluent communities. (One exception, St Michael's in Remuera, was opened in 1933, much later than the other denominations came to this suburb.)

In the eyes of Protestants, it was their attitude to thrift, consumption, alcohol and morality that kept the Irish Catholics poor. There is evidence from the church leadership that good relationships with the aspirations of the labouring class were deemed important, and the church reconciled itself to the Labour Party's version of socialism after 1916. Catholic commentaries often identified with the discontents of the poor. The 'Catholic Thought' page in the *Tablet* was often viewed by the Catholic middle class as 'straight-out propaganda for the Labour Party', although it did little more than reiterate the views found in papal encyclicals.[68]

There were rural and urban parishes with a different flavour. The Catholic Church had a lay elite who could easily get the ear of the bishops.[69] 'Lace curtain Catholics' (to use an American term) — the families of socially successful lawyers, business leaders and farmers — established superior Catholic schools that were out of the range of working-class families.

From the outset, the Church of England in New Zealand was viewed as a class-based institution. As a notoriously left-wing Anglican vicar of Cambridge, the Australian Charles Chandler, wrote in his column in the *Auckland Star*, 'the snob content of the Church of England, even in New Zealand, must be considerable'.[70] Of course given that Anglicans were nearly half the population, the social range of the church was huge. Anglicans dominated most parts of New Zealand north of the Presbyterian stronghold of Otago.

The many nominal working-class members of the church rarely graced it with their physical presence. Even in the colonial period, Bishop Harper observed that many Anglican labourers in New Zealand did not attend church, blaming this on the lack of free seats. South Dunedin was not an Anglican stronghold, but the percentage of working class in the Anglican congregation of Holy Cross was well below 20 per cent, where the typical figure was 25 per cent.[71] Keith Pickens notes from nineteenth-century marriage licences that every type of person was involved with the Anglican Church, but shows that rural social leaders stand out.[72] Marie Peters found that in the 1870s 'middling people' dominated St Michael's in Christchurch, but there were only two labourers in the 124 identified people.[73] In the 1921 census Anglicans had a high proportion of people in the professions (5 per cent of men), compared to Presbyterians, Methodists and Catholics. Anglicans were naturally the largest denomination in almost every type of work, but were particularly well represented in property, finance, law and in most official positions.

Pickens's study shows that in Canterbury large-business owners, professionals and gentlemen were bridegrooms in 11 per cent of marriages conducted in Anglican churches (which conducted 1010 of the 2308 marriages held in churches). Certainly the Congregationalist Church was almost exclusively an elite of businessmen, but its numbers were very small.[74] The wealthy runholders of Canterbury were solidly Anglican, apart from the original Deans family, who were Presbyterians. Even though Canterbury was not as Anglican as it intended to be, its elite was dominated by Anglicans.

Although from a humble background, Bob Lowe, the vicar of St Barnabas Fendalton from 1966 to 1986, exactly combined the easy relationship between the public world and the pulpit which exemplified that kind of wealthy religion — certainly neither academic nor reflective. These were the parishes with the stone churches, the robed choirs, the Oxford-educated clergy, where students attended the denominational secondary schools and where Ladies' Guilds ran very successful fairs. Erstwhile Baptist, Presbyterian and Methodist businessmen in these suburbs sometimes transferred to the Anglican Church as their respectability grew, although this is much less obvious in New Zealand than in England. Anglican vestries were generally comprised of the wealthy in the parish, and the working-class voice was, as observers noted, usually silent.[75]

In Auckland the equivalent parish was Remuera, which had some very prominent lay members. For example Sir George Arney, chief justice of the Supreme Court and farmer of the land that later became the beautiful Arney Crescent in Remuera, was accompanied to church by a valet, to whom his hat was always handed before the service commenced. He was only one of a group of members who walked to their rented pews in the church through the land owned by James Dilworth (whose estate was devoted to the creation of Dilworth School, the only private school in New Zealand that does not charge fees).

Garden parties were held by three other notable Remuera families, the J. P. Campbells, the James Russells and the Moore Joneses, to raise money for the parish, and were enjoyable social occasions. The original parish of St Mark's was readily able to raise the money for the branch church of St Aidan's in east or 'upper Remuera', and when St Aidan's was built in 1905 it was financed by free-will offerings and loans free of interest. Yet regular collections were always rather low.[76] As the 'red dean' Charles Chandler commented sarcastically, there was a fair bit of 'the Gospel with a Fendalton or Remuera touch' in the afternoon teas consumed by many an Anglican vicar.[77]

The choir was often a symbol of social aspirations. Anglicanism had a strong tradition of this because it retained cathedrals. In Christchurch the Cathedral Grammar School was particularly significant, but even in other parishes the robing of choirs and the achievement of a cathedral-like tone was very striking. Even though St Mark's parish was Low Church, the men in its choir were dressed in surplices from 1889, and finally in 1977 red-robed women were allowed to join them.

By the 1930s there was still much of this earlier style to be seen, for example in the church garden parties. St James' Lower Hutt sponsored a party in the home of Mrs Vivian Riddiford (the wife of the heir of the great Wellington runholder Daniel Riddiford), using the theme 'Olden styles of the British Isles', and when Bishop St Barbe Holland appeared he was definitely treated as the Lord Bishop.[78]

Christenings and weddings were great occasions in wealthy parishes. Most weddings in the nineteenth century were not elaborate affairs, but the Anglican society wedding was a sight to behold. The marriage of Annie Hadfield (daughter of Bishop Octavius Hadfield) to William Marshall of Marton in 1882 was an astonishing assemblage of tone and elaboration.[79] All the features that we recognise today in the society wedding were present, down to Mendelssohn's 'Wedding March' and the singing of a wedding hymn from *Hymns Ancient and Modern*. The happy couple then departed to stay with Lord Normanby, the Governor of Victoria and a powerful symbol of the British Empire, and Lady Normanby in Melbourne.

The Anglican Church thus reflected the elite of society, and it honoured them, whether they were the chiefs of the Māori or the judges, lawyers, merchants and runholders of the rural and urban European communities. It looked to them for finance, and it did not need to relate to its wider fraternity.

As a consequence of this, Anglicans could raise very large sums for building projects — the Wells Campaign was the most striking proof of this — but the level of regular giving by parishioners was far below that of equivalent Presbyterian congregations. Miserly sums were put in the plate by wealthy congregations. The secret of the Wells Campaign was selecting eminent people to front the committee and show an example in giving, and this encouraged others to give as generously.

The overall commitment of Anglican congregations was often frustratingly low. Bishop Samuel Nevill commented that 'I stand amazed at the willing and patient sacrifice they make of time and effort in the management of church affairs in synods, on vestries and committees of every kind for the promotion of her work'. But he also felt that 'definite and clear instruction should be given so that the future heads of families may know and value their privileges and the whole population will be impressed by the strength of our convictions'. He could not count on the enthusiastic support of many people.[80]

The Rev. Joseph Feron, vicar of Ashburton in the 1930s, bluntly attacked the 'deadheads' of his parish: 'The people who do not come to church, who will not pay, and who expect the same consideration as all you good people,' as the exasperated vicar put it. But more was to come. After declaring that it was a miserable position to be in to have to send the vestry out cadging subscriptions from those who never showed up at church, Mr Feron added, 'For my part, I would rather tell them to go to hell.' He went on (causing some consternation by his directness): 'Surely there can be no people more contemptible than those who use the Church as a public convenience; first for the social charm of a Church wedding, then disappearance until the Church naming ceremony of the infant (not a conscious bringing of it into the Master's Kingdom, mark you, but a pleasant formality), then disappearance again until the parson is called in for a burial.'[81]

The same nominality afflicted Anglican Māori. The future Bishop William Williams observed as early as 1834 that, 'We do not generally find that growth in grace among them which we desire. On admission into the Church, they seem, for the most part, satisfied to remain stationary, feeling that they have advanced a step beyond the multitude.'[82] Similarly Alfred Brown, visiting Matamata, noted:

> In conversation with a party at my tent to-night, one of them remarked that the belief of a Native was no part of himself, like his head; but that it was rather like a hat, which could be taken off or put on at pleasure. There is too much truth in this stinging satire; and it would be well if it were not as applicable to congregations in a civilized country, as to those surrounding us.[83]

ANGLICANS BENEFITED FROM WEALTHY and generous patrons who had their own very definite ideas of piety. In the nineteenth century the laity of the synods were rather more distinguished than most of the clergy. These leaders are so well known for their other roles that little has been made of their Anglicanism. One example is Richard John Seddon, Liberal prime minister of New Zealand from 1893, and this aspect of his life has been re-evaluated in a recent biography.[84]

Vestries were perhaps a little different. As one of the few parish historians to look at lay participation, Julia Stuart has noted that the task of vestry is rarely to advance the kingdom of God but more mundane responsibilities which often place them at odds with the vicar.[85] Some were relatively inarticulate in matters of faith, but deeply devoted to the administration of the church, on vestries and in lay offices in the dioceses. The laity of the Anglican Church were capable of stopping the plans of the bishops and clergy — and they did so at various times. And yet those laymen are frequently written out of the story except for their memorial plaques.

A singular group of laity helped Bishop Selwyn to fashion the church's constitution in 1857, after 257 people signed Sir George Grey's proposal, which was presented to Selwyn. Sir William Martin was prominent in the early judiciary, and was not only an architect of the constitution but also a member of the General Synod. The Martin family was based at Judge's Bay in Auckland, where they were hosts to Selwyn initially; Sir William supported the development of a native ministry and the Melanesian mission, and when he retired in 1874 the family settled in Lichfield where they were near Selwyn's residence.[86] William Swainson (1809–1884), attorney general of the colony, advocate for Māori and first speaker of the Legislative Council, was another who was involved in drafting the constitution. He was also a member of the Auckland Synod, and from 1866 until his death first chancellor of the Auckland Diocese.[87]

Others among the small group of laity who prepared the church's constitution at St Stephen's Chapel in 1857 included the premier, Edward Stafford; Henry Tancred of Christchurch; R. K. Prendergast of Wellington; and T. Hirst from New Plymouth.[88] Those at the first General Synod in 1859 included William Hall of Canterbury and Henry St Hill, a highly regarded Wellington settler. Bishop Hobhouse called the first Nelson Synod 'The oddest set of Church Legislators that ever assembled — Farmers, Captains, Majors, Lieutenants R.N., an Attorney, an Apothecary, and an ex barrister'.[89] They were the elite of Nelson society.

A frustrating aspect of many parish histories is that they do so little to identify leading members of the laity. But the names that do emerge are often very familiar to local historians. Take, for example, Edwin Mitchelson, chair of the board of Auckland Diocesan School, and also a key member of the Auckland Synod until ill-health forced his retirement in 1915. He was a very prominent Aucklander who had served as native minister and even premier, as well as on a raft of civic bodies.[90] Another member of the Diocesan School Board was Edwin Horton, of the newspaper-owning family.

Colonel Theodore Haultain (1817–1902), who came to New Zealand to take charge of the Fencibles and served prominently in the New Zealand wars, was a member of the committee that wrote the 1857 constitution. His is a frequent name in the nineteenth-century Auckland and General Synods, and he was founding chair of the Purewa cemetery, although he was himself buried at St John's College.[91] Francis Fenton (1820–98) was a noted magistrate throughout the Auckland province, a supporter of Māori in the face of Donald McLean's land acquisition policies, and later chief judge of the Native Land Court. Fenton was a parishioner of St Paul's Symonds Street for most of his life, a member of the Auckland Synod in the 1860s and 1870s, as well as a contributor to the choirs, orchestras and public parks of Auckland.[92]

Other members of this elite included Allan Taylor (1832–90), the owner of Alberton and squire of Mount Albert, where he held an annual 'hunt', merchant banker, patron of St Luke's Church and synod representative.[93] We might continue, but the list would seem little more than an identification of the bulk of the elite of colonial New Zealand. The extent of their involvement in the Anglican Church is not always clear, but certainly attending a synod in the nineteenth century meant giving up a full week. Among the synod representatives, clergy sons and lawyers often seemed important groups.

Over recent years these features of Anglican synods have changed somewhat, but the old legal, business and academic elite is still present, albeit in smaller numbers. Such laymen were very willing to challenge clergy in Synod and in the Standing Committee, which maintained the work of the Synod when it was not in session. The members of the Standing Committee in Auckland in Bishop Gowing's day were highly irritated at the way Gowing and especially his assistant bishop, Ted Buckle, made decisions without consulting them, then expected them to finance the outcome — for example, inviting the Franciscans to the diocese, or purchasing Buckle's car.[94]

The domination of the church by the elite was a somewhat sensitive issue. The seventh Bishop of Wellington, Henry Baines, raised the issue in his synod address in 1963. The local trade union magazine took up the theme, sparking a guilty Anglican reaction.[95] The vast majority of Anglicans were not from the elite. Most parishes had a very average range of people in the congregation, and they sometimes felt overlooked. After a remarkably successful series of mission services at St Jude's in Avondale, the vicar, Lloyd Cullen, commented: 'Some parishes are too "pukka". Their people have too much money. We don't suffer from that here.'[96]

There was also a Māori Anglican elite, and typically these were very prominent members of Māori society. Attendance at Te Aute College helped to shape many members of this elite, especially those in the Waiapu Diocese. It is only possible to mention a very few names here. One of the earliest was Hirini Te Kani, who was a synod representative along with Wiremu Pere and Ānaru Mātete and a member of the Standing Committee, although later he was caught up in responding to Pai

Mārire.[97] Turi or Alfred Thomas Carroll (1890–1975), of mixed Irish and Ngāti Kahungunu background, and a key member of the Pioneer Battalion, was an advocate of both Māori and European types of knowledge, a member of the Waiapu Synod for 20 years, and a people's warden.[98]

Hori Tupaea (1879–1944), from Te Hauke, was a prominent member of Ngāti Kahungunu and a great fundraiser for the Church Army and the Eastern Maori Patriotic Association, a supporter of the Pioneer Battalion, and very active in supporting the Māori Anglican newspaper, *Te Kopara*. He was a vigorous supporter of the Bishopric of Aotearoa at the General Synod in 1926, and insistent that Māori should hold the position — he was prepared to have Āpirana Ngata ordained if all else failed. Hori Tupaea spoke at the ordination of Frederick Bennett, Bishop of Aotearoa in 1928.[99] Paraire Tomoana (1874–1946) was a leader among Ngāti Kahungunu, a sportsman, and from 1900 lay representative on the 'Maori synods' and gatherings of the church. It would be interesting to know what impact his divorce in 1913 had on his relationship with the church.

The greatest Anglican layman was Āpirana Ngata (1874–1950) of Ngāti Porou, first Māori graduate, lawyer, farmer, MP, translator of the Māori Bible and prominent on the Synod.[100] Some Māori identified with more than just one denomination. Sir James Henare (1911–89) was baptised an Anglican but chose to go to Sacred Heart College in Auckland because his father was a friend of Bishop Cleary. He was a lay reader in the Anglican Church in the 1930s and for 20 years a member of the Auckland Synod, but neither he nor members of the family then became Catholics.[101]

MANY OF THE SCOTS and northern Irish who came to New Zealand in the early years were poor. The Rev. John Inglis noted that the early Scots settlers in the Hutt Valley, for example, were almost exclusively working class, but he was confident that as a result by their hard labour they would improve their lot.[102]

Presbyterian adherents were for many years rather more a rural group than others. Many were farmers; many other Presbyterians were involved in primary production, including some 27 per cent of Presbyterian males in 1921, much higher than any other denomination except the Lutherans. There were 8276 Presbyterian primary producers who were employers, and 9 per cent of all Presbyterians were employers; 10.5 per cent of males were self-employed, which was the highest of the larger denominations. Presbyterians were prominent in cropping, sheep farming and dairying. In the 1926 census they were noted as strong in all aspects of primary production except sawmilling, while few were in the building and construction industries, commerce and finance, personal service or administration.[103] Presbyterian ministers did not have a positive reputation with many of the poor.[104]

The typical Presbyterian congregation was more often rural than in other denominations. The church in Gore is an example of the traditional heartland of Presbyterianism. Here, solid and substantial farmers were so passionate about their Presbyterianism that they created three parishes — the original St Andrews in 1881, then East Gore in 1951 and Calvin Church in West Gore in 1960 — as well as a schism into a Congregational Church in 1892, after Presbytery rejected the sustentation fund to pay the stipend of a minister. No names stand out among the Gore laity, and yet the church attracted prominent and academic ministers, many of whom were leaders in the evangelical wing of the church. The women's groups, the choir and the brigades were solid and strong, and the church, its manse and its hall lacked for nothing.[105]

The liberal, educated side of Presbyterianism was evident in its leading city congregations, for example Knox in Dunedin or St Andrew's on the Terrace in Wellington. These were churches that selected educated and erudite ministers, and had congregations that included notable laity, businessmen, politicians and academics. The Presbyterian elite was always well educated.

Keith Pickens's study of Canterbury churches reveals quite a sharp difference between the Wesleyan Methodists and the Primitive Methodists. For example, 16 per cent of Wesleyan bridegrooms were unskilled, compared with 35 per cent of Primitive Methodist grooms.[106] In the Otago University study of Caversham in Dunedin, St Clair Methodist Church, located by the sea, had no working-class members, whereas Cargill Road Methodist Church reflected the proportion of working-class people in South Dunedin.[107]

In Auckland in 1882, the Primitive Methodist churches were in Alexandra Street, Franklin Road and Upper Pitt Street, all working-class communities. The Wesleyans were much more broadly based, including in their eight congregations Pitt Street, Grafton Road Ponsonby (where they had recently opened a fine spired church), Parnell, Newmarket, Union Street, Arch Hill and Devonport — while not salubrious suburbs, certainly respectable artisan and middle-class addresses.

Wesleyans were often the agents of order, a kind of moral police. Thus in the winter of 1871 Auckland Wesleyans hired the Theatre Royal to conduct Sunday afternoon services using revival hymns and a simple gospel style of preaching.[108] Alfred Fitchett, editor of the Wesleyan magazine (who later became an Anglican), derided the idea that Methodists had a special calling to the poor, insisting that there was nothing wrong in focusing on the more prosperous in an improving society.[109] Some suspected that Wesleyan preachers pandered to the rich and therefore let their ministry to the poor lapse.[110] During the strikes against the Union Steam Ship

Company in 1890 the prominent Wesleyan preacher Joseph Berry spoke to trade unions, praising them as organisations but critical of their threats.[111] Wesleyans focused on respectability. When the editor of the Wesleyan newspaper asked whether the Methodist Church wanted mass support, responses were unenthusiastic, and the general feeling was to leave the masses to the Salvation Army.[112]

Primitive Methodist chapels were strikingly lacking in wealthy sponsors, at least in the early years. In their cause in Timaru, for example, William Leggott, one of the founders of the church, was described at the opening of the new church as a working man, not a merchant prince but a prince in the eyes of God. In the list of trustees of their various buildings was a bootmaker, a labourer, a carter, a stonemason and a gardener, and the parsonage included also a watchmaker and a wheelwright, while the man with the 'highest' profession was Benjamin Gibson, a timber merchant.[113]

Reaching the working class was a constant concern for Methodists in England, and the same issues were much discussed in New Zealand. Methodism could attract reasonable numbers to special evangelistic meetings in working-class suburbs.[114] Ongoing involvement by the poor was rare.

In 1913 the Wesleyans and Primitive Methodists amalgamated. In the 1921 census, Methodists were quite distinctive in terms of their employment and work status. At that time Methodist males were second only to Presbyterians among the larger churches as employers (8 per cent) and lowest among the employees (41 per cent), and also quite high among the self-employed (11 per cent). So the union did not shift Methodism towards the industrial poor. A significant proportion were in commercial employment (11 per cent, exceeded only by Baptists, Congregationalists and Hebrews) or industrial (where again they were beaten by those smaller groups as well as by those of no religion).

This suggests that Methodists had a significant group of shopkeepers and small-scale industrial producers in urban communities. Methodists had 1156 industrial employers and 7314 employees, and 853 commercial employers and 4070 employees. No particular occupations stand out other than manufacturing and building trades. In 1926 the same patterns remained. Counting both men and women, only 28 per cent of Methodists were in employment (one of the lowest averages of any denomination and certainly the lowest of the larger denominations) and 61 per cent were either too young or too old to be employed. As a church it had the highest proportion aged above 60 and the greatest disproportion of women to men, for Methodism had been quite successful in recruiting new members in the late nineteenth century, but not so much thereafter. Consequently Methodism went into decline long before other denominations.

Methodists expected to attract the working class, but the Wesleyan strand rarely did so because it conflicted with their longing for respectability. Methodists often expressed sympathy with the poor, and were very aware of class tensions.[115] As a result they sought to play a bridging role in society. The rise of the labour movement cost Methodism dearly. Most observed that the Methodists were struggling with such people, and thought that only a body like the Salvation Army had any hope of breaking through. Methodist preachers sometimes called Methodism back to its supposed working-class roots. In his presidential address in 1908, for example, the Rev. William Slade, who was the second City Missioner in Dunedin, called Methodism to identify more strongly with the demands of the working class.[116]

A 1914 resolution of the Annual Conference expressed concern at 'the lot of the toiler' at a time when those workers were in a stand-off with the Reform Government. Inevitably the church advocated mutual cooperation and evolutionary social forces, for 'class-hatred and class-warfare are anti-social and anti-Christian'.[117] In 1919, the conference expressed its 'full sympathy with labour in its efforts to secure its fair and equitable rights', and in 1924 it adopted the Social Creed that had originally been developed by the Federal Council of Churches in the United States.[118]

In his history of the Upper Riccarton Methodist Church, the historian John Cookson notes the way in which Methodism was dominated by a small group of wealthy and socially influential members who were prominent in the large city congregations. He cites among others the Ballantynes, the famous retailers. In Auckland the Smith, Caughey and Preston families were equally dominant in retailing and in Methodism. Yet the congregation also included many poorer but hard-working and respectable people who wanted to get ahead.[119] Many Wesleyans in England agreed with the popular preacher Joseph Beet, who claimed that 'Methodism lays hold of the "top" of the working classes — not the scum, but the cream — the foremen, the sergeant-majors, the gangers — in short, the men who, through their own worth, rise to positions of trust and influence,' and claimed that such men were given responsibility in the circuit.[120] The young Spencer Ratcliffe, a Methodist home missionary in charge of some nine mission stations in the Nelson district, soon discovered that his congregations were largely there because it was respectable to attend.[121]

So perhaps a typical Methodist church might be Hawera Methodist Church, so carefully described by Helen Foy. It was a former mission station that became part of a long, straggly circuit dominated by English West Country Methodists. It flourished in the 1900s, building a huge church in 1906, rigidly organised by its circuit stewards, and financed by pew rents. It was constantly enlarging its buildings and its debt, lurching from revival to decline, dominated by a huge Sunday school and its annual celebrations — a place of enormous energy where there was no rich sponsor to support it, but very few poor either. The church community still exists today, much smaller but still in its fine church building.[122]

A SOCIAL PORTRAIT OF BAPTIST, Congregationalist and other such denominations reflects their commercial middle-class status, as in England. As Pickens notes from the Canterbury case, the English ethos of Congregationalism as a purely urban and predominantly middle-class denomination was accentuated in Canterbury at least — and there is reason to think that its failure came about from its domination by people of professional, clerical and financial occupations.[123] Keith Furniss's account of the Moray Place Congregational Church describes how in the nineteenth century this Dunedin congregation was supported by the local industrial elite, including Henry Shacklock (the manufacturer), William Coull (the publisher) and Percy Sargood (the merchant prince). Their early minister, Dr Thomas Roseby, went on to a distinguished ministry in Melbourne.[124]

There was little else to distinguish Congregationalism from Presbyterianism. It was more liberal in outlook than most Presbyterianism, but by 1966 when Moray Place merged with First Church in Dunedin there was little distinction to attract people to it. The same happened to Trinity Congregational Church in Christchurch, which merged with St Paul's Presbyterian Church, and the Beresford Street Congregational Church, which merged with St James Presbyterian Church in Auckland, even though that church had welcomed the first Cook Islanders to New Zealand and given them its hall in Edinburgh Street as a church.

In contrast, as most Baptist churches abandoned the 'dissenting' identity they moved in conservative directions. In social profile, Baptist adherents in 1921 were urban, commercial, self-employed or skilled manual workers, not unlike the Wesleyans and not as professional as Congregationalists. They were employees or small businessmen. As the Baptist scholar Brian Smith has shown, there was little room in the Baptist philosophy for identification with working-class aspirations, for class solidarity went against Baptist individualism.[125]

The success of the Salvation Army went beyond the working-class suburbs, partly because of its appeal to the rural poor; in the late nineteenth century it primarily attracted the poor. Fifty per cent of the Salvation Army's soldiers in the South Dunedin Citadel were unskilled, a higher proportion than in the wider community.[126] Why did the Salvation Army appeal to the poor? Language and music both played their part. The success of its formula reflected the appeal of the military to the jingoistic late-Victorian world and partly the media fascination with the Army's work and the opposition it initially attracted. Because the working class in New Zealand was less consciously alienated from other people in the community than in Britain, the Army soon found it helpful to broaden its appeal.[127]

Among other groups, the Brethren stood out as dairy farmers (572 of them in 1921) and as having minimal attraction to the poor.[128] Other evangelicals acknowledged that they were too rich to have any appeal to the poor, although the Great Depression changed this tone somewhat.[129]

Sectarianism, which rejected the mainstream churches in favour of loyalty to one true church, was prevalent among the working class. For example, the Christadelphians and the Jehovah Witnesses had a markedly working-class profile. Sects and sectarian thinkers often attacked the rich and saw the social elite as their opponents.[130]

In the 1880s, Robert Stout claimed that, 'As intelligence increases, heresy increases and crime lessens.'[131] The social identity of those professing no religion is curious but does not altogether bear out Stout's argument. In 1921 the small group of males with no religion is quite distinctive — 14 per cent of them were self-employed (second highest after the Lutherans), 54 per cent were employees (highest of all groups), and they had the third highest level of unemployment at 2 per cent. As for occupations, 7 per cent were professionals (the second highest figure) and 23 per cent were in industry (the highest level, and suggesting that the industrial working-class unionists were more likely to be freethinkers than others). Eighty-seven miners were freethinkers, as were a large group in the building industry, 82 working in the railways, and 68 in shipping. Freethinkers were in the strongly male-dominated industries, where hostility to religion was high, or in careers where auto-didacticism flourished.

As early as 1852, the absence of the working classes from the Anglican Church was a matter of public comment in the Canterbury settlement.[132] The Church of England constantly looked for means to reconnect with labourers, but never seemed to find the secret.[133] Concern about 'the church and the masses' had been made popular in England possibly by the late-nineteenth-century Dean of Canterbury Frederic Farrar. By the 1880s, Anglicans in England frequently discussed the issue in church congresses, and these were widely reported in New Zealand.[134] Frequently, Methodist magazines in the colony reported on English debates on why the working class did not go to church.[135]

Many observers felt that the church had failed to stand with the poor in support of their grievances. The eight-hour working day was the subject of lively debate, and some clergy were uncomfortable about taking sides on the issue. When the Rev. Richard Coffey questioned the cause in a sermon at St Mark's Church in Wellington, the poor in his congregation were outraged.[136]

The church was forced to recognise rising class tensions, however. In 1879, Edward Stuart, the new Bishop of Waiapu, called upon the church to play a healing role.[137] Several bishops spoke sympathetically of the struggles experienced by labourers and seamen during the 1890 strike, notably Bishop Churchill Julius of Christchurch. Bishop Suter of Nelson was convinced that the tough conditions of labour kept these men from attending church.[138]

The 1880s and the Long Depression was a critical time when New Zealand society was riven with economic crisis; there was a nett migration loss of 10,000 in the single year of 1886. Migration reflected the shortage of capital and growing pressure between rich and poor, with a rise in the numbers of people resorting to charitable aid, while sweated labour and strikes in which unions challenged capital became critical. While a certain amount of class tension could be dismissed as 'parrot prattle', rationalists observed and laughed at the panic among church leaders in the 1880s and their search for solutions.[139]

The churches' view of organised labour was generally not positive. Tensions between the churches and unions were higher in Australia, especially in the largest city of Australasia, Melbourne. Here, a conference between the churches and the labour unions took place in 1907 at which there was an appeal for a Labour Sunday.[140] Already some churches in New Zealand had supported the eight-hour movement, and there was intense interest among New Zealand church people in the efforts of the churches in London to reach the poor — and in their failure to convert them.[141]

The unions had eloquent supporters, but few churches fully understood the injustices they were addressing. At the Wesleyan Conference on 1890, strong statements were made about the value of trade unions, but the printing of the minutes of that conference was entrusted to a company that kept its prices down by using boy labour.[142]

In 1882 the *Auckland Star* copied the famous London survey of the previous year and sent people to count the attendance at every church in the town of Auckland. They ended up with a figure of about 26 per cent of the population. This survey led to much soul-searching. The Rev. G. B. Monro of St Luke's Presbyterian Church in Remuera identified issues that deterred the poor from attending — drink, getting over Saturday night, and youthful irresponsibility. But when he also criticised the scepticism of the poor, the *Star* leapt to the defence of 'honest enquiring scepticism'. It insisted that clergy were themselves to blame for low attendance, commenting that 'if there were more thought, greater freshness, wider reading, less antiquity, and fewer stereotyped expressions in their sermons their churches would be better filled'.[143]

In a final editorial the *Star* declared it had no problem with intelligent people not attending church, but was worried by the wholesale absence of the poor, suggesting: 'This is the class of people whom it is most desirable to have brought under religion's influences, as much for their own sakes as in the interest of the peace and comfort of the general public.'[144] Other correspondents to the newspapers were even more critical of the churches. One noted the failure of the clergy to make pastoral visits to the poor.[145]

Many of the unskilled in nineteenth-century New Zealand survived on millwork and labouring, so the category 'working class' must be defined carefully. Rural workers were not natural churchgoers, but they were not innately hostile to the church. Thus, for example, the Presbyterian minister John Ross, who was based in Turakina and the Wairarapa in the late nineteenth century, constantly visited working men and made himself popular because he spoke their language.[146] Brian Smith shows that unskilled workers in the milling and labouring world formed a significant sector of the Baptist world when ministers learned how to relate to them.[147]

Even in the working-class suburbs of South Dunedin, where factory employment dominated, there was little evidence of hostility to the church, although workers reacted swiftly to moralisers telling them what to do.[148]

Churches berated themselves in the nineteenth century that they had failed to be welcoming places for the poor. John Armitage, the Wesleyan minister, commented that the typical church was a cold, uninviting building.[149]

Sometimes evangelism touched working-class communities very deeply, though at other times it received minimal interest from the poor. The world of the poor was penetrated to a degree by revivalist religion, and Sankey songs continued to be popular in the rest homes of the elderly poor. After the great 1875 Moody and Sankey crusade in Scotland and London, New Zealand evangelicals were convinced that revivalism was smashing the resistance of the working-class communities to the gospel.[150] Evangelicalism did have some appeal. For example, Katikati was seen as a 'God forsaken place', although curiously the Presbyterian home missionary who went there commented ruefully that 'I went down there to evangelise them thinking that all they knew was whiskey and two-up, but I found some extremely religious people who tried to evangelise me'.[151] It was in such places that the evangelical sects — Brethren, Salvation Army, Primitive Methodists, and Adventists — often flourished.

THE AWKWARD ROLE THAT ministers played in times of class conflict was nowhere more evident than on the issue of alcohol use. Scottish Presbyterians and the upper-class elite of Anglicanism were hardly teetotallers. There was a fear that the educated classes would be suspicious of prohibition because it insulted their ability to control their drinking.[152] Although there were some attacks on middle-class pleasures, such as Alfred Fitchett's criticism of the lewdness of theatre-goers,[153] it sometimes seemed that temperance picked on the poor.

The temperance issue was a critical one in a rough working-class community like Temuka, which was deeply divided between northern and southern Irish. The local Anglican minister thought of himself as a moral policeman.[154] Prohibition often presumed an association between drunkenness and poverty;[155] drunkenness and failure to attend church were also seen as connected.[156] Nevertheless, the prohibition movement seriously sought to benefit the working classes by helping them out of poverty.[157] Temperance has been identified as a movement of the middle class and of women in hostility to the misbehaviour of working-class men, but it also had working-class support.[158]

From the early twentieth century the city missions sought to connect the church to the working-class community, using entertaining services, practical help and good food. William Ready, from one of the small Methodist groups, the Bible Christians, experimented with a direct ministry to the poor through the first city mission in Dunedin in 1890. Ready had been raised in George Muller's orphanage in Bristol and been helped by the London City Mission, with its distinctive combination of evangelism and social work. He was astonishingly successful at Garrison Hall, with congregations of up to 1500 people.[159]

The Tory Street Mission in Wellington used an orchestra and suppers very effectively to boost its numbers.[160] The Seamen's Mission aimed to make provision to the seamen who were so uncomfortable in ordinary churches.[161]

In 1902, the Diocese of Wellington decided to appoint a diocesan missioner to seek to reach the missing masses.[162] In 1904, the bishop authorised the appointment of a member of staff from the Evangelistic Brotherhood of the Church Army, and Brother Mutter and then Brother Fox were appointed to work among the flax workers in Foxton. Mutter lasted just under one year, being regarded with some suspicion by the local parish, which had to fund part of his salary. He had held services in the public hall, not using the prayer book, and started a men's club. It was all to no avail. In the end the parish saw no point in this work.[163]

In 1913 the Wellington diocesan magazine published a long article on the church and labour, grimly reflecting the difficulties of that year, and noting, 'A church from which the working classes hold aloof must be sadly lacking in the spirit of her Master.'[164] Some advocated the Christian Socialist solution. John Millar, the prominent seaman and union leader, and the member of the Legislative Council whose vote helped to bring down the Liberal Government in 1911, was a member of the Dunedin Anglican Synod in 1893, and saw socialism as the true practice of Christianity.[165] The way in which the Rev. Jasper Calder fell out with the Bishop of Auckland in 1919 suggests that his populism vaguely unnerved the Auckland elite, with his striking sermons delivered in tense times, advocating for the worker. The city missions and deaconess orders were created by people alert to these issues. The 1913 general strike, in which unions sought to block the ports in protest of working conditions, provoked some deep thinking in various Anglican quarters. A committee of the Waiapu Synod (Charles Tisdall, C. A. de Latour and the Rev. Frederick Chatterton) produced a series of relatively left-wing papers and proposed the introduction of deaconesses to provide a kindly contact with the poor.[166] This was not a particularly radical solution.

City missions faced obstacles in New Zealand, including the high cost of renting a theatre and the necessity of a larger staff, including deaconesses. Each aspect was important in what developed in this model, including the diaconal work of women like Sister Lena Button in Dunedin, who was as essential as William Ready with his oratorical skills. Other missioners such as Everil Orr, Colin Scrimgeour, Jasper Calder and Leslie Neale also depended on deaconesses. Missions also required generous donors — Miss Boot of the English firm Boots the Chemists was one who helped out at a time of financial need.[167]

Such examples suggest that the working class was not completely alienated from the churches. Spectacular and controversial subjects could easily attract a crowd of working-class men, as many a home missionary discovered.[168] Nevertheless, church visitors were struck by the levels of ignorance about religion. A door-to-door survey of thousands of people in the relatively working-class suburb of Onehunga revealed that some people had never been inside the door of a church and struggled to correctly name their denomination. The surveyors were also surprised at the huge variety of sectarian groups in small numbers throughout the suburb.[169]

Jasper Calder attracted huge crowds to his 'Church and Racing' and 'Church and Sport' services in a hall in working-class Grey Lynn in the 1920s.[170] In the process he did not endear himself to the sniffy church authorities, but he demonstrated that while lacking a habit of church attendance, working-class men in particular were not hostile to a warm-hearted religion. Perhaps this explains why Catholic working-class men more often had a habit of churchgoing. Methodists had a strong interest in a working-class audience, but could not avoid lecturing it on respectable values. The Methodist President in 1908, William Slade, had heard the anger of the poor who saw the church as a place for the privileged and well-heeled:

at church time on Sunday, either morning or evening, visit a populous street, inhabited by working men and notice how small a number that street contributes to church congregations. To these persons churches are associated with political disabilities, with social inequalities, with invidious class distinctions, with economic injustices, with pride of purse and pride of place. To them religion has seemed to be always the privilege of the rich and the strong.[171]

Lists of sins often sounded like lists of working-class pleasures, like gambling and drinking. As the Rev. Henry Ryan told the story in 1927, it was very easy to produce proselytes who were not really converted.

> This erring brother gets converted. To what? Often to nothing but a state of sleek respectability, and sometimes, even worse ... There is an atmosphere about the churches which exalts respectability as the open sesame to the Kingdom, and the man who is richly endowed with the things of this world has infinitely more chance in the average congregation than the man who is down and out. That is the spirit which has helped to drive a wedge between the Church and the masses of the people.[172]

When churches were hypocritical they heard about it.[173] Good churchmen sometimes had a bad reputation as harsh employers. The *Observer* reported angrily: 'There are rogues carrying prayer books in Auckland who extort high rents for hovels and who make their peace with God by putting a fraction of it in the church plate.'[174] Church attendance remained a badge of 'respectability'.

In working-class parishes the normal ways of operating often did not succeed. For example, in the 1950s, Alun Richards, who was unacceptable to most Presbyterians as a pacifist, was welcomed by Newtown parish in the poorer southern part of Wellington.[175] Working-class churches tended to embrace difference more easily than others.

The location of congregations and the concentration of denominations suggest that affinity with poor communities varied greatly. Thus in Christchurch the eastern suburbs had significantly weaker church life than the west and north. There was considerable hesitation, for example, about planting a Baptist church in Opawa, a poorer suburb in the south-east, and for a fair proportion of its life most of the congregation did not belong to the community.[176] The rediscovery of profound social need in the community and the greater openness of people in that situation has been very apparent in recent years.

HOW WAS CHRISTIANITY TO make any sense to the poor? New Zealand was suffused with Christian language, but much of what went on in churches was mysterious to outsiders. Religious codes were distinctly denominational as well. In the church service, reverent behaviour was culturally defined. Standing, sitting and kneeling, and kneeling at the altar carried different meanings in different denominations. The language of the churches was foreign. Shaped by intellectual and conceptual discourse, and not a little Latin, it was almost impossible to translate their message into the direct active language of the workers.

The tones of Anglicanism are easiest to pick, because of the role that educated elites played. The bishops, as direct imports from England, came with an upper-crust tone and the vocabulary of the Oxbridge educated. The Anglican clerical and lay hierarchy mimicked that tone. It was this that so obviously made the poor feel unwelcome.[177] The genius of the founder of the Auckland City Mission, Jasper Calder, was his ability to find the accents of the poor, even to swear a little like them, but this did not endear him to his bishop.

Other churches in New Zealand also sought to avoid 'vulgarity'. Methodists in particular felt the pull towards the elite, which affected their language and lost the attention of the less-educated person, although there were striking exceptions who sounded and acted as people from poorer communities. Bible Christians like William Ready and the Primitive Methodists certainly did not lose their connection with the poor.

In the first hundred years of Pākehā society the accent of the labourer was a vernacular far removed from standard English, reflecting various English dialects — cockney and many others. These were the sounds that were not heard in church. 'Me go to church on Sundays? Not likely. Well, no; it's not exactly because I don't believe in it, but why should I go? Do you reckon I'm not as good as some of the wowsers because I don't tog up on Sundays and give m' thrup'ny bitt?'[178]

The *Auckland Star* reporter captured the tone of working-class indignation at the pressure to attend church, and their reading of the motives behind it. The colourful testimony was always appreciated by a rough working-class audience,[179] but there was a risk that the patronising tone of a charity would prove offensive. Gradually a Kiwi tone and language emerged, but it was very slow to be heard in church services.

One factor was the shame of not renting a pew, and the sense that the church was after money from people who attended. As the *Auckland Star* editorialised in 1882: 'After being bundled about from pillar to post in search of a seat, snobbishly treated on the one hand or offensively patronised on the other, and finally badgered for a money subscription, they might be pardoned if they seriously questioned the sincerity of the motives of the good people who invited them . . .'[180] As far as this editor was concerned, pew rents were an abomination in the eyes of the poor. Another reason the poor did not enter churches was the dress code. This factor was very apparent to people of earlier generations. The issue was frequently a subject of comment.[181]

Church in the nineteenth century was a public place, and going to church therefore required dressing up. The working man's suit was always worn to church, and the low level of working-class attendance may have some connection with this. Certainly the feeling that people would look down on those who were shabbily dressed was often reported by those in touch with the poor.[182] As we have seen earlier, from the 1880s the leaders of the services — the clergy and the choir — were dressing ever more smartly. Propriety of dress was required — 'no straw hats, no puggarees or hat scarfs, no sun shades, no dust-coats, no secular tweed'.[183] Black suits were the normal dress for men.

IN CERTAIN RESPECTS, AS New Zealand politics became more sharply delineated in the twentieth century, politics became interconnected with class consciousness. Although, for example, Catholics have featured at every level of the New Zealand political arena from the earliest days, Catholic clergy (notably Patrick Moran, first Catholic Bishop of Dunedin) often nurtured a feeling of exclusion. Nevertheless, Sir Joseph Ward, the Liberal prime minister from 1906, was a powerful Catholic presence in the political system. Catholic voices were, however, significantly under-represented in the Reform Party. Sectarianism burst out at the end of World War I in the flourishing of the Protestant Political Federation. The situation changed with the rise of the Labour Party, when in effect the Catholic Church and then the Methodist Church found it necessary to reconcile themselves with that party.

By 1975, these politico-religious linkages were less clear: 41 per cent of Labour and 53 per cent of Values supporters did not attend church, but only 31 per cent of National supporters absented themselves from Sunday services. Catholics were predominantly Labour (14 per cent of Labour voters were Catholic, compared with 10.8 per cent of National voters); similarly, 4 per cent of Labour voters were Methodist, compared to 3.6 per cent of National voters. In contrast, National had a predominance of Anglican, Presbyterian and Baptist voters (28, 16 and 2 per cent of their vote compared to 20, 11 and 2 per cent, respectively). Most strikingly, 60 per cent of Anglican voters were National supporters compared to 26 per cent Labour supporters, and 58 per cent of Presbyterians supported National compared to 25 per cent Labour. The largest group of Catholics and Methodists also supported National (43 per cent and 48 per cent, respectively) but the Labour support was closer at 33.8 per cent and 33.9 per cent, respectively. Frequency of churchgoing was also interesting, for 27 per cent of National voters attended church regularly, compared to 22 per cent of Labour, 27 per cent of Social Credit, and 12 per cent of Values supporters.[184]

The political scientist Austin Mitchell did not sense that religion made much difference to politics in the 1960s and 1970s, except where it reflected social groups.[185] Another political scientist, Paul Reynolds, in a detailed thesis surveyed members of Presbyterian, Methodist and Baptist congregations in 1967. He estimated that those who actually attended church were strikingly pro-National, with the Presbyterian and Baptist figures more or less the same as Methodist (64 per cent National to 26 per cent Labour for Presbyterians, 60 per cent to 32 per cent for Methodists, and 53 per cent compared to 32 per cent for Baptists). Baptists also had a high proportion of Social Credit supporters and non-voters. Reynolds looked at the occupations of church voters and found that 52 per cent were business people or professionals, 31 per cent were white-collar employees, and 18 per cent were blue-collar workers. But he also noted the existence of a group of middle-class radicals among Presbyterians and Methodists.[186]

THE ISSUES OF SOCIAL division receded in New Zealand in the postwar years. Interestingly, by 1986 the Census showed that Anglican adherents made up by far the greatest proportion of the highest pay bracket (earning more than $40,000 per year), and of the second highest bracket ($30,000–40,000 per year). Just 7 per cent of that denomination could be described as working class.[187]

During the 1960s, the Anglican reputation had been subject to attack, following a period in the previous decade when the church had leased its extensive property in the Meadowbank area to private homeowners using what were known as 'Glasgow' leases. These were revalued every 21 years, leading to dramatic rises in rent. The simultaneous rise in these leases gave the church a bad name in its heartland in eastern Auckland, and an inquiry undertaken by Tony Lusk QC did not completely vindicate the church.[188] During this period the church ceased to be the National Party at prayer, and its occasional political interventions (often on behalf of the poor and needy) were not always welcome.

Work by Noel Derbyshire shows that the decline of the church since the 1980s has confined Anglicanism to parts of Auckland city with the lowest levels of deprivation. Parishes in the west of the city experienced a wholesale decline, while those in the east remained strong.[189]

Presbyterian congregations changed radically after the 1970s, with a loss of status and connections. The successful churches seem to have a broader range of social

Above The choir processes out of the Cathedral of St John the Evangelist in Napier in 1985, followed by Dean Murray Mills. Despite the pageant, the congregation is noticeably small and not all are formally dressed. WAIAPU ANGLICAN CATHEDRAL ARCHIVES

Below The Cook Islands Sunday school group outside the Pacific Islands Presbyterian Church in Newton, Auckland. PACIFIC ISLANDS PRESBYTERIAN CHURCH

contacts, with many Pasifika people among them. The old elite city churches became smaller enclaves of professional people. They have continued their support of liberal causes, including gay and lesbian people, while the denomination as a whole has become more conservative. Presbyterianism remains a denomination with deep respect for learning, but it now has a vaguer social profile.

Over the same period, Baptists were generally recognised as the mainstream evangelical denomination, which welcomed other Protestant refugees, although many did not understand their independent church government. Their social profile became more upwardly mobile in the later twentieth century. The Catholic Church continued to include a wide spread of people, but upward mobility has also been a feature of this church, while the Polynesian and other migrant communities have become the new poor.

The economic crisis of the 1980s made many local congregations more aware of the inequities in their society. The denominational social agencies became more active, and congregations sought to respond to the struggles they saw. Many Baptist congregations were growing rapidly, and some of those redirected their focus towards community needs. Several very different churches stand out in this respect. Spreydon Baptist Church in Christchurch, the largest Baptist church in the country, sponsored many transformative initiatives, including a range of financial, family and counselling services.[190] Mount Roskill Baptist, which sat at the conservative end of the Baptist spectrum, made space in its church buildings in 1978 for a Plunket clinic and then established a kindergarten. In 1983, the church added a new Lockwood building, known as the Helen Patteson Community Hall.[191]

Glen Eden Baptist Church, a charismatic church that encouraged its members to speak in tongues, began a drop-in centre and op shop in 1984, soon appointed a community pastor, then set up Baptist HomeCare Waitakere. Eventually it was contracted by the Ministry of Health to support hundreds of families, with its own community kindergarten, foodbank, budgeting service, social housing, counselling and training. It has grown into the 'Vision West Community Trust'.[192] Ponsonby Baptist Church in central Auckland, a small, radically minded church led by pastor Mike Riddell, established the Community of Refuge Trust in 1987 to provide housing for the mentally ill, and it gradually developed into one of the largest providers of social housing in New Zealand.[193] These are examples of a striking trend of churches becoming much more conscious of the social needs around them, and seeking to make faith more tangible in their communities.

By the 1990s, the prosperous no longer needed outward displays of religiosity to indicate their status. Today the elite use church schools, and sometimes church weddings and funerals, but infant baptisms are rare. The strongest presence of the church is now among the impoverished Pasifika community, and the poor still queue at the doors of the city missions. Ethnic factors are frequently markers of social status, and many new migrants are strongly associated with religion, although not necessarily Christian.

In effect, the traditional lines of class division have been replaced by new divisions. Traditional speech and dress as markers of division have faded. As church services have ceased to be recognised public events, the casual weekend dress codes apply to them, except among older people who remember the world as it was. The evangelical churches, with a higher proportion of young people, are particularly casual, thereby conceding that church is a leisure choice. In the Pasifika world, however, the church has a formal public status, and so their churches retain the formal Sunday dress of the Pacific.

Clergy dress has meantime became more elaborate in the traditional churches, and non-stipendiary clergy, who have been appointed for churches that cannot afford a minister, often wear robes. Pentecostal pastors dress so smartly that the Museum of New Zealand Te Papa Tongarewa decided to include one of Bishop Brian Tamaki's suits in its collection. The traditions of hierarchy have emerged in a new way in the Pentecostal senior pastors and apostles, while the Anglican and Catholic bishops are often given little respect.

These changes in status and hierarchy are, like many of the other changes we have observed, glimpses of a very different future for the churches. Nevertheless, that future will still be expressed in terms of the cultures and forms of the wider society. The change that is unfolding is bound to call forth new reflections on the way religion draws on and modifies existing cultural forms.

All Change

Previous St Philip's, Nikau Street, Kelston, west Auckland, assembled ready for family worship in 1956. The building had originally been in Glen Eden and was later moved. It ceased to be used and was finally sold in 1991. PAROCHIAL DISTRICT OF NEW LYNN (WELLS CAMPAIGN CANVASS BOOKLET), AUCKLAND, 1956

WE NEED TO PONDER the significance of the landscape sketched in this book in order to understand the significance of the cultures of faith, for the aim of this book is not simply to be an investigation of antiquarian customs. Customs carry values, and this book is a search for them.

One way to understand these cultures might be through the notion of social capital. Although criticised for its vagueness, the concept of social capital seeks to identify those assets with which people and communities are endowed and that may not have formal financial value. Thus it seeks to probe the value (including negative value) of culture to identify how significant religious communities are in their societies. As one team of scholars has argued, religion is an adaptive institution that functions as a significant cultural resource for individuals and groups. This is very evident in the way in which it promotes political mobilisation, civic participation and social incorporation.[1] If this is right, then there may be ways to detect a decline in these various types of engagement in society. The evident losses that have occurred within the decline of communities of faith might then be shown to have impoverished society as a whole.

We might alternatively invoke the concept of civil society. The proportion of people involved in churches over the history of modern New Zealand resulted in a vigorous contribution to civil society, given that church people participated in a culture that contributed to their community at various levels. These voluntary groups shared a set of values that by and large contributed to the welfare of society and made a significant difference, albeit not one that could be easily measured (except in the temperance poll). The decline of the religious role in society has been a favourite subject for sociologists, who have explained it through various interpretative tools, none more common than that of secularisation.

It is worth reflecting on secularisation as a cultural process. Secularisation theories are numerous, but most of them recognise the decline of a culture where high value is placed on the spiritual or transcendent in favour of the ordinary day-to-day empirical and material world. The strong version of secularisation sees this as a necessary and inevitable process in the history of society; religious ideas fade away as more adequate and grounded scientific explanations take away the mysteries, devaluing religious explanations or, more often, the excuses for inexplicable phenomena. Weaker theories of secularisation do not see this as an inevitable force, but rather contextualise it within modern Western societies that give absolute authority to science, even where its power to explain things is incomplete. Alternative explanations disconnect the various factors that are said to comprise secularisation, including the increasing authority of the state, open intellectual and social challenges to religion, and public discrediting of religion.

New Zealand is often described as a relatively secular society. This may be stating the obvious, for non-church society *is* secular, and culture reflects this. It is, however, worth pursuing the argument. From the commencement of the Pākehā settlement of New Zealand, religion faced many challenges simply because the established church was displaced, cultural reinforcement of religion was lost as people moved to a new land, and old customs had to be blended together, so that everyone's religious behaviour was forced to change.

There are some arguments in favour of this view. The CMS missionaries seem to have hoped for a very religious Māori society, in which religious arguments and values reframed Māori social practices, including carving, tattooing, and warfare and cannibalism. They were relatively successful in establishing the notion of a sacred cycle of the seven-day week, with a holy Sabbath devoted to worship and to rest. Such values were probably relatively easy for Māori society to adopt, but European warfare and the breach of sabbatarianism by British government troops must have rudely disrupted the notion that the Christian rules were honoured by all Western people. By the end of the 1840s Māori had learned that they needed to protect themselves by politics and armaments against the so-called Christian nation.

New Zealand and its European settlers were very much part of the Western world. In the eighteenth century the Enlightenment exposed the elites of Europe to a series of intellectual and cultural challenges to religion. Although there was a revival of religion in the post-revolutionary age, the flood of secular scientific, political and ideological reasoning of the great nineteenth-century transformation of society delivered a blow to religion at the popular level. The forces of urbanisation and global migration also removed people from the familiar religious customs of traditional societies.

This country's European settlers were not united as a religious community and did not as a group share common passions about the importance of religion. They were in no way comparable to the Pilgrim Fathers of America. Among the colonists were some more profoundly religious groups, notably the settlers in Otago, in Waipu, and some small groups of settlers who came with a religious vision for their new land. Yet during the nineteenth century religious commitments and enthusiasms increased markedly — more in some quarters than in others.

The historian James Belich wrote of a 'great tightening' in late-nineteenth-century New Zealand, in which economic and social ties to Britain increased. This was also a cultural tightening in which New Zealand gained a reputation as a more conservative British society and, as part of this, religious values gained greater status. The temperance movement and the Sunday school movement prospered in the wake of this. The 'tightening' also corresponded with a stronger religious culture in many parts of society, although church-going was never anywhere near universal. Certainly, the religious community was so deeply denominationalised that its cultural influence was dissipated.

Nevertheless, this book shows that much was shared across denominations. Anglicanism commanded a high proportion of church adherents in New Zealand north of the Waitaki, and Presbyterianism was the same south of the same line, so they had considerable cultural mana, and other denominations recognised their dominance. Presbyterianism operated more effectively than Anglicanism as a cultural force because the Otago Synod and the Presbyterian General Assembly had committees that regularly reviewed public and moral issues. Anglicans were much more restrained, reflecting the English confinement of the Anglican Church to religious matters. The high point of religious influence was reached in the 1890s if we are to judge from the growth of denominations, church attendance and voting on temperance issues. Thereafter, imperceptibly at first, the authority of the denominations was challenged in the public realm.

The decline of adherence to the churches was a sensitive subject. In 1889 Robert Sommerville, minister of the Grey Lynn Presbyterian Church, and a relatively liberal Presbyterian who was in favour of dropping confessional rules, found himself at odds with the *New Zealand Herald*. The newspaper had enthusiastically backed the Otago University professor (and former educator of Presbyterian ministerial candidates) Dr Salmond's call for Presbyterianism to no longer insist on the doctrine of Hell. This, argued the *Herald*, would help religion to prosper. Sommerville was outraged. The *Herald* had no right to tell the church what to do, and he thought that the public press was too often hostile to his church. The *Herald*'s argument was that there was public interest in preserving the moral power of religion, and that this was in danger of being lost.[2]

> We are desirous to see the question solved, as to why the educated classes are drifting away from the church. Of the services to civilisation, and freedom, and religious and civil liberty, which Presbyterianism has rendered, we have several times spoken. Our very affection for the Kirk has made incumbent upon us to notice the discussions in the Assembly and Presbyteries. We are only sorry that the gentleman who has constituted himself its champion in Auckland is filled with the spirit of sacerdotal tyranny, which resents the interference a newspaper exercises when that newspaper happens to be engaged in backing him up.[3]

It was not the first time, nor the last, that the church sought public support but grew tetchy in the face of public criticisms.

On the whole, New Zealand public opinion at the time was relatively kind to the church. In more recent years, perhaps as the 'great tightening' has been followed by a great loosening of traditions and conventions, columnists have been much freer with their criticisms, and reporters have been frequently ill-informed on religious matters. Religion's public profile is not the rosiest. Nevertheless, religious culture has continued undeterred within the shelter of the Christian community. Religious communities grew and adapted regardless of public opinion.

BY THE NINETEENTH CENTURY the Christian church had developed many formal institutions, which were replicated in New Zealand. These organisations, and new bodies established as ways to respond to new circumstances, worked relatively well in the period before 1950; contemporary people would be struck by the formality of social customs and conventions in the churches of the period, although that was little different from the wider world. The church's sense of hierarchy, of title, routine and system, made it one of the most formal parts of society, but this was consistent with middle-class patterns in New Zealand before the 1950s.

In the postwar world, and after 1960, these structures rapidly became anachronistic. The proposed plan for the united Church of Christ in New Zealand, which was issued in 1969, would have created a huge formal structure that was out of keeping with social and cultural trends. The merger did not take place. As a consequence, denominations that had placed many issues on hold for 15 years had to make their own individual responses to changing times. Denominations in particular suffered a serious loss of respect and authority with the younger generation. Radical shifts took place, sometimes with the creation of new congregations and organisations, and sometimes old titles and functions were subverted within congregations. For example, many congregations could no longer afford to fund ministers, and instead a plethora of non-stipendiary people were ordained as volunteer priests.

In the contemporary world voices of alarm frequently surface in church circles about the loss of direction and authority as change happens from below, with little control from denominational bodies. Many across the spectrum of the Christian community feel that the churches are losing their way. Some feel that the problem is the church itself, and its inability to attract or to retain people from the secular world. Some clearly think that the church is disposable. I am not so sure that it is this simple. Belief in God is socially mediated, and in a world where agnosticism and atheism as well as many religious beliefs are socially acceptable Christian belief is bound to struggle. In Western societies, with their emphasis on wealth, security, prosperity and wellbeing, fewer people feel the need for divine presence and intervention. Western secular culture has no room for the divine, and leaves believers out in the cold, and unless or until this sense of security is overturned, the demand for religion is bound to weaken.

In a fascinating book entitled *New Zealand Jesus,* Geoff Troughton has shown that various peoples in the history of this country have explored different dimensions of the person of Jesus. He notes how social campaigners, children's advocates and different genders have seen Jesus in different ways. One very interesting chapter shows that Jesus was often seen as a prophet by those who despised the church.[4] The decline of formal religious institutions does not in fact mean that the Christian story has lost its pertinence. There is every evidence of its power to generate new visions.

Sunday Best has focused on religion as a form of culture which nurtured and cocooned believers. That culture is necessarily sidelined in today's world. Families and groups of people are rarely united as participants in this religious culture today. The loss of communal participation is a very significant change. Religious behaviour today is something shown by individuals, like so much else in life — whether it be supporting a sports team, loving music, or planning travels. Our self-selected culture gathers a group of aficionados. Are they a community? Only in a very curious sense. Observers have noted that the Christian community is becoming more and more a subculture, or indeed a series of subcultures. People try out various options — 'Catholic', 'Anglican', 'Pentecostal' — as if they were fashions, involving no doctrinal adherence. The mega-churches, which have the resources to do new things, often succumb to secular cultural forms as they try to figure out what succeeds.

The churches are not on their own in this struggle. Culture wars are prevalent throughout many aspects of society, and many voluntary groups and associations have succumbed to commercial rivals. The churches have done better than Freemasons or Scouts or traditional women's organisations. There are commercial providers of religious products, but as yet no one has made a commercial bid for a church. Meanwhile different kinds of church have carried the same message in very different cultural carriers. Neighbourhood churches are being replaced by citywide or online organisations, but the medium is not the message.

So it would be wrong to end this book with a sense of the church being locked in a cultural crisis. Looking back at the customs and culture of New Zealand Christianity over the past 200 years, we can see a vast amount of change and development. This study indicates that we are in a period of great cultural rethinking and change. Not being a prophet, I cannot fully see where these changes are going, but I am sure that future historians will find plenty to write about.

Glossary

Previous Old St Paul's Church, the first parish church in Auckland. It stood on what was then Britomart Hill, near today's Emily Place. This watercolour by John Kinder, painted in 1861, shows the church from Symonds Street and is a somewhat idealised vision of the church at the centre of Auckland. AUCKLAND ART GALLERY TOI O TĀMAKI, GIFT OF HARRY KINDER, 1937

Acolyte: A server or assistant in liturgy or at the altar in Catholic churches.

Advent: The four weeks prior to Christmas in the Christian liturgical calendar.

Alb: A white outer garment worn by priests, ministers and lay people in the altar area of a church.

Apse: Traditionally the altar end of the church, especially when it is a separate section of the building or a recess. The place where the congregation sits is called the nave.

Cassock: A full-length tunic today used largely by priests during Catholic or Anglican services.

Catechism: A basic primer of Christian belief authorised by the churches and often memorised by children.

Chancel: The space around the altar, including the area for the choir.

Chasuble: The outer liturgical garment (worn over the alb), normally in the liturgical colour appropriate for the season of the Christian year.

Chimere: A sleeveless satin or silk coat, traditionally worn over the rochet by Anglican bishops.

Circuit: A group of congregations under the control of one Methodist minister (especially in the era when the minister rode on horseback between locations); today more usually called a parish.

Class meeting: The weekly small group meeting introduced by Methodism, traditionally the basis of membership of Methodism.

Confessional: The small, closet-like space in which the Catholic priest heard the confessions of parishioners, separated by a grille to ensure privacy.

Cope: A long cloak with a clasp at the front, often highly ornamented, worn in processions. Usually worn by bishops, although any rank of clergy may wear it. Some Anglican clergy wear it during Communion.

Creed: A formal statement of belief, recited in church. The most notable creed is the fourth-century Nicene Creed recited during Communion in Catholic and Anglican churches.

Doxology: A short declaration of praise or blessing often recited or sung at the end of hymns or at the end of a service.

Eirenic: Working for harmonious relationships (in this context, between churches).

Episcopal: Related to a bishop.

Epistle: In the church context, a section of the New Testament of the Bible, largely a series of letters by St Paul; usually the second reading in churches that follow the lexicon.

Eucharist: Another name for the Holy Communion or Mass.

Evensong: The Anglican afternoon or evening service.

Hymnody: The range of hymns sung in services.

Kīngitanga: The movement to support the Māori kings, first elected in 1857.

Lent: The six weeks before Easter, commencing with Ash Wednesday, in which Catholics, in particular, practise self-denial.

Lexicon: An agreed set of Bible readings. The revised common lectionary is shared by most of the liturgical churches, but previous to this most churches had their own lectionary.

Liturgy (sim. liturgical, liturgist): The set prayers for a service recited by priest and congregation.

Matins: The standard Anglican morning service which does not have Communion; these days largely replaced by Holy Communion.

Mitre: A bishop's hat, generally a folded high form with a pointed arch at the front.

Moderator: The chair of a Presbyterian or Methodist formal assembly.

Nave: The congregational end of a church.

Oblation: An offering, used by churches to refer to the gifts of bread and wine used in Communion.

Ordination: The laying on of hands to confer the office of a priest or minister.

Pentecost: The season of the Christian year in which the gift of the Holy Spirit is recalled. In England often called Whitsun; 50 days after Easter Sunday.

Precentor: In Anglican worship, the person in a service (especially in a cathedral) who prepares the worship and may lead the liturgy. In non-Anglican worship, traditionally the person who sets the tunes and commences unaccompanied hymns.

Presbyter: The word in Greek means 'elder', and it is used by some Protestant churches to refer to the pastor or minister.

Presbytery: 1. The residence of the Catholic priest; 2. The meeting of churches in a region (especially in Presbyterian usage), with responsibility over those churches, hence 'Auckland Presbytery'.

Primate: The senior bishop over a group of bishops, often called the archbishop.

Reformation: The period in church history in the sixteenth century when many churches split away from the Catholic Church on account of its doctrines and practices, which led in turn to a reform movement in the Catholic Church.

Rochet: A white gown falling to just below the knee, worn by a Catholic or Anglican bishop; worn by bishops other than in services.

Sacrament: A Christian rite that symbolises (and in Catholic usage, conveys) the grace of God. Protestants only recognise two: baptism and Holy Communion. Catholics recognise seven, including confirmation, penance, anointing, marriage and holy orders.

Sinecure: An office in the church that is largely a title and income, with little work expected.

Sodalities: Organisations within the church that have connections beyond the parish or diocese. Another name is a 'confraternity'. Lay people join these pious associations. The term is mostly used in the Catholic Church.

Soutane: A white, black or brown cassock used as the day dress of clergy (although this is unusual today).

Stole: A scarf worn during worship by clergy. In Anglican and Catholic usage, it is worn differently by priests and deacons.

Surplice: A white, sleeved tunic worn over the cassock either by clergy or by people serving in the chancel of the church.

Thurible: A metal censer, holding incense, on chains so it can be swung during worship in Catholic or High Anglican usage. The person who swings it is a thurifer.

Trent: The council of the Catholic Church which met in this town intermittently from 1545 to 1563, and reviewed and reformed Catholic theology and practice in the wake of the Protestant reformation.

Tridentine: Of or pertaining to the Council of Trent; for example, the text of the Mass agreed there.

Verger: The lay person who assists in the conduct of Anglican worship, especially in cathedrals, wearing a gown and conducting people to their 'stalls'. Also used for the person responsible for the church during the week.

Watchnight: A special service, usually held on New Year's Eve, particularly observed by Methodists.

Notes

Introduction

1. L. Guy, *Shaping Godzone: Public Issues and Church Voices in New Zealand 1840–2000* (Wellington: Victoria University Press, 2011).

Chapter One: The Sacred Day

1. See Alexis McCrossen, 'Sabbatarianism,' in *Encyclopedia of Protestantism*, vol. 4, ed. Hans Hillerbrand (London: Routledge, 2004), 1635–36. See David S. Katz, *Sabbath and Sectarianism in Seventeenth Century England* (New York: E. J. Brill, 1988).
2. John Wigley, *The Rise and Fall of the Victorian Sunday* (Manchester: Manchester University Press, 1980).
3. H. R. Jackson, *Churches and People in Australia and New Zealand 1860–1930* (Wellington: Allen & Unwin, 1987), 109.
4. See J. Ward, 'The Invention of Papahurihia' (PhD thesis, Massey University, 2016), 263–304.
5. Samuel Marsden to Josiah Pratt, 30 September 1814, Marsden Archive. http://www.marsdenarchive.otago.ac.nz/MS_0054_055
6. Reverend Samuel Marsden's Journal from 13 February 1820 to 25 November 1820, 19, 32, 36, 75, 124, Marsden Archive. http://www.marsdenarchive.otago.ac.nz/MS_0177_002
7. Henry Williams to Josiah Pratt, 10 November 1823, 11, Marsden Online Archive, http://www.marsdenarchive.otago.ac.nz/MS_0498_305
8. Augustus Earle, *Narrative of a Residence in New Zealand in 1827; Together with a Journal of a Residence in Tristan d'Acunha* (London: Longman, Rees, Orme, Brown, Green & Longman, 1832), 146–47.
9. 'Narrative of a Journey Through Part of the North island of New Zealand in 1849,' *New Zealander* 5, no. 386 (26 December 1849): 2.
10. J. N. Coleman, *Memoir of Rev Richard Davis, for Thirty-nine Years a Missionary in New Zealand* (London: James Nisbet, 1865), 308–09.
11. Peter Clayworth, 'Weekends — Origins of the Weekend — the Sunday Sabbath,' Te Ara — the Encyclopedia of New Zealand, updated 8-Jul-13, http://www.TeAra.govt.nz/mi/weekends/page-1
12. See, for example, James Buller, 'Our Maori Mission,' *New Zealand Wesleyan* (1 July 1873), 97–98, citing the missionary C. H. Schnackenberg. Also 'In a Sabbatarian Village,' 31 March 1850, in James Cowan, *Sir Donald Maclean: The Story of a New Zealand Statesman* (Wellington: Reed, 1940), 150.
13. W. A. Taylor, *Lore and History of the South Island Maori* (Christchurch: Bascands, 1952), 167.
14. 'On Keeping the Sabbath,' *New Zealand Evangelist* (August 1849), 47–49; 'The Sabbath a Privilege,' *New Zealand Evangelist* (October 1849), 124–29; W. White, 'Antiquity of the Sabbath,' *New Zealand Evangelist* (December 1849), 185–86.
15. 'Tired Pedestrian,' to the editor, *Christian Observer* (February 1870), 26.
16. A. J. Clarke, 'Feasts and Fasts: Holidays, Religion and Ethnicity in Nineteenth Century Otago' (PhD thesis, University of Otago, 2003).

17 G. A. Selwyn, *Letters from the Bishop of New Zealand to the Society for the Propagation of the Gospel*, 3rd ed. (London, 1847), 31. Cited in P. J. Lineham, 'How Institutionalised was Protestant Piety in Nineteenth-century New Zealand?' *Journal of Religious History* 13, no. 4 (1985): 370–82 at 372.
18 See Lineham, 'Protestant Piety,' 375; P. Lineham, 'The New Zealand Christmas and the Interweaving of Culture and Religion,' in *Sacred Histories in Secular New Zealand*, ed. G. Troughton and S. Lange (Wellington: Victoria University Press, 2016), 154–70.
19 W. Downie Stewart, 'The Law of the Sabbath Day,' *New Zealand Evangelist* (January 1872), 3–5 and *New Zealand Evangelist* (February 1872), 35–41.
20 Cited in L. Guy, *Shaping Godzone: Public Issues and Church Voices in New Zealand 1840–2000* (Wellington: Victoria University Press, 2011), 110; A. Clarke, 'A Godly Rhythm: Keeping the Sabbath in Otago, 1870–1890,' in *Building God's Own Country: Historical Essays on Religions in New Zealand*, ed. J. Stenhouse and J. Thomson (Dunedin: University of Otago Press, 2004), 46–59.
21 *New Zealand Presbyterian* 1, no. 2 (March 1866), 3.
22 Sutherland, letter to editor, *Otago Daily Times*, 16 May 1871, p. 3; letters in reply, *Otago Daily Times*, 17 May 1871, p. 3; 18 May 1871, p. 3, 19 May 1871, p. 3.
23 *New Zealand Presbyterian* (1885), cited in Clarke, 'A Godly Rhythm,' 49.
24 Details in Guy, *Shaping Godzone*, 113–14.
25 Ibid., 113.
26 Cited in M. N. Garing, 'Against the Tide: Social, Moral and Political Questions in the Presbyterian Church of New Zealand, 1840–1970' (PhD thesis, Victoria University of Wellington, 1989), 91.
27 *White Ribbon* 2, no. 22 (1897): 6–7. For details see L. Guy, 'The Rise and Fall of the Sabbath in New Zealand 1860–2000,' *Pacific Journal of Baptist Research* 5, no. 2 (2009): 3–38.
28 W. J. Habens, 'The Lord's Day and the Museum,' *New Zealand Wesleyan* (August 1873), 113–14. See other comments in *New Zealand Wesleyan* (February 1873), 23; *New Zealand Wesleyan* (July 1873), 104–105; *New Zealand Wesleyan* (October 1873), 149.
29 *New Zealand Wesleyan* (March 1880), 63.
30 *New Zealand Wesleyan* (March 1881), 65.
31 *New Zealand Wesleyan* (July 1880), 158.
32 Patsy Martin, *Knox Alive! A Celebration of 150 Years of the Presbyterian Church in the Hutt Valley* (Lower Hutt: Knox-St Columba Presbyterian Church, 2002), 24.
33 G. Urquhart et al., *100 by the Grace of God; Somervell Memorial Presbyterian Church 100 Years of Grace 1905–2005* (Auckland: Somervell Church, 2005), 16–17.
34 Clarke, 'A Godly Rhythm,' 50.
35 See Presbyterian Church of New Zealand, *Proceedings of General Assembly*, 1890, Appendix xvi, pp. 66–67; Lineham, 'Protestant Piety,' 378.
36 Cited in Christopher William Collins, 'Leisure and Christianity: The Case of the Brethren' (MA thesis, Victoria University of Wellington, 1990), 162.
37 *New Zealand Wesleyan* (April 1881), 86.

38 Cited in Guy, 'Rise and Fall', 15.
39 Ayson Clifford, cited in Guy, ibid., 21
40 Guy, *Shaping Godzone*, 122–24.
41 Garing, 'Against the Tide,' 109.
42 WCTU Convention Minutes, 19 March 1895.
43 Garing, 'Against the Tide,' 93; Guy, *Shaping Godzone*, 117–22.
44 'Mr Heaurndall at Albert Street Congregational Church Soiree,' *New Zealand Herald*, June 19, 1867, 5.
45 Slade, 'Retiring Address,' *Outlook* (7 March 1908), 32.
46 Lady Barker, 'Looking for a Congregation', in *Station Amusements in New Zealand* (London: William Hunt, 1873), 122.
47 W. M. W. Brookfield, 'Life of William Johnstone Will,' typescript at Otago Settlers Museum, cited in A. Clarke, 'The Presbyterian Way of Life in Nineteenth-century New Zealand,' http://www.presbyterian.org.nz/archives/presresnetworkoct09.pdf, 4.
48 Collins, 'Leisure and Christianity,' 160–61 includes several citations.
49 WCTU Auckland, Minutebook, 11 December 1889.
50 WCTU Convention Minutes, 22 March 1909.
51 See 'Sabbath Recreations,' *Observer*, 6 May 1882, 115.
52 http://www.teara.govt.nz/mi/cartoon/39776/seddon-and-the-sabbatarians-1904
53 See Guy, *Shaping Godzone*, 109–110.
54 *New Zealand Parliamentary Debates (NZPD)*, vol. 53 (House of Representatives, September 10, 1885), 671.
55 Ernest H. Edwards, *Norman Hyde: His Life and Work* (Auckland: H. L. Thatcher, Bible House, 1945), 64.
56 Henry Ryan, 'The Church and Our Age,' *New Zealand Methodist Times* (27 December 1930), 3.
57 See the accounts in 'Religion Today,' *Auckland Star*, 22 June 1935, 7; 'The Shepherdless Sheep,' *New Zealand Methodist*, 6 July 1935, 1.
58 See Guy, *Shaping Godzone*, 125; Bill Cooke, *Heathen in Godzone: Seventy Years of Rationalism in New Zealand* (Auckland: New Zealand Association of Rationalists and Humanists, 1998), 50–56.
59 Guy, *Shaping Godzone*, 126–28, and Guy, 'Rise and Fall,' 23–28.
60 WCTU Convention Minutes, 26 March 1917.
61 Guy, *Shaping Godzone*, 131; P. Lineham, 'The Inter-Church Council on Public Affairs: An Exercise in Ecumenical Political Influence,' in *Christianity, Modernity and Culture: New Perspectives on New Zealand History*, ed. J. Stenhouse and G. A. Wood (Adelaide, ATF Press: 2005), 269–310.
62 *Proceedings of the Synod of Otago and Southland* (Dunedin: J. Wilkie, 1895), Appendix, 41.
63 *Otago Witness*, 31 March 1892, 18; 'WCTU 1891 Convention,' *Star* (Christchurch), 5 March 1891, 3; WCTU Convention Minutes, 19 & 20 March 1895.
64 WCTU Convention Minutes, 14 February 1910.

65 Anglican General Synod Social Service Committee, 1922, in Guy, 'Rise and Fall,' 22.
66 N. Daniels, *St Mary's in Merivale: A History of Merivale and the Anglican Parish of Merivale in Christchurch, New Zealand and the Ministry of Its Fifteen Vicars from 1866 to 2000* (Christchurch: Merivale Parish, 2004), 119.
67 Guy, 'Rise and Fall,' 36.
68 P. Budge, *Legacy of Faith 1926–1996: A Chronicle of St Stephens and St Aidans Presbyterian Churches Lower Hutt* (Lower Hutt: St Stephens and St Aidans, 1997), 17, 23, 29–30.
69 Cited in Collins, 'Leisure and Christianity,' 161.
70 See Lineham, 'Protestant Piety,' 376.
71 M. Sharpe, 'Anzac Day in New Zealand 1916–39,' *New Zealand Journal of History* 15, no. 2 (1981): 104.
72 A. Clarke, *Holiday Seasons: Christmas, New Year and Easter in Nineteenth Century New Zealand* (Auckland: Auckland University Press, 2007), 120–27.
73 'Sacred Day,' *Auckland Star*, 20 April 1935, 6.
74 F. Murray, *Knox Church 1881–1980* (Christchurch: Centennial Committee of Knox Church, 1980), 41, 66.
75 Lineham, 'The New Zealand Christmas,' 154–70.
76 Ibid.
77 Clarke, *Holiday Seasons*, 120–27.
78 D. Menefy, *You Shall Be My People: Ko Koutou Hei Iwi Maku: A History of St Francis Xavier Parish Whangarei 1897–1997* (Whangarei: St Francis Xavier Parish, 1997), 42.
79 See *New Zealand Herald*, 28 March 1929, 4. Also *New Zealand Herald*, 19 April 1930, 13.
80 *Auckland Star*, 24 April 1882, 2.
81 *New Zealand Primitive Methodist* (May 1893), 42; *New Zealand Herald*, 30 March 1929, 8.
82 Presbyterian Church, *Proceedings of General Assembly*, 1930, 25, 207. See Clarke, *Holiday Seasons*, 128–35.
83 See 'Sunday,' *Waiapu Church Gazette* (April 1917), 76.
84 James Obelkevich, *Religion and Rural Society: South Lindsay 1825–1875* (Oxford: Oxford University Press, 1976), 158.
85 *Nelson Examiner*, 23 February 1870, 3.
86 This comment is made by Clarke, *Holiday Seasons*, 144.
87 R. E. Clevely, *The Bunnythorpe Wesleyan-Methodist Church* (Palmerston North: The Church, 1987), 10, 26.
88 'Presbyterian Youth,' *Outlook* (15 June 1963), 25.
89 Garing, 'Against the Tide,' 117–24. Presbyterian Church of New Zealand, General Assembly 1960, 110a–111a. This was further reviewed in 1969. See Presbyterian Church General Assembly Reports of Committees [White Book], 1969, 158.
90 See Anne-Marie Kennedy, 'Keep Sunday Free: Social Engineering through Shop Trading Hours in New Zealand' (PhD thesis, Auckland University of Technology, 2009).
91 Chris Saunders, 'The Response of Grassroots Christians to the Introduction of Sunday Trading to New Zealand in 1989: By What Authority Are You Doing These Things and

Who Gave You This Authority?' (MTh thesis, University of Otago, 2011).

92 See *The Essential Vygotsky*, ed. Robert W. Rieber and David K. Robinson, in collaboration with Jerome Bruner et al. (New York: Kluwer Academic, 2004), 1–8.

Chapter Two: The House of God

1   Geoff Park, *Nga Uruora, Ecology and History in a New Zealand Landscape* (Wellington: Victoria University Press, 1995).
2   Ernest Merrington, 'God of Eternity,' in *Spirit in a Strange Land: A Selection of New Zealand Spiritual Verse*, ed. Paul Morris, Harry Ricketts and Mike Grimshaw (Auckland: Godwit, 2002), 20.
3   Francis Pound, *The Invention of New Zealand: Art & National Identity, 1930–1970* (Auckland: Auckland University Press, 2009), 16–60.
4   Blanche Baughan, from 'Summer Estuary,' in *Spirit in a Strange Land*, ed. Morris, Ricketts and Grimshaw, 27.
5   See in particular B. McKay and J. Ussher, *Worship: A History of New Zealand Church Design* (Auckland: Godwit, 2015); L. Burgess, *Historic Churches: A Guide to Over 60 Early New Zealand Churches* (Auckland: Random House, 2015).
6   Tom Brooking, 'Use It or Lose It: Unravelling the Land Debate in Late Nineteenth Century New Zealand,' *New Zealand Journal of History* 30, no. 2 (1996): 141–62 at 141.
7   Nicely portrayed in M. Rae, 'Auckland Landmarks: Architecture and the Shaping of National Identity,' in *Making Our Place: Exploring Land Use Tensions in Aotearoa-New Zealand*, ed. J. Ruru, J. Stephenson and M. Abbott (Dunedin: Otago University Press, 2011), 125–41.
8   G. Maclean and J. A. Phillips, *The Sorrow and the Pride: New Zealand War Memorials* (Wellington: GP Books, 1990).
9   S. Deed, *Unearthly Landscapes: New Zealand's Early Churchyards, Cemeteries and Urupā* (Dunedin: Otago University Press, 2015), 55, 66–72.
10 'Clock Cross Worries Atheist,' *New Zealand Herald*, 29 September 2003; 'Clock Cross Tower Takes a Dive,' *Manawatu Standard*, 1 December 2012. Hans-Georg Betz, in *Movements of Exclusion: Radical Right-wing Populism in the Western World* (New York: Nova, 2005), 35.
11 'Statue of Mary Has a Lean On,' *Dominion Post*, 28 September 2009; 'Miracle Virgin Statue Dominates Paraparaumu,' *Dominion Post*, 25 May 2015.
12 Allen Curnow, 'Magnificat,' in *Spirit in a Strange Land*, ed. Morris, Ricketts & Grimshaw, 61.
13 Deed, *Unearthly Landscapes*, 30–41; R. Joseph, 'Nga Pakanga no Wahi Tapu: Battles Over Sacred Places,' in *Making Our Place*, ed. Ruru, Stephenson and Abbott, 173–83.
14 Philip Carrington, 'Rangiora' (first published in *Treasury of New Zealand Verse*, 1926), in *Spirit in a Strange Land*, ed. Morris, Ricketts and Grimshaw, 47–49.
15 Lauris Edmond, 'Another Christmas Morning,' in *Spirit in a Strange Land*, ed. Morris, Ricketts and Grimshaw, 55.
16 See Geoff Park, *Theatre Country: Essays on Landscape and Whenua* (Wellington:

Victoria University Press, 2006), especially Chapter 6, 76–94 (although this deals with Darwinism in a later era).

17 See the illustration in R. A. Sundt, *Whare Karakia: Maori Church Building, Decoration and Ritual in Aotearoa New Zealand, 1834–1863* (Auckland: Auckland University Press, 2010), 14.

18 Jonathan Mane-Wheoki, 'Selwyn the Ecclesiologist: In Theory and in Practice,' in *A Controversial Clergyman, essays on George Selwyn, Bishop of New Zealand and Lichfield, and Sarah Selwyn*, ed. A. K. Davidson (Wellington: Bridget Williams Books, 2011), 128–45.

19 Sundt, *Whare Karakia*, 11.

20 Speaking to the Auckland Wesleyan Missionary Associations, *New Zealander*, 14 February 1852, 2.

21 P. Brooks, *By the Name of Mary: Tauranga Catholic Church, 1840–2000* (Tauranga: The Author, 2000), 34–35. The quotation from Gisborne is at 34. Further quotations from *Daily Southern Cross*, 26 April 1869, 4.

22 See Roger Neich, *Carved Histories: Rotorua Ngati Tarawhai Woodcarving* (Auckland: Auckland University Press, 2001), 196–97.

23 J. K. E. Dieffenbach, *Travels in New Zealand*, 1843, cited by Geoff Park in *Theatre Country*, 101.

24 C. H. Laws, *Methodism in Napier: The Story of the First Decade* (Auckland: Wesley Historical Society, 1943), 5.

25 N. Crawshaw, *A Lasting Faith: A History of St Canice's Parish Westport* (Westport: The Parish, 2012), 5, 9.

26 Kathleen Hawkins, 'Church Sunday,' in *Spirit in a Strange Land*, ed. Morris, Ricketts and Grimshaw, 36.

27 'Old St Mary's,' *Timaru Herald*, 20 August 1880, 3.

28 See my discussion of this in P. Lineham, *Ventures of Faith and Community: The Development of Churches on the North Shore, Auckland* (Auckland: Wesley Historical Society and Anglican Historical Society, 2014).

29 F. A. Bull, *Malvern Presbyterian Church 1878–1978* (Christchurch: The Parish, 1978), 3–4.

30 For example, Patsy Martin, *Knox Alive! A Celebration of 150 Years of the Presbyterian Church in the Hutt Valley* (Lower Hutt: Knox-St Columba Presbyterian Church, 2002), 35.

31 M. J. Greathead and H. S. Kings, *Greytown Glimpses: A History of the Fortunes of One Hundred and Ten Years of Methodism in the Wairarapa, Particularly Relating to Greytown and Featherston* (Greytown: Methodist Church Book Committee, 1967), 5.

32 *Auckland Star*, 12 April 1882, 2; 25 April 1882, 2; 28 April 1882, 2. I am grateful to Alison Clarke for her analysis of the figures, and also to Michael Powell, 'The Church in Auckland Society, 1880–1886' (MA thesis, University of Auckland, 1970).

33 'Places of Worship,' *Results of a Census of the Colony of New Zealand*, Wellington, 1875, 114.

34 1878 *Census*, 349.

35 1881 *Census*, 117, 305.
36 1886 *Census*, 119.
37 *Auckland Star*, 25 April 1882, 2.
38 Mane-Wheoki, 'Selwyn the Ecclesiologist,' 138.
39 Margaret Alington, *Frederick Thatcher and St Paul's* (Wellington: NZ Historic Places Trust, 1965), 20–22.
40 Ian Lochhead, *A Dream of Spires: Benjamin Mountford and the Gothic Revival* (Christchurch: Canterbury University Press, 1999), 89–90.
41 Ibid., 64.
42 Ibid.
43 C. R. Knight, *The Selwyn Churches of Auckland* (Wellington: A.H. & A.W. Reed, 1972), 19.
44 Ibid., 20–21.
45 Margaret Alington, *Godly Stones and Timbers: A History of St Mary's Church, New Plymouth* (New Plymouth: St Mary's Church, 1988), 3–40.
46 Cited, for example, in Foxton; see E. C. Murphy, *Century of Faith 1876–1976: A History of All Saints Church Foxton* (Foxton: The Parish, 1976), 57.
47 See R. Brownson, ed., *John Kinder's New Zealand* (Auckland: Random House and Auckland Art Gallery Toi o Tamaki, 2004), 58, 62.
48 *Taranaki Herald*, 15 March 1856, 3.
49 R. B. Keey, *To Him Be the Glory: The Story of Trinity Congregational Church Christchurch* (Christchurch: St Paul's Trinity-Pacific Presbyterian Church, 1974), 14.
50 Marie Peters, *Christchurch-St Michael's: A Study in Anglicanism in New Zealand* (Christchurch: University of Canterbury, 1986), 102.
51 Lochhead, *Dream of Spires*, 205–207.
52 Ibid., 201–203.
53 Ibid., 299.
54 See ibid., 299; 'St Thomas Church,' *Auckland Star*, 22 January 1886, 4.
55 Lochhead, *Dream of Spires*, 173–80.
56 See N. Ledgerwood, *R. A. Lawson: Victorian Architect of Dunedin* (Dunedin: Otago University Press, 2013).
57 *North Otago Times*, 13 April 1865, 2; *North Otago Times*, 20 April 1865, 2.
58 See Robert A. Orsi, *History and Presence* (Cambridge, Mass: Bellknap Press, 2016).
59 'First Communion at St Mary's Church, Napier,' *Tablet*, 17 December 1880, 11.
60 See 'St Mary's Church,' *Colonist*, 1 June 1891, 3.
61 Greathead and Kings, *Greytown Glimpses*, 28.
62 F. Fyfe, *The Quick Steeple Fix: An Eketahuna Tale from the 1930s* (Greytown: Wakelin House, 1991).
63 H. Wilson, *The Church on the Hill: The Story of St James Presbyterian Church Newtown*. (Wellington: St James Presbyterian Church, 1982), 70.
64 G. F. Angas, *Savage Life and Scenes in Australia and New Zealand*, vol. 1 (London: Reed, 1847), 2.
65 Brooks, *By the Name of Mary*, 67.

66 'Cenotaph or Bells,' *Manawatu Standard*, 2 August 1922, 5.
67 'Letter to Editor,' *Evening Post*, 23 April 1925, 9.
68 N. Daniels, *St Mary's in Merivale: A History of Merivale and the Anglican Parish of Merivale in Christchurch, New Zealand and the Ministry of its Fifteen Vicars from 1866 to 2000* (Christchurch: Merivale Parish, 2004), 151.
69 'Those Bells,' *Evening Post*, 7 November 1910, 8.
70 'Fetch 'em,' *Auckland Star*, 6 March 1915, 8.
71 *Church & People* (October 1961), 4; *Church & People* (August 1962), 5.
72 W. E. Morris, *The Centennial History of St Peter's Presbyterian Church and the Presbyterian Movement in the Western Bay of Plenty* (Tauranga: Editorial Committee, 1978), 16.
73 Peters, *Christchurch-St Michael's*, 81.
74 'St Mary's Church Annual Meeting,' *Taranaki Daily News*, 20 April 1910, 7.
75 F. Ciaran, 'Stained Glass in Canterbury, New Zealand, 1860 to 1988' (DPhil, University of Canterbury, 1992), and F. Ciaran, *Stained Glass Windows of Canterbury New Zealand: A Catalogue Raisonne* (Dunedin: University of Otago Press, 1998).
76 F. Ciaran, 'Are These New Zealand's Oldest Victorian Stained Glass Windows?' *Historic Places* 20 (1988): 20–22.
77 'Consecration of St Peter's Church Riccarton,' *Lyttelton Times*, 10 April 1858, 4.
78 'Letter to the Editor,' *Christian Observer* (November 1870), 171–72.
79 'Thorndon Church,' *Lyttelton Times*, 20 December 1851, 6.
80 A. Harris, *The Beauty of Your House: The Nelson Catholic Parish 1844–1994* (Nelson: St Mary's Parish, 1994), 24.
81 M. McCormick, *We Remember, We Celebrate, We Believe: Catholic Parish of Tainui, St Brigid's Church 1951–2001* (Dunedin: The Parish of Tainui, 2001), 22.
82 Sundt, *Whare Karakia*, 30–31.
83 Peters, *Christchurch-St Michael's*, 42.
84 H. B. Laurenson, *In this Familiar Place: The Mt Eden Village Methodist Church Centenary 1899–1999* (Auckland: The Church, 2005), 32.
85 Daniels, *St Mary's in Merivale*, 284, 289, 298.
86 Murphy, *Century of Faith*, 42.
87 'Opening of New Church,' *Patea Mail*, 19 December 1881, 3.
88 Permitted in the Privy Council judgment of 1889. See 'Letter of Ritualism,' *Southland Times*, 23 February 1881, 3; 'St Thomas Church,' *Auckland Star*, 22 January 1886, 4; 'High Church Services,' *New Zealand Herald*, 23 March 1928, 14.
89 Daniels, *St Mary's in Merivale*, 44, 47, 70.
90 'Vicar and Vestry Differ,' *Auckland Star*, 4 December 1912, 5.
91 F. A. Lane, *Light in the Clearing: A Historical Survey of Methodism in Rangiora* (Rangiora: Trustees, Methodist Church, 1965), 35.
92 R. E. Clevely, *The Bunnythorpe Wesleyan-Methodist Church: A Centennial Survey 1887–1987* (Palmerston North: The Church, 1987), 2.
93 A. MacLeod, *The First Hundred Years: A Centennial History of Oxford Terrace Baptist*

Church Christchurch 1863–1963 (Christchurch: The Church, 1963), 92.
94 J. B. Bennett, *Christchurch Wanganui: The Continuing Story* (Wanganui: Christchurch Parish Vestry, 1976), 111–12.
95 Joan Mary Bythell, *The Golden Jubilee of St Christopher's Sunday School Redwoodtown 1909–1959 with an Account of the Years 1905–1908* (Blenheim: The Vestry, 1959), 40.
96 Lane, *Light in the Clearing*, 50, 57.
97 These figures from Wanganui East in 1966 — J. B. Bennett, *Steps in Faith: A History of All Saints' Church Wanganui East 1909–1984* (Wanganui: The Parish, 1987), 76.
98 Methodist Church, *The Church in the Midst* (Christchurch: Church Building and Load Fund Committee, c1960), 3.
99 Ibid., 6.
100 Morris, *The Centennial History of St Peter's Presbyterian Church*, 31–33.
101 Keith Rowe, *Beyond the Tamaki: Celebrating 150 Years of Methodism in Howick-Pakuranga 1852–2002* (Auckland: Barry Crichton for Trinity Methodist Church, 2002), 33.
102 Elaine E. Bolitho, *First a Church: The Continuing Story of Ngaio Methodist, Presbyterian and Union Churches* (Wellington: Ngaio Union Church, 2004), 100–102.
103 Bennett, *Steps in Faith*, 52–53, 64–65, 85, 103–104.
104 Helen Phibbs, *A Short History of Christ Church, Warkworth: Its Building and Its Life 1876–1976* (Auckland: St Alban's Church Office Balmoral, 1976), 65.
105 See G. O'Brien and N. Bevin, *Futuna: Life of a Building* (Wellington: Victoria University Press, 2016).
106 K. Ward, *Against the Odds: Murray Robertson and Spreydon Baptist Church* (Auckland: Archer Press, 2016), 35–36, 41, 104–105.
107 'Removal of Pews Upsets Parishioners,' *Marlborough Express*, 27 November 2014, http://www.stuff.co.nz/marlborough-express/news/63581206/removal-of-pews-upsets-parishoners, accessed 4 December 2016.
108 http://www.stpeter.org.nz/information/loft, accessed 4 December 2016.
109 See Federated Farmers of New Zealand, Women's Division, *A Tapestry of Tarras* (Tarras: WDFF Tarras Branch, 1998).
110 Tom Isern, 'Past Like a Mask, or, The Trouble with "The Trouble with Wilderness",' *Journal of New Zealand Studies*, 16 (2013): 158–71 at 161.
111 Survey results from the Church Life Survey Administration Committee database.
112 Questions C6, C7 and C8 in the 2007 survey.
113 K. Pickles, 'Postcolonial Environments,' in *Making a New Land: Environmental Histories of New Zealand*, ed. E. Pawson and T. Brooking (Dunedin: Otago University Press, 2013), 261–76 at 274.

Chapter Three: Gathered to Worship

1 Marsden Journal for 25 December 1814, in *The Letters and Journals of Samuel Marsden, 1765–1838*, ed. J. R. Elder (Dunedin, 1932), 93–94.
2 Henry Williams Journal for 11 November 1833, in *The Early Journals of Henry Williams, 1826–1840, Senior Missionary in New Zealand of the Church Missionary Society*,

ed. L. M. Rogers (Christchurch: Pegasus Press, 1961), 345; also cited in *Transplanted Christianity*, ed. A. K. Davidson and P. J. Lineham, 5th edn (Auckland: Kereru Press, 2015), document 1.18.

3   H. W. Williams, *A Bibliography of Printed Maori*, Dominion Museum Monograph No. 7, 1924, items 4a, 6, 7. See P. Parkinson, '"A Language Peculiar to the Word of God": The Anglican Liturgy in the Maori Language,' *Publishing History* 54 (2003): 19–65.

4   R. A. Sundt, *Whare Karakia: Maori Church Building, Decoration and Ritual in Aotearoa New Zealand, 1834–1863* (Auckland: Auckland University Press, 2010), 3.

5   For Catholic practice, see A. Harris, *The Beauty of Your House: The Nelson Catholic Parish 1844–1994* (Nelson: St Mary's Parish, 1994), 192.

6   Anglican 29th General Synod Proceedings Central Radio Advisory Committee Report, 1943, 147.

7   Helen Phibbs, *A Short History of Christ Church, Warkworth: Its Building and Its Life 1876–1976* (Auckland: St Alban's Church Office Balmoral, 1976), 33.

8   I. Breward, 'Claimant Needs Determined Battlers', in *Presbyterians in Aotearoa 1840–1990*, ed. D. McEldowney (Wellington: Presbyterian Church of New Zealand, 1990), 46.

9   H. B. Laurenson, *In this Familiar Place: The Mt Eden Village Methodist Church Centenary 1899–1999* (Auckland: The Church, 2005), 58.

10 P. Barclay, *The Word and Work of Christ in New Zealand: Sermons Preached in St Paul's Church, Napier, with Two Addresses on Church-work in that Colony* (Edinburgh: John MacLaren, 1871).

11 See Joseph Feron, *The British: Whence Came They?* (Napier: British Israel, c.1970). See also Feron in M. Blain, 'Blain Biographical Directory of Anglican Clergy in the South Pacific Ordained before 1931', http://anglicanhistory.org/nz/blain_directory/bibliography.pdf

12 J. B. Bennett, *Steps in Faith: A History of All Saints' Church Wanganui East 1909–1984* (Wanganui: The Parish, 1987), 67.

13 'Public Worship,' *New Zealand Evangelist* (September 1848), 63–66.

14 Barclay, *The Word and Work of Christ*, 239.

15 P. Lineham, 'How Institutionalised was Protestant Piety in Nineteenth-century New Zealand?' *Journal of Religious History* 13, no. 4 (1985): 370–82 at 373.

16 R. Randerson, *Slipping the Moorings: A Memoir Weaving Faith with Justice, Ethics and Community* (Wellington: Matai Press, 2015), 29.

17 W. M. Ryburn, *A City Set on a Hill: The Story of St David's Presbyterian Church Auckland 1864–1964* (Auckland: Len Bolton & Co., 1964), 97.

18 A. K. Davidson, 'Depression War New Life', in *Presbyterians in Aotearoa 1840–1990*, ed. D. McEldowney (Wellington: Presbyterian Church of New Zealand, 1990), 110.

19 Ryburn, *A City Set on a Hill*, 24.

20 A. Clarke, 'Popular Piety: The Sacraments and Calvinism in Colonial New Zealand,' in *Calvin: The Man and the Legacy*, ed. M. Rae, P. Matheson and B. Knowles (Adelaide: ATF Theology, 2014), 189–212.

21 See, for example, 'Our City Missions,' *Outlook* (5 August 1905), 42.

22 Graeme Ball, '"The Amazing Jasper" Calder, the Auckland City Mission and Welfare Provision 1920–1946' (MA thesis, University of Auckland, 1997), 27.
23 N. Daniels, *St Mary's in Merivale: A History of Merivale and the Anglican Parish of Merivale in Christchurch, New Zealand and the Ministry of its Fifteen Vicars from 1866 to 2000* (Christchurch: Merivale Parish, 2004), 70.
24 Harris, *The Beauty of Your House*, 112–13.
25 P. Brooks, *By the Name of Mary: Tauranga Catholic Church, 1840–2000* (Tauranga: The Author, 2000), 73, 75.
26 J. B. Bennett, *Christchurch Wanganui: The Continuing Story* (Wanganui: Christchurch Parish Vestry, 1976), 76–77, 79.
27 Daniels, *St Mary's in Merivale*, 40.
28 M. Peters, *Christchurch-St Michael's: A Study in Anglicanism in New Zealand* (Christchurch: University of Canterbury, 1986), 42.
29 Bennett, *Christchurch Wanganui*, 108.
30 A. Clarke, '"Days of Heaven on Earth": Presbyterian Communion Seasons in Nineteenth-century Otago,' *Journal of Religious History* 26, no. 3 (2002): 274–97.
31 Ibid. See also Patsy Martin, *Knox Alive! A Celebration of 150 Years of the Presbyterian Church in the Hutt Valley* (Lower Hutt: Knox-St Columba Presbyterian Church, 2002), 21.
32 Laurenson, *In this Familiar Place*, 32.
33 Ibid., 58.
34 E. Bisseker and I. Giles, *Kaiapoi Baptist Church 1899–1999. Souvenir booklet.* (Kaiapoi: The Church, 1999), 12–13.
35 A. MacLeod, *The First Hundred Years: A Centennial History of Oxford Terrace Baptist Church Christchurch 1863–1963* (Christchurch: The Church, 1963), 66.
36 See http://www.materialreligion.org/documents/may98doc.html, accessed 29 December 2016.
37 D. G. and J. S. Jardine, *Mountain Parish, 1867–1990* (Queenstown: Frankton APW, 1990), 32.
38 *New Zealand Methodist Times* (March 1955), 372.
39 For example, James Hunter Brown, *High Churchmen and Their Rights* (Dunedin: Jas. Braithwaite, 1888).
40 'Use of Eucharistic Vestments,' *Press*, 17 December 1912, 2; Peters, *Christchurch-St Michael's*, 103–104.
41 'High Church Services,' *New Zealand Herald*, 23 March 1928, 14.
42 See, for example, 'High Church Services,' *New Zealand Herald*, 28 April 1927, 14.
43 J. Dickson, *Shall Ritualism and Romanism Capture N.Z.? Their Ramifications in Protestant Churches* (Dunedin: Otago Daily Times, 1912), 38.
44 F. A. Bull, *Malvern Presbyterian Church 1878–1978* (Christchurch: The Parish, 1978), 126.
45 W. T. Blight, *A House Not Made with Hands: A History of Durham Street Methodist Church Christchurch Since the Present Church Building Was Erected 1864–1964* (Christchurch: The Trustees, 1964), 89.

46 *New Zealand Methodist Times* (May 1965), 26–27.
47 *New Zealand Methodist Times* (June 1965), 68.
48 MacLeod, *The First Hundred Years*, 88.
49 Matthew Calder, *Sin in the City: Broadcast Talks* (Wellington: Whitcombe & Tombs, 1966).
50 J. Tucker, 'The Ancient Word in the Modern World: The Preaching of J.J. North', in *Sacred Histories in Secular New Zealand*, ed. G. Troughton and S. Lange (Wellington: Victoria University Press: 2016), 139–53.
51 F. W. Boreham, *When the Swans Fly High* (London: The Epworth Press, 1931), 131.
52 M. J. Hanrahan, *The Warm Wind of Faith: A History of the Catholic Church in Ashburton* (Ashburton: Higgins & Co. for the Parish, 1981), 50.
53 Daniels, *St Mary's in Merivale*, 214.
54 See [Anglican Church] Province of New Zealand, *Proceedings of 29th General Synod* (Christchurch: Coulls Somerville Wilkie, 1943), appendices a-b, 145–54.
55 See J. W. Bartrum, 'Some Observations of Church Broadcasting,' *Church & People*, December 1954, 12.
56 See Ken Coates, 'Church Could End Up Talking to Itself,' *Church & People*, 11 December 1972, 10.
57 See Church of the Province of New Zealand, *Proceedings of 34th General Synod*, 1958, 171ff; Church of the Province of New Zealand, *Proceedings of 39th General Synod*, 1970, 173 ff. For a general survey, see G. Dallard, *The 'God Slot': The Church and its Broadcasting* (Wellington: Presbyterian Church of New Zealand, 1989).
58 Spencer Ratcliffe, 'The Average Minister's Greatest Problem,' *New Zealand Methodist Times* (3 July 1926), 6.
59 For example, *New Zealand Baptist* (April 1916): 77.
60 Gwynne Urquart et al., *100 Years by the Grace of God: Somervell Memorial Presbyterian Church 100 Years of Grace 1905–2005* (Auckland: Somervell Church, 2005), 10.
61 J. Wilson, *Mt Roskill Baptist Church (Formerly White Swan) 75th Anniversary Celebrations: A History* (Auckland: The Church, 1989), 29.
62 See *New Zealand Methodist Times* (December 1965), 274.
63 *Press*, 2 January 1871, 2.
64 See H. M. Foy, 'Methodism in Hawera 1874–1918' (BA Hons diss., University of Otago, 1980), 74–78.
65 'Auxiliary Bible Society, Annual General Meeting,' *Press*, 5 May 1868, 2.
66 *New Zealand Herald*, 13 April 1936, 12.
67 Anglican Diocese of Auckland *Yearbook*, 1963, 24.
68 Lloyd Martin, *One Faith, Two Peoples: Communicating Across Cultures Within the Church* (Paraparaumu: Salt Company Publishers, 1991), 20–27.
69 See D. Menefy, *You Shall Be My People: Ko Koutou Hei Iwi Maku: A History of St Francis Xavier Parish Whangarei 1897–1997* (Whangarei: St Francis Xavier Parish, 1997), 21.
70 *New Zealand Herald*, 24 August 1885, 3. See G. E. Mason, *Round the Round World on a Church Mission* (London: S.P.C.K., 1892).

71 E. C. Millard, *What God Hath Wrought: An Account of the Mission Tour of the Rev G. C. Grubb, M.A. (1889–1890) Chiefly from the Diary Kept by E. C. Millard One of his Companions, in Ceylon, South Africa, Australia, New Zealand, Cape Colony* (London: E. Marlborough, 1891), and E. C. Millard, *The Same Lord: An Account of the Mission Tour of the Rev. George C. Grubb in Australia, Tasmania and New Zealand from April 3rd 1891, to July 7th 1892* (London: E. Marlborough, 1893).
72 There is as yet no history of the Mission of Help, and I am grateful for the help of the Rev. Michael Blain.
73 'Wesleyan Anniversary Soiree,' *Southland Times*, 27 September 1872, 2.
74 See for example, 'Blown Up,' *Feilding Star*, 3 May 1904, 4; 'The Chapman Cadge,' *Truth*, 18 January 1913, 4; 'World-Wide Wowserism,' *Truth*, 1 June 1918, 4.
75 R. Evans and R. McKenzie, *Evangelical Revivals in New Zealand: A History of Evangelical Revivals in New Zealand and an Outline of Some Basic Principles of Revivals* (Paihia: Colcom Press, 1999); P. J. Lineham, 'When the Roll is Called up Yonder, Who'll Be There? An Analysis of Nineteenth Century Trans-Atlantic Revivalism in New Zealand and Canada,' in *'Rescue the Perishing': Comparative Perspectives on Evangelism and Revivalism*, ed. D. Pratt (Auckland: College Communications, 1989), 1–22; B. D. Gilling, 'Retelling the Old Old Story: A Study of Six Mass Evangelistic Missions in Twentieth Century New Zealand' (PhD thesis, University of Waikato, 1990); J. Simpson, 'Joseph W. Kemp: Prime Interpreter of American Fundamentalism in New Zealand in the 1920s,' in *'Rescue the Perishing'*, ed. Pratt, 23–42.
76 G. M. Troughton, 'Moody and Sankey Down-under: A Case Study in "Trans-Atlantic" Revivalism in Nineteenth Century New Zealand,' *Journal of Religious History* 29, no. 2 (2005), 145–62.
77 H. R. Jackson, *Churches and People in Australia and New Zealand 1860–1930* (Wellington: Allen & Unwin, 1987), Chapter XX; D. Jull, 'The Knapdale Revival (1881): Social Context and Religious Conviction in 19th Century New Zealand,' *Australasian Journal of Pentecostal Studies* 7 (2003). www.aps-journal.com
78 P. Lineham, 'Brethren Revivalism: A Second Look at New Zealand,' in *The Growth of the Brethren Movement: National and International Experiences. Essays in Honour of Harold H. Rowdon*, ed. N. T. R. Dickson and T. Grass (Carlisle: Paternoster, 2006), 154–75.
79 B. Gilling, 'Rushing into the Kingdom of Heaven: William "California" Taylor and New Zealand Revivalism,' *Stimulus* 12, no. 1 (2004): 7–12.
80 Blight, *A House Not Made with Hands*, 21, 33, 37, 41, 42, 43, 47, 48, 52, 55, 72, 74, 99, 101.
81 Gilling, 'Retelling the Old Old Story.'
82 Bisseker and Giles, *Kaiapoi Baptist Church 1899–1999*, 14.
83 Editorial, *New Zealand Methodist Times* (23 August 1884), 4.
84 Spencer Ratcliffe, 'The Average Minister's Greatest Problem,' *New Zealand Methodist Times* (3 July 1926), 7.
85 H. Scott, *A Pioneering Ministry: Presbyterian Home Missionaries in New Zealand 1862–1964* (Wellington: Presbyterian Church, 1983).

86 See M. J. Greathead and H. S. Kings, *Greytown Glimpses: A History of the Fortunes of One Hundred and Ten Years of Methodism in the Wairarapa, Particularly Relating to Greytown and Featherston* (Greytown: Methodist Church Book Committee, 1967), 27.
87 John Armitage, 'Qualifications and Duties of the Lay Preacher,' *New Zealand Wesleyan* (1 September 1874), 149–50.
88 R. E. Clevely, *The Bunnythorpe Wesleyan-Methodist Church: A Centennial Survey 1887 1987* (Palmerston North: The Church, 1987), 27.
89 'Church Work Society,' *Press*, 9 January 1880, 3.
90 'Bishop Julius in South Canterbury,' *Timaru Herald*, 26 May 1890, 3.
91 'The Gore Wesleyan Church,' *Mataura Ensign*, 28 March 1890, 4.
92 Ibid.
93 Sarah Hart, ed., *St Matthew's: Oruanui's Community Church* (Taupo: The Church, 2011), 54, 80–87.
94 Comment by William Saunders, 'Moray Place,' *Outlook* (3 November 1906), 36; J. Featherston, *New Zealand Methodist Times* (9 October 1920), 10.
95 'Sunday School Manual,' *Church Gazette* (July 1931), 37.
96 *New Zealand Methodist Times* (19 August 1933), 5.
97 *New Zealand Methodist Times* (5 June 1937), 42.
98 *New Zealand Methodist Times* (6 November 1937), 219.
99 *New Zealand Methodist Times* (21 July 1945), 96.
100 *Church & People* (October 1947), 11, describes the regular family service on the day of the consecration of St Mary's Cathedral. See *Church & People* (December 1947), 8, for a similar service at St Matthew's Hastings. The Paeroa services are described as the fifth Sunday in *Church & People* (February 1950), 12, but monthly services were reported as taking place in Plimmerton, ibid., 13.
101 *Church & People* (October 1948), 7.
102 *Church & People* (December 1948), 6–7.
103 *Church & People* (June 1950), 14.
104 *Church & People* (November 1950), 11.
105 See Dickson, *Shall Ritualism and Romanism Capture N.Z.?*, 27.
106 See *Church & People* (August 1953), 5; (October 1953) 15.
107 *Church & People* (September 1953), 5. See also his article, 'Are Sunday Schools Helping or Hindering the Church,' *Church & People* (April 1954), 6.
108 *Church & People* (November 1954), 5.
109 'Mixed Pickles,' *Observer*, 23 April 1887, 9.
110 Boreham, *When the Swans Fly High*, 1.
111 'Fetch Em,' *Auckland Star*, 6 March 1915, 8.
112 'A Kinema Church,' *Auckland Star*, 7 February 1920, 19, citing the *Weekly Dispatch*.
113 L. Guy, *Shaping Godzone: Public Issues and Church Voices in New Zealand 1840–2000* (Wellington: Victoria University Press, 2011), 130.
114 'Church Holds Rally,' *New Zealand Herald*, 16 June 1930, 11.
115 D. Pratt, *An Ordered Faith: Faith and Order in the Methodist Church of New Zealand*

1950–1984 (Auckland: Wesley Historical Society N.Z., 1989), 42–43.
116 J. Grayland, *It Changed Overnight! Celebrating New Zealand's Liturgical Renewal, 1963 to 1970* (Auckland: Te Hepara Pai, 2003).
117 Barbara Harper, *The Harvest: History of the Catholic Church in Timaru 1869–1969* (Timaru: Centennial Committee, 1969), 141.
118 Harris, *The Beauty of Your House*, 112–13, 163.
119 Bennett, *Steps in Faith*, 81, 97, 106.
120 Phibbs, *A Short History of Christ Church, Warkworth*, 60–61.
121 See http://www.beingfrank.co.nz/kneeling, accessed December 4, 2016.
122 R. B. Keey, *To Him Be the Glory: The Story of Trinity Congregational Church Christchurch* (Christchurch: St Paul's Trinity-Pacific Presbyterian Church, 1974), 54–55.
123 E. Wilson, *Blessed to be a Blessing: 50 Years of Glen Eden Baptist Church 1959–2009* (Auckland: Glen Eden Baptist Church, 2009).
124 Ibid., 25–26.
125 A. MacLeod, *Long Bay Baptist Church: The Third Decade 1998–2008* (Auckland: The Church, 2008), 27.
126 See K. Ward, *Against the Odds: Murray Robertson and Spreydon Baptist Church* (Auckland: Archer Press, 2016), 83–85, 105–108, 136–38.

Chapter Four: The Music and Words of Faith

1 See, for example, Edith L. Blumhofer and Mark A. Noll, eds., *Singing the Lord's Song in a Strange Land: Hymnody in the History of North American Protestantism*, Religion & American Culture series (Tuscaloosa, AL: University of Alabama Press, 2004); Philip Bohlman, Edith L. Blumhofer and Maria M. Chow, eds., *Music in American Religious Experience* (Oxford: Oxford University Press, 2006); Richard Mouw and Mark A. Noll, eds., *Wonderful Words of Life: Hymns in American Protestant History and Theology* (Grand Rapids, MI: William B. Eerdmans, 2004).
2 See Peter Lineham, *Bible and Society: A Sesquicentennial History of the Bible Society in New Zealand* (Wellington: Bible Society in New Zealand & Daphne Brasell Associates, 1996), 5–12.
3 J. L. Nicholas, *Narrative of a Voyage to New Zealand Performed in the Years 1814 and 1815 in Company with the Rev Samuel Marsden*, vol. 2 (London: James Black, 1817), 348.
4 See D. F. McKenzie, *Oral Culture, Literacy and Print in Early New Zealand: The Treaty of Waitangi* (Wellington: Victoria University Press & Alexander Turnbull Library, 1985).
5 H. W. Williams, *A Bibliography of Printed Maori to 1900* (Wellington: Dominion Museum Monograph, 1924), item 9, p. 4.
6 P. Lineham, 'Tampering with the Sacred Text: The Second Edition of the Maori Bible,' in *A Book in the Hand: Essays on the History of the Book in New Zealand*, ed. P. Griffith, P. Hughes and A. A. Loney (Auckland: Auckland University Press, 2000), 29–47.
7 *Missionary Register*, 1829, 458.
8 Mervyn McLean and Margaret Orbell, *Traditional Songs of the Maori* (Auckland: Auckland University Press, 1975).

9 For example *Missionary Register*, 1817, 524.
10 *Missionary Register*, 1819, 308.
11 *Missionary Register*, 1823, 188, letter from Samuel Leigh. Other reports follow this.
12 *Missionary Register*, 1828, 128.
13 *Missionary Register*, 1829, 464.
14 L. M. Rogers, *The Early Journals of Henry Williams, 1826–1840, Senior Missionary in New Zealand of the Church Missionary Society* (Christchurch: Pegasus Press, 1961), 345 [10 November 1833].
15 Ibid., 364 [16 March 1834].
16 For example, ibid., 459 [1 December 1839].
17 Ibid., 347 [14 November 1833].
18 William Williams, *The Turanga Journals 1840–1850: Letters and Journals of William and Jane Williams, Missionaries to Poverty Bay*, ed. F. Porter (Wellington: Price Milburn for Victoria University Press, 1974), 457 [28 November 1847].
19 Original Correspondence, letter two, *New Zealander*, 12 February 1848, 3.
20 J. A. Wilson, *Missionary Life and Work in New Zealand 1833–1862: Being the Private Journal of the Late Rev. John Alexander Wilson* (Auckland: Auckland Star, 1889), 7 (29 December 1833 at Puriri), 24 (23 August 1834). The first hymn is No. 130 in *He Himene Mo te Karakia Ki te Atua* (Auckland: Sunday School Union, 1916), 110–11; the latter is No. 96, p. 86.
21 In order these are 1837 (23), 1839 (37, 39), Wesleyan 1839 (36), 1844 (104, 105); Colenso's hymns (161); 1850 hymns (210a); 1860 (211, 212, 213, 214), later editions (320–24, 849, 650a); Wesleyan book (327, 559, 878). The references are to Williams's bibliography.
22 'Monganui War,' *Daily Southern Cross*, 3 June 1843, 4.
23 'H. Williams (Pukekaraka) to editor,' 7 February, in *Church Gazette* (March 1878), 29. The hymn was named for the Rev. Matiu Tautari.
24 William Williams, *The Turanga Journals*, 102 [May 1840].
25 Some information is available at http://www.folksong.org.nz/tama_ngakau_marie/index.html
26 'Church Music,' *New Zealand Evangelist* (February 1850), 257 [1407/1740].
27 'Anniversary Soiree, Albert Street Congregational Church,' *New Zealand Herald*, 19 June 1867, 5.
28 *New Zealand Evangelist* (November 1869), 19–20.
29 J. M. Andrewes, 'The Whistling Kirk,' in *Building God's Own Country: Historical Essays on Religions in New Zealand*, ed. J. Stenhouse and J. Thomson (Dunedin: University of Otago Press, 2004), 60–71 at 62.
30 *New Zealand Evangelist* (May 1870), 156–57; 'Synod Report,' *New Zealand Evangelist* (February 1872), 213; *New Zealand Evangelist* (October 1872), 310, 313–14.
31 'Pitcairn's Island,' *Lyttelton Times*, 18 September 1852, 8.
32 M. Peters, *Christchurch-St Michael's: A Study in Anglicanism in New Zealand* (Christchurch: University of Canterbury, 1986), 40.
33 D. Davie, *A Gathered Church: The Literature of the English Dissenting Interest, 1700–*

1930 (London: Routledge, 1978); see also H. Davies, *Worship and Theology in England*, vol. 3: *From Watts and Wesley to Maurice*, and vol. 4: *From Newman to Martineau* (Princeton and London: Princeton University Press, 1962). A significant new analysis of the language of religion in the early period is in I. Rivers, *Reason, Grace, and Sentiment: A Study of the Language of Religion and Ethics in England, 1660–1780*, vol. 1: *Whichcote to Wesley* (Cambridge: Cambridge University Press, 1991). On hymns, see J. R. Watson, *The English Hymn: A Critical and Historical Study* (Oxford: Oxford University Press, 1999).

34 'The Chorale or Psalm Tune,' *Daily Southern Cross*, 14 October 1856, 4. The source is John Antes Latrobe, *The Music of the Church Considered in its Various Branches, Congregational and Choral: An Historical and Practical Treatise* (London: Thames Ditton, 1831).

35 P. Lineham, 'How Institutionalised was Protestant Piety in Nineteenth-century New Zealand?', *Journal of Religious History* 13, no. 4 (1985): 370–82 at 374.

36 'Easter Hymn,' *New Zealander*, 3 April 1847, 4.

37 Margaret Deck's poem, cited by P. Lineham, 'The Significance of J. G. Deck,' in *Christian Brethren Research Fellowship (NZ) Journal* 107 (November 1986): 13–34.

38 'Auxiliary Bible Society,' *New Zealander*, 5 September 1846, 2.

39 *Wellington Independent*, 24 February 1847, 3.

40 For example, 'Wesleyan Missionary Society,' *Wellington Independent*, 4 October 1848, 4; 'Wanganui Wesleyan Methodist Church,' *Wellington Independent*, 27 September 1859, 5; E. W. Hames, *Out of the Common Way: The European Church in the Colonial Era* (Auckland: Wesley Historical Society of New Zealand, 1972); *Proceedings* 27, nos 3–4 (1972): 86–87, 136–37.

41 'Baptist Chapel Anniversary,' *Colonist*, 22 February 1861, 2.

42 'Diocesan Synod,' *Lyttelton Times*, 13 July 1861, 3; see W. P. Morrell, *The Anglican Church in New Zealand* (Dunedin: Church of the Province of New Zealand, 1973), 98.

43 Information from J. D. Julian, *A Dictionary of Hymnology: Origin and History of Christian Hymns and Hymnwriters of All Ages and Nations, Together with Biographical and Critical Notices of Their Authors and Translators* (London: John Murray, 1892) and from hymnary.org

44 *New Zealand Presbyterian* (February 1867), 25–28.

45 'Diocesan Synod,' *Press*, 27 November 1866, 2.

46 'To the Editor,' *New Zealand Herald*, 13 October 1865, 5, and 14 October1865, 5.

47 'To the Editor,' *New Zealand Herald*, 18 October 1865, 5.

48 Letter by 'Not lining it out', *Christian Observer* (January 1870), 9. The claim that singing was now faster is in 'Anniversary Soiree,' *Daily Southern Cross*, 22 March 1872, 3.

49 'Tonic Solfa,' *Christian Observer* (July 1870), 110.

50 Expressed by Mr Wilson at Prebbleton, *Lyttelton Times*, 17 July 1865, 2.

51 C. Kingsley, 'Musical Instruments in Churches,' *Christian Observer* (August 1870), 119. Also see *Christian Observer* (April 1870), 50.

52 A. MacLeod, *The First Hundred Years: A Centennial History of Oxford Terrace Baptist*

Church Christchurch 1863–1963 (Christchurch: The Church, 1963), 24.
53   Letter in *Evangelist* (November 1869), 19–20.
54   N. Derbyshire, *Serving the Community: The Story of Pukekohe's Anglican Parish* (Christchurch: Wily Publications, 2016), 56.
55   D. G. and J. S. Jardine, *Mountain Parish, 1867–1990* (Queenstown: Frankton APW, 1990), 28–29, 31.
56   http://www.ponsonbybaptist.org.nz/organ.html, accessed 29 November 2016.
57   *New Zealand Herald*, 5 January 1881, 3.
58   Information supplied by an informant.
59   W. T. Blight, *A House Not Made with Hands: A History of Durham Street Methodist Church Christchurch Since the Present Church Building Was Erected 1864–1964* (Christchurch: The Trustees, 1964), 30, 32, 63.
60   *New Zealand Wesleyan* (July 1872), 107; *New Zealand Wesleyan* (August 1872), 124.
61   R. G. Newton, *Organ Cantueariensia: Organs in Canterbury 1850–1885* (Christchurch: School of Music, University of Canterbury, 1992), 1–5.
62   F. A. Lane, *Light in the Clearing: A Historical Survey of Methodism in Rangiora* (Rangiora: Trustees, Methodist Church, 1965), 40, 45, 58.
63   H. L. Fiebig, *Cuba Street Methodist Church Diamond Jubilee Souvenir 1893–1943* (Palmerston North: The Church [Kerslake & Billens Print], 1943), 11.
64   E. W. Hames, *100 Years in Pitt Street: Centenary History of the Pitt Street Methodist Church, Auckland* (Auckland: Pitt Street Methodist Trustees, 1970), 14, 42.
65   There is a fine account of precentors at Knox Church in Dunedin in Andrewes, 'The Whistling Kirk', 60–62.
66   *Presbyterian Magazine* (1863), 31; (1864), 28–29; *New Zealand Presbyterian* (February 1866), 13, 23, 26–27; *Otago Witness*, 2 December 1865, 5.
67   'St Paul's Presbyterian Church,' *Nelson Examiner and New Zealand Chronicle*, 10 January 1867, 6.
68   'Report on the Otago Synod,' *Otago Witness*, 22 January 1876, 7–9. See coverage of Presbyterian worship in *Presbyterians in Aotearoa 1840–1990*, ed. D. McEldowney (Wellington: Presbyterian Church of New Zealand, 1990).
69   Andrewes, 'The Whistling Kirk,' 83–84.
70   W. E. Morris, *The Centennial History of St Peter's Presbyterian Church and the Presbyterian Movement in the Western Bay of Plenty* (Tauranga: Editorial Committee, 1978), 53, 84, 109.
71   *New Zealander*, 30 May 1849, 2.
72   'The Choral Society,' *Daily Southern Cross*, 21 September 1858, 2.
73   Peters, *Christchurch-St Michael's*, 40.
74   'Primitive Methodist Chapel, Thorndon,' *Wellington Independent*, 5 December 1857, 3.
75   Andrewes, 'The Whistling Kirk,' 65.
76   'Thames,' *Christian Observer* 1, no. 7, 110.
77   William Greenwood, *Woodlands Street: The Story of a Timaru Church* (Timaru: Woodlands Street Methodist Church, 1984), 20.

78   For example in Napier, with a harmonium delivered from Clyde. *Hawke's Bay Herald*, 13 December 1861, 3.
79   Helen Phibbs, *A Short History of Christ Church, Warkworth: Its Building and Its Life 1876–1976* (Auckland: St Alban's Church Office Balmoral, 1976), 61.
80   *New Zealand Evangelist* (May 1871), 134; (February 1873), 36; *Christian Observer* (January 1870), 9, (July 1870), 110; W. M. Grant, MS Book of Ministries, 168 [20 April 1883], Hocken Library, Dunedin; *New Zealand Presbyterian*, 1 October 1881, 62–63.
81   *Colonist*, 28 December 1866, 2; *Nelson Examiner and New Zealand Chronicle*, 10 January 1867, 6.
82   Diocese of Christchurch, *Proceedings of Synod Session*, 1871, Bishop's address.
83   F. K. Tucker, *J. C. Bradshaw Mus.D. F.R.C.O., L.R.A.M., A.R.C.M., Hon. F.R.M.C.M.: A Memoir* (Christchurch: Caxton Press Print, 1955).
84   Roger Couper and Don Hamilton, *Jubilate: The Story of a Choir School* (ChristChurch: Cathedral Grammarian Association, 2006).
85   David Gee, 'Singing the Praises of a Man Who Loves Music,' *Press*, 30 January 1999; Obituary, *Press*, 21 December 1999, 3.
86   Bishop Cowie praised Vicesimus Lush for just such reasons; *New Zealand Herald*, 5 January 1881, 3.
87   'Soiree of the Dunedin Young Men's Christian Association,' *Otago Daily Times*, 14 August 1863, 4.
88   See Lloyd Keating, 'Surpliced Choirs,' *New Zealand Herald*, 26 February 1884, 3.
89   'Vicar and Vestry Differ,' *Auckland Star*, 4 December 1912, 5.
90   Blight, *A House Not Made with Hands*, 89, 97.
91   Andrewes, 'The Whistling Kirk,' 69.
92   Raymond White, *Joy in the Singing: The Choral Commitment of St Paul's Cathedral Choir Dunedin, New Zealand, 1859–1989* (Dunedin: Musick Fyne, 1989).
93   Rachael M. Hawkey, 'Griffiths, Thomas Vernon', from the Dictionary of New Zealand Biography. Te Ara – the Encyclopedia of New Zealand, updated 2-Oct-2013. URL: http://www.TeAra.govt.nz/en/biographies/4g21/griffiths-thomas-vernon. See also Rachael M. Hawkey, 'Vernon Griffiths (1894–1985): His Life and Philosophy of Music Education as Demonstrated in His Collected Papers' (PhD thesis, University of Canterbury, 1993).
94   See E. Salmon, *Peter Godfrey: Father of New Zealand Choral Music* (Wellington: Makaro Press, 2015).
95   White, *Joy in the Singing*.
96   'Anglican Dean Asked to Leave,' *New Zealand Herald*, 4 July 2000. www.nzherlad.co.nz/nz/news/142916.
97   R. A. Matthews, *100 Years on Emerald Hill: A History of the Epsom Presbyterian Church* (Auckland: Epsom Presbyterian Church, 2006), 92.
98   See Lineham, 'Protestant Piety,' 375, and *Echo*, 1 May 1880.
99   'Motueka,' *New Zealand Wesleyan* (1 May 1874), 70.
100 Ira D. Sankey, *Sacred Songs and Solos 1200 hymns* (London: Marshall Morgan & Scott, 1921).

101 'Farewell Soiree to the Rev George Smith,' *Thames Advertiser*, vol. XIII, issue 3572, 27 March 1880, 3; Hames, *Out of the Common Way; Proceedings* 27, nos 3–4 (1972): 86–87.
102 *Christian Observer* (February 1870), 26.
103 John Kent, *Holding the Fort: Studies in Victorian Revivalism* (London: Epworth Press, 1978), 215–35.
104 F. T. Bullen, *With Christ at Sea* (London: Hodder & Stoughton, 1900), 87–89.
105 'Congregational Church Anniversary Soiree,' *Wellington Independent*, 3 June 1869, 4.
106 *New Zealand Wesleyan* (1880), 34.
107 See Julian, *Dictionary of Hymnology*, 1587, 1692.
108 *Truth*, 18 January 1901, 3.
109 Keith Cole, 'Robert Harkness,' in Australian Dictionary of Evangelical Biography, http://webjournals.ac.edu.au/ojs/index.php/ADEB/article/view/1118/1115
110 French E. Oliver, *Oliver's Songs of Deliverance* (Kansas City: Author, n.d.).
111 The Billy Graham New Zealand Crusades, *Billy Graham Crusade Songs* (Minneapolis: Rodeheaver Corporation, 1959).
112 http://en.wikipedia.org/wiki/Redemption_Hymnal. See Brett Knowles, 'Is the Future of Western Christianity a Pentecostal One? A Conversation with Harvey Cox,' in *The Future of Christianity: Historical, Sociological, Political and Theological Perspectives from New Zealand*, ATF series, ed. John Stenhouse and Brett Knowles (Adelaide: ATF Press, 2004), 39–59.
113 C. R. Bradwell, 'An Outline History of the Salvation Army in N.Z. History' (MA thesis, University of New Zealand Canterbury University College, 1950), 61–64, 93–95.
114 *Outlook* (26 August 1961), 2.
115 See W. Scott, cited in *Church & People* (November 1965), 2.
116 I am indebted for information from Harvey Rees Thomas's draft history of Elizabeth Street Chapel, due for publication in 2017.
117 G. H. Kerslake et al., *St John's Methodist Church Diamond Jubilee 1895–1955: A Brief Record and Historical Survey* (Levin: The Church, 1955). Information from Ed Matla, Petrus Matla's son.
118 See *Church News* (Christchurch) (February 1938), 7; *Church Gazette* (Auckland) (May 1938), 3; *Church & People* (July 1960), 18.
119 *Church & People* (July 1961), 9.
120 Elaine E. Bolitho, *First a Church: The Continuing Story of Ngaio Methodist, Presbyterian and Union Churches* (Wellington: Ngaio Union Church, 2004), 89, 119, 146.
121 A. Goulstone et al., *Opawa Baptist Church: Our Centenary. From Then Until Now, 1911–2011* (Christchurch: Opawa Baptist Church Outreach Press, 2011), 31, 39, 43, 46, 67.
122 *New Zealand Baptist* (October 1983), 14.
123 Goulstone et al., *Opawa Baptist Church*, 46, 67.
124 'Current Comment,' *Treasury* 69 (1967): 14.
125 Wyn Fountain in Dale Garrett, *The Profile of a Pioneer: Mentors to a Future Generation* (Auckland: Earthmovers, 1993), x, 42. Introduction to *Scripture in Song. Vol. 1, Songs of Praise* (Auckland: Scripture in Song, 1979). http://www.davidanddalegarratt.com/garrattfamilystory.html

126 The National Library has a record of this EP.
127 Garrett, *The Profile of a Pioneer*, 61. Dale Garrett, *The Pleasure of Your Company* (Eastbourne: Kingsway, 1983), 102, 131–32.
128 http://www.hymnary.org/text/this_is_the_day_this_is_the_day_that_th
129 D. R. Wood, *A Tale of Two Seasons: Tawa-Linden Baptist Church, 1948–2000*, vol. 2 (Wellington: TLBC Organising Committee, 2005), 29–96.
130 http://en.wikipedia.org/wiki/Parachute_Music.
131 C. Gibson, 'Mapping the New Zealand Landscape: A Survey of the Hymnic Tradition,' in *Mapping the Landscape: Essays in Australian and New Zealand Christianity. Festschrift in honour of Professor Ian Breward*, ed. S. and W. W. Emilsen (New York: Peter Lang, 2000), 238–54.
132 http://sounz.org.nz/works/show/13893 and http://sounz.org.nz/contributor/composer/1173
133 http://www.hymnology.co.uk/c/colin-gibson
134 http://www.hopepublishing.com/html/main.isx?sub=27&search=64
135 'Hymn Writer Stresses the Power of Words,' *Spanz*, December 2009, http://www.presbyterian.org.nz/publications/spanz-magazine/2009/december-2009/hymn-writer-stresses-the-power-of-words
136 http://www.hymnary.org/person/Wallace_. Also http://www.methodist.org.nz/resources/hymns/the_mystery_telling/about_the_author
137 http://www.selahpub.com/CongregationalSong/HymnCollections/125-435-MysteryTelling.html
138 http://jocelynmarshall.org/bio.html
139 *Songs for Prayer and Praise*, ed. R. J. Muller (Christian Advance Ministries, 1973).
140 National Library sources; I have a copy of 'Rejoice Young One,' 1979.
141 http://www.hymnary.org/person/Gillard_R and http://unitedmethodistreporter.com/2012/08/08/history-of-hymns-new-zealand-composer-bases-best-known-song-on-call-to-servanthood/
142 http://www.hymnary.org/person/Chambers_B
143 See http://www.nzcf.org.nz/page.php?page=83 and http://www.nzcf.org.nz/news.php?id=178&sza.
144 *Servant Songs*, ed. Guy E. Jansen and Felicia Edgecombe (Sutherland, NSW: Albatross Books, 1987).
145 http://sounz.org.nz/contributor/composer/1806
146 See *New Zealand Praise* (Hastings: New Zealand Christian Resource Trust, 1988), Update One (Hastings, 1990), Update Two (Upper Hutt, 1993).
147 'Wesleyan Musical Festival,' *Press*, 21 June 1872, 2; see also *New Zealand Wesleyan* (June 1872), 92.
148 See Chandler, 'The Religion of England,' *Auckland Star*, 18 March 1939, 6.
149 See P. J. Lineham, *Bible & Society*.
150 Chris Gardner, 'Controversial Revision of Bible Receives Approval,' *Waikato Times*, 28 April 2012, http://www.stuff.co.nz/waikato-times/life-style/6329890/Controversial-

revision-of-Bible-receives-approval

151 See *Christian Guardian*, (May 1972), 1–2; Christian Guardian Reporter (May 1973).

Chapter Five: Clergy Culture

1. See A. K. Davidson, 'Culture and Ecclesiology: The Church Missionary Society and New Zealand,' in *The Church Mission Society and World Christianity 1799–1999*, ed. K. Ward and B. Stanley (Grand Rapids, MI, and Surrey, UK: Eerdmans and Curzon, 2000), 198–227.
2. Peter J. Lineham, 'Pahewa, Hakaraia', from the Dictionary of New Zealand Biography. Te Ara – the Encyclopedia of New Zealand, http://www.TeAra.govt.nz/en/biographies/3p2/pahewa-hakaraia, accessed 27 January 2017.
3. J. E. Fitzgerald to H. Selfe, 27 December 1851, Selfe papers, vol. 1, no. 17, Canterbury Museum.
4. K. Orr-Nimmo, '"Who Am I That Should Undertake This Great Work?" Bishop Harper's Clergy,' in *Shaping a Colonial Church: Bishop Harper and the Anglican Diocese of Christchurch 1856–1890*, ed. C. Brown, M. Peters and J. Teal (Christchurch: Canterbury University Press, 2006), 83–110.
5. *Hastings Standard*, 22 February 1909, 21.
6. A. MacLeod, *The First Hundred Years: A Centennial History of Oxford Terrace Baptist Church Christchurch 1863–1963* (Christchurch: The Church, 1963), 30.
7. See, for example, Anglican layman, 'Letter to editor,' *Dominion*, 18 September 1917, 6.
8. Cowie to Synod, *New Zealand Herald*, 31 October 1876, 3.
9. See *Church & People* (November 1949), 1–2.
10. 'Recruiting for the Ministry,' *Church & People* (September 1949), 4.
11. A. K. Davidson, *Selwyn's Legacy: The College of St John the Evangelist Te Waimate and Auckland 1843–1992; A History* (Auckland: St John's College, 1993).
12. J. H. Simmonds, 'Ministerial Studies,' *New Zealand Wesleyan* (August 1875), 17.
13. J. Hislop, *History of Knox Church, Dunedin* (Dunedin: John Wilkie & Co. for the Office Bearers, 1892), 38.
14. L. B. Mannes, *Golden Jubilee: Holy Cross College Mosgiel, New Zealand; A History of the College Through Fifty Years 1900–1950* (Christchurch: Whitcombe & Tombs, 1949); D. P. O'Neill, *Mosgiel '75: 1900–1975* (Mosgiel: New Zealand Tablet, 1975); P. J. Norris, *Southernmost Seminary: The Story of Holy Cross College Mosgiel (1900–97)* (Auckland: Holy Cross Seminary, 1999).
15. See *Tablet*, 3 March 1910, 1.
16. Presbyterian Church, *Book of Order* (1908), 90 (1906 resolution); C. W. Casey et al., *Meeanee and Greenmeadows 1890–1955: A Survey, Historical and General of the New Zealand Marist Scholasticate* (Greenmeadows, Napier: Marist Fathers, 1955); Marist Brothers, *Souvenir of the Golden Jubilee of Highden Novitiate, Awahuri, Palmerston North, New Zealand 1924–1974* (Palmerston North: Marist Fathers, 1974).
17. Davidson, *Selwyn's Legacy*, 209.
18. D. Pratt, *An Ordered Faith: Faith and Order in the Methodist Church of New Zealand*

1950–1984 (Auckland: Wesley Historical Society, 1989), 33.
19 S. J. Thompson, *Knowledge and Vital Piety: Education for Methodist Ministry in New Zealand from the 1840s* (Auckland: Wesley Historical Society, 2010), 83, 89–90, 93, 168.
20 'Student Regulations,' *Book of Order* (Christchurch: Presbyterian Church of New Zealand, 1960), clause 7, 175.
21 Anglican Diocese of Auckland, *Yearbook* (1975), 114.
22 J. C., 'The Parson: Some Rural Memories,' *Auckland Star*, 27 August 1932, 1.
23 *Outlook* (7 March 1908), 35–36.
24 'Presbyterian Synod,' *Otago Witness*, 22 January 1870, 6, 8.
25 R. B. Keey, *To Him Be the Glory: The Story of Trinity Congregational Church Christchurch* (Christchurch: St Paul's Trinity-Pacific Presbyterian Church, 1974), 29.
26 Para 37, Parish Statute 1929, in *Statutes and Standing Orders of the Diocese of Auckland* (1947), 52; N. Daniels, *St Mary's in Merivale: A History of Merivale and the Anglican Parish of Merivale in Christchurch, New Zealand and the Ministry of Its Fifteen Vicars from 1866 to 2000* (Christchurch: Merivale Parish, 2004), 29, 132.
27 *Truth*, 9 April 1910, 5.
28 Para 4, Parish Statute 1929, Para 12 of Parochial Districts Statute 1929, in *Statutes and Standing Orders of the Diocese of Auckland* (1947), 47, 59.
29 Anglican Diocese of Auckland, *Yearbook* (1964), 37.
30 M. McCormick, *We Remember, We Celebrate, We Believe: Catholic Parish of Tainui, St Brigid's Church 1951–2001* (Dunedin: The Parish of Tainui, 2001), 18, 36.
31 Despite suggestions in *Truth*, 12 December 1908, 1.
32 J. Cowan, *Settlers and Pioneers* (Wellington: Department of Internal Affairs, 1940), 138–39.
33 Primate's address, *Proceedings of Fifth General Synod*, Dunedin, 1871, 8–11.
34 For a complaint, see 'The Press and the Clergy,' *Otago Daily Times*, 12 July 1929, 12.
35 'Bishop Julius in South Canterbury,' *Timaru Herald*, 26 May 1890, 3.
36 'Farewell Soiree to the Rev George Smith,' *Thames Advertiser*, 27 March 1880, 3.
37 *Auckland Star*, 26 April 1882.
38 J. C., 'The Parson: Some Rural Memories,' *Auckland Star*, 27 August 1932, 1.
39 Alan Mulgan, 'The Church', in *The Golden Wedding and Other Poems* (London: J. M. Dent, 1932), 17–18.
40 Letters beginning with *Otago Daily Times*, 5 July 1929, 13; 9 July 1929, 13; 10 July 1929; 12 July 1929, 12; 13 July 1929, 24; 15 July 1929, 10; 17 July 1929, 6. The discussion began with a report by presbytery complaining of gambling, 3 July 1929, 3.
41 McCormick, *We Remember, We Celebrate, We Believe*, 6–8, 35–36, 43–44.
42 See P. Matheson, 'The Settler Church', in *Presbyterians in Aotearoa 1840–1990*, ed. D. McEldowney (Wellington: Presbyterian Church of New Zealand, 1990), 15–42.
43 See editorial in *New Zealand Gazette*, 31 July 1844, 2.
44 Memoirs of Thomas Norrie, MSX-5906, Alexander Turnbull Library, Wellington. See M. Atchison, *Clevedon Presbyterian Church centenary 1858–1958* (Auckland: The Parish, 1958), 4, 8–9.

45 See Public Questions Committee Minutes, 16 August 1948, Presbyterian Archives, Dunedin.
46 Editorial, *Bruce Herald*, 12 September 1873, 5.
47 *Outlook* (1968), 30.
48 William Greenwood, *Woodlands Street: The Story of a Timaru Church* (Timaru: Woodlands Street Methodist Church, 1984), 19.
49 Daniels, *St Mary's in Merivale*, 128.
50 See A. Trapeznik and A. Gee, 'Laying the Victorians to Rest: Funerals, Memorials, and the Funeral Business in Nineteenth-century Dunedin,' in *Australian Economic History Review* 56, no. 3 (2016): 317–36; A. Clarke, '"Tinged with Christian Sentiment": Popular Religion and the Otago Colonists, 1850–1900,' in *Christianity, Modernity and Culture: New Perspectives on New Zealand History*, ed. J. Stenhouse and G. A. Wood (Adelaide: ATF Press, 2005), 103–31; S. Hewlett, 'Funerary Rites and Their Significance in the Western Bay of Plenty 1950–2000' (MA research exercise, Massey University, 2001).
51 Letter to editor, *Observer*, 5 October 1889, 9.
52 'Clergy Deceived,' *New Zealand Herald*, 16 May 1914, 10.
53 In Christchurch this was an abiding concern at St Michael's according to M. Peters, *Christchurch-St Michael's: A Study in Anglicanism in New Zealand* (Christchurch: University of Canterbury, 1986), 20–22. See also D. H., 'Letter to editor,' *Evening Post*, 17 October 1893, 4.
54 *Tablet*, 3 March 1910, 1.
55 *New Zealand Herald*, 25 October 1875, 2.
56 *Colonist*, 1 April 1876, 3.
57 See 'Report of Synod,' *Church Chronicle* (1 August 1902), 126.
58 *Tablet*, 28 October 1892, 5.
59 D. G. and J. S. Jardine, *Mountain Parish, 1867–1990* (Queenstown: Frankton APW, 1990), 32.
60 Helen Phibbs, *A Short History of Christ Church, Warkworth: Its Building and Its Life 1876–1976* (Auckland: St Alban's Church Office Balmoral, 1976), 34, 36.
61 'Presentations,' *Tablet*, 3 March 1910, 1.
62 Phibbs, *A Short History of Christ Church, Warkworth*, 36–37.
63 W. E. Morris, *The Centennial History of St Peter's Presbyterian Church and the Presbyterian Movement in the Western Bay of Plenty* (Tauranga: Editorial Committee, 1978), 105.
64 For example, C. H. Laws, 'The Arrest of the Church,' *New Zealand Methodist Times* (6 April 1912), 1.
65 Maurice Andrew, *Set in a Long Place: A Life from North to South* (Christchurch: Hazard Press, 1999), 249, 251.
66 See, for example, Walter McDonald, 'A Missionary from Mooncoin,' *Tablet*, 12 April 1917, 54.
67 For example, 'The Wearing of Cassocks,' *New Zealand Herald*, 5 July 1928, 12.
68 *Truth*, 28 August 1930, 4.
69 *Auckland Star*, 24 July 1934, 3; 18 November 1937, 19; 11 June 1938, 7.

70 'My Predecessor,' *New Zealand Methodist Times* (15 June 1889), 2.
71 See 'Retirement of Bishop Sprott,' *Evening Post*, 6 December 1935, 13.
72 See Dr Stenhouse's comments (originally on women) and responses to them, *Otago Daily Times*, 28 June 1888, 3 (Otago Educational Institute), and letters and Dr Stenhouse's response in *Otago Daily Times*, 1 July 1888, 3; 3 July 1888, 3; 4 July 1888, 3.
73 Anglican Diocese of Auckland, *Yearbook* (1974), 23.
74 1929 statute, *Statutes and Standing Orders of the Diocese of Auckland*, 1947, 47.
75 R. A. Matthews, *100 Years on Emerald Hill: A History of the Epsom Presbyterian Church* (Auckland: Epsom Presbyterian Church, 2006), 53.
76 J. T. Pinfold, *Fifty Years in Maoriland* (London: Epworth Press, 1930), 148.
77 The Auckland Diocese regulations are in Financial Regulations Statute, para. 14 and Diocesan Handbook C. 4 section 10 & appendix 4. http://www.auckanglican.org.nz/Anglican/media/Images/PDF/Chapter-4.pdf. Presbyterian regulations are in the rules for a call, http://www.presbyterian.org.nz/for-parishes/book-of-order/old-appendices/appendix-e-17-ministry-regulations, but these regulations reflect the abandonment of the requirement to own a manse.
78 Phibbs, *A Short History of Christ Church, Warkworth*, 45–46. For a more positive story, see Patsy Martin, *Knox Alive! A Celebration of 150 Years of the Presbyterian Church in the Hutt Valley* (Lower Hutt: Knox-St Columba Presbyterian Church, 2002), 21.
79 See 'Nuda Verba, District Meeting Recommendations,' *New Zealand Wesleyan* (15 January 1883): 6, and *Laws and Regulations of the Methodist Church*, 1969, clause 509, p. 104.
80 Salvation Army Orders and Regulations, c.1920. Thanks to Raewyn Hendy for this.
81 C. B. Oldfield, *Woodville Methodist Circuit Hawke's Bay, N.Z.: 75 Years of Methodism in Woodville 1876–1951* (Auckland: Wesley Historical Society, 1951), 17.
82 M. J. Hanrahan, *The Warm Wind of Faith: A History of the Catholic Church in Ashburton* (Ashburton: Higgins & Co. for the Parish, 1981), 31, 35.
83 Ibid., 25.
84 *Tablet*, 3 March 1910, 1.
85 See 'Clerical Tourists,' *Auckland Star*, 16 November 1927, 6.
86 Hislop, *History of Knox Church, Dunedin*, 100–101.
87 Barbara Harper, *The Harvest: A History of the Catholic Church in Timaru 1869–1964* (Timaru: Centennial Committee, 1969), 85–86.
88 Wesleyan Methodist Church 1891 Conference, 87; 1893 Conference, 104.
89 For example, 'Farewell Meeting,' *Wellington Independent*, 20 December 1870, 3.
90 For example, see MacLeod, *The First Hundred Years*, 40, 52, 60.
91 Peters, *Christchurch-St Michael's*, 48–49.
92 P. Lineham, *Ventures of Faith and Community: The Development of Churches on the North Shore, Auckland* (Auckland: Wesley Historical Society and Anglican Historical Society, 2014), 46–49.
93 See W. Morley, 'An Evening in the Anglican Synod,' *New Zealand Wesleyan* (July 1874), 114.
94 See A. W. Averill, 'Address to Synod,' *Church Gazette* (December 1915 Supplement), 4–5.
95 See *New Zealand Primitive Methodist Magazine* (1890–91), 6.

96 See Presbyterian Public Questions Committee Minutes, 22 April 1938, Presbyterian Archives, Dunedin.
97 *Laws and Regulations of the Methodist Church*, 1969, clause 513, p. 118.
98 *New Zealand Census*, 1921, Part VII: Religions (Wellington: Government Printer, 1923), 39, 42; *New Zealand Census*, 1921, Religious Professions, 36.
99 *New Zealand Census*, 1936, vol. VI, Religious Professions (Wellington: Government Printer, 1940), v, 27.
100 N. W. Derbyshire, 'An Anatomy of Antipodean Anglicanism: The Anglican Church in New Zealand 1945 to 2012' (PhD thesis, Massey University, 2013), 316.
101 See *Church Gazette* (December 1936), and *Auckland Star*, 3 December 1936, 22.
102 See Letters, *Church Gazette* (March 1873), 40.
103 *Fifth General Synod*, 1871, President's address, 9.
104 H. Scott, *A Pioneering Ministry: Presbyterian Home Missionaries in New Zealand 1862–1964* (Wellington: Presbyterian Church, 1983).
105 Derbyshire, 'An Anatomy of Antipodean Anglicanism', 316.
106 P. Lineham in *Living Legacy: A History of the Anglican Diocese of Auckland*, ed. A. K. Davidson (Auckland: Anglican Diocese, 2011), 260–61.
107 See P. Lineham, *Destiny: The Life and Times of a Self-made Apostle* (Auckland: Penguin, 2013), 35–36.
108 L. M. Flett, *A Full-er Gospel? Pentecostal Proclamation in New Zealand, 1990–2008* (Auckland: Archer Press, 2015).
109 C. G. Ashby, 'Principles in Practice: A Historical Analysis of the Trend Towards Employing Pastors in the Open Brethren Churches of New Zealand' (BA Hons diss., Massey University, 2013).
110 E. Bolitho, 'In this World: Baptist and Methodist Churches in New Zealand 1948–1988' (PhD thesis, Victoria University of Wellington, 1992), part 5.
111 Laurie Ennor, reporting from the Presbytery report of April adapted to July.
112 Stephanie Robson to Peter Lineham, email 27 June 2016.

Chapter Six: Convictions of the Faithful

1 P. Lineham, *No Ordinary Union: The Story of the Scripture Union, Children's Special Service Mission and Crusade Movements of New Zealand 1880–1980* (Wellington: Scripture Union of New Zealand, 1980), 7–8.
2 'Ko te Hunga o te Hahi,' William Colenso, Ahuriri, 1851 (Hawke's Bay Libraries). See P. Lineham, 'Paihia Versus Kororareka: Protestant Versus Catholic: Bible and Prayer Book in Catholic, Anglican and Methodist Missionary Strategy in New Zealand,' in *The French Place in the Bay of Islands: Te urunga mai o te iwi Wiwi: Essays from Pompallier's Printery*, ed. K. Martin and B. Mercer (Kororāreka Russell: Matou Matauwhi with Rim Books, 2011), 56–73.
3 Lady Barker, cited in Jeanine Graham, 'Settler Society,' in *Oxford History of New Zealand*, ed. W. H. Oliver with B. R. Williams (Wellington: Oxford University Press, 1981), 128, citing Mrs Barker's Journal for 3 January 1851.

4   For this, see P. J. Lineham, 'How Institutionalised was Protestant Piety in Nineteenth-century New Zealand?' *Journal of Religious History* 13, no. 4 (1985), 370–82.
5   M. Gee, *Plumb* (Oxford: Oxford University Press, 1979), 78. See D. McEldowney, 'Maurice Gee's "Plumb",' in *The World Within the Word*, ed. W. T. G. James (Hamilton: Waikato University, 1983), 61–73; also Geoff Chapple, in *New Zealand Listener*, 3 November 1984.
6   Lineham, *No Ordinary Union*, 15–20, 140–41.
7   Data from Christian Research Association's *Church Life Survey, 1996–2011*, and Bible Society, *New Zealand Report on Bible Engagement*, 2008.
8   See E. Larkin, 'The Devotional Revolution in Ireland, 1850–75,' *American Historical Review* 77 (June 1972): 625–52. For New Zealand, see M. King, *God's Farthest Outpost: A History of Catholics in New Zealand* (Auckland: Penguin, 1997), 11–29.
9   'Public Holiday, Grand Demonstration of Loyalty,' *Press*, 31 March 1868, 2.
10   'Church Parade,' *Wanganui Chronicle*, 5 February 1900, 2.
11   'Volunteer Parade,' *Auckland Star*, 12 February 1900, 6.
12   *Southland Times*, 1 June 1900, 2.
13   R. E. Clevely, *The Bunnythorpe Wesleyan-Methodist Church: A Centennial Survey 1887–1987* (Palmerston North: The Church, 1987), 11.
14   Church and Society Commission, NCC, *The Observance of Anzac Day* (Auckland: Church and Society Commission, 1972); M. Sharpe, 'Anzac Day in New Zealand 1916–39,' *New Zealand Journal of History* 15, no. 2 (1981): 97–114; M. Pickering, 'The Insubstantial Pageant: Is There a Civil Religious Tradition in New Zealand?' (MA thesis, University of Canterbury, 1985); S. Clarke, 'The One Day of the Year: Anzac Day in Aotearoa/New Zealand 1946–1990' (MA thesis, University of Otago, 1995); D. Amos, 'Hamilton Remembers Two Wars: An Investigation of Collective Remembrance 1917–2004' (BA Hons research exercise, University of Waikato, 2005); G. F. Davis, 'Anzac Day Meanings and Memories: New Zealand, Australian and Turkish Perspectives on a Day of Commemoration in the Twentieth Century' (PhD thesis, University of Otago, 2009); H. A. Robinson, 'Remembering the Past, Thinking of the Present: Historic Commemorations in New Zealand and Northern Ireland, 1940–1990' (PhD thesis, University of Auckland, 2009).
15   *New Zealand Herald*, 10 January 1880, 6.
16   See Clarence Eaton's address to the Annual North Canterbury Synod, *New Zealand Methodist Times* (3 December 1837), 246.
17   J. Button, *Love and Faithfulness: Stories of St Mary's, Timaru, 1860–2010* (Timaru: The Parish, 2010), 13–14.
18   H. M. Foy, 'Methodism in Hawera 1874–1918' (BA Hons diss., University of Otago, 1980), 92. See also H. Peterson, *Glasshouses But No Haughty Culture* (Wellington: David F. Jones, n.d.), 19.
19   *Christian Observer*, 1 June 1870, 92.
20   Hilary Reid, *St Mark's Anglican Church Remuera: The Story of a Parish 1847–1981* (Auckland: Vestry of St Mark's, 1982), 18.
21   *Otago Daily Times*, 8 June 1915, 5.

22 See *Observer*, 4 March 1905, 2.
23 Calder, Bible Society to Temple, London office, 17 February 1937. Bible Society records in Wtu.
24 Auckland Anglican Diocese, *Yearbook*, 1979, 105.
25 *Otago Daily Times*, 17 July 1876, 3.
26 See D. Menefy, *You Shall Be My People: Ko Koutou Hei Iwi Maku: A History of St Francis Xavier Parish Whangarei 1897–1997* (Whangarei: St Francis Xavier Parish, 1997), 49.
27 C. van der Krogt, 'Catholic Religious Identity and Social Integration in Interwar New Zealand,' *Catholic Historical Review* 86, no. 1 (2000): 47–65; C. van der Krogt, 'Good Catholics and Good Citizens,' in *Godly Schools? Some Approaches to Christian Education in New Zealand*, ed. B. Gilling (Hamilton: University of Waikato & Colcom Press, 1993), 17–39.
28 'Current Comment,' *Treasury* (March 1967), 14.
29 'The Curse of Auckland,' *Observer*, 16 May 1914, 2.
30 P. Lineham, 'The Great Bible Demonstration,' in *Scholarship and Fierce Sincerity: Henry D.A. Major, The Face of Anglican Modernism*, Clive Pearson, Allan Davidson and Peter Lineham (Auckland: Polygraphia, 2006), 199–214.
31 See Brother Juniper, 'Doctrinal Standards,' *New Zealand Methodist Times* (28 March 1935), 4.
32 J. Stenhouse, '"The Wretched Gorilla Damnification of Humanity": The "Battle" Between Science and Religion over Revolution in 19th Century New Zealand,' *New Zealand Journal of History* 18, no. 2 (1984): 154. Stenhouse's article shows that in general Christians did not find evolution unacceptable.
33 There are striking debates; for example, the dispute over Dr Pettit's anti-evolutionary lecture in Wellington, in *Evening Post*, 4 July 1929, 18, and 6 July 1929, 17.
34 H. D. A. Major's visit provoked a sharp debate in the correspondence pages of the *New Zealand Herald*, beginning on 16 March 1929, 16, and continuing almost daily until 26 April 1929.
35 See P. Lineham, 'The Fundamentalist Agenda and Its Chances,' *Stimulus* 14, no. 3 (2006): 2–14; J. Evans, 'The New Christian Right in New Zealand,' in *'Be Ye Separate': Fundamentalism and the New Zealand Experience*, ed. B. Gilling (Hamilton: University of Waikato & Colcom Press, 1992), 69–106.
36 J. Bluck, *Killing Us Softly: Challenging the Kiwi Culture of Complaint* (Christchurch: Shoal Bay Press, 2001) 34–42.
37 Alf Adams' memories, V. W. Hamill, Maerewhenua Goldfield, Alexander Turnbull Library (ATL), MS papers 2347.
38 See Lineham, 'Protestant Piety,' 378.
39 *Truth*, 25 January 1908, 5.
40 Menefy, *You Shall Be My People*, 12.
41 Sarah Dalton, 'The Pure in Heart: The NZWCTU and Social Purity' (MA thesis, Victoria University of Wellington, 1993); M. N. Garing, 'Against the Tide: Social, Moral and Political Questions in the Presbyterian Church of New Zealand, 1840–1970' (PhD thesis,

Victoria University of Wellington, 1989), Chapter 6; and Jolene A. McKay, 'The Tie That Binds: Christianity in the NZWCTU' (BA Hons diss., University of Otago, 1997).

42 See M. Powell, 'The Church in Auckland Society' (MA thesis, University of Auckland, 1970), 142–65.
43 See 'Baptist Assembly,' *New Zealand Baptist* 32 (November 1915), 383.
44 See Dalton, 'The Pure in Heart,' 63–72.
45 For example, C. O. Mules, 'Jubilee Shadows and Jubilee Hopes,' *New Zealand Church Messenger* (July 1887), 63.
46 *Press*, 5 June 1893, 5; J. Berry, *Private Lecture to Young Men Upon an Avoided but Important Subject* (Wellington: Edwards & Co., 1888); *New Zealand Baptist* (1880): 74.
47 New Zealand Defence Department, lectures by Dr Pettit, AD1 37/61, National Archives.
48 William Coull, 'The Church and the Masses of London,' *Evening Star*, 12 May 1894, 1.
49 *New Zealand Wesleyan* (January 1880), 4; 1878 Wesleyan Methodist Conference, 45; 1879 Wesleyan Methodist Conference, 39.
50 *Echo*, 8 July 1882, 2.
51 *New Zealand Wesleyan* (February 1880), 31.
52 WCTU Convention Minutes, 4 March 1898, ATL; WCTU Convention Minutes, 23 March 1917, ATL.
53 T. H. Salmon, 'Why I Stopped Smoking,' *Reaper* 8, no. 3 (1930): 69.
54 J. Cocker, 'Roland Tremain's Wife,' *New Zealand Methodist Times* (16 February 1918), 7.
55 See *New Zealand Methodist Times* (July 1964), 82.
56 For example P. W. Fairclough, 'Gambling,' *Outlook* (2 August 1902), 23.
57 'The Gambling Vice,' *Otago Daily Times*, 3 July 1929, 2; letters in comment, *Otago Daily Times*, 5 July 1929, 13; 9 July 1929, 13; 10 July 1929, 12; 12 July 1929, 12; 17 July 1929, 6.
58 For example the testimony at a conscientious objector's appeal, *Auckland Star*, 26 July 1946.
59 *New Zealand Methodist Times* (3 August 1935), 100.
60 See, for example, WCTU Minutes of Third Annual Meeting, 1888, President's address, 19–31.
61 *Reaper* 4, no. 1 (March 1926): 12.
62 See A. E. Hunt comments and 'Public Meeting, Congregational Annual Meetings,' *Outlook* (29 February 1908), 36.
63 Congregational Union, *Yearbook*, 1896, 7.
64 *New Zealand Methodist Times* (3 August 1935), 100.
65 See 'The Temperance Crusade,' *New Zealand Methodist Times* (27 April 1889), 4.
66 'New Zealand Alliance, visit of Mark Guy Pease,' *Prohibitionist*, 2 January 1892, 8.
67 See Dalton, 'The Pure in Heart,' 15–27.
68 See A. R. Grigg, 'Prohibition, the Church and Labour: A Programme for Social Reform 1890–1914,' *New Zealand Journal of History* 15, no. 2 (1981): 135–54.
69 See for example the society in Wellington in 1849, *New Zealand Evangelist* (October 1849), 140–41.
70 See, for example, 'Total Abstinence Society,' *Daily Southern Cross*, 23 March 1863, 4.

71 See P. Grimshaw, *Women's Suffrage in New Zealand* (Auckland: Auckland University Press, 1972), 57.
72 'Wesleyan Methodist Conference, Temperance Report,' *New Zealand Methodist Times* (12 February 1887), 4; Mrs Fulton, 'to Editor,' *Prohibitionist* (16 January 1892), x.
73 *New Zealand Evangelist* (August 1869), 20; (September 1869), 22.
74 *New Zealand Evangelist* (November 1870), 321–22.
75 See A. Drummond, ed., *The Thames Journals of Vicesimus Lush* (Christchurch: Pegasus, 1975), 205–206 [8 December 1879].
76 W. Morley, *History of Methodism,* (Wellington: McKee, 1900), 377–78.
77 Congregational Union, *Yearbook*, 1888, 21; *Protestant Ensign*, 15 September 1889, 26; *Outlook* (25 November 1899), 26; (10 November 1900), 4; (8 June 1901), 7–8; (15 June 1901), 6.
78 See *New Zealand Baptist* (May 1895): 65; Congregational Union, *Yearbook*, 1897, 8.
79 'Temperance Committee Report,' *New Zealand Methodist*, 12 February 1887, 4.
80 Geoffrey Troughton, 'Richard Booth and Gospel Temperance Revivalism,' in *The Spirit of the Past: Essays on Christianity in New Zealand History*, ed. Geoffrey Troughton and Hugh Morrison (Wellington: Victoria University Press, 2011), 112–25.
81 For a Baptist example see *New Zealand Baptist* (April 1895), 62.
82 See *Freethought Review* (June 1885), 1; (July 1885), 5; (August 1885), 1.
83 See *New Zealand Methodist* (July 1884), 4; (23 August 1884), 4.
84 C. H. Hinman in *Treasury* 2 (1900), 15.
85 Drummond, *The Thames Journals of Vicesimus Lush*, 205–206 [8 December 1879].
86 Methodist Annual Conference Minutes, 1949, p. 70.
87 W. H. Judkins, 'Social Unrest: The Inequalities of To-day,' *Vanguard* (January 1907), 11.
88 Congregational Union, *Yearbook*, 1903, 12.
89 J. Hislop, *History of Knox Church, Dunedin* (Dunedin: John Wilkie & Co. for the Office Bearers, 1892), 41.
90 *Auckland Star*, 20 April 1935, 6; *New Zealand Herald*, 23 March 1940, 13; 31 March 1945, 8.
91 'Los Angeles Easter Morning,' *Poverty Bay Herald*, 28 June 1919, 6. See also 'Easter in Hollywood,' *Auckland Star*, 4 April 1931, 12; 'Easter Observance,' *New Zealand Herald*, 20 April 1935, 12.
92 'Sunrise Service,' *Evening Post*, 25 March 1940, 4; 'Easter Sunrise Service,' *Evening Post*, 14 April 1941, 5.
93 *Evening Post*, 21 March 1940, 4; 25 March 1940, 4; 14 April 1941, 5; 27 March 1945, 7; 29 March 1945, 6; 2 April 1945, 4.
94 Y. Fer, 'Des "marches pour Jésus" à l'Anti-Smacking Referendum (1972–2009): Histoire d'une offensive évangélique en Nouvelle-Zélande,' in *La Politisation du Religieux en Modernité*, ed. N. Caron and G. Marche (Rennes: Presses Universitaires de Rennes, 2015), 145–58.
95 See P. Lineham *Destiny: The Life and Times of a Self-made Apostle* (Auckland: Penguin, 2013), 12–22.
96 G. Bond, 'Evangelistic Performance in New Zealand: The Word and What is Not Said'

    (PhD thesis, University of Canterbury, 2008).
97 M. Mawson, 'Believing in Protest: The Liberal Ideal of Separation of Religion and Politics in Two Recent Religious Protests,' *New Zealand Sociology* 21, no. 2 (2006): 196–214.
98 'Timaru,' *Tablet*, 14 October 1920, 22, for example.
99 *New Zealand Herald*, 5 February 1940, 9.
100 'Jubilee Days,' *Tablet*, 10 February 1921, 25.
101 'Diocese of Auckland,' *Tablet*, 8 November 1923, 27.
102 P. Budge, *Legacy of Faith 1926–1996: A Chronicle of St Stephens and St Aidans Presbyterian Churches Lower Hutt* (Lower Hutt: St Stephens and St Aidans, 1997), 17–18.
103 'Methodist Central Mission Dunedin,' *Christian Bridgeheads* (1942), 17.
104 See J. W. Bartrum, 'Some Observations of Church Broadcasting,' *Church & People* (December 1954), 12.
105 For example, Report of Provincial Broadcasting and Television Committee, Proceedings of 39th General Synod, 1970, 173. See also Dunedin Presbytery Minutes, vol. 10 (1932), 132.
106 Ken Coates, 'Church Could Be Talking to Itself,' *Church & People* (December 1972); see also George Dallard, *The 'God Slot': The Church and its Broadcasting* (Wellington: Presbyterian Church of New Zealand, 1989).
107 See *Outlook* (16 November 1963), 24.
108 See D. Wooding, *Never Say Never: The Story of the Rhema Broadcasting Group; A Modern-day Miracle* (Auckland: Rhema Broadcasting Group, 2003).
109 See D. Harding, 'Quake, Place and the End of the English: The New Zealand Christchurch Cathedral as Symbolic of Christchurch Place Identity' (2011). www.interdisciplinary.net

Chapter Seven: The Money in the Bag

1 *A Potter's Field to Bury People In* (Auckland: John Brame, 1880), cited in *New Zealand Methodist Times* (1880), 245.
2 For example in the Anglican report on clergy recruitment, *Church & People* (November 1949), 1.
3 'Anniversary Soiree,' *Daily Southern Cross*, 22 March 1872, 3.
4 *Otago Witness*, 1 February 1900, 48.
5 Letters to the editor, *Daily Southern Cross*, 30 September 1873, 2.
6 R. Creed Meredith, 'Synod Sermon', in *Church Chronicle* (September 1928), 148.
7 'Anniversary Soiree,' *Daily Southern Cross*, 22 March 1872, 3.
8 Marie Peters, *Christchurch-St Michael's: A Study in Anglicanism in New Zealand* (Christchurch: University of Canterbury, 1986), 79.
9 M. J. Hanrahan, *The Warm Wind of Faith: A History of the Catholic Church in Ashburton* (Ashburton: Higgins & Co. for the Parish, 1981), 18–19.
10 'Congregational Church Anniversary Soiree,' *Wellington Independent*, 3 June 1869, 4.
11 'News,' *Otago Daily Times*, 2 May 1874, 3.
12 *Timaru Herald*, 17 January 1910, 5.
13 'St Peter's Church,' *Akaroa Mail and Banks Peninsula Advertiser*, 10 May 1932, 4.

14 D. Menefy, *You Shall Be My People: Ko Koutou Hei Iwi Maku: A History of St Francis Xavier Parish Whangarei 1897–1997* (Whangarei: St Francis Xavier Parish, 1997), 31, 34–35.
15 There are many quotations of this, but see *Mataura Ensign*, 1 May 1900, 2. I cannot find the original source, which raises some concerns about the accuracy of the story.
16 C. B. Oldfield, *Woodville Methodist Circuit Hawke's Bay, N.Z.: 75 Years of Methodism in Woodville 1876–1951* (Auckland: Wesley Historical Society, 1951), 14.
17 J. Hislop, *History of Knox Church, Dunedin* (Dunedin: John Wilkie & Co. for the Office Bearers, 1892), 75.
18 See, for example, Bishop Mules, 'Jubilee Shadows and Jubilee Hopes,' *New Zealand Church Messenger* (July 1887), 63. Also see 'Orthodox,' to the editor, *Lyttelton Times*, 26 September 1855, 5.
19 R. L. Button to Temple (BFBS, London), 25 July 1940 in BFBS letterbook 80-179-41/5, Cambridge University Library.
20 *Star* (Christchurch), 21 February 1871, 4.
21 W. T. Blight, *A House Not Made with Hands: A History of Durham Street Methodist Church Christchurch Since the Present Church Building Was Erected 1864–1964* (Christchurch: The Trustees, 1964), 65, 71, 89, 91.
22 'Pitt Street Wesleyan Church Annual Soiree,' *New Zealand Herald*, 16 October 1872, 2.
23 P. P. Cahill, *St. Mary's Parish, Blenheim, Marlborough: Being an Account of One Hundred Years' Development 1864–1964* (Wellington: For the Parish, 1964), 52.
24 D. G. and J. S. Jardine, *Mountain Parish, 1867–1990* (Queenstown: Frankton APW, 1990), 32.
25 Ian Lochhead, *A Dream of Spires: Benjamin Mountford and the Gothic Revival* (Christchurch: Canterbury University Press, 1999), 49. See Peters, *Christchurch-St Michael's*, 27, 30.
26 *Lyttelton Times*, 2 May 1873, 2–3.
27 *Waikato Argus*, 21 October 1903, 2.
28 *Colonist*, 26 October 1917, 6; 5 July 1919, 5.
29 R. B. Keey, *To Him Be the Glory: The Story of Trinity Congregational Church Christchurch* (Christchurch: St Paul's Trinity-Pacific Presbyterian Church, 1974), 33, 34.
30 See 'Fetch Em,' *Auckland Star*, 6 March 1915, 8.
31 Jardine, *Mountain Parish*, 31, 33.
32 E. C. Murphy, *Century of Faith 1876–1976: A History of All Saints Church Foxton* (Foxton: The Parish, 1976), 38.
33 For example, Redwoodtown in Blenheim. See Joan Mary Bythell, *The Golden Jubilee of St. Christopher's Sunday School Redwoodtown 1909–1959 with an Account of the Years 1905–1908* (Blenheim: The Vestry, 1959), 28, 31.
34 M. J. Greathead and H. S. Kings, *Greytown Glimpses: A History of the Fortunes of One Hundred and Ten Years of Methodism in the Wairarapa, particularly relating to Greytown and Featherston* (Greytown: Methodist Church Book Committee, 1967), 24–25.
35 See the sarcastic reference in *Hawke's Bay Herald*, 28 January 1890, 2.

36 For example, J. B. Bennett, *Steps in Faith: A History of All Saints' Church Wanganui East 1909–1984* (Wanganui: The Parish, 1987), 42, 69.
37 Helen Phibbs, *A Short History of Christ Church, Warkworth: Its Building and Its Life 1876–1976* (Auckland: St Alban's Church Office Balmoral, 1976), 19–20.
38 Murphy, *Century of Faith*, 46–47.
39 M. McCormick, *We Remember, We Celebrate, We Believe: Catholic Parish of Tainui, St Brigid's Church 1951–2001* (Dunedin: The Parish of Tainui, 2001), 8–9.
40 Barbara Harper, *The Harvest: History of the Catholic Church in Timaru 1869–1969* (Timaru: Centennial Committee, 1969), 61, 67.
41 Ibid., 78.
42 Menefy, *You Shall Be My People*, 43.
43 Phibbs, *A Short History of Christ Church, Warkworth*, 68.
44 'Pitt Street Wesleyan Church Annual Soiree,' *New Zealand Herald*, 16 October 1872, 2.
45 'Anniversary Soiree,' *Daily Southern Cross*, 22 March 1872, 3.
46 'Popotunoa Church Soiree,' *Bruce Herald*, 22 April 1873, 7.
47 Blight, *A House Not Made with Hands*, 35, 38.
48 B. Iveson et al., *The First Hundred Years: Centennial Survey of Masterton Methodism 1858–1958* (Wesley Historical Society, 1958), 20.
49 'St Mary's Church Annual Meeting,' *Taranaki Daily News*, 20 April 1910, 7.
50 See http://www.materialreligion.org/documents/jan98doc.html, consulted 29 December 2016.
51 W. M. Ryburn, *A City Set on a Hill: The Story of St David's Presbyterian Church Auckland 1864–1964* (Auckland: Len Bolton & Co., 1964), 40, 68.
52 For example, 'St Peter's Church,' *Akaroa Mail and Banks Peninsula Advertiser*, 10 May 1932, 4.
53 For example, A. Harris, *The Beauty of Your House: The Nelson Catholic Parish 1844–1994* (Nelson: St. Mary's Parish, 1994), 103, 113.
54 For example *Wanganui Chronicle*, 15 February 1890, 2.
55 Ryburn, *A City Set on a Hill*, 45–46.
56 R. L. Button to Temple (BFBS, London), 25 July 1940 in BFBS letterbook 80-179-41/5.
57 Phibbs, *A Short History of Christ Church, Warkworth*, 52.
58 N. W. Derbyshire, 'An Anatomy of Antipodean Anglicanism: The Anglican Church in New Zealand 1945 to 2012' (MA thesis, Massey University, 2013), 83–85.
59 Harris, *The Beauty of Your House*, 113–14.
60 See P. Budge, *Legacy of Faith 1926–1996: A Chronicle of St Stephens and St Aidans Presbyterian Churches Lower Hutt* (Lower Hutt: St Stephens and St Aidans, 1997), 36.
61 See P. Lineham, Destiny: The Life and Times of a Self-made Apostle (Auckland: Penguin, 2013), 218–42.
62 See http://www.teara.govt.nz/en/pacific-churches-in-new-zealand/page-3.
63 Bernard Hickey, 'Biggest Insurer of Church and Heritage Sites Ends Earthquake Cover,' *New Zealand Herald*, 30 September 2011. http://www.nzherald.co.nz/business/news/article.cfm?c_id=3&objectid=10755440

Chapter Eight: A Sociable Religion

1. Cited in V. Graham and D. Payne, *Cross Currents: 125 Years of Settler Methodism in Kirikiriroa-Hamilton* (Hamilton: Hamilton Parish History Committee, 1989), 19.
2. W. R. Ward, *Religion and Society in England 1790–1850* (London: Batsford, 1972).
3. See the letters in *Transplanted Christianity: Documents Illustrating Aspects of New Zealand Church History*, ed. A. K. Davidson and P. J. Lineham, 5th edn (Auckland: Kereru, 2015), documents 1.30, 1.31 and 1.32.
4. N. Crawshaw, *A Lasting Faith: A History of St Canice's Parish Westport* (Westport: The Parish, 2012), 10–11.
5. Elaine E. Bolitho, *First a Church: The Continuing Story of Ngaio Methodist, Presbyterian and Union Churches* (Wellington: Ngaio Union Church, 2004), 92.
6. P. Brooks, *By the Name of Mary: Tauranga Catholic Church, 1840–2000* (Tauranga: The Church, 2000), 67.
7. *North Otago Times*, 15 September 1864, 3; 29 September 1864, 3; 28 April 1868, 2; see also K. C. McDonald, *The Way We Came: A Centennial History of St. Paul's Presbyterian Church Oamaru* (Oamaru: The Parish, 1963), 17.
8. J. Hislop, *History of Knox Church, Dunedin* (Dunedin: John Wilkie & Co. for the Office Bearers, 1892), 74.
9. A. MacLeod, *The First Hundred Years: A Centennial History of Oxford Terrace Baptist Church Christchurch 1863–1963* (Christchurch: The Church, 1963), 11, 15, 18.
10. See 'Nota Bene,' *Outlook* (June 1962), 31.
11. See, among a very large literature, W. P. Morrell, *The Anglican Church in New Zealand* (Dunedin: Church of the Province of New Zealand, 1973); Peter Hinchliff, *The One-sided Reciprocity: A Study in the Modification of the Establishment* (London: Darton, Longman & Todd, 1966).
12. See 'Church of England Meeting,' *New Zealander*, 8 May 1852, 2.
13. 'Churchmen's Club,' *Press*, 13 May 1890, 5.
14. Keith Rowe, *Beyond the Tamaki: Celebrating 150 Years of Methodism in Howick–Pakuranga 1852–2002* (Auckland: Barry Crichton for Trinity Methodist Church, 2002), 6–7.
15. 'St Paul's Church Annual Soiree,' *North Otago Times*, 14 April 1868, 2.
16. *Wanganui Herald*, 19 October 1874, 2.
17. 'Thanksgiving Service at St. Paul's,' *Otago Witness*, 23 November 1872, 2.
18. 'Bishop Julius in South Canterbury,' *Timaru Herald*, 26 May 1890, 3.
19. E. C. Millard, *What God Hath Wrought: An Account of the Mission Tour of the Rev G. C. Grubb, M.A. (1889–1890) Chiefly from the Diary Kept by E. C. Millard One of His Companions, in Ceylon, South Africa, Australia, New Zealand, Cape Colony* (London: E. Marlborough, 1891), 230.
20. David Pratt, cited in David Pratt and David S. Mullan, *Following the Dream: Memories and Reflections on the Century of Russell Methodist Church* (Red Beach: Colcom Press, 2014), 39.

21 Anglican Diocese of Auckland, *Yearbook*, 1970, 25.
22 Jenny Dawson, *A Radical Theology of Baptism: A Critical Investigation of Baptism as the Key Element in the Ecclesiology of the Anglican Church in Aotearoa, New Zealand and Polynesia* (Porirua: The Author, 2011).
23 P. Barclay, *The Word and Work of Christ in New Zealand: Sermons Preached in St. Paul's Church, Napier, With Two Addresses on Church-work in that Colony* (Edinburgh: John MacLaren, 1871).
24 M. Sutherland, 'Downgrade Down Under: Conflict and Cohesion and New Zealand Baptists,' *Baptist Quarterly* (1998), 351–63.
25 William Greenwood, *Woodlands Street: The Story of a Timaru Church* (Timaru: Woodlands Street Methodist Church, 1984), 29–30.
26 Greenwood, *Woodlands Street*, 29.
26A R. A. Nisbet, *The Sociological Tradition* (London: Heinemann, 1967), 208–11.
27 P. Lineham, *Ventures of Faith and Community: The Development of Churches on the North Shore, Auckland* (Auckland: Wesley Historical Society & Anglican Historical Society, 2014).
28 Kathleen Hawkins, 'Church Sunday,' in *Spirit in a Strange Land: A Selection of New Zealand Spiritual Verse*, ed. Paul Morris, Harry Ricketts and Mike Grimshaw (Auckland: Godwit, 2002), 38.
29 L. R. Spencer, *Memoirs of the History of Methodism in Levin* (Levin: Methodist Parish, 1969), 3.
30 *New Zealand Evangelist* (January 1850), 246–54.
31 *Lyttelton Times*, 6 March 1893, 6; *Outlook* (15 June 1901), 3–4.
32 *Freethought Review* (April 1884), 3.
33 *New Zealand Herald* 29 July 1884, 5; 4 August 1884, 5.
34 *Rationalist* (November 1885), 4; *Freethought Review* (May 1885): 4.
35 Michael O'Meeghan, *Held Firm by Faith: A History of the Catholic Diocese of Christchurch 1840–1987* (Christchurch: The Catholic Diocese of Christchurch, 1988), 214.
36 See *Wellington Independent*, 27 May 1859, 3.
37 I am indebted to David Hood of the Caversham Project of the University of Otago for supplying me with this data, which I used in my article 'Religion and Genealogy ... What was Inherited from Britain?' in *Centred on Nelson 2005: Proceedings of the 2005 Conference of the New Zealand Society of Genealogists* (Nelson: Society of Genealogists, 2005).
38 See, for a study of one such movement, M. N. Garing, 'Four Square for Christ: The Presbyterian Bible Class Movement 1902–1972: Its Background, Its Rise, Its Influence and Its Decline' (MA thesis, Victoria University of Wellington, 1986).
39 *New Zealand Evangelist* (June 1850), 405–406.
40 Crusader Leaders letter, 1964, Scripture Union Archives, Laidlaw College, Auckland.
41 *Tablet*, 12 November 1941, 17.
42 P. Lawlor, *The Demanding God: Some Boyhood Recollections* (Dunedin: New Zealand Tablet, 1972), 97.

43 R. E. Clevely, *The Bunnythorpe Wesleyan-Methodist Church: A Centennial Survey 1887 1987* (Palmerston North: The Church, 1987), 8; 'News of the Church,' *New Zealand Baptist* (February 1883), 25, 26, 27.
44 'Motueka,' *New Zealand Wesleyan* (1 May 1874), 70.
45 'News,' *New Zealand Baptist* (March 1890), 35.
46 W. E. Morris, *The Centennial History of St Peter's Presbyterian Church and the Presbyterian Movement in the Western Bay of Plenty* (Tauranga: Editorial Committee, 1978), 79–80.
47 See A. Clarke, 'A Godly Rhythm: Keeping the Sabbath in Otago, 1870–1890,' in *Building God's Own Country: Historical Essays on Religions in New Zealand*, ed. John Stenhouse and Jane Thomson (Dunedin: University of Otago Press, 2004), 55. For a Methodist example, see 'The President on Sunday Golf,' *New Zealand Methodist Times* (4 December 1937), 259.
48 *New Zealand Herald*, 11 March 1929, 10.
49 *Outlook* (23 March 1963), 6, although others were critical — see Arthur Gunn's letter, *Outlook* (4 May 1963), 30 and (1 June 1963), 10–11; (15 June 1963), 25; (29 June 1963), 10, 32, when correspondence was closed.
50 For one example, see Presbyterian Public Questions Committee Minute Book GA21, Presbyterian Archives, 92/29 AL16/1, 21 April 1939.
51 'Whangarei Presbyterian Soiree,' *Daily Southern Cross*, 10 February 1869, 3.
52 *Southland Times*, 7 June 1869, 1.
53 'St Paul's Church Annual Soiree,' *North Otago Times*, 14 April 1868, 2.
54 *Southland Times*, 7 June 1869, 1.
55 C. Bradwell, *Marching as to War: A History of the Linwood Citadel Corps of the Salvation Army 1888–1988* (Christchurch: Linwood Citadel Corps Council, 1988), 22.
56 For a nice description, see Clevely, *The Bunnythorpe Wesleyan-Methodist Church*, 8–9.
57 *New Zealand Wesleyan* (May 1872), 77–78.
58 See Lineham, *Ventures of Faith and Community*, 75.
59 B. Buckley, 'The Holy Name Society: A Short History of the Society in Auckland' (MA thesis, Massey University, 2001).
60 R. Sweetman, *Faith and Fraternalism: A History of the Hibernian Society in New Zealand 1869–2000* (NZ: Hibernian Society, 2002); see in particular p. 83.
61 See reports in *Grey River Argus*, 18 December 1869, 2; 30 December 1869, 2; *Westport Times*, 23 December 1869, 2 (two reports); Crawshaw, *A Lasting Faith*, 12–13.
62 'Two Bishops Consecrated,' *Evening Star*, 13 December 1920, 2.
63 K. Furniss, 'Moray Place Congregational Church, Dunedin: History' (BA Hons thesis, University of Otago, 1975). See also Keith Furniss, 'Moray Place Congregational Church: A Social History, 1862–1966,' in *Building God's Own Country: Historical Essays on Religions in New Zealand*, ed. John Stenhouse and Jane Thomson (Dunedin: University of Otago Press, 2004), 75–83.
64 *Southland Times*, 7 June 1869, 1.
65 'Letter of Veritas,' *New Zealand Wesleyan* (February 1872), 25.

66 'Church Holds Rally,' *New Zealand Herald*, 16 June 1930, 11.
67 'Old English Custom,' *Evening Post*, 12 July 1934, 10.
68 *Southland Times*, 7 June 1869, 1.
69 *Bruce Herald*, 3 July 1872, 9.
70 'Congregational Church,' *Wellington Independent*, 3 June 1869, 4.
71 'Maungaturoto Recognitions Soiree,' *New Zealand Herald*, 5 April 1880, 6.
72 See the essays by A. Davidson and P. Lineham in *Where the Road Runs Out: Research Essays on the Ecumenical Journey and the Conference of Churches in Aotearoa New Zealand*, ed. G. Cant (Christchurch: Conference of Churches in Aotearoa New Zealand, 2005).
73 K. Loan, *Wainuiomata Union Parish 25th Anniversary* (Wainuiomata: The Parish, 1978), 16.
74 'Religious World, Present Day Outlook,' *Auckland Star*, 6 June 1931, 3.
75 A. Harris, *The Beauty of Your House: The Nelson Catholic Parish 1844–1994* (Nelson: St Mary's Parish, 1994), 151–56.
76 Noel Derbyshire, *Serving the Community: The Story of Pukekohe's Anglican Parish* (Christchurch: Wily Publications, 2016), 201–204.
77 M. A. Reid, 'But By My Spirit: A History of the Charismatic Renewal in Christchurch 1960–1985' (PhD thesis, University of Canterbury, 2003), 183–96. See also M. Reid, *'Thus Far': A Centennial History of Hornby Presbyterian Church 1908–2008* (Christchurch: Verve, 2008).
78 For example, at the Tory Street Mission, *Outlook* (3 October 1908), 35, and at Ashburton by the Wesleyans, *Ashburton Guardian*, 11 March 1910, 3.
79 *New Zealand Baptist* (April 1973), 28.
80 *New Zealand Baptist* (September 1964), 241; (August 1965), 214; (November 1966), 294.
81 *New Zealand Baptist* (November 1971), 35; (February 1972), 29; 'Murray's Bay,' ibid. (September 1972), 26.
82 W. M. Ryburn, *A City Set on a Hill: The Story of St David's Presbyterian Church Auckland 1864–1964* (Auckland: Len Bolton & Co, 1964), 110.
83 *New Zealand Baptist* (November 1973), 28; ibid. (November 1979), 14; ibid. (April 1980), 14. For discussion see *New Zealand Baptist* (May 1981), 8 (Epsom); (November 1982), 109 (Masterton).
84 See for example 'New Lynn and Glenfield Baptist,' *New Zealand Baptist* (March 1986), 10.
85 'Food is for Fellowship,' *New Zealand Baptist* (March 1984), 15.
86 *Church & People* (October 1949), 14.
87 *S. Sepulchre's Parish Magazine* (January 1875) to (December 1877).
88 N. Daniels, *St Mary's in Merivale: A History of Merivale and the Anglican Parish of Merivale in Christchurch, New Zealand and the Ministry of its Fifteen Vicars from 1866 to 2000* (Christchurch: Merivale Parish, 2004), 83, 123.
89 M. McCormick, *We Remember, We Celebrate, We Believe: Catholic Parish of Tainui, St Brigid's Church 1951–2001* (Dunedin: The Parish of Tainui, 2001), 34–35.
90 See, for example, M. J. Hanrahan, *The Warm Wind of Faith: A History of the Catholic*

Church in Ashburton (Ashburton: Higgins & Co. for the Parish, 1981), 67.
91 Anglican Diocese of Auckland, *Yearbook*, 1969, 23; C Van der Krogt, '"The Evils of Mixed Marriages": Catholic Teaching and Practice,' in *The Spirit of the Past: Essays on Christianity in New Zealand History*, ed. G. Troughton and H. Morrison (Wellington: Victoria University Press, 2011), 142–55.
92 Anglican Diocese of Auckland, *Yearbook*, 1972, 25.
93 M. Brown, 'Losing Touch: Bible Disengagement in New Zealand,' *Stimulus* 15, no. 1 (2007): 2–4.

Chapter Nine: The Gendered Church

1 See the work of Cathy R. Ross, '"More than Wives": A Study of Four Church Missionary Society Wives in Nineteenth Century New Zealand' (PhD thesis, University of Auckland, 2003). See also C. Ross, *Women With a Mission: Rediscovering Missionary Wives in Early New Zealand* (Auckland: Penguin, 2006).
2 See Ross, *Women With a Mission*, 97–133.
3 A. Wanhalla, 'The "Natives Uncivilize Me": Missionaries and Interracial Intimacy in Early New Zealand,' *in Missions, Indigenous Peoples and Cultural Exchange*, ed. P. Grimshaw and A. May (Eastbourne: Sussex Academic Press, 2010), 24–36.
4 See *New Zealand Baptist* (September 1893), 158.
5 Alfred Brown, CMS Journal 1835–38, 2 June 1837, 111, CMS microfilms.
6 See, for example, William Fairburn Journal V, August–November 1835, entry for 23 August, CMS microfilms.
7 See Brown, Journal 1835–38, 15 May, 63.
8 E. Fairbrother and J. P. Te Paa, eds., *Our Place, Our Voice: Explorations in Contextual Theology: Women in the Anglican Church of Aotearoa New Zealand and Polynesia* (Auckland: Council for Anglican Women's Studies, 2012), 37.
9 Wendy Scott's story in ibid., 7.
10 J. Munro, *The Story of Suzanne Aubert* (Auckland: Auckland University Press & Bridget Williams Books, 1996), 83–86.
11 Julia Stuart, 'Unrepresented: A Mere 80%,' *Church & People* (12 June 1972), 3.
12 Numia Tomoana, in ed. Fairbrother and Te Paa, *Our Place, Our Voice*, 33–53.
13 *New Zealand Herald*, 27 June 2003. http://www.nzherald.co.nz/nz/news/article.cfm?c_id=1&objectid=3507564 accessed December 31, 2016.
14 J. T. Pinfold, *Fifty Years in Maoriland* (London: Epworth Press, 1930), 145–46.
15 Raewyn Dalziel, 'The Colonial Helpmeet: Women's Role and the Vote in Nineteenth-century New Zealand,' *New Zealand Journal of History* 11, no. 2 (1977): 112–23.
16 *New Zealand Wesleyan* (1872), 115–17.
17 Nancy Robertshawe, Thora Holland and Barbara Archer, *A History of the Mothers' Union and the Association of Anglican Women in New Zealand* (Wellington: Association of Anglican Women, 1980), part 1, 2.
18 *Leader*, 20 July 1888, 101.
19 J. E. Malone, 'What's Wrong with Emma? The Feminist Debate in Colonial Auckland,'

in *Women in History: Essays on European Women in New Zealand*, ed. B. Brookes, C. Macdonald and M. Tennant (Wellington: Allen & Unwin/Port Nicholson Press, 1986), 81.
20 *Christian Observer* (August 1870): 3–4.
21 *Christian Observer* (August 1870), 115; (August 1870), 138.
22 For example, 'Editorial Notes,' *New Zealand Methodist Times* (23 August 1884), 4.
23 In black quarto book, first page, 'On prayer by Hardwick,' lent to me by a member of Epsom Baptist Church.
24 'Comment at Ladies Benevolent Society AGM,' *New Zealand Herald*, 15 March 1873, 3.
25 Sarah Dalton, 'The Pure in Heart: The NZWCTU and Social Purity' (MA thesis, Victoria University of Wellington, 1993), 45 ff.
26 'Editorial,' New *Zealand Methodist Times* (25 November 1922), 8.
27 Dalton, 'The Pure in Heart,' 15 ff.
28 'Mothers' Meetings,' *Daily Southern Cross*, 27 August 1866, 4.
29 *Tablet*, 15 October 1941, 5. See also 'Editorial,' ibid., 26 September 1945, 7.
30 Robertshawe et al., *A History of the Mothers' Union*, part 1, 1–5.
31 J. Cocker, 'Roland Tremain's Wife,' *New Zealand Methodist Times* (16 February 1918), 7.
32 P. J. Lineham, *There We Found Brethren: A History of Assemblies of Brethren in New Zealand* (Palmerston North: Gospel Publishing House, 1977), 99; Colleen Main in Dictionary of New Zealand Biography, http://www.teara.govt.nz/en/biographies/1s19/squires-catharine; Squires' diaries are in the Early Settlers Museum in Dunedin.
33 See Ruth Fry, *Out of the Silence: Methodist Women of Aotearoa 1822–1985* (Christchurch: Methodist Publishing, 1987), 49.
34 M. W. Stack, 'The Women of Dunedin,' *Otago Daily Times*, 6 August 1870, 3.
35 P. Brooks, *By the Name of Mary: Tauranga Catholic Church, 1840–2000* (Tauranga: The Author, 2000), 78.
36 *Treasury* 34 (1932): 29; ibid. 52 (1950): 11; ibid., 53 (1951): 137; ibid., 55 (1953): 155.
37 N. Daniels, *St Mary's in Merivale: A History of Merivale and the Anglican Parish of Merivale in Christchurch, New Zealand and the Ministry of its Fifteen Vicars from 1866 to 2000* (Christchurch: Merivale Parish, 2004), 119.
38 For example 'Editorial,' *Christian Observer* (July 1870), 98–99.
39 *Evening Star*, 2 April 1883, 2.
40 T. G. Carr, 'My Life Story,' MS Papers 316, Alexander Turnbull Library (ATL), Wellington, 1926: 65, p. 45.
41 See Fry, *Out of the Silence*, 178–82.
42 Daniels, *St Mary's in Merivale*, 25–26, 55, 59, 118, 124.
43 I am relying on a set of clippings on the revival in the Waituna Valley in the 1880s in the Baptist Archives.
44 Letter of Mrs Jack Johnson, 30 October 1936, Baptist Archives.
45 *Freethought Review* (July 1885), 8.
46 J. E. Crawford, 'Mrs Hampson and the "hot gospel",' in *The Spirit of the Past: Essays on Christianity in New Zealand History*, ed. G. Troughton and H. Morrison (Wellington: Victoria University Press, 2011), 98–111.

47 See her obituary, *New Zealand Methodist Times* (15 June 1912), 14–15; Morley, *History of Methodism* (Wellington: McKee, 1900), 41, 495, 503, 506; Carr, 'My Life Story,' 33; Pybus Papers, Hocken Library, 534/m.
48 *New Zealand Primitive Methodist Magazine* (April 1889), 5; (April 1890), 7; (July 1890), 2; (January 1891), 3. See J. Crawford, 'Prim Preachers,' *Vashti's Voice* 14 (2006): 13–16.
49 'Owaka Baptist Church: Its Beginning and Development,' *Clutha Leader*, 25 November 1936, 3.
50 See the comments of W. J. Williams in his obituary, *New Zealand Methodist* (18 October 1890).
51 Cited in J. B. Chambers, *'A Peculiar People': Congregationalism in New Zealand 1840–1984, Including the Congregational Union of New Zealand 1884–1984* (Wellington: Congregational Union, 1984), 13.
52 'Ladies Benevolent Society,' *New Zealand Herald*, 15 March 1873, 3.
53 Congregational Union, *Yearbook*, 1891, 11.
54 Daniels, *St Mary's in Merivale*, 65, 90.
55 Fry, *Out of the Silence*, 65–74.
56 This was the comment of the Bible Society to England on 20 December 1944, 80-179/41-5, Cambridge University Library.
57 Marie Peters, *Christchurch-St Michael's: A Study in Anglicanism in New Zealand* (Christchurch: University of Canterbury, 1986), 93.
58 'My Predecessor,' *New Zealand Methodist Times* (15 June 1889), 2.
59 Fry, *Out of the Silence*, Chapter 17 analyses Methodist parsons' wives. Hilda Minnie Ford, in *Through Many Doors* (Ilfracombe: Arthur H. Stockwell, 1954), 54, says her husband called her his curate.
60 The Wells organisation's work is discussed in N. W. Derbyshire, 'An Anatomy of Antipodean Anglicanism: The Anglican Church in New Zealand 1945 to 2012' (PhD thesis, Massey University, 2013). For the changing roles of women, see Jane M. R. Simpson, 'Liberal Christianity and the Changing Role of Women in New Zealand Society: A Study of the National Council of Churches and the League of Mothers 1939 to 1959' (PhD thesis, University of Otago, 1992).
61 Charlotte Macdonald, 'Between Religion and Empire: Sarah Selwyn's Aotearoa/New Zealand, Eton and Lichfield, England, c.1840s–1900,' *Journal of the Canadian Historical Association* 19, no. 2 (2008): 43–75; Beverley Reeves, *Looking for Mrs Cowie: The Life and Times of a Colonial Bishop's Wife* (Auckland: The Author, 2005).
62 R. Roberts, *Diary of a Voyage* [1896], 111, 113–14, 117, 142.
63 *New Zealand Evangelist* (1870), 345.
64 V. Johnson and H. Jensen, *A History of Diocesan High School for Girls, Auckland, 1903–1953* (Auckland: Whitcombe & Tombs, 1956); K. Carpenter, *Marsden Women and Their Worlds: A History of Marsden School 1878–2003* (Wellington: Samuel Marsden Collegiate School, 2003).
65 J. Hislop, *History of Knox Church, Dunedin* (Dunedin: John Wilkie & Co. for the Office Bearers, 1892), 32.

66 Margaret Tennant, 'Pakeha Deaconesses and the New Zealand Methodist Mission to Maori, 1893–1940,' *Journal of Religious History* 23, no. 3 (October 1999): 309–26.
67 Sister Dorothy Pointon, *Memoirs of D. M. Pointon (Sister Dorothy) including her work among the Maori people 1939–1953* (Auckland: The Author, 1993).
68 L. Paterson, 'The Rise and Fall of Women Field Workers Within the Presbyterian Māori Mission, 1907–1970,' in *Mana Māori and Christianity*, ed. H. Morrison, L. Paterson, B. Knowles and M. Rae (Wellington: Huia, 2012), 179–204.
69 Alf Peters & John Edie, 'A Few Reminiscences of the Owaka Baptist Church' [1936], 10. Baptist Archives.
70 H. D. Morrison, *Pushing Boundaries: New Zealand Protestants and Overseas Missions 1827–1939* (Dunedin: Otago University Press, 2016), 12–13, 111–17.
71 *Treasury* 5 (1903): 26.
72 *New Zealand Census*, 1921, part VII: Religions (Wellington: Government Printer, 1923), 42.
73 *New Zealand Census*, 1926, vol. VIII: Religious Professions (Wellington: Government Printer), 37
74 Mary Betz, 'Women and the Changing Face of the Christian God,' *Women's Studies Journal* 20, no. 2 (Spring 2006): 23–40.
75 Mike Subritsky in Richard Laurenson, *1902–2002: One Hundred Years: Parish School of St Joseph, Waihi: Ever Faithful* (Waihi: Parish of St Joseph, 2002), 27.
76 See M. Damian, *Sing No Sad Songs for Me: We Religious: Who We Are and What We Are About* (Wellington: A. H. & A. W. Reed, 1971). And see D. Strevens, 'Some Issues Around Writing the Histories of Catholic Religious Congregations for Women in Aotearoa New Zealand,' in *The Spirit of the Past: Essays on Christianity in New Zealand History*, ed. G. Troughton and H. Morrison (Wellington: Victoria University Press, 2011), 69–82; S. Smith, 'Religious Life in Aotearoa New Zealand: A Brief History,' in *A Church in Change: New Zealand Catholics Take Their Bearings*, ed. H. Bergin and S. Smith (Auckland: Accent Publications, 2016), 77–91. Among the many fine accounts, see: Diane Strevens' account of the Brown Joes, D. Strevens, *MacKillop Women: The Sisters of St Joseph of the Sacred Heart Aotearoa New Zealand 1883–2006* (Auckland: David Ling, 2008); M. D. Kirk, *Remembering Your Mercy: Mother Cecelia Maher and the first Sisters of Mercy in New Zealand 1850–1880* (Auckland: Sisters of Mercy, 1998); A. Trotter, *Mary Potter's Little Company of Mary: The New Zealand Experience 1914–2002* (Wellington: Bridget Williams Books for Little Company of Mary, 2003); S. Grant, *Windows on a Women's World: The Dominican Sisters of Aotearoa New Zealand* (Dunedin: Otago University Press, 2017).
77 See Diane Strevens, 'Some Issues Around Writing the Histories of Catholic Religious Congregations for Women in Aotearoa New Zealand,' in *The Spirit of the Past: Essays on Christianity in New Zealand History*, ed. Geoffrey Troughton and Hugh Morrison (Wellington: Victoria University Press, 2011), 69–82.
78 Hislop, *History of Knox Church, Dunedin*, 32.
79 *Lyttelton Times*, 28 August 1893, 3.
80 See J. M. A. Tuck, 'The Devil's Half-acre, 1900–1910: The Work of the Dunedin City

Council and St Andrew's Presbyterian Church in the Slum Area Known as the Devil's Half-acre' (MA thesis, University of Otago, 1983); M. Tennant, 'Sisterly Ministrations: The Social Work of Protestant Deaconesses in New Zealand,' *New Zealand Journal of History* 32, no. 1 (1998): 3–22.

81 K.-M. Piercy, 'Patient and Enduring Love: The Deaconess Movement, 1900–1920,' in *Building God's Own Country: Historical Essays on Religions in New Zealand*, ed. J. Stenhouse and J. Thomson (Dunedin: University of Otago Press, 2004), 196–208.

82 *Outlook* (3 August 1901), 8; (10 August 1901), 37; (14 September 1901), 35.

83 M. Evans, 'Women and Ministry and Leadership in the Baptist Churches of New Zealand,' *New Zealand Journal of Baptist Research* 9 (2004): 49–71.

84 M. Tennant, '"Sometimes When My Heart Was Sad with Snubs and Coldness . . ." Narrative of Maori Mission Work,' *History Now: Te Pae Tawhito o Te Wa* 7, no. 3 (2001): 14–18.

85 A. Matthews, 'An Easy Passage? An Anglican Female Priesthood in New Zealand,' in *Building God's Own Country*, ed. J. Stenhouse and J. Thomson, 209–22.

86 Ian Fraser, *'Neither Male nor Female': A Study of the Place of Women in the Church* (Christchurch: Presbyterian Bookroom, 1950), 13–14.

87 See G. Lewis, *Kept by the Power: Insights and Memories from My Life* (Christchurch: Hazard Press, 1999).

88 M. McClure, *Saving the City: The History of the Order of the Good Shepherd and the Community of the Holy Name in Auckland, 1894–2000* (Auckland: David Ling, 2002); L. Strahan, *Out of the Silence: A Study of a Religious Community for Women: The Community of the Holy Name* (Melbourne: Oxford University Press, 1988); R. Fry, *Community of the Sacred Name: A Centennial History* (Christchurch: Community of the Sacred Name, 1993).

89 *Marlborough Express*, 7 December 1912, 2.

90 Peters, *Christchurch-St Michael's*, 88, 93.

91 Anne O'Brien, '"A Church Full of Men": Masculinism and the Church in Australian History,' *Australian Historical Studies* 25, no. 100 (1993): 439.

92 Ibid.

93 'Clarence Eaton's Address to the Annual North Canterbury Synod,' *New Zealand Methodist Times* (3 December 1937), 246.

94 London Churchwarden, 'Heartiness in Public Worship,' in *Church Quarterly* (July 1866), 9. For Bishop Julius see G. and A. Elworthy, *A Power in the Land: Churchill Julius, 1847–1938* (Christchurch: Private publication, 1971), 109–14.

95 Presbyterian General Assembly State of Religion Report 1908, 64–65.

96 Louise Mitchell, 'Where the River Widens,' *New Zealand Methodist Times* (29 May 1915), 4.

97 'Melanesia,' *Evening Post*, 15 January 1914, 2.

98 Guy D. Thornton, *With the Anzacs in Cairo: The Tale of a Great Fight* (London, 1917). See also his work *The Wowser* (London, 1916).

99 M. King, 'Contradictions', in *One of the Boys? Changing Views of Masculinity in New Zealand*, ed. M. King (Auckland: Heinemann, 1988), 135–155 at 143.

100 *White Ribbon* (December 1896), 2–3, for example.
101 'The Temperance Crusade,' *New Zealand Methodist Times* (27 April 1899), 4.
102 Cited in P. Grimshaw, *Women's Suffrage in New Zealand* (Auckland: Auckland University Press, 1972), 57.
103 Daniels, *St Mary's in Merivale*, 119, 139.
104 P. P. Cahill, *St. Mary's Parish, Blenheim, Marlborough: Being an Account of One Hundred Years' Development 1864–1964* (Wellington: For the Parish, 1964), 65.
105 O'Brien, 'A Church Full of Men,' 449–51.
106 'The Rev H. S. Woolcombe,' *West Coast Times*, 1 February 1910, 1. See H. Le Couteur, 'Where Are All the Men: An Attempt by the Anglican Church in Australia to Counter Secularisation at the Beginning of the Twentieth Century,' in *Secularisation: New Historical Perspectives*, ed. C. Hartney (Newcastle upon Tyne: Cambridge Scholars Press, 2014), 68–89.
107 See 'Church work,' *Evening Post*, 17 April 1914, 4.
108 See Anglican Diocese of Auckland, *Yearbook*, 1965, 23, 37, 89.
109 J. E. Cookson, *Upper Riccarton Methodist Church: A Centennial Retrospect 1886–1986* (Christchurch: Upper Riccarton Methodist Church, 1986), 24.
110 See H. D. Morrison, '"It Is Our Bounden Duty": The Emergence of the New Zealand Protestant Missionary Movement 1868–1926' (PhD thesis, Massey University, 2004).
111 H. L. Fiebig, *Cuba Street Methodist Church Palmerston North New Zealand: Jubilee Souvenir 1893–1943* (Palmerston North: The Church [Kerslake & Billens Print], 1943), 14.
112 Fry, *Out of the Silence*, 114–25; Alice Henderson, *Women's Work for Missions: The Story of the Beginnings and Growth of the Presbyterian Women's Missionary Union of New Zealand* (Christchurch: Presbyterian Bookroom, 1939); Vera L. McLennan, *These Seventy-Five Years: A Short History of the Baptist Women's Missionary Union* (Palmerston North: BWMU, 1978). I have explained the development of national religious organisations in Peter J. Lineham, 'Finding a Space for Evangelicalism: Evangelical Youth Movements in New Zealand,' in *Voluntary Religion, Studies in Church History*, vol. 29, ed. W. J. Sheils and Diana Wood (Oxford: Blackwell, 1986).
113 For example, G. Urquhart et al. *100 by the Grace of God; Somervell Memorial Presbyterian Church 100 Years of Grace 1905–2005* (Auckland: Somervell Church, 2005), 13.
114 See, for example, *New Zealand Methodist Times* (May 1965), 25.
115 Anglican Diocesan of Auckland, *Yearbook*, 1961, 125.
116 Anglican Diocese of Auckland, *Yearbook*, 1972, 20.
117 See *Treasury* 69 (1967): 16.
118 Maurice Andrew, *Set in a Long Place: A Life from North to South* (Christchurch: Hazard Press, 1999), 257.
119 For example see the correspondence in *Church & People* (May 1965), 15.
120 Anglican Diocese of Auckland, *Yearbook*, 1978, 84.
121 *New Zealand Methodist Times* (November 1963), 228.
122 See Helen Arndt and J. D. Salmond, *Outlook* (June 1962), 3, 13; Alexa Fraser in ibid. (14 July 1962), 13, 25–26 (the latter a letter by six writers from the PWMU).

123 Christine Cheyne, *Made in God's Image: A Project Researching Sexism in the Catholic Church in Aotearoa (New Zealand)* (Wellington: Catholic Commission for Justice, 1990).
124 S. Smith, *Call to Mission: The Story of the Mission Sisters of Aotearoa New Zealand and Samoa* (Auckland: David Ling, 2010).
125 *Reaper* 17 (July 1939), 132.
126 *New Zealand Baptist* (November 1912), 25–26, cited in S. Hewlett, '"Adam's Helper": Women's Roles in Evangelical Churches in New Zealand from Colonial Times to the End of the 20th Century' (MA thesis, Massey University, 2004), 20.
127 *Outlook* (17 April 1940), 10–11.
128 See 'Clarence Eaton's Address to the Annual North Canterbury Synod,' *New Zealand Methodist Times* (3 December 1937), 246.
129 Hewlett, '"Adam's Helper",' 24.
130 *New Zealand Methodist Times* (19 February 1944), 255.
131 *Methodist Annual Conference*, 1944, 80, 87.
132 For example, P. M. Burns, *The New Zealand Laity Today* (Catholic Coordinating Committee, 1969), where Dorothy Smith of the Catholic Women's league opposed married women working.
133 Daniels, *St Mary's in Merivale*, 173.
134 See Jan Jamieson letter in *Outlook* (10 March 1962), 14. Defended, ibid., (21 April 1962), 30; *New Zealand Methodist Times* (December 1963), 276.
135 Fraser, 'Neither Male Nor Female', 11–12.
136 Laws and Regulations of the Methodist Church Ministry 111, 16.
137 Stuart, 'Unrepresented', 3.
138 SU Executive Committee, Minutes, 18 November 1965.
139 P. J. Lineham, *No Ordinary Union: The Story of the Scripture Union, Children's Special Service Mission and Crusader Movement of New Zealand 1880–1980* (Wellington: Scripture Union in New Zealand, 1980), 148.
140 See P. J. Lineham, 'The Gender Issue in New Zealand Evangelical History,' in *Reconsidering Gender: Evangelical Perspectives*, ed. M. Habets and B. Wood (Eugene, OR: Pickwick Publications [Wipf & Stock], 2011), 75–104.
141 R. E. Low, 'The Debate on the United Nations Convention for the Elimination of All Forms of Discrimination Against Women: Motivated by Fear or a Clash of Ideologies?' *Stimulus* 13, no. 4 (2005): 23–30.
142 See https://www.aboverubies.org.au/about.
143 P. Lineham, *Destiny: The Life and Times of a Self-made Apostle* (Auckland: Penguin, 2013), 131–32, 205–206.
144 See I. Vodanovich, 'Women's Place in God's World,' *New Zealand Women's Studies Journal* 2, no. 1 (1985): 68–79.
145 See Lineham, *Destiny*, 132 and footnotes on p. 282.
146 T. T. Mailiko, 'The Hierarchy of Voice: The Context of the Congregational Christian Church of Samoa (CCCS) in New Zealand' (MTh thesis, University of Auckland, 2000), 206, 257.

147 P. Budge, *Legacy of Faith 1926–1996: A Chronicle of St Stephens and St Aidans Presbyterian Churches Lower Hutt* (Lower Hutt: St Stephens and St Aidans, 1997), 73.
148 Anglican Diocese of Auckland, *Yearbook*, 1981, 93.
149 Anglican Diocese of Auckland, *Yearbook*, 1984, 25–26.
150 R. E. Low, 'A Magnificent Tapestry of Women: "Women and Ministry Conferences" and the Developing Woman-Church Movement in Aotearoa 1980–1994' (MA thesis, Massey University, 1999).
151 'Association of Pentecostal Churches,' *New Zealand Times* (1976), 1.

Chapter Ten: Children and Young People and Church

1   G. Bateman, 'Signs and Graces: Remembering Religion in Childhood in Southern Dunedin, 1920–1950' (PhD thesis, University of Otago, 2013).
2   'Jubilee Days,' *Tablet*, 10 February 1921, 25.
3   P. P. Cahill, *St Mary's Parish, Blenheim, Marlborough: Being an Account of One Hundred Years' Development 1864–1964* (Wellington: For the Parish, 1964), 31.
4   G. Troughton, 'Religion, Churches and Childhood in New Zealand, c.1900–1940,' *New Zealand Journal of History* 40, no. 1 (2006): 44–46.
5   Cahill, *St Mary's Parish*, 59.
6   N. Daniels, *St Mary's in Merivale: A History of Merivale and the Anglican Parish of Merivale in Christchurch, New Zealand and the Ministry of its Fifteen Vicars from 1866 to 2000* (Christchurch: Merivale Parish, 2004), 26.
7   W. M. Ryburn, *A City Set on a Hill: The Story of St David's Presbyterian Church Auckland 1864–1964* (Auckland: Len Bolton & Co., 1964), 37.
8   New Zealand Census for the listed years.
9   J. Buller, 'Opening of Canterbury Museum,' *New Zealand Wesleyan* (1 July 1874), 117. *The Observer*, 18 September 1915, 2.
10 Frank Hanson, *The Sunday School in New Zealand Methodism* (Auckland: Wesley Historical Society (NZ), 1998), 15.
11 Marie Peters, *Christchurch-St Michael's: A Study in Anglicanism in New Zealand* (Christchurch: University of Canterbury, 1986), 84.
12 Joan Mary Bythell, *The Golden Jubilee of St. Christopher's Sunday School Redwoodtown 1909–1959 with an Account of the Years 1905–1908* (Blenheim: The Vestry, 1959), 54–56.
13 J. A. Pittman in *Church & People* (April 1954): 6.
14 Nuda Verba, a Methodist, complained of this in *New Zealand Wesleyan* (January 1883), 194.
15 See the letter by 'A Quondam Teacher,' *New Zealand Wesleyan* (30 April 1872), 58.
16 Hanson, *The Sunday School in New Zealand Methodism*, 37.
17 D. S. Keen, 'Feeding the Lambs: The Influence of Sunday Schools on the Socialization of Children in Otago and Southland, 1848–1901' (PhD thesis, University of Otago, 1999).
18 Ibid., chapters 8–9, 164–230.
19 H. Morrison, 'Settler Childhood, Protestant Christianity and Emotions in Colonial New Zealand, 1880s–1920s,' in *Childhood, Youth and Emotions in Modern History*, ed. S.

Olsen (London: Palgrave Macmillan, 2015), 76–94.
20 See A. Harris, *The Beauty of Your House: The Nelson Catholic Parish 1844–1994* (Nelson: St Mary's Parish, 1994), 87.
21 A. Sangster, 'Anglican Reaction to the 1877 Education Act' (MA thesis, Massey University, 1984).
22 G. Urquhart et al., *100 By the Grace of God: Somervell Memorial Presbyterian Church 100 Years of Grace 1905–2005* (Auckland: Somervell Church, 2005), 17.
23 K. Baljit et al., *Empire, Education, and Indigenous Childhoods: Nineteenth-century Missionary Infant Schools in Three British Colonies* (Farnham, and Burlington, VT: Ashgate, 2014), 186–224; L. Prochner et al. '"The Blessings of Civilisation": Nineteenth-century Missionary Infant Schools for Young Native Children in Three Colonial Settings — India, Canada and New Zealand 1820s–1840s,' *Paedagogica Historica: International Journal of the History of Education* 45, nos 1–2 (2009): 83–102.
24 L. Paterson, 'The Rise and Fall of Women Field Workers Within the Presbyterian Māori Mission, 1907–1970,' in *Mana Māori and Christianity*, ed. H. Morrison, L. Paterson, B. Knowles and M. Rae (Wellington: Huia, 2012), 179–204.
25 Wendy Scott in *Our Place, Our Voice: Explorations in Contextual Theology: Women in the Anglican Church of Aotearoa New Zealand and Polynesia*, eds. E. Fairbrother and J. P. Te Paa (Auckland: Council for Anglican Women's Studies, 2012), 17–18.
26 A. MacLeod, *The First Hundred Years: A Centennial History of Oxford Terrace Baptist Church Christchurch 1863–1963* (Christchurch: The Church, 1963), 62.
27 Urquhart et al. *100 By the Grace of God*, 17.
28 W. E. Morris, *The Centennial History of St Peter's Presbyterian Church and the Presbyterian Movement in the Western Bay of Plenty* (Tauranga: Editorial Committee, 1978), 53, 84, 109.
29 'First Communion at St Mary's Church, Napier', *Tablet*, 17 December 1880, 11.
30 'Church work,' *Evening Post*, 17 April 1914, 4.
31 G. Bateman, 'Signs and Graces: Children's Experiences of Confirmation in New Zealand, 1920s–1950s,' in *Creating Religious Childhoods in Anglo-world and British Colonial Contexts, 1800–1950*, ed. H. Morrison and M. C. Martin (London: Routledge, 2017), 201–21.
32 J. B. Bennett, S*teps in Faith: A History of All Saints' Church Wanganui East 1909–1984* (Wanganui: The Parish, 1987), 50–51.
33 Anglican Diocese of Auckland, *Yearbook*, 1962, 22.
34 Diocesan Youth Council, Anglican Diocese of Auckland, *Yearbook*, 1961, 44–46.
35 Anglican Diocese of Auckland, *Yearbook*, 1979, 115. The first instance seems to be Anglican Diocese of Auckland, *Yearbook*, 1971, 26. Also ibid., 1970, 37.
36 See J. Dawson, *A Radical Theology of Baptism: A Critical Investigation of Baptism as the Key Element in the Ecclesiology of the Anglican Church in Aotearoa, New Zealand and Polynesia* (Porirua: The Author, 2011).
37 See John Silvester comments, *New Zealand Methodist Times* (June 1963), 58–59; letter in ibid. (October 1963), 205.

38　See for example *Believer's Magazine* (Kilmarnoch), 7 (a response to a question from G.F.B. of New Zealand); *New Zealand Baptist* (1916), 103.
39　V. H. Hamill, Maerewhenua Goldfield (MS papers, 2347, Wtu).
40　*New Zealand Wesleyan* (August 1881), 208–209.
41　Anglican Diocese of Auckland, *Yearbook*, 1983, 24; N. Derbyshire, *Serving the Community: The Story of Pukekohe's Anglican Parish* (Christchurch: Wily Publications, 2016), 188.
42　Chris Brickell's *Teenagers: A New Zealand History* (in press, 2017) should illuminate this for New Zealand. Hugh Morrison has pointed me to two works on the parallel Australian phenomenon: M. Bellanta, *Larrikins: A History* (St Lucia: University of Queensland Press, 2012), and S. Sleight, *Young People and the Shaping of Public Space in Melbourne, 1870–1914* (London & New York: Routledge, 2016; Farnham: Ashgate, 2013).
43　'Larrakinism Rampant,' *Auckland Star*, 16 April 1886, and various other references.
44　*Auckland Star*, 19 March 1887, 8.
45　See for example *Auckland Star*, 8 July 1887, 4.
46　For example, C. H. Yolland, *Reaper* (July 1942), 104–105.
47　Editorial, *Primitive Methodist Magazine* 1 (1889), 9.
48　B. McLennan, *YMCA New Zealand: The First 125 Years* (Wellington: National Council of YMCAs of NZ, 1981); C. Taylor, *Body, Mind and Spirit: YMCA Auckland Celebrating 150 years 1855–2005* (Auckland: Reed, 2005).
49　'Churchmen's Club,' *Press*, 13 May 1890, 5.
50　S. Coney, *Every Girl: A Social History of the Women and the YWCA in Auckland 1885–1985* (Auckland: YWCA, 1986); H. K. Lovell-Smith, *The Story of the Christchurch Young Women's Christian Association: A Venture with Youth from 1883–1894 – 1901–1960* (Christchurch: Christchurch YWCA, 1961).
51　'The Girls Friendly Society,' *Church Gazette* (December 1884), 118.
52　*New Zealand Baptist* 9 (1892), 119, 154, 156. See M. N. Garing, 'Four Square for Christ: The Presbyterian Bible Class movement 1902–1972: Its Background, Its Rise, Its Influence and Its Decline' (MA thesis, Victoria University of Wellington, 1986), 49.
53　*Proceedings of the Synod of the Presbyterian Church of Otago and Southland*, 1895, 39.
54　'Conference of Christian Workers,' *Auckland Star*, 19 March 1887, 8.
55　*Zealandia*, 25 March 1937, 2e.
56　As cited in M. E. Hoare, 'Training in Manliness' (DipEd thesis, Massey University, 1979), 6.
57　M. E. Hoare, *Faces of Boyhood: An Informal Pictorial Record of the Boys' Brigade in New Zealand 1886–1982* (Wellington: Boys Brigade, 1982), 14–16.
58　Ibid., 20–21.
59　Ibid., 17–21; Methodist Church, *Minutes of Annual Conference*, 1959, 86.
60　For the general trend, see J. A. Mangan and J. Walvin, ed., *Manliness and Morality: Middle-class Masculinity in Britain and America 1800–1914* (Manchester: Manchester University Press, 1987).
61　T. Brooking, 'Wheels,' in *One of the Boys? Changing Views of Masculinity in New*

Zealand, ed. M. King (Auckland: Heinemann, 1988), 166.
62 For the Crusader movement see P. J. Lineham, *No Ordinary Union: The Story of the Scripture Union, Children's Special Service Mission and Crusader Movement of New Zealand, 1880–1980* (Wellington: Scripture Union in New Zealand, 1980), 44, 72, 75, 76, 122–24.
63 See, for example, 'Public Meeting, Congregational Union,' *Outlook* (29 February 1908), 36.
64 C. Sage, 'Jubilee History of the Young Men's Presbyterian Bible Class Union of New Zealand', unpublished MS, Presbyterian Archives, 1952, 29.
65 E. P. Blamires, *Youth Movement: The Story of the Rise and Development of the Christian Youth Movement of the Churches of New Zealand — As Seen By a Methodist* (Auckland: Forward Books with Wesley Historical Society, 1952), 1–20, 44–45.
66 Ibid., 94–96.
67 'Religious Youth Groups,' in G. Woolford and M. Law, *Youth in Perspective: A Study of Youth Services in New Zealand* (Wellington: National Youth Council of New Zealand, 1980), 175; Garing, 'Four Square for Christ'.
68 For example, *Church & People* (December 1950), 7; *Outlook* (7 April 1962), 7. They were defended in *Outlook* (21 April 1962), 30.
69 *Outlook* (May 1962), 32a reports an experiment along these lines in Waverley.
70 Bythell, *The Golden Jubilee of St. Christopher's Sunday School Redwoodtown*, 55.
71 'Retiring Address,' *New Zealand Methodist Times* (7 March 1914), 1–4.
72 Congregational Union, *Yearbook*, 1899, 18.
73 See Peters, *Christchurch-S. Michael's*, 88–89.
74 M. J. Hanrahan, *The Warm Wind of Faith: A History of the Catholic Church in Ashburton* (Ashburton: Higgins & Co. for the Parish, 1981), 30.
75 See for example *New Zealand Baptist* (April 1894), 49.
76 *Christian Outlook* (18 July 1896), 296–97.
77 See 'Local Preacher,' letter, *New Zealand Methodist Times* (1 September 1888), 8.
78 J. T. Pinfold, *Fifty Years in Maoriland* (London: Epworth Press, 1978), 62.
79 W. Colenso to the Editor, *Hawke's Bay Herald*, 12 June 1890, 3.
80 Troup to the Editor, *Outlook* (May 1903), 5.
81 Wm B. Scott, 'Athletics, Football and their Application to Christianity,' *Outlook* (April 1905), 23.
82 *State of Religion Report, PCNZ Proceedings of General Assembly*, 89–91.
83 'Clean Sport,' *Outlook* (September 1905), 21–22.
84 *Evening Post*, 4 July 1945.
85 Garing, 'Four Square for Christ,' 70–71.
86 Allan Davidson, *St Luke's Hockey Club, 2013*. [Notes provided by Allan Davidson.]
87 *Church & People* (August 1953), 7.
88 For example, see 'The Canterbury Y.M.B.C. Easter camp,' *New Zealand Methodist Times* (27 April 1918), 7.
89 Hanrahan, *The Warm Wind of Faith*, 30.
90 *Reaper* (March 1943), 8.

91 *New Zealand Evangelist* (June 1850), 397–407.
92 *Echo*, 21 October 1882, 2.
93 *Echo*, 28 April 1883, 2.
94 *Outlook* (June 1901), 36; (13 July 1901), 35–36; (July 1901), 6.
95 'Opunake,' *Taranaki Daily News*, 13 February 1917.
96 *Tablet*, 12 November 1941, 17; see P. Lawlor, *The Demanding God: Some Boyhood Recollections* (Dunedin: New Zealand Tablet, 1972), 37, 79.
97 See 'Letters to the Editor,' *Otago Daily Times*, 28 November 1924, 8.
98 *Proceedings of the General Assembly of the Presbyterian Church*, 1939, 55–56.
99 Minutes of the Methodist Annual Conference, 1938, 52–57.
100 Minutes of the Methodist Annual Conference, 1937, 50–51.
101 Minutes of the Methodist Annual Conference, 1938, 53.
102 Minutes of the Methodist Annual Conference, 1938, 54–57.
103 Minutes of the Methodist Annual Conference, 1943, 55; ibid., 1944, 59; ibid., 1945, 60; ibid., 1946, 59, 61; ibid., 1958, 56; Laws, clause 296, 46.
104 Lineham, *No Ordinary Union*, 72–73.
105 R. A. Matthews, *100 Years on Emerald Hill: A History of the Epsom Presbyterian Church* (Auckland: Epsom Presbyterian Church, 2006), 48.
106 Bythell, *The Golden Jubilee of St. Christopher's Sunday School Redwoodtown*, 55.
107 A. H. Reed, 'Church and Sunday School,' *New Zealand Methodist Times* (24 January 1931), Supplement, 4.
108 Henry Ryan, 'The Church and Our Age,' *New Zealand Methodist Times* (27 December 1930), 3.
109 For example, Goulstone et al., *Opawa Baptist Church: Our Centenary: From Then Until Now, 1911–2011* (Christchurch: Opawa Baptist Church Outreach Press, 2011), 44.
110 Scott Thomson, *Church Standing Tall: A People's History of St John's in the City 1853–2003* (Wellington: Steele Roberts Ltd, 2003), 119–123. See also Patsy Martin, *Knox Alive! A Celebration of 150 Years of the Presbyterian Church in the Hutt Valley* (Lower Hutt: Knox-St Columba Presbyterian Church, 2002), 93.
111 See the comments in Lorna Jenkins, 'Where Are We Going on Saturday Night?' *New Zealand Baptist* (October 1964), 258–59.
112 *Outlook* (June 1963), 18–19; (July 1962), 3–4.
113 Bennett, *Steps in Faith*, 55, 100.
114 'Nota Bene,' in *Outlook* (May 1963), 31.
115 R. A. Lowe, 'Looking for a Youth,' *Outlook* (18 April 1964), 6–7.
116 See Rory Sweetman, *Spire on the Hill: A History of St Andrew's Church in the Epsom District 1846–1996* (Auckland: St Andrew's Parish, 1996), 163–64.
117 *Outlook* (7 March 1964), 30.
118 Ewing Stevens, *Sunday Alive: A Story of Youth and the Church* (Dunedin: John McIndoe, 1970).
119 Ibid.
120 Woolford and Law, *Youth in Perspective*, 176, 177–79.

121 Much of this is based on interviews conducted in the 1980s with Cecil Marshall and Ken Wright.
122 Woolford and Law, *Youth in Perspective*, 179–86.
123 *Challenge Weekly*, 13 May 1967, 5. See Leah Haines, 'The Gospel According to Ian Grant,' *New Zealand Herald*, 6 August 2006. http://www.nzherald.co.nz/nz/news/article.cfm?c_id=1&objectid=10394825
124 See N. Reid, 'A New World Through a New Youth: The Life and Death of the Catholic Youth Movement in New Zealand,' in *The Spirit of the Past: Essays on Christianity in New Zealand History*, ed. G. Troughton and H. Morrison (Wellington: Victoria University Press, 2011), 156–68.
125 Blamires, *Youth Movement*.
126 *Outlook* (19 March 1966), 1.
127 *New Zealand Baptist* (September 1960), 222; see also (May 1963), 117.
128 *New Zealand Baptist* (November 1962), 302 and (August 1964), 213.
129 *Challenge* (18 September 1965), 3; (25 September 1965), 4, 6, 7.
130 *New Zealand Baptist* (November 1965), 302.
131 New Zealand Baptist (January 1966).
132 *Challenge*, May 20, 1967, 7, interview with John Hawkesby. I have been given access to John Hawkesby's files. One cutting from 1968: 'Drift Inn Venture Proves Popular by Eileen Johnson' [*Auckland Star*?].
133 *Challenge*, 19 April 1969, 12.
134 *Challenge*, 20 May 1967, 7.
135 *Challenge*, 19 April 1969, 12.
136 Hanrahan, *The Warm Wind of Faith*, 67.
137 Jemima Tiatia, *Caught Between Cultures: A New Zealand-born Pacific Island Perspective* (Auckland: Christian Research Association, 1998).
138 Goulstone et al., *Opawa Baptist Church*, 79–80.
139 See U. F. Nokise, 'A History of the Pacific Islanders' Congregational Church in New Zealand 1943–1969' (MTh thesis, University of Otago, 1978), 53.

Chapter Eleven: Status, Hierarchy and Faith

1 H. R. Niebuhr, *Christ and Culture* (New York: Harper & Row, 1951); H. R. Niebuhr, *The Social Sources of Denominationalism* (New York: New American Library, 1929, 1957).
2 B. R. Wilson, *Religion in Secular Society* (London: Penguin, 1968); B. R. Wilson, *Religion in Sociological Perspective* (Oxford: Oxford University Press, 1982).
3 See, for example, K. S. Inglis, *Churches and the Working Classes in Victorian Britain* (London: Routledge Kegan Paul, 1963).
4 John Stenhouse, 'God, the Devil and Gender,' in *Sites of Gender: Women, Men and Modernity in Southern Dunedin, 1890–1939*, ed. B. Brookes, A. Cooper and R. Law (Auckland: Auckland University Press, 2003), 313–47; J. Stenhouse, 'Christianity, Women, and the Working Class: A Dunedin Case Study 1885–1935,' in *Christianity, Modernity and Culture: New Perspectives on New Zealand History*, ed. J. Stenhouse and

G. A. Wood (Adelaide: ATF Press, 2005), 157–79; J. Stenhouse, 'Christianity, Gender, and the Working Class in Southern Dunedin, 1880–1940,' *Journal of Religious History* 30, no. 1 (2006): 18–44.

5   John Stenhouse, Alison Clarke and I are working on a joint project on this subject.
6   *New Zealand Evangelist* (September 1848), 63–66.
7   *Auckland Star*, 17 April 1882, 2. The minister who spoke, the Rev. Monro, forgot that large numbers would have attended Newmarket Methodist congregations and the Catholic church in Parnell; nevertheless, churchgoing does seem very low in the district.
8   *Observer*, 29 April 1882, 99.
9   'Notes and Comments,' *Outlook* (29 June 1901), 25.
10 For example James Buller in *New Zealand Wesleyan* (1 January 1877), 10.
11 Y. M. Wilkie, *Weaving Vision, Heritage and Hope: 150 Years of the Presbyterian Synod of Otago and Southland 1866–2016* (Dunedin: Presbyterian Synod of Otago and Southland, 2016), 11.
12 E. R. Simmons, *Pompallier: Prince of Bishops* (Auckland: C. P. C. Publishing, 1984), 67–71.
13 'Old St Mary's', *Timaru Herald*, 20 August 1880, 3.
14 Barbara Harper, *The Harvest: History of the Catholic Church in Timaru 1869–1969* (Timaru: Centennial Committee, 1969), 80.
15 For example 'Bishop Selwyn's Bull,' *Nelson Examiner*, 24 June 1848, 65.
16 N. W. Derbyshire, 'The "English Church" Revisited: Issues of Expansion and Identity in a Settler Church: The Anglican Church in New Zealand 1891–1945' (MA thesis, Massey University, 2006); N. W. Derbyshire, 'An Anatomy of Antipodean Anglicanism: The Anglican Church in New Zealand 1945 to 2012' (PhD thesis, Massey University, 2013), 155–58.
17 Geoffrey M. R. Haworth, *Marching as to War? The Anglican Church in New Zealand During World War II* (Christchurch: Wily Publications, 2008), 45.
18 Cited in C. Brown, '"We Should Settle in New Zealand": H. J. C. Harper: Colonist and Bishop,' in *Shaping a Colonial Church: Bishop Harper and the Anglican Diocese of Christchurch 1856–1890*, ed. C. Brown, M. Peters and J. Teal (Christchurch: Canterbury University Press, 2006), 35–58 at 56.
19 Ibid.
20 K. Orr-Nimmo, '"Who Am I That Should Undergo This Great Work": Bishop Harper's Clergy', in *Shaping a Colonial Church: Bishop Harper and the Anglican Diocese of Christchurch 1856–1890*, ed. C. Brown, M. Peters and J. Teal (Christchurch: Canterbury University Press, 2006), 83–110 at 86.
21 Brown, '"We Should Settle in New Zealand"', 56.
22 'Letter of Cantankerous to the Editor,' *Dominion*, 15 June 1915, 8 (to which the editor offered a defence of the title).
23 For example, R. Hattaway and M. Willis, *When All the Saints: Celebrating 150 Years of All Saints Church — Howick* (Auckland: The Parish, 1997), 72.
24 *New Zealand Herald*, 20 October 1875, 2.
25 Cited in P. P. Cahill, *St. Mary's Parish, Blenheim, Marlborough: Being an Account of One*

Hundred Years' Development 1864–1964 (Wellington: For the Parish, 1964), 27.
26 Derbyshire, 'An Anatomy of Antipodean Anglicanism,' 158–60, 269–70.
27 Ibid., 159–60.
28 Advertisement for visit to St James, Lower Hutt, *Church & People* (October 1960), 16.
29 C. Brown, *Vision & Reality: Christchurch's Cathedral in the Square* (Christchurch: Cathedral Chapter, 2000), 116.
30 'General Notes on Episcopal Dress and Ornaments,' Archives of the Anglican Diocese of Auckland, thought to have been prepared by Bishop Simkin, c.1960.
31 Title of '"My Lord" not wanted,' *Church & People* (November 1968), 1.
32 Colin Brown, *Dictionary of New Zealand Biography*, vol. 5, ed. Claudia Orange (Auckland: Auckland University Press, 2000), 426–27.
33 40th General Synod, 1972, 168.
34 *Church & People* (May 31, 1968), 9.
35 'Primary Charge at the second session of the seventeenth session of the diocese of Auckland, 1903,' Stout collection http://nzetc.victoria.ac.nz/tm/scholarly/tei-Stout77-t4-body-d1-d14.html
36 H. Anderson, *The Anglican Church in Auckland and Its Lands* (Auckland: The Diocese, 1977), 30. (Bound copy in Auckland Diocesan Archives.)
37 *Press*, 2 June 1927, 4, photo at City Library. http://anglicanliving.co.nz/wp-content/uploads/2016/03/290415-A-brief-history-of-Bishopspark.pdf
38 http://www.stuff.co.nz/the-press/news/70576918/demolition-order-for-historic-bishopscourt
39 *Wellington Independent*, 27 May 1859, 3.
40 https://osphistory.org/2016/08/03/the-people-of-bishopscourt/
41 http://www.heritage.org.nz/the-list/details/7475
42 Heritage New Zealand, http://www.heritage.org.nz/the-list/details/2147
43 http://www.heritage.org.nz/the-list/details/555; see *Tablet*, 13 April 1894, 6.
44 D. G. Hamilton, *College! A History of Christ's College* (Christchurch: Caxton Press for Christ's College Board of Governors, 1996); B. and D. Hamilton, *Never a Footstep Back: A History of the Wanganui Collegiate School, 1854–2003* (Wanganui: Board of Trustees, Wanganui Collegiate School, 2003); B. Hamilton, *O Floreat Semper: The History of King's College, 1895–1995* (Auckland: Board of Governors, King's College, 1995).
45 John Barrington, *Dictionary of New Zealand Biography*, vol. 2, ed. Claudia Orange (Wellington: Bridget William Books, 1993), 539.
46 'Synod Discussion,' *Auckland Star*, 22 October 1918, 6.
47 *New Zealand Methodist Times* (7 March 1891).
48 John Davison, 'Church Schools, Do We Value Them?' *Church & People* (May 1960), 8.
49 V. Johnson and H. Jensen, *A History of Diocesan High School for Girls, Auckland, 1903–1953* (Auckland: Whitcombe & Tombs, 1956), 11.
50 Ibid., 49.
51 J. Sharfe and J. Teal, *We Kindle This Light: A History of St Margaret's College* (Christchurch: Caxton Press for St Margaret's College, 2010).

52 John Ross, 'Leading Libber Hits Out at Society's Double Standards,' *Church & People* (8 May 1982), 6.
53 *Te Karere* (October 1935), 375.
54 G. McLean, *The Governors: New Zealand's Governors and Governors-General* (Dunedin: Otago University Press, 2006), 131, 245, 263, 269.
55 See, for example, *Zealandia*, 8 July 1937, 8.
56 *Press*, 22 July 1933, 2.
57 https://marsden.ultranet.school.nz/WebSpace/1024/; for references see *Evening Post*, 22 May 1937, 18; 6 May 1941, 4; *Church & People* (June 1954), 14.
58 'Reunion Ball,' *New Zealand Herald*, 8 July 1940, 20.
59 See *Church & People* (October 1952), 11.
60 *Church & People* (September 1952), 9.
61 *Press*, 24 August 1939, 2.
62 See *Press*, 16 July 1932, 2.
63 Anglican Diocese of Auckland, *Yearbook*, 1961, 44. For Catholics, see *Zealandia*, 8 July 1937, 8.
64 Stenhouse in *Christianity, Modernity and Culture*, 165.
65 K. Pickens, 'Denomination, Nationality and Class in Canterbury,' *Journal of Religious History* 15, no. 1 (1988): 131.
66 See 'The Clergy and the Poor,' *Observer*, 5 October 1889, 9.
67 See the analysis by C. Van der Krogt, '"Typical of the New Zealand Occupational Distribution"? A Reconsideration of Catholic Interwar Employment Patterns,' *Journal of New Zealand Studies* n.s. vol. 2–3 (2003): 173–96.
68 *Tablet*, 14 February 1940, 5.
69 B. F. Cadogan, '"Lace Curtain Catholics": The Catholic Bourgeoisie of the Diocese of Dunedin, 1900–1920' (BA Hons diss., University of Otago, 1984).
70 Charles Chandler, 'The Religion of England,' *Auckland Star*, 18 March 1939, 6.
71 See Stenhouse, 'Christianity, Gender, and the Working Class in Southern Dunedin,' 31.
72 Pickens, 'Denomination, Nationality and Class in Canterbury,' 130.
73 M. Peters, *Christchurch-St Michael's: A Study in Anglicanism in New Zealand* (Christchurch: University of Canterbury, 1986), 45.
74 Pickens, 'Denomination, Nationality and Class in Canterbury,' 131.
75 'Layman,' in *Church Chronicle* (2 September 1890), 167.
76 See Hilary Reid, *St Mark's Anglican Church Remuera: The Story of a Parish 1847–1981* (Auckland: Vestry of St Mark's, 1982), 16, 18, 23, 28, 60.
77 Chandler, 'The Religion of England,' 6.
78 *Hutt News*, 10 March 1937, 5.
79 'Diocesan Intelligence,' *Church Chronicle* (1 December 1882), 566.
80 H. T. Purchas, *A History of the English Church in New Zealand* (Christchurch: Simpson & Williams, 1914), x–xi.
81 *Church Chronicle* (June 1939), 243.
82 W. Williams letter, 23 February 1834, in *Missionary Register*, 1835, 426.

83 Brown Journal, 10 October 1838, in *Missionary Register*, 1840, 58.
84 T. Brooking, *Richard Seddon King of God's Own: The Life and Times of New Zealand's Longest Serving Prime Minister* (Auckland: Penguin, 2014), 15, 47.
85 Julia Stuart, *For Everything Its Season: A History of Anglicans in Eastbourne* (Eastbourne: Parish of Eastbourne Trust Board, 2010), 81.
86 G. P. Barton, *Dictionary of New Zealand Biography*, vol. 1, ed. W. H. Oliver (Wellington: Allen & Unwin, 1990), 277–79.
87 Graeme Reid, *Dictionary of New Zealand Biography*, vol. 1, ed. W. H. Oliver (Wellington: Allen & Unwin, 1990), 412–13.
88 W. P. Morrell, *The Anglican Church in New Zealand* (Dunedin: Church of the Province of New Zealand, 1973), 63.
89 Hobhouse to Miss Hobhouse, 29 August 1859, cited in ibid., 68.
90 *Church Gazette*, 1915 Supplement to no. 12, p. 1 (Synod Supplement); Johnson and Jensen, A *History of the Diocesan High School*, 23–25; Janice C. Mugford, *Dictionary of New Zealand Biography*, vol. 2, ed. Claudia Orange (Wellington: Bridget William Books, 1993), 331–32.
91 Gerald Hensley, *Dictionary of New Zealand Biography*, vol. 1, ed. W. H. Oliver (Wellington: Allen & Unwin, 1990), 179–80.
92 William Renwick, *Dictionary of New Zealand Biography*, vol. 1, ed. W. H. Oliver (Wellington: Allen & Unwin, 1990), 121–23.
93 John Stacpoole, *Dictionary of New Zealand Biography*, vol. 2, ed. Claudia Orange (Wellington: Bridget William Books, 1993), 511.
94 Anderson, 'The Anglican Church in Auckland and its Lands,' 19.
95 'Church and Worker,' *Church & People* (September 1963), 2. Citing *The Clarion*, magazine of the Labourers Union.
96 'Successful Avondale Mission Attracts Many,' *Church & People* (November 1961), 5.
97 Steven Oliver, *Dictionary of New Zealand Biography*, vol. 1, ed. W. H. Oliver (Wellington: Allen & Unwin, 1990), 457–58.
98 Jinty Rorke, *Dictionary of New Zealand Biography*, vol. 4, ed. Claudia Orange (Auckland: Auckland University Press, 1998), 91–92.
99 Angela Ballara, *Dictionary of New Zealand Biography*, vol. 4, ed. Claudia Orange (Auckland: Auckland University Press, 1998), 537–38.
100 M. P. K. Sorrenson, *Dictionary of New Zealand Biography*, vol. 3, ed. Claudia Orange (Auckland: Auckland University Press, 1996), 359–63.
101 Puna and Robin McConnell, *Dictionary of New Zealand Biography*, vol. 5, ed. Claudia Orange (Auckland: Auckland University Press, 2000), 214–15.
102 Patsy Martin, *Knox Alive! A Celebration of 150 Years of the Presbyterian Church in the Hutt Valley* (Lower Hutt: Knox-St Columba Presbyterian Church, 2002), 10, citing the *Home & Foreign Record*, c.1850.
103 *Census of Population 1921*, Part VII: Religions (Wellington: Government Printer, 1923), 10–11, 36–40; *Census of Population 1926*, Part VII: Religions (Wellington: Government Printer, 1928), 36–38.

104 See 'The Clergy and the Poor,' *Observer*, 5 October 1889, 9.
105 J. F. McArthur, *From the Kirk on the Hill 1881–1981: A History of the Presbyterian Church in Gore* (Gore: Presbyterian Church, 1981).
106 Pickens, 'Denomination, Nationality and Class in Canterbury,' 131.
107 Stenhouse, in *Christianity, Modernity and Culture*, 165, 168.
108 *New Zealand Wesleyan* (31 July 1871), 107.
109 'The Present Position of Wesleyan Methodism,' *New Zealand Wesleyan* (September 1873), 136.
110 'Does the Church Really Want the Masses,' *New Zealand Methodist Times* (17 May 1890), 8.
111 Joseph Berry, *Unionism Boycotting* (Wellington: John Watt, 1890).
112 *New Zealand Methodist Times* (17 May 1890), 8.
113 W. Greenwood, *Woodlands Street: The Story of a Timaru Church* (Timaru: Woodlands Street Methodist Church, 1984), 39–40.
114 See, for example, *Outlook* (29 July 1905), 32 (Young men's forward movement).
115 For example, Clarence Eaton, 'Address to Annual District Synod,' *New Zealand Methodist Times* (4 December 1937), 246.
116 'The President's Retiring Address,' *Outlook* (7 March 1908), 31–34.
117 *Methodist Conference*, 1914, 57.
118 *Methodist Conference*, 1919, 122; ibid., 1924, 75. For a discussion of this see L. Guy, *Shaping Godzone: Public Issues and Church Voices in New Zealand 1840–2000* (Wellington: Victoria University Press, 2011), 216, 217, 221–22, 223–26.
119 J. E. Cookson, U*pper Riccarton Methodist Church: A Centennial Retrospect 1886–1986* (Christchurch: Upper Riccarton Methodist Church, 1986), 2–12.
120 Cited by *New Zealand Methodist Times* (22 February 1890), 8.
121 S. Ratcliffe, 'The Average Minister's Greatest Problem,' *New Zealand Methodist Times* (3 July 1926), 6.
122 H. M. Foy, 'Methodism in Hawera 1874–1918' (BA Hons diss., University of Otago, 1980). See E. V. Crosby and A. Robinson, *Wesley Methodist Church, Hawera: Centenary 1876–1976* (Hawera: Church Centennial Committee, 1976); 'Hawera's Season of Celebration,' *Touchstone*, June 2006.
123 Pickens, 'Denomination, Nationality and Class in Canterbury,' 130.
124 K. Furniss, 'Moray Place Congregational Church: A Social History, 1862–1966,' in *Building God's Own Country: Historical Essays on Religions in New Zealand*, ed. J. Stenhouse and J. Thomson (Dunedin: University of Otago, 2004), 75–83.
125 B. K. Smith, 'Baptists and the Working Class in New Zealand' (MA thesis, University of Birmingham, 1990). See B. Smith, '"Wherefore Then This Thusness?" The Social Composition of Baptist Congregations in New Zealand,' *New Zealand Journal of Baptist Research* 3 (1998): 71–83.
126 Stenhouse, in *Christianity, Modernity and Culture*, 131.
127 See the comments in 'Fetch Em,' *Auckland Star*, 6 March 1915, 8.
128 'Plymouth Brethren,' *New Zealand Wesleyan* (March 1876), 48 ff.

129 *Reaper* 13 (October 19350), 195.
130 For example, H. Ellingworth, *Light in the Darkness* (Auckland, c.1944), 8.
131 *Echo*, 6 January 1882, 2.
132 'Lyttelton Meeting of Members of the Church of England,' *Lyttelton Times*, 27 March 1852, 5.
133 Peters, *Christchurch-St. Michael's*, 46–47, 233.
134 See especially *Church Chronicle* (1 December 1880), 485–87.
135 There are early accounts of British concerns, for example in a report on 'A Quaker School,' extracted from *The Christian World* in *The Christian Observer*, 1 August 1870, 117. There are very strong words in the British prize essay by William Hunter, 'Why the Working Classes Do Not Go to Church,' *Advocate*, 1 January 1898, 850.
136 See *Evening Post*, 11 October 1893, 2 and letters to the editor on the days following.
137 Waiapu Diocese, *Proceedings*, First Session of Eighth Synod, Napier, 1880, 10.
138 'Bishop's Address at Opening of Synod,' *New Zealand Church Messenger* (December 1890), 99.
139 *Echo*, 18 March 1882, 2; *Freethought Review* (January 1885), 1.
140 'Labour and the Churches,' *Outlook* (12 October 1907), 28.
141 See for example the talk by William Coull, 'The Church and the Masses of London,' *Evening Star*, 12 May 1894, 1.
142 *Press*, 10 February 1890, 3; 15 February 1890, 6; 'Editorial Notes,' *New Zealand Methodist Times* (22 February 1890), 4–5.
143 Editorial, 'Church Attendance in Auckland,' *Auckland Star*, 18 April 1882, 2. For discussion of the results, see M. Powell, 'The Church in Auckland Society, 1880–1886' (MA thesis, University of Auckland, 1970).
144 *Auckland Star*, 28 April 1882, 2.
145 'T. H. C. to the Editor', *Auckland Star*, 21 April 1882, 3.
146 'Assembly Jottings,' *Outlook* (3 March 1899), 4.
147 Smith, '"Wherefore Then This Thusness?",' 71–83.
148 Stenhouse, 'Christianity, Gender, and the Working Class in Southern Dunedin,' 18–44. But see the letter of William Coull, *Evening Star*, 12 May 1894, 1.
149 J. Armitage, 'Faults in Public Worship,' *New Zealand Wesleyan* (1 July 1874), 105.
150 For example see various letters to the editor, *Bruce Herald*, 15 June 1875, 5.
151 W. E. Morris, *The Centennial History of St Peter's Presbyterian Church and the Presbyterian Movement in the Western Bay of Plenty* (Tauranga: Editorial Committee, 1978), 29–30.
152 For example, A. S. Adams, *Professor Salmond's Blunder — Prohibition: An Effective Social Reform* (Wellington: New Zealand Alive, 1911).
153 A. R. Fitchett, 'The Right and Wrong in Amusements,' *New Zealand Wesleyan* (31 May 1872), 65.
154 *New Zealand Wesleyan* (December 1871), 173.
155 For example Adams, *Professor Salmond's Blunder*.
156 For example Monro, *Auckland Star*, 17 April 1882, 2.

157 See 'How Shall We Spend Our Sundays?' *Church Gazette* (November 1889), 126.
158 P. J. Lineham, *New Zealanders and the Methodist Evangel: An Interpretation of the Policies and Performance of the Methodist Church of New Zealand* (Auckland: Wesley Historical Society, 1983).
159 See L. H. Court, *Ready, Aye Ready: The Story of a Romantic Career* (London: Epworth Press, 1935).
160 *Outlook* (3 October 1908), 35.
161 'Seamen's Mission Dunedin,' *New Zealand Wesleyan* (1 August 1874).
162 'Diocesan Synod Report,' *Church Chronicle* (August 1902), 125–26.
163 E. C. Murphy, *Century of Faith 1876–1976: A History of All Saints Church Foxton* (Foxton: The Parish, 1976), 43.
164 Editor, 'The Church and Labour,' *Church Chronicle* (September 1913), 136.
165 Herbert Roth, *Dictionary of New Zealand Biography*, vol. 2, ed. Claudia Orange (Wellington: Bridget Williams Books, 1993), 326–27.
166 'Committee on Social Questions,' *Waiapu Church Gazette*, December 1913, 74ff.
167 See newspaper clipping in Lewis Court collection, John Rylands Library, Manchester. For studies of city missions see J. W. Parker, *In the Midst of the City: The Rise and Growth of the Auckland Methodist Central Mission* (Auckland: Auckland Methodist Central Mission, 1971); I. F. Faulkner, *The Decisive Decade: Some Aspects of the Development and Character of the Methodist Central Mission Auckland, 1927–1937* (Auckland: Wesley Historical Society [New Zealand], 1982); N. Gill, *Mission Accomplished: The Establishment of the Christchurch Methodist Mission* (Christchurch: Christchurch Methodist Mission, 1991); T. Leah, *Leslie Bourneman Neale: A Man of Faith and Vision* (Dunedin: Dunedin Methodist Mission, 2000); D. Phillips, *Mission in a Secular City: Methodist Mission Northern 1851–2001* (Auckland: Methodist Northern Mission, 2001).
168 Spencer Ratcliffe, 'The Average Minister's Greatest Problem,' *New Zealand Methodist Times* (3 July 1926), 6.
169 See the accounts in 'Religion Today,' *Auckland Star*, 22 June 1935, 7; 'The Shepherdless Sheep,' *New Zealand Methodist* (6 July 1935), 1.
170 *New Zealand Herald*, 5 January 1914, 8; *Dominion*, 6 January 1914, 6.
171 *Outlook* (7 March 1908), 35.
172 Henry Ryan, 'The Pulpit and Sin,' *New Zealand Methodist Times* (30 July 1927), 8.
173 See, for example, 'Incongruities of Pulpit and Pew,' *Christian Observer* (October 1870), 3.
174 'The Curse of Auckland,' *Observer*, 16 May 1914, 2.
175 Maurice Andrew, *Set in a Long Place: A Life from North to South* (Christchurch: Hazard Press, 1999), 137.
176 A. Goulstone, et al. *Opawa Baptist Church: Our Centenary: From Then Until Now, 1911–2011* (Christchurch: Opawa Baptist Church Outreach Press, 2011), 3, 21–22.
177 See, for example, *Church Chronicle* (December 1880), 485.
178 'Fetch Em,' *Auckland Star*, 6 March 1915, 8.
179 'Helping Hand Mission Freeman's Bay,' *Auckland Star*, 12 October 1887, 2.
180 'A Church Problem,' *Auckland Star*, 28 April 1882, 2.

181 See, for example, *Church Chronicle* (December 1880), 485. 'A Church Problem,' *Auckland Star*, 28 April 1882, 2.
182 'Fetch Em,' *Auckland Star*, 6 March 1915, 8.
183 Cited from a description of Dunedin in 1874 by A. Clarke, 'A Godly Rhythm: Keeping the Sabbath in Otago, 1870–1890,' in *Building God's Own Country: Historical Essays on Religions in New Zealand*, ed. J. Stenhouse and J. Thomson (Dunedin: University of Otago Press, 2004), 49.
184 S. Levine and A. Robinson, *The New Zealand Voter: A Survey of Public Opinion and Election Behaviour* (Wellington: Price Milburn, 1976), 132–134.
185 A. Mitchell, *Politics and People in New Zealand* (Christchurch: Whitcombe and Tombs, 1969), 211.
186 P. L. Reynolds, 'Religion and Voting in Auckland,' *Political Science* 24, no. 1 (1972): 38–48.
187 Figures analysed by Brian Smith in his thesis, "Baptists and the Working Class in New Zealand,' 34.
188 Anderson, 'The Anglican Church in Auckland and Its Lands,' 34–40.
189 Derbyshire, 'An Anatomy of Antipodean Anglicanism,' vol. 1, 364–68, and appendix 13, vol. 2, 366–76.
190 J. Davidson, *Stepping Stone to New Life: Ten Years On* (Christchurch: Stepping Stone Trust, 2000); K. Ward, *Against the Odds: Murray Robertson and Spreydon Baptist Church* (Auckland: Archer Press, 2016).
191 J. Wilson, *Mt Roskill Baptist Church (formerly White Swan) 75th anniversary Celebrations: A History* (Auckland: The Church, 1989), 43–44.
192 E. Wilson, *Blessed to Be a Blessing: 50 Years of Glen Eden Baptist Church 1959–2009* (Auckland: Glen Eden Baptist Church, 2009), 28, 55–60.
193 M. McClure, *Community of Refuge: A History of the Community of Refuge Trust* (Auckland: Community of Refuge Trust, 2005).

Chapter Twelve: All Change

1 J. Z. Park, J. G. Rogers, M. Neubert and K. D. Dougherty, 'Workplace — Bridging Religious Capital: Connecting Congregations to Work Outcomes,' *Sociology of Religion* 75, no. 2 (2014): 310.
2 Editorial, *New Zealand Herald*, 11 May 1889, 4; Letter of Sommerville, *New Zealand Herald*, 14 May 1889, 6; Editorial, ibid., 4; Letter of Sommerville, ibid., 17 May 1889, 3.
3 Editorial, *New Zealand Herald*, 11 May 1889, 4.
4 G. Troughton, *New Zealand Jesus: Social and Religious Transformations of an Image, 1890–1940* (Bern: Peter Lang, 2011).

Index

Page numbers in bold denote illustrations.

A
Above Rubies 301–2
Abraham, Caroline & Charlie 272–3, 274
Acland, Emily (née Harper) 344
Adams, G. O. 109
Adams, Susan 302–4
agnostic 364, 379–80, 382–3
Albertland Nonconformist settlement 263
alcohol *see* food & alcohol; temperance
Alexander, Charles M. 120, 154
Alexander, Mrs 339
All Age Sunday School 330
Allen Home 314
altars *see* church buildings, design
Amos, John Frederick 183
Ānaru Mātete 358
Anderson, A. R. 149, **149**
Andrew, Maurice 182, 297
Angas, George French 81
Anglican Church 364–5, 372
  All Saints Churches 64, 66, 81, 94
  Anglican bishops, 1890 343, **343**
  Anglican Church Pastoral Aid Society 155
  Anglican Loyalty Dinner 239, **239**
  Anglican Sunday school hall & pupils, Glen Eden, 1956 312, **312–3**
  Anglican Youth Movement 331
  Association of Anglican Women 297–8
  Cathedral of St John the Evangelist, Napier, 1985 373, **373**
  ChristChurch Cathedral, Christchurch 148–50
  church building 63–7, 68–72, 78–9
  Church of England Men's Society 296
  Church Work Society 123
  Churchmen's Club 248
  clergy 169–74, 188, 190, 342–6
  history & structure 13–4, 18, 20, 248–9, 357–8
  Holy Sepulchre church, Khyber Pass Rd **87**
  Holy Trinity Cathedral, Auckland 79, 96
  Holy Trinity Church, Avonside
  70–1, 71
  Holy Trinity Church, Fitzroy, New Plymouth 165, **165**
  Ladies of St Peter's Anglican Church, Onehunga, 1940s 284, **284–5**
  Ladies of the New Lynn Anglican parish meeting, 1956 283, **283**
  Māori 13, 14–5, 181, **181**
  music & hymns 140, 142–4, 145–8, 150, 153–4
  Northcote Anglican Church fair, stallholders 1904 252, **252**
  Old St Paul's Church, Auckland 381–2, 383
  Old St Paul's Church, Wellington 65, **65**, 66
  Rangiātea Church, Ōtaki 53, **53, 54**
  St George's Anglican church, 1973 **222–3**, 224
  St George's Church, Papatoetoe 109, **109**
  St Hilda, Mount Wellington 83
  St John's College, Meadowbank 64, 84, 172–3
  St Jude's Avondale loyalty dinner, 1956 234, **234–5**
  St Margaret's Church, Taihape 59, **59**
  St Mary's Pro-Cathedral, Parnell, choir 142, **142–3**, 152, **152**
  St Matthew's Church, Auckland 59, **59**, 83, **83**, 237, **237**
  St Michael and All Angels Church hall, 1905, Christchurch 229, **229**
  St Michael's, Christchurch 343, **343**
  St Paul's Church, Waiwhetu **105**
  St Peter's Church, Onehunga, 1860 24–5
  St Peter's Church, Te Kopuru 46–7
  St Peter's Onehunga choir, 1952-1955 149, **149**
  St Thomas's Anglican Church, Māori confirmation, Auckland, 1950 323, **323**
  Takanini, service in a hall 109, **109**
  tradition & festivals 28, 30, 32, 38, 39–41, 103–6, 108–10, 122–7, 203–4
  Waikato, fête, 1885 229, **229**
  Wells Campaign dinner,
  Avondale, 1956 239, **239**
Ans Westra 80
Āpirana Ngata 359
Apostolic Church 302
Archer, John 178, 216
architecture *see* church buildings
Armitage, John 366
Arney, George 354
Arnold, C. H. 171
Assembly of God 159–60, 162
Associated Church of Christ 98–9, 100
Association of Anglican Women 297–8
atheist 364, 379–80, 382–3
Aubert, Mary Joseph 288–9
Aubert, Suzanne 13, 287
Auckland
  All Saints Anglican Church & vicarage, Ponsonby 94, **166–7**, 168
  All Saints Anglican Church, Howick 64, 66, 81
  Auckland Choral Society 147
  Auckland Diocesan Immigration Committee **196–7**, 198
  Auckland Diocesan School for Girls 346
  Auckland Rainbow Church 304
  Auckland Sunday School Union 311
  Congregational Christian Church of Samoa, Grey Lynn, Samoan White Sunday 128, **128–9**
  Glen Eden, Anglican Sunday school hall & pupils, 1956 312, **312–3**
  Holy Sepulchre church, Khyber Pass Rd **87**
  Holy Trinity Cathedral 79, 96
  Ladies' guild of the Dominion Road Methodist Church,1943 303, **303**
  Ladies of the New Lynn Anglican parish meeting, 1956 283, **283**
  Māori confirmation at St Thomas's Anglican Church, Newton, Auckland, 1950 323, **323**
  Northcote Anglican Church fair, stallholders, 1904 252, **252**
  Old St Paul's Anglican Church 381–2, 383
  Onehunga, Manukau Harbour and Heads, 1860 24–5
  Rosehill Presbyterian Church

knitting group, Papakura, 1982 305, **305**
St George's Anglican Church, Papatoetoe 109, **109**
St George's Presbyterian Church, Takapuna 61, **61**
St Hilda, Mount Wellington **83**
St John's College, Meadowbank 64, 84, 172–3
St Jude's Avondale loyalty dinner, 1956 234, **234**–5
St Mary's Pro-Cathedral, Parnell, choir 142, **142**–3, 152, **152**
St Matthew's Anglican Church 59, **59**, 83, **83**, 237, **237**
St Patrick's Catholic Church 74–5
St Peter's, Onehunga, choir, 1952-1955 149, **149**
St Philip's, Kelston, Auckland **376**–7, 378
St Thomas's, Sunday school, New Lynn, 1956 271, **271**
Swanson, bible class group 323, **323**
Takanini, Anglican service in a hall 109, **109**
Temperance Ladies' Brass Band of Auckland, 1910s 283, **283**
Titirangi, Cub pack, Soldiers Memorial Church, 1956 265, **265**
Unitarian Church, Ponsonby Rd 61, **61**
Averill, Alfred W. 'Wally' 112, 181, **181**, **196**–7, 198, 343, **343**, 347, **347**
Ayrton, Majorie 315

B

Bailey, Ebenezer 148
Baines, Henry 316, 345, 358
Ballantyne family 362
bands *see* music & hymns
Bands of Hope 321
baptism 12, 106–7, 178–9, 203, 315, 319 *see also* missions; traditions & festivals; specific denominations
Baptists 17–8, 130, 246, 316, 363, 374
Baptist HomeCare Waitakere 374
Baptist Women's Missionary Union 298
Brooklyn Baptist Church Sunday school procession 319, **319**

clergy 170–1, 193–4
conversion & confirmation 95, 119
Mosgiel, Baptist Sunday school, 1913 252, **252**
Sabbath observance 33–4, 38
services 106, 110, 113–4, 142, 144, 147, 158–9
tradition & festivals 106, 110
Valley Road Baptist Church singing group 159–60
vestments 112–3
Baragwanath, Owen 113, 266–7
Barber, E. C. 105
Barclay, Peter 103, 104, 146, 249
Barker, Dorcas 275
Barker, Mary Anne 34, 36, 200–2
Barnett, Graham 259
Barraud, Charles 53, **53**
Barrows, Cliff 154
Bateman, Grace 309, 316
Baughan, Blanche 49
Baumber, William 119, 123
Bavin, Rainsford 320–1
Baxter, Richard 180
Beere, Daniel Manders 240–1, 242
Beere, Joan 297
Beere, Lionel **166**–7, 168
Beet, Joseph 362
Belich, James 380–1
belief *see* Christian culture; convictions; traditions & festivals; specific denominations
Bell, David 162
Bell, Gordon **196**–7, 198
bells *see* church buildings, steeples & bells; music & hymns
Bennett, Francis 85
Bennett, Frederick 359
Berry, Joseph 119, 211, 361
Betz, Mary 288
Bible Christians 367
Bible classes 256, 266, 294–6, 322–4, 325–7, 330, 335
Bible Class Union 352
Lower Hutt, bible class picnic on Labour Day, 1941 265, **265**
Swanson, bible class group, Auckland 323, **323**
Bible Reading Fellowship 202
Bible Society 141, 163, 164, 202, 208
bibles & scripture 11, 102, 135–9, 163–4, 202, 203, 209, 270, 275
Bicknell, Ivan 183
Bishopscourts **336**–7, 338, 346–8

Black, Bower 106
Blenheim
Redwoodtown, Children of St Christopher's Sunday school, 1908 255, **255**
St Mary's Parish, Presentation Ball 351, **351**
Bliss, Philip 151–3
Bluck, John 210
Bodington, Charles 118, 154
Bond, Greta 219
Book of Order 173, 189–90
Booth, Catherine 282
Booth, Richard 215
Boots, Miss 368
Boreham, Frank 114, 125
Boulton-Smith, L J. 113
Bowen, Annette Laura 350
Boy Scouts 265, **265**, 321
Boyd, Vivienne 297
Boys' Brigades 321–2
Bradfield, Mary A. 287
Bradshaw, John 150
Brady, Nicholas 140
Brethren 17, 33, 95, 111, 135, 238, 364
bibles & scripture 163–4
music & hymns 141, 142, 153, 159
Sabbath observance 37, 38–9
women 287–8, 301
Brett, Henry 61
British Children's Special Service Mission 155
Brodie, Bishop 350
Brokenshire, John **166**–7, 168
Brooking, Tim 322
Brooking, Tom 50
Broomfield, John 245
Brough, Luke 333
Brown, Alfred N. 275, 356
Brown, Claud L. B. 181, **181**
Brown, Ian 130
Brown, Nigel 96
Browne, Charles Foster 150
Browne, Thomas Gore 31
Bruce, David 225
Buchanan, Samuel 250
Buckle, Ted 358
Bull, Herbert Walter 180
Buller, James 54, 169, 277
Burnett, H. B. 326
Burnett, Matthew 120
Burns, Thomas 31, 74
Button, Lena 368
Byrne, F. H. 261

C

Cahill, Patrick P. 351, **351**
Calder, Jasper 115, 126, 262–3, 293, 368, 370
Calder, Matthew 114
Cambridge Camden Society 64
Cameron, James 'Rev.' 183
Campbell, Dalton 131, **131**
Campbell, J. P. 354
Campbell, Nancy 301–2
Campbell, Thomas 227
Capital Teen Convention 160
Carlyon, Hubert 111–2
Carr, Clyde 178
Carrington, Bishop 14
Carrington, Philip 51–2
Carrol, Alfred Thomas (Turi) 359
Carterton, Sunday school picnic, Zabell's Paddocks, Carterton 258, **258**
Cathedral Grammar School 148–50, 355
Catholic Church
 The Basilica of the Sacred Heart, Timaru 76, **76–7**
 Catholic charity ball, 1936 351, **351**
 Catholic Literary and Debating Society 325
 Catholic Women's League's float, 1966 271, **271**
 Catholic Youth Movement 333
 church building 74–8
 clergy 169–70, 172–5, 177–8, 185, 187–8, 190, 195, 298
 First Communion at Our Lady of Lourdes church, Palmerston North, 1930s 317, **317**
 funding 226, 227, 232, 236
 Futuna Chapel, Karori 94
 history & structure 15–6, 75, 94, 126–7, 200, 244–5
 missions 12, 13, 102, 243
 music & hymns 142, 147–8, 159
 Ōtaki Church 74, 84
 Ōtūmoetai chapel, 1840 54–5, **56–7**
 parish schools 314
 sodalities 208, 261, 269, 333
 sport 326
 St Mary of the Angels, Wellington 93
 St Patrick's School, Sister of Mercy & class, Dunedin, 1959 329, **329**
 tradition & festivals 16, 30, 39–41, 102, 107–8, 114, 126–7, 202–3, 208, 219–20
 Tua Marina, Marlborough Sounds **131**
 Wellington, Catholic parade, 1940 217, **217**
 women 288–90, 298
Caughey family 362
Caversham Project 254–6
Celebration Singers 162
cemeteries 50, 181, **181**
Central Committee on Broadcasting 155
Central Religious Advisory Committee 115, 220
Certain Sounds 160
Chambers, Brent 159, 162
Chandler, Charles 353, 355
Channing, Frederick 164
Chapman, Wilbur 120, 154
Chapple, James 202
Charismatic churches 17–8, 128, 158–9, 162, 193, 202, 264–6
charity 179–80, 368, 374 see also specific charitable organisations
Chartist Movement 340
Chas Begg & Co 156
Chatterton, Frederick 368
Cherrington, Cecil 182, 352
Cheyne, Christine 298
Chidwell, F. 82
children & young people 309–35 see also services, family; Sunday Schools
 church membership 309–10, 324, 340
 youth groups & sport 320–2, 330–1
Childs, David T. 150
Chiniquy, Charles 245
Choudhary, Ashraf 50
Christadelphians 286, 364
Christchurch
 Anglican diocese 14
 Bishopscourts **336–7**, 338, 348
 Cathedral of the Blessed Sacrament 78
 Catholic diocese 16
 ChristChurch Cathedral 148–50
 Christchurch Inter-Church Soccer League 334
 Durham Street Wesleyan Chapel 67, 68, **68–9**, 119–20
 First Communion group at Addington, 1954 317, **317**
 Holy Trinity Church, Avonside **70–1**, 71
 Linwood Citadel, Salvation Army dinner, 1910 255, **255**
 St Michael and All Angels Anglican Church hall, 1905 229, **229**
 St Michael's 343, **343**
christening see baptism
Christian Advance Ministries 162
Christian culture 199–221 see also traditions & festivals; specific denominations
 discipline & judgement 199, 200, 203, 208, 210–3, 218
Christian Endeavour 32, 321
Christian Life Church 160
Christmas 11, 27, 31, 39–40, 42, 44, 101, 115 see also traditions & festivals
Church Army 359
church buildings 49–99 see also traditions & festivals; specific denominations
 design 85–6
 funding see funding
 furnishings 84–90, 95, 280
 halls 251–3
 housing 166–7, 168, 184–5, **336–7**, 338, 346–9
 steeples & bells 79–84
 windows 84, 95–6
Church Missionary Society 14, 101, 169–70, 200, 243, 275
churches 8–9, 10, 52–3, 85
 missions 11–2, 20, 52, 380
 women 314–5
Church of Christ 17
Church of Christ, Associated **98–9**, 100
Church of England see Anglican Church
Church of England Men's Society 296
Church of Scotland see Presbyterian Church
Church of the Province of New Zealand see Anglican Church
Church Service Society 106
Church Work Society 123
Churchmen's Club 248
City Impact Church, Northcross 267
Clark, Francis 321
Clark, Joseph 33–4
Clarke, Alison 30–1, 36, 110
Clarkson, Percy 59, **59**
class 339–75
Cleary, Henry 342
Clere, Frederick de Jersey 75
clergy 169–95, 190–5, 292–3, 341–9 see also laity; traditions

& festivals; vestments; specific denominations
education 172–3
entertainment & leisure 187
funding 192–5, 225–6
housing 166–7, 168, 184–5, **336–7**, 338, 346–9
marriage & family 173–4, 177, 183–4, 193, 194, 286
parishes 187–8
in politics 178, 189
remuneration 174–5
retirement 188–90
travel 180–2, 342
vocation 194–5
women 287–91, 290, 300–2
clothes, for church 33, 54, 102–3, 126, 127–8, 280–1, 300, 315, 371
see also vestments
Coad, Mr 120
Cocker, James 279–80
coffee bars 333–4
Coffey, Edmund 226
Coffey, Richard 253, 364
Colegrove, Richard 208
Colenso, Elizabeth (née Fairburn) 275
Colenso, William 11, 138, 200, 201, 325
collection plate *see* funding
Collins, Chris 33
Colville, A. H. 103
communion 41, 86, 94, 101–4, 107–11, 124–5, 200, **201**, 214–5
see also confirmation & first communion; missions; services; traditions & festivals; specific denominations
communities 250–3 *see also* sociability
Community Church 162
Community of Refuge Trust 374
Community of the Sacred Name 291
Condliffe, John 110–1
confirmation & first communion 117, 172, 189, 248, 266, 315, 319
see also communion; conversion
First Communion at Our Lady of Lourdes church,Palmerston North, 1930s 317, **317**
First Communion group at Addington, Christchurch,1954 317, **317**
Congregational churches 17, 32, 68, 127–8, 153, 188, 284, 363
Congregational Christian Church of Samoa, Grey Lynn,
Samoan White Sunday 128, **128–9**
Congregational Union 213
Connor, Charles 245
Connor, George 123
convents 185
conversion 116–21, 125, 365–9
see also missions; specific denominations
convictions 199–221 *see also* traditions & festivals; specific denominations
discipline & judgement 199, 200, 203, 208, 210–3, 218
Cook, Thomas 120
Cookson, John 362
Cooneyites 326
Copland, James 187
Costall, Jane 38
Cotton, Shane 96
Cotton, William 54
Coull, William 363
Coulthard, Edward 148
Council of Christian Women 298
Council of Churches in Aotearoa New Zealand 18
Cowan, Grant **196–7**, 198
Cowan, James 175
Cowie, William 145, 171, 342, 343, **343**
Croke, Bishop 348
Crosby, Fanny 151–3
Cruikshank, George **196–7**, 198, 344
Crump, John 144
Cub pack, Soldiers Memorial Church, Titirangi, 1956 265, **265**
Cullen, Lloyd 358
Cullen, Paul 203
culture, religions 22, 101–31 *see also* specific denominations
Cunningham, Loren 159
Curnow, Allen 50–1
Cutler family 323, **323**

D

Daldy, Amy 294
Dalton, Sarah 211, 279
Dalziel, Raewyn 277
dancing 253, 257, 262, 322, 327–8, 331–2, **332**, 350–2, **351**
Daniell, A. H. 233
Daniell, Charles 81
Darwinism 210
Daughters of Our Lady of Compassion 288–9
Davidson, Allan 173
Davis, Richard 28

de Jong, Mark 160
de Latour, C. A. 368
Deck, James George 141
Delargey, Reginald 333
Dell, Miriam 297
denominations *see also* schisms; specific denominations
attendance & numbers *see* membership of religions
rifts between 244–50, 360
unification & cooperation 18, 204, 209, 249, 262–6, 316, 319, 363, 382
Derbyshire, Noel 236, 342, 344, 372
design *see* church buildings, design
Destiny Church 96, 118, 193, 219, 220–1, 238
Dickie, Jane (née Smith) 281–2
Dickson, John 112, 245
Dieffenbach, Johann Karl Ernst 55
Dilworth, James 354
Dixon, Gray 106
Dixon, Haddon 122
Dobby, Eleanor 290
Dolamore, Decimus 246
Donachie, B. G. 131
Douglas, Mrs 282
Drake, Alfred 181, **181**
Drift Inn 333–4
Driver, Annie 300
Dudley, Raymond 113
Duggan, Eileen 131, 344–5
Duncan, Christabel 290, 300
Dunedin
Anglican diocese 14
Bishopsgrove 348
Catholic diocese 16
First Church 72–3, **73**, 78
Holy Cross College 172–3
Knox Church 72–3, **73**
St Columba College 348
St Patrick's School, Sister of Mercy & class, 1959 329, **329**
Dunmore, John 101
Dunn, J. S. 50
Duplex Envelope System 233–4

E

Earle, Augustus 28
East Coast 11, 13
Easter *see* traditions & festivals
Easter Bible class camps 256
Eastern Maori Patriotic Association 359
Eaton, Clarence 292
ecumenism *see* denominations,

unification & cooperation
Edgecombe, Felicity 162
Edger, Samuel 263
education 254, 314–5, 330, 349, 350 *see also* Sunday Schools
  girls' schools 349–52
  integration into state system 20–1, 208
  religion in schools 20–1, 349
  Sacred Heart Convent School, Wanganui, 1912 294, **294–5**
  St Patrick's School, Sister of Mercy & class, Dunedin, 1959 329, **329**
  Te Aute College 349, 358
  women 286–7
Edwards, Henry 85, 189
Elim churches 159–60, 193–4
Ellena, Vic 155
Elliott, Howard 125, 245
Ellis, Robert 96
Elmslie, John 113
Enough is Enough campaign 219
Ensor, Harold 112
entertainment & leisure 34–7, 253, 256–7, 328 *see also* sociability; sport
Evangelical movement 14, 15, 17–8, 115–7, 118–21, 130, 209, 366
  Evangelical Alliance 30
  Evangelical Fellowship of New Zealand 18
  Evangelistic Brotherhood of the Church Army 367
  funding 238
  music & hymns 158–9
Evans family 252, **252**
Everell, Roy **109**
Everyboys & Everygirls rallies 322
Excel School of Performing Arts 160
Exclusive Brethren *see* Brethren

F

faith *see* Christian culture; convictions; traditions & festivals; specific denominations
Falconer, Alexander 153
Fancourt, William 347, **347**
Farr, Samuel 68
Farrar, Frederic 364
Fenians 204, 244, 261
Fenton, Francis 358
Ferguson, Robert 61, **61**
Feron, Joseph F. 104, 263, 356
Festival Singers 162

festivals *see* traditions & festivals; specific denominations
Field-Dodgson, Robert 150
Fielding, Presbyterian Women's Missionary Union members, 1930 305, **305**
Fields, John 224
films 125–6, 254
finances *see* funding
Finney, Charles 117
Firth, A. K. 82
Fisher, John 323, **323**
Fitchett, Alfred 119, 162–3, 188–9, 210, 360, 367
Fitchett, William 344
Fitzgerald, James Edward 170
Fletcher, James 91
food & alcohol 33, 36, 212–6, 253, 292–4, 366–7 *see also* temperance
Forces Service Book 155
Ford, Leighton 120
Forrester, Thomas 74
Forsaith, Thomas 172
Fountain family 158–9
Fowler, Dad & 'Jimmy' 122
Fox, Brother 367
Fox, William 36
Foxton, All Saints 86–7
Foy, Helen 362
Fraser, Ian 291, 300
Free Church *see* Presbyterian Church
Freemasons 104, 206, 208
Frost, Fred L. 189
Froud, Canon 114
Fry, Ruth 286
funding 225–39, 250, 268
  Anglican Loyalty Dinner 239, **239**
  church buildings 227–8
  clergy 192–5, 225–6 *see also* specific denominations
  collections & pledges 225, 233–6
  debt 226–7, 228
  fund raising **229**, 231–2, 254, 259–60, 354–6
  ladies guilds 84, 90, 231, 232, 296
  pew rents 228–31, 370–1
  St Jude's Avondale loyalty dinner, 1956 234, **234–5**
  St Matthew's, Auckland, fair 237, **237**
  St Thomas's Church bazaar, Wellington, 1898 239, **239**
  Stallholders at the Northcote

Anglican Church fair, 1904 252, **252**
  tithes 228
  Waikato, fête, 1885 229, **229**
funerals 179, 180, 245
furnishings *see* church buildings, furnishings
Furniss, Keith 363

G

Galt, Margaret 193
gambling 212, 231–2, 253
Garin, Antoine 4, 85
Garrett, David & Dale 158–9
Garrett, Les 159
Gavin, James 178
Gee, Maurice 202
Geering, Lloyd 209
George Croft & Co 146
Gerard, George 344
Gibb, James 341, 347, **347**
Gibson, Colin 161
Gibson, Dean 268
Gifford, Algernon 248
Gilbert, Hannibal 112
Gillam, William 119
Gillard, Richard 162
Gillies, William 214
Gisborne **8–9**, 10, 79
Gisborne, William 55
Glover, T. W. 215
Godfrey, Peter 151, 162
Godfrey, Richard **196–7**, 198
Goetz, Greville 331
Goffin, Henry 155
Golden, John 175
Good Templars 214
Gowing, Eric 183–4, 249, 345, 346, 352, 358
Grace, Thomas 169
Graham, Billy 120, 154, 156
Grant, Ian 331–3
Gray, Mrs 298
Green, Matthew 178
Greenmeadows Scholisticate 173
Griffiths, Thomas Vernon 151
Grimes, John 342
Grocott, Horace & Ada 321
Grubb, George 118, 249
Guthardt, Phyllis 300–1
Guy, Laurie 21, 34, 37
Gwynn, Robin 42

H

Habens, William 32
Hadfield, Octavius 53, **53**, 54, 169, 314, 343, **343**, 348
hahunga 28

Hakaraia Pahewa 170
Hall, John 285
Hall, William 357
halls *see* church buildings, halls
Hampson, Margaret 282
Hanne, Tony 333
Hanson, Frank 312
Harkness Music Company of Pasadena 154
Harkness, Robert 154
Harmonic Society 150
harmoniums 145–7, 151 *see also* music & hymns
Harper, Emily 272–3, 274
Harper, Henry, Archdeacon 123, 344
Harper, Henry, Bishop 148, 171–2, 175, 189, 342, 343, **343**, 344, 346, 353
Harris, Murray 164
Harrison, Charles 220
Hart, Frederick 184
Hart, Hannah 275
Hauhau 13
Haultain, Theodore 357–8
Hawkesby, John 333
Hawkins, Hector 181, **181**
Hawkins, Kathleen 58, 251
Hay, Keith 92
Heavey, William 351, **351**
Helen Patteson Community Hall 374
Henare, James 359
Hennebery, Patrick 215, 230
Henry, Duke of Gloucester 347, **347**
Hercus, Duncan 106
Hewson, Margaret 299, **299**
Hibernian Society 206, 261–2
hierarchy 339–75
Hīkoi of Hope 219
Hill, James 147
Hillsong Church 160
Hinman, Charles 215
Hirini Te Kani 358–9
Hirst, T. 357
Hobhouse, Bishop 348, 357
Hogben, J. M. 349
Hoki 276
Holland, Herbert St Barbe 344, 348, 352, 355
Holland, John 345
Holley, Dean 188
Holy Name Society 261
Home Acquirement Fund 190
Hope 35
Hori Tupaea 359
Horton, Edwin 357

Hosking, John 211
housing **166–7**, 168, 184–5, **336–7**, 338, 346–9
The Hub 334
Hughes, Indra 151
Hunt family 252, **252**
hymns *see* music & hymns

I
Inglis, John 359
Inter-Varsity Fellowship 256
Isern, Tom 95
Isherwood, Mrs 283, **283**
Isitt, Frank 226
Isitt, Leonard 178, 215

J
Jackson, Revelle 271, **271**
Jamieson, John 326
Jansen, Guy 162
Jehovah Witnesses 364
Jellie, William 61
John McGlashan College 314
Johnston, Allen 345
Johnston, Mrs W. H. O. 299, **299**
Joint Commission of Church Union 18
Jones, Michael 42, 44
Jones, Moore 354
Jones, Mrs P. W. 282
Joplin, Robert Croudace 141
Judkins, W. H. 215–6
Julius, Churchill 112, 123, 175, 204–5, 248, 249, 292, 320, 346, 365

K
Kaitaia cemetery, 1920s 181, **181**
Kedgley, Sue 350
Keen, David 314
Keen, Kevin 178
Keep Sunday Free 42
Keey, R. B. 68
Kelly, Graham 159
Kelly, James 309
Kempthorne, Sampson 64–6
Ken, Bishop 141
Kendall, Thomas 210
Kennerley, Roy 160
Kent, John 153
Keretene, Wiremu 196–7, 198
Kerr, Mrs 282
Kinder, John 24–5, 67, **381–2**, 383
King Movement 12–3
Kingsley, Charles 180
Kirkwood, Anna 300
Kiwi Records 161

Knight, Cyril 66
Knox College 173
Koo, T. Z. 264

L
Ladies Benevolent Association 284
ladies, church involvement 84–90, 95, 231, 232, 280, 296
Ladies' guild of the Dominion Road Methodist Church, 1943 303, **303**
Ladies of St Peter's Anglican Church, Onehunga, 1940s 284, **284–5**
Ladies of the New Lynn Anglican parish meeting, 1956 283, **283**
Ladies of the Order of Fine Things 95
laity, as church officials 14, 101, 122, 127, 169, 171, 357–9, 368
Lamb, Captain 61
Lamb of God community 266
land wars 12
Larkin, Emmet 202–3
Latrobe, John Antes 141
Laud, Archbishop 86
Law, Brian 150
Lawry, Samuel 324
Lawson, Robert A. 72–4
Le Menant des Chesnais, Fr. 254
leadership, spiritual 169–95
League of Mothers 279
Leavitt, Mary 214, 282
Lefanu, Miss 282
Leggott, William 361
leisure *see* entertainment & leisure
Lemalu, Jonathan 154
Lesser, Norman 345
Lewis, John 349
LGBT community 304
Life Church 160, 302
Lifepoint Assembly of God Church 193–4
Light of Christ Covenant Community 266
Lind, Derek 160
Lingard, Edward 248–9
Linton, Mrs 282
Liston, James Michael 219–20, 351, **191**, **351**
liturgy *see* services & liturgy; traditions & festivals; specific denominations
Living Inn 334
Lohse, Mrs 350
Lord's Day Observance Society 27

Loten, Terrence 124
Low, Bonnie 162
Lowe, Bob 115, 220, 354
Lower Hutt **105**, 265, **265**
Luck, Francis A. 175
Luck, John Edmund 349
Lush, Vicesimus 215, 224, 248
Lusk, Tony 372
Lutheran church 244

M

Macé, Luke 54–5
Macfarlane, John 15, 178
Macky, Katherine Faith 161
MacMurray, George **196–7**, 198
Maher, Celia 288
Mainstage 333
Major, Henry 209
Malcolm, Margaret 301
Mane-Wheoki, Jonathan 64
Mangungu 11
Manuteke *see* Church Missionary Society
Māori 275–6, 315, 358–9 *see also* Pai Mārire; Ringatū
   Anglican Church 13, 14–5, 181, **181**
   bibles, scripture & hymns 135–9
   Catholic Church 55
   clergy 170, 276, 287
   Eastern Maori Patriotic Association 359
   land 12, 50–2
   Māori churches & parishes 8–9, 10, 54–5, **56–7**, 81, 101–2, 117–8, 123–4, 200
   Maori Methodist Mission Waiata Choir 149, **149**
   Maori Women's Welfare League 276
   Sabbath observance 28–30
   St Thomas's Anglican Church, Newton, confirmation, 1950 323, **323**
Marist order 13, 16, 131, 169–70, 173, 188, 322, 342
Marlborough Sounds, Tua Marina **131**
marriage 179, 245, 254–6, 269, 276, 277–9, 297, 354, 355
Marsden, Samuel 11, 28, 101
Marshall, Annie (née Hadfield) 355
Marshall, Jocelyn (née Crabtree) 162
Marshall, Russell 178
Marshall, William 355
Martin, Margaret Reid 300–1

Martin, William 357
Mason, G. E. 118, 154
Masterton **43**, 246, **246–7**, 332, **332**
Matla, Petrus 156
Maude, Sybilla 291
Maunsell, Robert 54, 169
McAleese, Patrick 178
McAllister, James **306–7**, 308
McCahon, Colin 49
McCaw, James 33
McClymont family 252, **252**
McDowell, W. C. W. 321
McGrail, Bruce 159–60, 162
McIntosh, Averil 301
McKeefry, Peter 344–5
McKenzie, John 34, 310, 330
McLaren, George 326
McLean, David 358
McPherson, Aimee Semple 301
membership of religions 97, 230, 248, 288, 339–40, 352–4, 359, 371–4, 381 *see also* conversion; specific denominations
   attendance 21, 34, 62–3, 365–6
   children & young people 309–10
   recruitment 116–7, 125, 365–9
Meredith, Creed 110
Methodist Church 16–7, 67–8, 92, 112–4, 119–21, 123, 126, 360–3
   children & young people 311–2, 324
   class ticket for Māori 201, **201**
   clergy 169, 172–3, 185, 188, 189–90
   Dominion Road Methodist Church, Ladies' guild,1943 303, **303**
   Durham Street Wesleyan Chapel, Christchurch 67, 68, **68–9**, 119–20
   funding 228–30, 233
   Hawera Methodist Church 362–3
   Liardet St Wesleyan Church, New Plymouth 67–8
   Masterton, harvest festival **43**
   Methodist Superannuation Fund 189
   missions 11, 13, 243
   Moxham Ave, church, Wellington 19, **19**
   music & hymns 141, 142, 144, 145–7, 150–1, 153
   Palmerston North Methodist Mutual Improvement Society, 1889 206, **206**

St Luke's schoolroom, Masterton, dinner 246, **246–7**
Temperance Committee of the Wesleyan Church 214–5
tradition & festivals 34, 36, 104, 110
Wesleyan Connexion 120
Wesleyan Helping Hand Mission 319–20
Wesleydale 11
women's involvement 282, 286, 290
Mill Hill Fathers 13
Millar, John 367–8
Miller, Ray 333
Mills, Murray 373, **373**
Milne, D. S. 210
Minchin, Miss 38
Mission of Help 118
missions 11–2, 101, 169, 205–6
   see also conversion
   Presbyterian Women's Missionary Union members, Feilding, 1930 305, **305**
   women 287–8, 296–7, 300
Mitchell, Austin 372
Mitchelson, Edwin 357
Moffat, James 163–4
Mohi Turei 181, **181**
Monro, G. B. 365
Monro, George 176
Moody & Sankey 366
Moody Bible Institute 116
Moody, Dwight 145, 151–3
Moran, Patrick 208, 371
Moreau, Fr. 180
Morgan, Maria (née Coldham) 275
Morkane, Fr. 182
Morley, William 205, 341
Morrison, Hugh 287–8, 314
Morrow, Anne 216, 301
Morton, Annie 287
Mosgiel, Baptist Sunday school, Mosgiel, 1913 252, **252**
Mothercraft 179
Mothers' Union 277, 279, 297–8
Mount Cook Bible class hockey team, 1908 332, **332**
Mountfort, Benjamin 66, 68, 71–2
Mountfort, Cyril 71
movies 125–6, 254
Mulgan, Alan 176
Muller, George 367
Mumford, Bob 266
Murray, Bruce 38
Murray, John Stewart 161
Murray, Malton 213

INDEX 457

Murray, Puti 277
Murray, Shirley 161
Murray, Shona 160
music & hymns 130, 134–65 *see also* bells; harmoniums; organs
　bands 153, 155, 158, 163, 253, 283, **283**
　choirs 142, **142–3**, 147–51, 149, **149**, 151, 154, 315, 355 *see* music & hymns
　hymn books & recordings 136, 139, 142, 144, 151, 153, 154, 155–6, 159, 161, 162
　singing 36, 49, 101, 103, 115, 117, 123, 127–8, 141
　women 281
Music of the Church 141
Musica Sacra 151
Mutter, Brother 367

N

Napier
　Cathedral of St John the Evangelist, 1985 373, **373**
Nash, Walter 178, 216, 296
National Council of Churches 18
National Council of Women 297
National Youth Choir 162
Natives assembled to celebrate the Lord's Supper at Orona, Taupo, New Zealand, 1845 **29**
Neale, Leslei 368
Neligan, Moore Richard 170, 293, 342, 346
Nelson 14, 348
Nevill, Samuel 249, 343, **343**, 348, 355–6
New Life Campaign 236
New Life Movement 251–3
New Plymouth 66, 67–8, 165, **165**
New York Bible Society 164
New Zealand Christian Network 18
New Zealand Christian Resource Trust 162
New Zealand Church Fellowship 39
New Zealand Hymnbook Trust 155–6, 161
New Zealand Jesus 383
Newton, Henry Edward 175
Ngāruawāhia Sunday school picnic, 1880s **240–1**, 242
Ngāti Kahungunu 359
Ngāti Maru 138
Ngāti Pikiao 55
Ngāti Porou 13, 181, 359
Niebuhr, Richard 339
Noll, Mark 135
non-religious 364, 379–80, 382–3
Nordmeyer, Arnold 178
Norrie, Thomas 179
North, Alfred 245
North, John 114, 245
Northland 11, 52–4, 102, 348
Numia Tomoana 276

O

Oakley Pinfold & Turvey 94
O'Brien, Anne 291–2
O'Connor, Michael 151
Oddfellows 254
O'Donnell, David 120
O'Donnell, Dean 114
Olding, John 159
Oliver, French 154
Onehunga, Manukau Harbour and Heads, 1860 **24–5**
O'Neill, Hugh, consecration, 1943 191, **191**
Orange, William 172
Orbell, Margaret 137
Order of St Stephen 333
Order of the Good Shepherd 291
organs 15, 144–7, 156–8, 315 *see also* music & hymns
Orr, Everil 368
Orr-Nimmo, Kathy 170
Orthodox church 244
O'Shea, Thomas & clergy, 1930s 191, **191**
Otago 15, 16, 31–2
Ōtaki 12, 53, **53**, 54, 74, 94
Owen, Richard 345

P

Pai Mārire 13, 30
Palau, Luis 120
Palmer, Mrs Joseph 229, **229**
Palmerston North
　clock tower & cross 50
　First Communion at Our Lady of Lourdes church, 1930s 317, **317**
　Palmerston North Methodist Mutual Improvement Society, 1889 206, **206**
　Salvation Army Citadel & band **132–3**, 134
　Women of the Salvation Army corps in Broadway 303, **303**
Pānapa, Wiremu 352
Parachute music festival 160, 333
Paraire Tomoana 359
Paraparaumu, Our Lady of Lourdes statue 50–1
Parihaka 13
Parker, Joseph 334
Pasifika influence 17, 21, 42, 44, 96, 127–8, 244, 375
　children & young people 334–5
　clergy 190
　funding 238
　music & hymns 154, 160
　women 302
Paterson, James 153, 226, 262, 263
Patoromu Tamatea 55
Pearse, Mark Guy 120
Pearson, Frederick 59
Peata 276
Pengelly family 252, **252**
Pentecostal movement 17–8, 96, 118, 130, 193, 238, 269, 331
　music & hymns 159–60
　women 301–2, 304
Pere, Wiremu 358
Peters, Marie 148, 354
Peters, Vic 150
Peters, Winston 50
Peterson, John W. 159
Petitjean, Fr. 180
Petre, Francis 76, 78, **93**
Pettit, William 210, 211
pews *see* church buildings, furnishings
Pezant, Fr. 55
Phillips, Jock 50
Phillips, John 164
Pickens, Keith 354, 360, 363
Pickerill, Cecily 59, **59**
Pickles, Katie 97
Pinfold, James 277, 325
Pittman, John 125
Pius IX 200, 260
Pius X 148
Planned Giving 236
Plunket Society 179, 279
Pointon, Dorothy 287
Police Offences Act 33, 36–8
politics & church 178, 189, 204–5, 208–9, 219, 364–5, 368, 371–2
Pollard, Vic 38
Pompallier, Jean-Baptiste 12, 15–6, 54–5, 102, 111, 169–70, 342, 348
Powell, Shirley 159
Poynton, Thomas 102
prayers 20, 101–4, 108, 116, 123–4, 127, 136, 199, 202
　prayer books 14, 85, 102, 104, 202
preachers 101–3, 106, 113–5, 122–5, 130 *see also* specific denominations
Prebble, Ken 158–9

Preece, Mary Ann (née Williams) 275
Prendergast, R. K. 357
Presbyterian Church
  church building 72–4
  Church Service Society 106
  clergy 172–4, 188, 192
  First Church, Dunedin 72–3, **73**, 78
  funding 231–3
  history & structure 15
  Knox Church, Dunedin 72–3, **73**
  membership 359–60
  missions 13
  music & hymns 140, 145–7, 151
  Presbyterian New Life Movement 91–2
  Presbyterian Women's Missionary Union members, Feilding, 1930 305, **305**
  Rosehill Presbyterian Church knitting group, Papakura, 1982 305, **305**
  sermons & services 106, 110
  St George's Church, Takapuna 61, **61**
  St Mary's Parish, Presentation Ball, Blenheim 351, **351**
  tradition & festivals 30, 31–2, 34, 40–1, 104, 106, 110
  vestments 112–3
  women's involvement 290–1, 299, **299**, 300
Preston family 362
Primitive Methodists *see* Methodist Church
Proclamation for the Encouragement of Piety and Virtue, 1787 27
profanities 30, 212
Protestant Political Association 125
Pryatt, Allan 345
Prynne, George Rundle 139
Pugin, Augustus 64, 76
Pugin, Peter Paul 349
Pulling, Mary Etheldred 350
Purchas, Arthur 142, 154
Pyatt, Allan 348

Q
Quakers 17, 107
Quayle, Tom 42
Quinn, Fr. 187

R
radio & television 37, 115, 155, 161, 220

Radio Church of the Helping Hand 220
Randerson, Richard 104–6
Ranfurly, Lord 59
Rātana Church 13, 79
Rātana, Tahupotiki Wiremu 13, 79
Ratcliffe, Spencer 362
Rationalists 37
Ready, William 367, 368
Redemptorist Fathers 118, 234, 293
Redwood, Francis 180, 191, 342
Reed, A. H. & A. W. 155, 314, 330
Rees, Tom 154
Reeves, Paul 237, **237**
Reid, Jessie 145
Returned Services' Association 205
revivalists *see* Evangelical movement
Reynolds, Paul 372
Rhema Group 220
Richards, Alun 369
Richardson, John 286–7
Richmond, Christopher 150
Riddell, Mike 374
Riddiford, Vivian 355
Ringatū 13, 30, 79
rituals *see* traditions & festivals; specific denominations
Robertson, Murray 95
Robley, Horatio Gordon 55, **56**–7
Ropetu, Marie 302
Roseby, Thomas 363
Ross, Cathy 275
Ross, John 366
Royal Christchurch Music Society 150
Royal School of Church Music 155
Ruatara 28, 101
Rudman, Brian 82
Ruskin, John 76
Russell, James 354
Russell, Rosemary 162
Ryan, Henry 37, 330, 369
Rymer, John 208

S
Sabbath observance 27–45, 253, 311 *see also* traditions & festivals
Sabbath Observance Committee 38
sacred days *see* traditions & festivals
Sacred Heart Convent School, Wanganui, 1912 294, **294**–5
sacred places 12, 50–2, 181, **181**

Sadlier, William 348
Salmond, Dr 381
Salmond, Miss 300
Salvation Army 17, 18, 107, 115, 200, 282, 290, 363–4
  clergy 185, 188
  conversion & confirmation 119, 121
  Linwood Citadel, Salvation Army dinner, Christchurch, 1910 255, **255**
  music & hymns 153, 155
  Palmerston North Citadel & band **132–3**, 134
  Women of the Salvation Army corps in Broadway, Palmerston North 303, **303**
Sangster, Margaret E. 278
Sankey, Ira D. 145, 151–4, 366
Sargood, Percy 363
Saultalk 160
Saunders, J. M. 234–6
Save Our Families campaign 216
Scanlon, Nell 309–10
schisms 244–50, 360 *see also* denominations, rifts
Scott, George Gilbert 71
Scott, Joan 119–20, 282
Scott, John 94
Scott, Wendy 315
Scrimgeour, Colin 125–6, 209, 220, 368
Scripture Union 202
Seamen's Mission 367
secular state 20–1, 42, 44, 379–80
Seddon, Richard John 'Dick' 36, 356
Selwyn, George Augustus 12, 14, 18, 20, **29**, 31, 111, 145, 189, 230, 243, 248, 342, 346, 357
  church building 54, 63–6, 85, 165
Selwyn, John 343, **343**
Selwyn, Sarah **272–3**, 274, 344
sermons 101–3, 106, 113–5, 122–5, 130 *see also* specific denominations
Serpell, Samuel 243
services & liturgy 36–7, 39–41, 88–9, 101–4, 115–7, 121–31, 123–7, 135, 155 *see also* communion; membership of religions; missions; Sabbath observance; specific denominations
  family services 124–5, 158, 266–7, 315, **376–7**, 378
Shacklock, Henry 363
Shalders, Richard 261

Shaping Godzone 21
Sharplin, Thomas 84–5
Shaw, George Bernard 78
Shea, George Beverly 154
Sheehy, Sister Cecil 162
shopping, Sabbath observance 33, 42
Simkin, John 125, **166–7**, 168, 239, 345
Simkin, William 172
singing *see* music & hymns
Singspiration 159
Sister Mary Perpetua 289
Sister of Mercy & class, St Patrick's School, Dunedin, 1959 **329**, 329
Sisters of Compassion, singing, 1984 157, **157**
Sisters of Mercy 16, 298
Sisters of St Joseph 294, **294–5**
Slade, William 174, 362, 368–9
Smalley, Joseph 89, 120, 212
Smith, Brian 363, 366
Smith family 362
Smith, James McCosh 218
smoking 211–2
sociability 243–70, 251–3, 259–60, 261, 268, 294–6, 297 *see also* communities; entertainment & leisure; Sunday Schools
Bible class picnic on Labour Day, Lower Hutt, 1941 265, **265**
camps 256, 268, 324
Children of St Christopher's Sunday school, Redwoodtown, Blenheim, 1908 255, **255**
Cub pack, Soldiers Memorial Church, Titirangi, 1956 265, **265**
refreshments 266–7, 333–4, 367
Salvation Army dinner, Linwood Citadel, Christchurch, 1910 255, **255**
Society of Mary 12, 15–6
Sommerville, Robert 381
song *see* music & hymns
South Island Organ Company 156
Speight, W. J. 349
sport 38, 253, 256–7, 325–6, 332, **332**, 334 *see also* entertainment & leisure
Spurgeon, Charles Haddon 171
Spurgeon, Thomas 88, 114
Squires, Catharine (née Dewe)
St Columba College, Dunedin 348
St Hill, Henry 357
St Paul's Musical Singers 160, 162
Stafford, Edward 357

Star of Hope Mission 250
status 339–75
steeples *see* church buildings, steeples & bells
Stenhouse, John 210, 340, 352
Stewart, Downie 30
Stobo, Andrew 118–9, 262, 263
Stout, Robert 37, 212, 364
Strahan family 323, **323**
Stuart, Donald 174, 187, 188, 218, 227–8, 245–6
Stuart, Edward 343, **343**, 365
Stuart, Julia 357
Student Christian Movement 256, 264
Stych, W. H. 48
Subritzky, Bill 158–9
Sullivan, Martin 345
Sunday *see* Sabbath observance
Sunday Schools 32, 124–5, 139, 257–9, 310–4, 319–20, 330, 334 *see also* education; sociability
Brooklyn Baptist Church Sunday school procession **318–9**, 319
Children of St Christopher's Sunday school, Redwoodtown, Blenheim, 1908 255, **255**
Sunday school picnic, Zabell's Paddocks, Carterton 258, **258**
Sunday school, St Thomas's, New Lynn, 1956 271, **271**
Sunday school unions 154–5, 311–2, 335
Sundt, Richard 54, 102
Surville, Jean François Marie de 101
Suter, Andrew 343, **343**, 365
Sutherland, George 31–2
Swainson, William 357
Swan, John 59
Syrton, Margery 33

T

Tablet 245, 326, 353
Tahupotiki Wiremu Rātana 13, 79
Taihape, St Margaret's Anglican Church 59, **59**
Tallis, Thomas 141
Tamaki, Hannah 193, 302
Tāmihana, Wiremu Te Waharoa 12, 136
Tana, Diana 276–7
Tancred, Henry 357
Taranaki church **306–7**, 308
Tate, Nahum 140
Taupo, N*atives assembled to celebrate the Lord's Supper at*

Orona, Taupo, New Zealand, 1845 **29**
Tauranga, Ōtūmoetai chapel, 1840 54–5, **56–7**
Taylor, Allan 358
Taylor, 'California' 119
Taylor, Kenneth 164
Te Kooti Arikirangi 13
Te Kopuru, St Peter's Anglican Church **46–7**
Te Pouhere 15
Te Rau 170
Te Rauparaha 53, **53**, 54
Te Ua Haumēne 12–3
Te Whiti o Rongomai 13
tea meetings *see* sociability
Teen Challenge 331
television 37, 115, 155, 161, 220
temperance 261, 279, 282–3, 286, 321, 381 *see also* food & alcohol; Women's Christian Temperance Union
Temperance Ladies' Brass Band of Auckland, 1910s 283, **283**
Tennant, Margaret 287, 290
Thames, St George's Anglican church, 1973 **222–3**, 224
Thatcher, Frederick 54, 64–6, **67**, 68, 71, 84, 165, 346
Thiem, Ben 76
Thompson, Susan 173
Thomson, George Samuel 'Rev.' 183
Thorburn, Stan 334
Thornton, Guy 293
Thornton, James 246
Thornton, John 349
Tiatia, Jemima 334
Timaru 58, 76, **76–7**
Tisdall, Charles 368
Titore 137
Tollemache, Algernon 348
Tönnies, Ferdinand 250–1
Torrey, Reuben 120, 154
Toy, Richard 94, 168
traditions & festivals 27–8, 30–1, 39–42, **43**, 94–6, 101–2, 124, 370 *see also* Christian culture; specific denominations
transport, Sabbath observance 33–4
Treaty of Waitangi 12
Trigge, Val 120
Troughton, Geoff 119, 383
Troup, George 322, 325
Truman, Frank **83**
Tubman, Dean 188
Turnbull, Richard 37

Tutty, Thomas Claude 326

U

unification *see* denominations, unification & cooperation
Unitarian Church, Ponsonby Rd 61, **61**
United Church of Christ in New Zealand 382
United Maori Mission 118
Upper Hutt, Catholic Women's League's float, 1966 271, **271**
urupā 50, 181, **181**
Ussher, Jane **65**

V

van der Krogt, Chris 208
Van Dijk, Fr. 245
Vanguard 215
Varley, Henry 211
Venimore, Colin 104
Vernon, Michael 342
vestments & clerical dress 111–3, 126, 150–1, 182–3, 291, 341–3, 345, 355, 375 *see also* clothes, for church; specific denominations
Vision College 160
Vision West Community Trust 374
Volkner, Carl Sylvanus 12
Vygotsky, Lev 44

W

Waddell, Rutherford 113, 290, 325
Waiapu 14, 170
Waikato 11, 14
  Anglican fête, 1885 229, **229**
Waimate North 11, 52, 54
Walker, Alan 113
Wallace, 'Bill' William Livingstone 161–2
Wanganui 79, **80**, 294, **294–5**
Wanhalla, Angela 276
war 20–1, 37, 81, 84, 139, 155, 171, 204–5, 326
Ward, Joseph 38, 371
Ward, Josiah 19
Warren, Alwyn 125
Warren, Doreen 348
Watson, Cecil 88, 150
Watts, Isaac 140–2
Webb, Mrs E. M. 299, **299**
Weber, Max 225
Weir, John 162
Welfare of the Church Committee 327–8

Wellington
  Anglican diocese 14
  Brooklyn Baptist Church Sunday school procession 318–9, 319, **319**
  Catholic diocese 16, 170
  Catholic parade, 1940 217, **217**
  Mount Cook Bible class hockey team, 1908 332, **332**
  Moxham Ave, Methodist church 19, **19**
  Old St Paul's Anglican Church 65, **65**, 66
  Sabbath observance 37
  St Mary of the Angels 93, **93**
  St Thomas's Church bazaar, Wellington, 1898 239, **239**
Wells, Herbert F. & campaigns 91–2, 105, 109, 236, 239, **239**, 355
Welsh, Mrs 290
Wesleyan Church *see* Methodist Church
Wesleyan Connexion 120
Wesleyan Helping Hand Mission 319–20
Wesleydale 11
West Taieri Total Abstinence Society 214
West-Watson, Campbell 338, 342–4, 346–7
Wanganui 79, **80**, 294, **294–5**
Whangaroa mission 11
White, Raymond 151
Whyte, James 191, **191**
Wilberforce, William 27
Wilkinson, John & family **186–7**, 187
Will, William 36
Willett, Lennox 150
Williams, Edward 138
Williams, Henry 11–2, 28, 101–2, 138
Williams, Herbert 344
Williams, Jane (née Nelson) 11, **272–3**, 274
Williams, Marianne (née Coldham) 275
Williams, William 11, 135, 138–9, 169–70, 189, 344, 356
Wilson, Benson 154
Wilson, Bryan 339
windows *see* church buildings, windows
Winnington-Ingram, Arthur **196–7**, 198
Winstone, George 146
Wishart, Guy 160
women, church involvement 275–304, 340, 368 *see also* church buildings, furnishings; funding, ladies guilds
  catering 266–7, 281
  missions 275–6, 287–8, 300
  moral code 279–80
Women's Christian Temperance Union 36–8, 212, 214, 277, 294
Women's Division of the Federated Farmers, Tarras 95
Women's Fellowships 298
Women's Missionary Unions 296–7
Women's Union 324
Wood, Cecil **336–7**, 338, 346
Wood, David 160
Woods, Sam 300
Woollcombe, Harry 296
working bees 260–1
Wright, Mrs J. L. 282

Y

Yate, Sarah 276
Yate, William 102, 135, 276
YMCA 261, 320, 321–2
young people *see* children & young people
Youth dance, St Matthew's, Masterton, 1957 332, **332**
Youth for Christ 160, 331–3
YWCA 320–1

Z

Zachariah, Joseph 'Zak' 332, **332**

About the author

PETER LINEHAM is Professor of History at Massey University and Regional Director of the College of Humanities and Social Sciences on Massey's Albany campus. He is a respected scholar whose interests cover a range of subject areas that can loosely be categorised under history and religion. He has written articles on many aspects of English and New Zealand religious history and his books include *There We Found Brethren*, *No Ordinary Union* and *Bible and Society*. He co-edited the standard text on New Zealand's religious history, *Transplanted Christianity*. In 2013 his book on Brian Tamaki and the Destiny Church, *Destiny*, was published by Penguin. His interpretations of trends in religion in New Zealand are also frequently reported by the media. He has long been active in a range of churches, Christian organisations and in tertiary chaplaincy coordination and prisoner support. His MA is from the University of Canterbury, his BD from the University of Otago, and his DPhil. from the University of Sussex.

First published in 2017 by Massey University Press
Private Bag 102904, North Shore Mail Centre
Auckland 0745, New Zealand
www.masseypress.ac.nz

Text copyright © Peter Lineham, 2017
Images copyright © as credited, 2017

Design by Kate Barraclough
Front cover image: Major General Horatio Robley's painting of the Roman Catholic chapel at Ōtūmoetai, Tauranga, 1865. Museum of New Zealand Te Papa Tongarewa, ref: 1992-0035-1705. Back cover image: First Communion at Our Lady of Lourdes Church, Palmerston North. Ian Matheson City Archives.

The moral right of the author has been asserted

All rights reserved. Except as provided by the Copyright Act 1994, no part of this book may be reproduced, stored in or introduced into a retrieval system or transmitted in any form or by any means (electronic, mechanical, photocopying, recording or otherwise) without the prior written permission of both the copyright owner(s) and the publisher.

A catalogue record for this book is available from the National Library of New Zealand

Printed and bound in China by Everbest Ltd

ISBN: 978-0-9941407-7-7